ARAMAIC
(ASSYRIAN/SYRIAC)

Swadaya–English
Turoyo–English
English–Swadaya–Turoyo

Dictionary & Phrasebook

Nicholas Awde,
Nineb Lamassu &
Nicholas Al-Jeloo

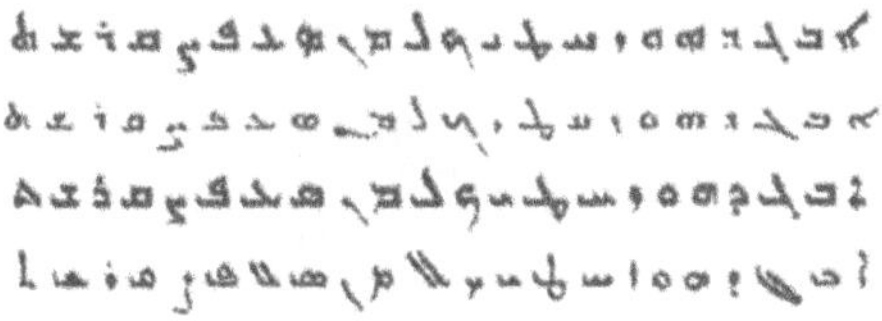

HIPPOCRENE BOOKS INC
New York

Typeset & designed by Desert♥Hearts

ISBN-13: 978-0-7818-1087-6
ISBN-10: 0-7818-1087-6

For information, address:
HIPPOCRENE BOOKS, INC.
171 Madison Avenue
New York, NY 10016
www.hippocrenebooks.com

Printed in the United States of America

CONTENTS

- An Assyrian person is a *S:* **Suraya** *m*/ **Surayta** *f*, **Suryaya** *m*/**Suryayta** *f*, or **Athuraya** *m*/**Athurayta** *f*; *T:* **Suroyo** *m*/ **Surayto** *f*, **Suryoyo** *m*/**Suryayto** *f*, or **Othuroyo** *m*/**Othurayto** *f*. This is also the adjective for Assyrian people and things.

- Assyrians call themselves *S:* **Suraye**, **Suryaye**, or **Athuraye**; *T:* **Suroye**, **Suryoye**, or **Othuroye**.

- The Aramaic, or Assyrian, language is *S:* **Surit** or **Athuraya**; *T:* **Surayt** or **Suryoyo**.

- Swadaya, or Madinkhaya, the Eastern Aramaic (or Syriac) language, is *S:* **Madinkhaya**; *T:* **Madinḥoyo**.

- Turoyo, or Ma'erboyo, the Western Aramaic (or Syriac) language, is *S:* **Maˁirwaya**; *T:* **Ṭuroyo**.

- Assyria is *S:* **Athur**; *T:* **Othur**. Mesopotamia is *S:* **Bet-Nahrain**; *T:* **Beth-Nahrin**.

A NOTE ON LANGUAGE: The terms Aramaic, Syriac and Assyrian are often used interchangeably in this dictionary/ phrasebook when referring to the modern spoken language. Note also that, where appropriate, we have included commonly used alternatives or loan words for the Turoyo entries only, in order to reflect the fact that the language is less standardized than Swadaya.

ABBREVIATIONS USED IN THIS BOOK:

S	Swadaya
T	Turoyo
m	masculine
f	feminine
pl	plural

INTRODUCTION

Against all adversity, the Assyrian nation has survived centuries of major political and social upheavals and has entered the 21-first century with its unique cultural identity intact, which it proudly displays for all those who are willing to take the time to embrace it.

Spread across adjoining areas of Iraq, Syria, Iran and Turkey, Northern Mesopotamia is a mountainous country, dominated by the continuous chain of mountains from the Hakkari uplands to the rugged Tur-Abdin plateau. The highest mountain in the traditional Assyrian homeland, Mt. Jilu (present Cilo Dagi), stands at 4,168 meters high.

Although the region has been populated since time immemorial – it is renowned as being the "Cradle of Civilization" – the modern Assyrians gradually arose from the ashes of the ancient civilizations of Assyria and Babylonia in the seventh century B.C. Yet for centuries, the local inhabitants were caught up in the bloody conflicts of a succession of rival empires and kingdoms which competed with each other to dominate the region. Among these was the Persian Achaemenid Empire, founded by Cyrus the Great in the sixth century B.C. and subsequently toppled by Alexander the Great in the fourth century. The Seleucids, Alexander's successors, held sway over the land until the warring empires of Rome and Parthia transformed northern Mesopotamia with Assyria in the center into little more than a buffer zone.

Prior to the arrival of Christianity the Assyrians had a number of small states across northern Mesopotamia, among them Edessa, Hatra and

Adiabene. In the first century B.C. the ruling family of Adiabene converted to Judaism, which paved the way for the later widespread acceptance of Christianity. This is also why there is still a large East Syriac-speaking Jewish community.

The First Christians

In 33 A.D. King Abgar the Black of Edessa corresponded with Christ himself and was converted to Christianity soon after the crucifixion by St. Thaddeus the Apostle. From then on the new faith became the official religion of the kingdom and quickly spread to the other Assyrian kingdoms, making them the first people in the world to accept Christianity. From then on, Christianity became a vital part of the nation's identity, which it remains to this day.

It was not long before Adiabene and Hatra fell to the powerful Sassanian Empire to the East and Edessa to the Romans in the West. The fledgling Assyrian Church also became the target of the Sassanians and Romans as they fought to keep each other at bay. The Patriarch at Antioch theoretically oversaw all of the Christian communities in Syria, Mesopotamia and all else to east. But due to the difficulty of managing such a large and divided area, it was clear that the position of Catholicos had to be created to administer the faithful across the border. The Catholicosate of the East was established in the early second century A.D. by elevating the rank of the Metropolitan of the twin cities of Seleucia-Ctesiphon, then the Persian imperial capital. The Catholicos's sway extended over all Metropolitans and Bishops in the Persian Empire and the East. Traditionally, all candidates for the Catholicosate would go to Antioch for selection, and the successful one was ordained personally by the Patriarch of Antioch.

But the imperial powers still suspected the Assyrians on either side to be spying for the other simply because of their shared ethnicity. This led to violent massacres and assassinations of leaders on both sides. In 191 A.D. the Romans seized the Patriarch of Antioch and the two candidates for the Catholicosate of the East and condemned them to be crucified. Between 330 and 379, the Sassanian emperor Shapur II launched a vicious campaign to eradicate Christianity and impose the state religion, Zoroastrian. During this time three Catholicoses were put to death along with many clergymen and more than 16,000 people. The Catholicosate of the East thus remained vacant for many years at a time.

Caught in the middle between the warring imperial giants, the Assyrian leadership did the only thing it could to survive. The Patriarchate of Antioch made a decree allowing future Catholicoses to be ordained locally. But soon, with the theological debates of the fifth century, the divide became more pronounced. In the year 421, the Church of the East gravitated towards Nestorianism, and fell out of communion with the rest of the church. They consequently became known as "Nestorian" and were deemed heretical. In 424, the Church of the East formally proclaimed itself independent of Antioch and the Catholicos was elevated in rank to Patriarch.

The Council of Chalcedon in 451 provoked a further split in the Patriarchate of Antioch. This time it was between the Hellenised upper class and the Aramaic/Syriac-speaking common people. The council's teachings were enforced by the Byzantine imperial authorities in the cities, but they were largely rejected in the countryside. Those that did not reject these teachings were labelled "Melkites" (i.e. the "Emperor's Men"). In the sixth century, the Bishop of Edessa, Jacob Baradaeus, ordained many bishops and priests to carry on the faith of those who rejected Chalcedon in the face of imperial opposition. Consequently this church, known officially today as the Syriac Orthodox Church of Antioch, became known as "Jacobite".

Scholars and Missionaries

The seventh century brought in new overlords as the Muslim Arabs fought their way north to take over the eastern domains of Byzantium, which was slowly crumbling through political infighting. Under the fast-expanding Islamic Empire, most Assyrians were reduced to *dhimmi* status – this was reserved in Islamic law for all conquered peoples that belonged to the People of the Book, the group of religions recognised by Islam, i.e. Christians, Jews and Sabaeans (linked to the Zoroastrians). Because the vast majority of them refused to convert to Islam, they were forced to pay a tax called *jizya*, which gave those worse off the incentive to convert to Islam. Some Assyrians in the more inaccessible highlands were nevertheless permitted to rule themselves.

Overall, the conquest of northern Mesopotamia by the Arabs ended Persian and Byzantine persecution and created conditions favouring a period of revival and further development. Aramaic/Syriac scholarship flourished in the famous universities of Edessa, Nisibis and Gundishapur and the nation also possessed schools of theology, philosophy, history and science. Ancient Greek masterpieces were translated into Syriac and then Arabic, later sparking the renaissance in Europe.

The Church of the East expanded through missionary activity into areas as far away as India, Tibet, China and Mongolia. By 1318 there were some 30 metropolitan sees and 200 suffragan dioceses stretching from Egypt and Cyprus in the west to

Japan and Indonesia in the East. The Syriac Orthodox Church had 20 metropolitan sees and 103 dioceses extending as far to the east as Afghanistan, as well as communities without bishops as distant as Turkestan (Central Asia) and Sinkiang (western China). The combined membership of these churches at this time is estimated to have numbered well over 80 million, outnumbering the Greek and Roman Churches of the time.

The nation's fortunes changed after the Kurdish invasions in the eleventh century and the Mongol invasions under Tamerlane in the late fourteenth century, during which most churches and monasteries were destroyed and the Assyrians were almost annihilated. This marked the beginning of a long period of gradual decline. By 1450 the office of the Patriarch and some other metropolitan and episcopal sees of the Church of the East had become hereditary (within one family), usually being passed down from uncle to nephew. This often produced unqualified leaders of the church who at times were elected at a very young age. The Assyrian churches were then further weakened by the formation of Catholic counterparts in the sixteenth and seventeenth centuries – the Chaldean and Syriac Catholic Churches.

Caught up in the relentless march for power by larger neighbours, the next trial for the Assyrians was their absorption into the Ottoman Empire. They were ruled by the Sultans and their viziers in Istanbul, and for many years their fortunes were tied to the vicissitudes of that empire's struggles with the Iranian Safavid Empire.

Revival, Genocide and Survival

The Assyrians isolated themselves during the Ottoman Empire and contributed little to the cultural, political and administrative life of the Empire.

But their fortunes changed sharply as the Empire began to decline steadily during the nineteenth century. A new threat to its borders had emerged to the north, that of the Tsar's Russia, which greedily looked to taking Ottoman territories around the Black Sea, Caucasus and Persia.

By the 1830s Western missionaries began to establish themselves in Assyrian centres in Turkey and Iran. The influx led to the establishment of schools, colleges, printing presses and libraries and a general revival of Assyrian culture. This ultimately sparked books, newspapers, magazines and the birth of the Assyrian national movement. But in the 1840s, in the shadow of Ottoman attempts to centralize power over the crumbling empire, the Kurds massacred nearly 50,000 Assyrians in their attempt to create a break-away independent state. This had the effect of greatly reducing the autonomy enjoyed by the Assyrians of Hakkari and Tur-Abdin.

By the 1870s, Tsarist Russia and Ottoman Turkey had come to blows and in the fallout, during the reign of Sultan Abdul Hamid II, Armenians and Assyrians living in Turkey were massacred. Between 1894-1896, an estimated 55,000 Assyrians were slaughtered. In 1909, a further 3,000 Assyrians were massacred at Adana in Cilicia. Yet despite such a horrific fate, the Assyrians continued to develop their dreams for an independent Assyria. But, between 1914-1924, tragedy struck once again for the Armenians and Assyrians. An estimated 750,000 Assyrians were again massacred wholesale in a genocidal act by the Turkish government of the Young Turks – and little more than 300,000 survivors were forced into exile.

The end of the First World War brought a short-lived period of semi-independence as the Assyrians administered a protectorate under the French colonial authority in the Jazira region of northeast Syria between 1919 and 1922. This was cut short by the colonial policies of Britain, which had no interest in an Assyrian state and wanted to retain the Assyrians as a mercenary force in what was to become Iraq.

In 1919 an Assyrian delegation attended the Paris Peace Conference to request the formation of an Assyrian state in northern Mesopotamia. The 1920 Treaty of Sevres consequently stipulated full safeguards for the protection of the "Assyro-Chaldeans" within either Turkey or a Kurdish state formed by plebiscite. But the 1923 Treaty of Lausanne made no mention of the Assyrians – despite there being an Assyrian delegate at the conference. Assyrians were placed under the broad banner of "non-Muslim minorities" and, until recently, even the meager rights they were entitled to have been denied by the Turkish state. Many Assyrians migrated to Syria, Iraq and Lebanon as a result.

The Assyrians in Iraq were, however, no better off after the country's independence in 1924. In August 1933 more than 3,000 Assyrian civilians were disarmed and put to death by the Iraqi military over a period of less than ten days, and 65 Assyrian villages were sacked, destroyed or burnt to the ground. Nearly 15,000 Assyrians escaped to Syria later that year and established 35 new villages on the banks of the Khabour River.

For a brief period of time, the Soviet Union was the only modern state to make Assyrian one of its national languages, guaranteeing limited but protected use of it in publications as well as primary school education. But the Assyrians (known as "Aysors") under Soviet rule soon lost this right and were repressed, experiencing much hardship as a great many of them were deported to Siberia and Central Asia.

Struggle for Identity

The Assyrians of Iraq and Turkey have since continually been caught in the conflicts between the Kurds and the ruling governments. Between 1961-1988, during the Kurdish revolt and the Anfal campaign, the Iraqi government destroyed 189 villages in northern Iraq. As a result hundreds of people were killed, nearly 5,000 families were displaced and about 80 ancient churches and monasteries were destroyed.

The Assyrians of Turkey also underwent displacement as they came between government forces and the Kurdish Workers' Party (P.K.K.). Between 1992 and 1996 more than 30 Assyrian villages in the Tur-Abdin and Bohtan regions were evacuated and destroyed. Many Assyrians went missing as they tried to return to their homes. At the same time many Assyrian children, mostly girls, were kidnapped and many community leaders were murdered. Because of all this the 40,000 Assyrians that lived in that region in 1978 have dwindled to the present 2,000.

In 1979 Saddam Hussein began his reign of terror in Iraq. This was marked by repeated attempts to Arabize Assyrians and to erase their unique ethnic identity. They were forced to register as Arabs or Kurds in the regular national census and were discriminated against along ethnic rather than religious lines. All nationalistic organisations went underground and their activities were held in secret. Assyrian migration from Iraq was widely encouraged and made quite simple. In the later years of his rule, Saddam even forced Assyrian parents to give their children Arab or Muslim names.

Also in 1979, the Islamic Revolution in Iran changed the Assyrian community of that country forever. On the eve of the revolution Assyrians numbered 80,000 throughout Iran but after decades of strict Islamic law and blatant discrimination against indigenous Christians and other minorities, the community had shrunk to little more than 15,000 by 2002.

After the end of the First Gulf War in 1991 a vast area of northern Iraq, known officially as the "Kurdistan region", was given protection and a large degree of local autonomy. The Assyrians there were free for the first time in decades to work in politics, form new political parties, open offices and produce all kinds of publications and media freely as well as offer primary and secondary education completely in Aramaic/Syriac. Despite that and the Assyrians holding the balance of power – five seats and a ministry – in the regional parliament, the rift and inevitable civil war between the Kurdistan Democratic Party (K.D.P.) and the Patriotic Union of Kurdistan (P.U.K.) rendered them ineffective and left the Assyrians in the middle of another unwanted conflict.

In the years that followed 52 Assyrian villages were at least partially occupied by Kurdish forces. Kurds also settled in most of the nearly 200 Assyrian villages that had been previously destroyed and continue to expropriate Assyrian land. There have also been a number of unsolved murders, terrorist attacks and assassinations of Assyrian leaders, as well as blockades of Assyrian villages and regions.

Assyrians today remain a stateless minority scattered between Iraq, Syria, Turkey and Iran, but also with communities in other Middle Eastern countries as well as the Caucasus. They have representatives in the parliaments of Syria and Iran, as well as the newly created Iraqi Governing Council, but are yet to be recognized as an ethnic minority in Turkey.

Focus for the Diaspora

The Diaspora was born from the region's turbulent history and has given rise to the creation of innumerable Assyrian communities around the world – which are a cause for celebration as they continue to flourish and keep alive their culture and traditions. There are an estimated three million Assyrians around the world including half a million in the U.S.A., with large centers in Chicago, Detroit and California.

Despite the long history of persecution and their present situation, there is much hope that the Assyrians in the new Iraq will be given a prominent role as well as cultural, linguistic and administrative rights. There is also hope that the governments of Syria, Turkey and Iran, as they increasingly open up to the rest of the world, will concede more rights to their Assyrian minorities to create a secure future for all.

■ For some further background information, see *The Iraqis* (Bennett & Bloom, forthcoming).

A VERY BASIC GRAMMAR

Reflecting their complex history, the two languages in this dictionary/phrasebook are known by various names. Although the languages here – which many prefer to be seen as dialects of a single language – are jointly called Aramaic, individually they are usually called East Syriac (**Swadaya** or **Madinkhaya**) and West Syriac (**Ṭuroyo** or **Ma'erboyo**). These both belong to the Aramaic branch of the Semitic language family, and their speakers share a long history of common literature and can sometimes understand each other with varying ease. Note that many speakers prefer the term Assyrian instead of Syriac and both are used in this book.

Other members of this family include Hebrew (note that the Jews of the time of Jesus Christ spoke Aramaic not Hebrew), Arabic, Akkadian (Ancient Assyro-Babylonian), Mandaic (the language of an ethno-religious minority in southern Iraq and Iran), and, more distantly, Amharic, spoken in Ethiopia. Aramaic is written in its own unique script – this book uses an easy-to-understand Latin transliteration throughout.

—Structure

Like English, the linguistic structure of Aramaic is basically a simple one, e.g.

Do you *(m/f)* speak English?
S: **Msawtit/Msawtat lishana Englishaya?**
T: **Kibokh/Kibekh mijgholat Inglishoyo?**
(literally: "Speak-you language English?")

—Nouns

"A/AN and THE" – Aramaic has no words for "a" or "an" in the same way as English does – instead the meaning is generally understood from the context, e.g. *S:* **gawra**, *T:* **gawro** can mean "a man" or just simply "man".

Gawra in Swadaya also means "the man", since it has no particular word for "the". Turoyo, however, adds to the beginning of a word **u-** (to a masculine singular word), **i-** (to a feminine singular word), **a-** (to a plural word of either gender) or **an-** (if the plural word begins with a vowel), e.g. **u-gawro** "the man", **i-athto** "the woman", **a-bnotho** "the girls/daughters", **an-abne** "the sons".

GENDER – As with many other languages, such as French, Spanish and Arabic, Aramaic divides words according to gender, i.e. whether they are masculine or feminine. This can be predictable, e.g. *S:* **athta**, *T:* **athto** "woman" (feminine) and *S:* **gawra**, *T:* **gawro** "man" (masculine); or not, e.g. *S:* **radita**, *T:* **radhayto** "car" (feminine) and *S:* **bayta**, *T:* **bayto** "house" (masculine). Adjectives and verbs agree according to this gender, e.g.

> The (male) doctor has arrived.
> *S:* **Asya mṭile.**
> *T:* **Maṭi u-osoyo.**
>
> The (female) doctor has arrived.
> *S:* **Asita mṭila.**
> *T:* **Maṭyo i-ositho.**
>
> The boy is happy.
> *S:* **Yala psikha ele.**
> *T:* **U-ʿlaymo fṣiḥoyo-yo.**
>
> The girl is happy.
> *S:* **Brata psikhta ela.**
> *T:* **I-bartho fṣiḥayto-yo.**

Gender is often reflected in the form the verb takes, depending on the gender of both the verb's subject and object:

I *(m/f)* understand.
S: said by a male: **Ana prama wen.**
said by a female: **Ana prama wan.**
T: said by a male: **Ko-fohamno.**
said by a female: **Ko-fuhmono.**

We need it *(a masculine thing).*
S: **Sniqe wikh.**
T: **Ko-lozam-lan.**

We need it *(a feminine thing).*
S: **Sniqa wikh.**
T: **Ko-luzmo-lan.**

We need them.
S: **Sniqehe wikh.**
T: **Ko-luzmi-lan.**

PLURALS – Nouns form their plural by replacing the masculine ending *S:* **-a**, *T:* **-o** with *S/T:* **-e**, or the feminine ending *S:* **-ta/-tha**, *T:* **-to/-tho** with *S:* **-atha**, *T:* **-otho**, e.g. *S:* **qanya** → **qanye**, *T:* **qanyo** → **qanye** "pens"; *S:* **midrashta** → **midrashatha**, *T:* **midrashto** → **midrashotho** "schools".

There are some irregular plurals – analogous to occurrences in English like "man/men" or "child/children", e.g. *S:* **brona** → **bnone**, *T:* **abro** → **abne** "sons"; *S:* **brata** → **bnate**, *T:* **bartho** → **bnotho** "daughters/girls"; *S:* **attha** → **neshe**, *T:* **athto** → **neshe** "women"; *S:* **bayta** → **bate**, *T:* **bayto** → **bote** "houses", *S:* **khona** → **khonwate**, *T:* **ahuno** → **ahunone** "brothers", *S:* **khata** → **khatwate**, *T:* **hotho** → **ahwotho** "sisters".

Plurals of females or feminine things that are loan words from other languages add **-at/-wat**, e.g. *T:* **kachikke** → **kachikkat** "daughters/girls", **radio** → **radiowat** "radios".

"OF" – The word **d-**, attached to the beginning of words, is used to denote "of", e.g. *S:* **ktawa d-brata**, *T:* **kthowo di-bartho** = "the girl's book" (or "the book of the girl"), *S:* **monaᶜa d-bayta**, *T:* **mhawyonutho du-bayto** = "the house's address" (or "the address of the house"), *S:* **kharița d-Qamishli**, *T:* **karțo di-Qamishlo** = "map of Qamishli", *S:* **qunțrun d-mdita**, *T:* **qențrun di-mdhitho** = "city center", or *S:* **brona d-khona**, *T:* **abro d-ahuno** = "nephew" ("son of brother"). Note that for sound reasons, there are several forms of **d-**.

D- can also have other uses and mean other things. It can introduce a quote or direct speech. It is also used when introducing a relative clause, e.g. *S:* **hu nasha d-zille**, *T:* **u-nosho d-azze** "the man who went", *S:* **hay brata d-khzeli**, *T:* **i-bartho d-hze-li** "the girl whom I saw". It can be used to mean "that" after verbs of knowing, saying, suspecting or thinking, e.g. *S:* **Yadᶜin d-...**, *T:* **K-odhaᶜno d-…** "I know *(masculine form)* that …", *S:* **Miri d-...**, *T:* **Mir-li d-…** "I said that…"

—Adjectives

Adjectives are like nouns in that they can take the same endings. They always come after the nouns, e.g.

"new"	*S:* **khadta** *(m)*/**khdatta** *(f)* *T:* **hatho** *(m)*/**hathto** *(f)*
"new hotel"	*S:* **bet-bawta khadta** *T:* **hotel hatho**
"new car"	*S:* **radhita khdatta** *T:* **radhayto hathto**
"old"	*S:* **ᶜatiqa** *(m)*/**ᶜatiqta** *(f)* *T:* **ᶜatiqo** *(m)*/**ᶜatiqto** *(f)*
"old hotel"	*S:* **bet-bawta ᶜatiqa** *T:* **hotel ᶜatiqo**

"old car"	*S:* **radhita ʿatiqta** *T:* **radhayto ʿatiqto**

Some other basic adjectives are:

open	*S:* **ptikha** *(m)*/**ptikhta** *(f)* *T:* **ftiho** *(m)*/**ftihto** *(f)*
shut	*S:* **dwira/dwirta** *T:* **skhiro/skhirto**
quick	*S:* **msarhiwa/msarhiwta** *T:* **khayifo/khayifto**
slow	*S:* **nekha** *(m/f)* *T:* **hedi hedi** *(m/f)*
cheap	*S:* **shawya/shwita** *T:* **lo ṭimo** *or* **arzon** *(m/f)*
expensive	*S:* **yaqura/yaqurta** *or* **ṭema** *(m/f)* *T:* **ṭimo** *(m/f)*
hot	*S:* **shakhina/shakinta** *T:* **shahino/shahinto**
cold	*S:* **qarira/qarirta** *T:* **qariro/qarirto**
young	*S:* **zʿora/zʿorta** *T:* **naʿimo/naʿimto**
old *person*	*S:* **sawa/sawta** *T:* **sowo/sawto**
old *thing*	*S:* **ʿatiqa/ʿatiqta** *T:* **ʿatiqo/ʿatiqto**
new	*S:* **khatda/khadta** *T:* **ḥatho/ḥathto**
near	*S:* **qariwa/qariwta** *T:* **qariwo/qaruto**
far	*S:* **rakhuqa/rakhuqta** *T:* **rahuqo/rahuqto**
good	*S:* **ṭawa/ṭawta** *T:* **ṭowo/ṭowto**
bad	*S:* **kherba** *(m/f)* *T:* **ḥarbo** *(m/f)*
big	*S:* **raba/rabta** *T:* **rabo/rabtho**

small	*S:* **zʿora/zʿorta**
	T: **naʿimo/naʿimto**
long	*S:* **yarikha/yarikhta**
	T: **yarikho/yarikhto**
short	*S:* **karya/kreta**
	T: **karyo/kritho**
rich	*S:* **ʿatira/ʿatirta** *or* **zangina/zanginta**
	T: **ʿatiro/ʿatirto** ***or*** **zangin** *(m/f)*

—Adverbs

Adverbs have a single form which seldom changes. Some examples:

here	*S:* **lakha** *or* **harka**; *T:* **harke**
there	*S:* **tama**; *T:* **tamo**
up	*S:* **lʿel**; *T:* **lalʿlel**
down	*S:* **ltekhet**; *T:* **laltaḥt**
well	*S:* **ṭawa**; *T:* **ṭowo** *(m)*/**ṭowto** *(f)*
bad(ly)	*S:* **kherba**; *T:* **ḥarbo**
now	*S:* **hadiya** *or* **hasha**; *T:* **uʿdo**
tomorrow	*S:* **qudme** *or* **lamkhar**; *T:* **ramḥel**
again	*S:* **medre**; *T:* **naqqa ḥreto**
truly	*S:* **b-ishara**; *T:* **b-shrolo**
probably	*S:* **kbar** *or* **balki**; *T:* **balki**
immediately	*S:* **har hadiya**; *T:* **bar-shoʿtho**

—Preposition

Aramaic has prepositions – where words like "in", "at" and "to" come before the noun, just as in English. Most are joined to the word itself, or a definite article that precedes it:

to/for	*S/T:* **l-**
like	*S:* **akh**, *T:* **khid**
in/at/on	*S/T:* **b-/bi-**
under	*S:* **tkhet**, *T:* **taḥt**
upon	*S/T:* **ʿal/ʿl**
with	*S/T:* **ʿam/ʿm**
in front of	*S:* **qam**, *T:* **qum/qm**

behind	*S:* **batir** *or* **bar**; *T:* **bithir**	
opposite *S*	*:* **barqul,** *T:* **mqabel d-**	
for	*S:* **meṭul** *or* **qad**, *T:* **lajan**	

e.g. *S:* **qam mashreta,** *T:* **qm u-mashryo** "in front of *(m)* the station", *S:* **ʿal da shquqa,** *T:* **ʿal u-shqoqano** "on this street", *S:* **b-ʿidta,** *T:* **bi-ʿidto** "at the church", *S:* **zilli ʿam-e,** *T:* **azzino ʿam-e** "I *(said by a male)* went with him".

—Pronouns

Basic forms are as follows:

SINGULAR

I	*S:* **ana**	*T:* **ono**
you *(m)*	*S:* **at**	*T:* **hat**
you *(f)*	*S:* **ate**	*T:* **hate**
he/it	*S:* **haw**	*T:* **huwe** *or* **hiye**
she/it	*S:* **hay**	*T:* **hiya**

PLURAL

we	*S:* **akhnan**	*T:* **aḥna**
you	*S:* **akhtu**	*T:* **hatu**
they	*S:* **ane**	*T:* **hinne**

Unlike French and Armenian, there is no polite form which uses the plural. As subject pronouns, like Spanish or Italian, you tend to use them for emphasis only, since the verb already tells you who is speaking.

Possessive pronouns in Turoyo are generally used with "the" attached (Italian also does this, e.g. "la mia casa" for "mia casa" – both mean "my house"). Note that, again similar to Italian, in Swadaya the forms agree with the gender of the word they modify:

SINGULAR

my	*S:* **diyi** *or* **didi**	*T:* **didhi**
your *(m)*	*S:* **diyokh** *or* **didokh**	*T:* **didhokh**

your *(f)*	*S:* **diyakh** *or* **didakh**	*T:* **didekh**
his/its	*S:* **diye** *or* **dide**	*T:* **didhe**
her/its	*S:* **diya** *or* **dida**	*T:* **didha**

PLURAL

our	*S:* **diyan** *or* **didan**	*T:* **didhan**
your	*S:* **diyokhon** *or* **diyakhu**	*T:* **dithkhu**
their	*S:* **diyae** *or* **didhay**	*T:* **dithe**

e.g. *S:* **khona diyokh;** *T:* **u-ahuno didhokh**
"your *(m)* brother"
S: **ktawa diyi;** *T:* **u-kthowo didhi**
"my book"
S: **radhita diyan;** *T:* **i-radhayto didhan**
"our car"
S: **radhiyata didan;** *T:* **i-radhayotho didhan**
"our cars"

The forms above are generally used for emphasis, there is system of "streamlined" forms that are contractions of the above and join onto a noun (which usually loses its final vowel):

SINGULAR

my	*S:* **-i**	*T:* **-aydhi**
your *(m)*	*S:* **-okh**	*T:* **-aydhokh**
your *(f)*	*S:* **-ekh**	*T:* **-aydekh**
his/its	*S:* **-e**	*T:* **-aydhe**
her/its	*S:* **-a**	*T:* **-aydha**

PLURAL

our	*S:* **-an**	*T:* **-aydhan**
your	*S:* **-khon**	*T:* **-athkhu** *or* **-khu**
their	*S:* **-wae**	*T:* **-athe**

e.g. *S:* **qritwae,** *T:* **i-qrithathe** "their village"
S: **baytan,** *T:* **u-baytaydhan** "our house"
S: **karmane,** *T:* **a-karmaydhe** "his vineyards"

Simple demonstratives in Aramaic are:

this	*S:* **aha** *(m)*/**aya** *(f) or* **hana** *(m)*/**hadhe** *(f)*
	T: **hano** *(m)*/**hathe** *(f)*
these	*S:* **anna**
	T: **hani**
that	*S:* **awa** *(m)*/**aya** *(f)*
	T: **hawo** *(m)*/**hayo** *(f)*
those	*S:* **anna**
	T: **hanik**

In the spoken language of Turoyo, people tend to shorten the words and attach them to shortened forms of the words they describe, e.g. *T:* **u-gawrano** "this man" (from *T:* **u-gawro-hano**, literally "the man this"), *T:* **a-nosh-ani** "these people" (from *T:* **a-noshe-hani**, "the people those"), *T:* **u-baytawo** "that house" (from *T:* **u-bayto-hawo** "the house that"), *T:* **a-radhayothanik** "those cars" (from *T:* **a-rad-hayotho-hanik**, "the cars those"). Note that the fuller forms in brackets are purely to illustrate the derivations and are not used.

—Verbs

Verbs are easy to form, adding a number of prefixes and suffixes to the basic verb form. In fact the underlying structure of Aramaic verbs shares similar concepts to those of some European languages and so its system of regularities and irregularities may appear familiar. Every Aramaic verb has a basic form that carries a basic meaning. To this are added smaller words or single vowels/consonants that add further information to tell you who's doing what and how and when, e.g.

"to write" – *S:* **ktawa**, *T:* **kthowo**

"I am writing"
S: **ktawa win** *(m)*/**ktawa wan** *(f)*
T: **ko-kothawno** *(m)*/**ko-kuthwono** *(f)*

"I will write"
S: **bid katwin** *(m)*/**bid katwan** *(f)*
T: **gid-kothawno** *(m)*/**gid-kuthwono** *(f)*

"I must write"
S: **zadiq d-katwin** *(m)*/**zadiq d-katwan** *(f)*
T: **k-lozim kothawno** *(m)*/**kuthwono** *(f)*

Some verbs, as in Western European languages, have sound changes for different tenses, completely different forms, or combinations of these, e.g. in Turoyo, *T:* **ihobo** "to give" – "I *(m)* give" **k-obeno**, "I gave" **huw-li**; **mazlo** "to go" – "I *(m)* am going" **k-izzino**, "I *(m)* went" **azzino**.

We saw the personal pronouns above, but these are only for emphasis. Like French or Spanish, the verb already gives this information. The following endings are for imperfect (and some perfect) verb forms:

SINGULAR		
I *(m)*	*S:* **-win**	*T:* **-no**
I *(f)*	*S:* **-wan**	*T:* **-ono**
you *(m)*	*S:* **-wit**	*T:* **-at**
you *(f)*	*S:* **-wat**	*T:* **-at**
he/it	*S:* **-u**	*T:* *(no ending)*
she/it	*S:* **-wa**	*T:* **-o** *or* **-uw**
PLURAL		
we	*S:* **-wikh**	*T:* **-ina**
you	*S:* **-witon** *or* **-utu**	*T:* **-utu**
they	*S:* **-wi**	*T:* **-i/-in**

e.g.

I *(m)* write	*S:* **katwin**	*T:* **kothawno**
I *(f)* write	*S:* **katwan**	*T:* **kuthwono**
you *(m)* write	*S:* **katwit**	*T:* **kuthwat**
you *(f)* write	*S:* **katwat**	*T:* **kuthwat**
she/it writes	*S:* **katwa**	*T:* **kuthwo**
he/it writes	*S:* **katuw**	*T:* **kothuw**

we write	*S:* **katwikh**	*T:* **kuthwina**
you *(pl)* write	*S:* **katwiton** *or* **katwitu**	*T:* **kuthwutu**
they write	*S:* **katwi**	*T:* **kuthwi/kuthwin**

The following endings are for most of the perfect verb forms:

SINGULAR

I		*S/T:* **-li**
you *(m)*		*S/T:* **-lokh**
you *(f)*		*S/T:* **-lekh**
he/it		*S/T:* **-le**
she/it		*S/T:* **-la**

PLURAL

we	*S/T:* **-lan**	
you	*S:* **-lokhon**	*T:* **-lkhu**
they	*S:* **-lon**	*T:* **-e/-len**

e.g.

I wrote	*S:* **ktuwa-li**	*T:* **kthuw-li**
you wrote *(m)*	*S:* **ktuwa-lokh**	*T:* **kthuw-lokh**
you wrote *(f)*	*S:* **ktuwa-lekh**	*T:* **kthuw-lekh**
he/it wrote	*S:* **ktuwa-le**	*T:* **kthuw-le**
she/it wrote	*S:* **ktuwa-la**	*T:* **kthuw-la**
we wrote	*S:* **ktuwa-lan**	*T:* **kthuw-lan**
you *(pl)* wrote	*S:* **ktuwa-lokhon**	*T:* **kthuw-lkhu**
they wrote	*S:* **ktuwa-lon**	*T:* **kthuw-e/kthuw-len**

These are the most commonly used endings, but note they can take different forms according to the tense used.

"Not" is *S:* **la/layt**, *T:* **lo/lat** (which can be joined to the following word), e.g. *S:* **la ela rikhqa**, *T:* **lat-yo rahuqo** "it's not far", *S:* **layt-li zawna**, *T:* **lat-li zabno** "I don't have time". Meaning "no" and also used with commands are *S:* **la**, *T:* **lo**, e.g. *S:* **la kalit!**,

T: **lo kolat!** "don't stop!", *S:* **la gayshit b-iye!**, *T:* **lo gayshat b-uwe!** "don't touch him/it!"

—Essential Verbs

—"To be" *S:* **hwayta** (or **ituta**), *T:* **hwoyo** (or **ithutho**)
The present is:

SINGULAR

I am	*S:* **-win** *(m)*/**-wan** *(f)*	*T:* **-no**
you *(m)* are	*S:* **-wit**	*T:* **-hat**
you *(f)* are	*S:* **-wat**	*T:* **-hat**
he/it is	*S:* **ile**	*T:* **-yo**
she/it is	*S:* **ila**	*T:* **-yo**

PLURAL

we are	*S:* **-wakh**	*T:* **-na**
you are	*S:* **-ton**	*T:* **-hatu**
they are	*S:* **ilay**	*T:* **-ne**

The negative form is:

SINGULAR

I'm not	*S:* **la-win** *(m)*/**la-wan** *(f)*	*T:* **lat-no**
you *(m)* aren't	*S:* **la-wit**	*T:* **lat-hat**
you *(f)* aren't	*S:* **la-wit**	*T:* **lat-hat**
he/it isn't	*S:* **la-ile**	*T:* **layto**
she/it isn't	*S:* **la-ila**	*T:* **layto**

PLURAL

we aren't	*S:* **la-iwakh,**	*T:* **lat-na**
you aren't	*S:* **la-iton**	*T:* **lat-hatu**
they aren't	*S:* **la-ilay**	*T:* **lat-ne**

The simple past is:

SINGULAR

I was	*S:* **-nwa**	*T:* **-wayno/-nowa**
you were	*S:* **-twa**	*T:* **-watwa**
he/she/it was	*S:* **-wa**	*T:* **-wa**

PLURAL

we were	*S:* **-khwa**	*T:* **-wayna**
you were	*S:* **-tuwa**	*T:* **-waytu/–tuwa**
they were	*S:* **-w**	*T:* **-wen**

e.g. "I am a doctor"
S: **asya-win** *(m)*/**asita-wan** *(f)*
T: **osyo-no** *(m)*/**ositho-no** *(f)*

"You were not a doctor"
S: **Laytwa asya/asita.**
T: **Lo-watwa osyo/ositho.**

"Where is the hotel?"
S: **Ika ile bet bawta?**
T: **Ayko-yo u-hotel** (*or* **fundqo**)**?**

—"To have"
Corresponding to the English verb "to have", Aramaic prefers to use the expression "there is to (me/you/him/her, etc)" – *S:* **it-/et-**, *T:***kit-** "there is/are". Therefore "I have" is translated as *S:* **et-li**, *T:***kit-li** (literally "there is/are to me").

SINGULAR

I have	*S:* **et-li**	*T:***kit-li**
you *(m)* have	*S:* **it-lokh**	*T:***kit-lokh**
you *(f)* have	*S:* **it-lakh**	*T:***kit-lekh**
he/it has	*S:* **it-le**	*T:***kit-le**
she/it has	*S:* **it-la**	*T:***kit-la**

PLURAL

we have	*S:* **it-lan**	*T:***kit-lan**
you have	*S:* **it-lokhon**	*T:***kit-khu**
they have	*S:* **it-lon**	*T:***kit-te/kit-len**

e.g. "Do you *(pl)* have any rooms free?"
S: **Itlokhon tawana spiqta?**
T: **Kit-khu qlayotho khalye?**

"I have medical insurance"
S: **Et-li ʿurawa kholmanaya.**
T: **Kit-li shuroro ḥulmonoyo.**

—"To go" *S:* **zalta**, *T:* **mazlo**

SINGULAR

I'm going *(m)*	*S:* **bizalawin**	*T:* **k-izzino**
I'm going *(f)*	*S:* **bi-zalewan**	*T:* **k-izzono**
you're going *(m)*	*S:* **bi-zalawet**	*T:* **k-izzokh**
you're going *(f)*	*S:* **bi-zalewat**	*T:* **k-izzekh**
he/it is going	*S:* **bi-zalale**	*T:* **k-izze**
she/it is going	*S:* **bi-zalela**	*T:* **k-izza**

PLURAL

we're going	*S:* **bi-zalawekh**	*T:* **k-izzano**
you're going	*S:* **bi-zalaton**	*T:* **k-izzokhu**
they're going	*S:* **bi-zalalay**	*T:* **k-izzin**

—"To come" *S:* **teta**, *T:* **mathyo**

SINGULAR

I'm coming *(m)*	*S:* **bi-tayawin**	*T:* **k-otheno**
I'm coming *(f)*	*S:* **bi-tayewan**	*T:* **k-uthyono**
you're coming *(m)*	*S:* **bi-tayewit**	*T:* **k-othat**
you're coming *(f)*	*S:* **bi-tayewat**	*T:* **k-othat**
he/it is coming	*S:* **bi-tayele**	*T:* **k-othe**
she/it is coming	*S:* **bi-tayela**	*T:* **k-uthyo**

PLURAL

we're coming	*S:* **bi-tayewikh**	*T:* **k-othina**
you're coming	*S:* **bi-tayeton**	*T:* **k-othutu**
they're coming	*S:* **bi-tayelay**	*T:* **k-othin**

Note that the particles *S:* **bi-** and *T:* **k-** are added to indicate continuous action, e.g. "I am ...ing", "you are ...ing", "he is ...ing", etc.

PRONUNCIATION GUIDE

Aramaic letter	*Aramaic example*	*Approximate English equivalent*
a	*S:* **alpa**, *T:* **alfo** "thousand"	c***a***t *or* f***a***ther
b	*S:* **bayta**, *T:* **bayto** "house"	***b***ox
ch	*S/T:* **chaykhana** "tea house"	***ch***urch
d	*S:* **dusha**, *T:* **dawsho** "honey"	***d***og
dh	*S:* **pladha**, *T:* **fulodho** "steel"	***th***at
e	*S:* **en**, *T:* **e** "yes"	p***e***t
f	*S:* **ferna**, *T:* **farmo** "notebook"	***f***at
g	*S:* **glida**, *T:* **glidho** "ice"	***g***ot
gh	*S:* **ṭroghe**, *T:* **eṭrugho** "orange"	*see notes*
h	*S/T:* **hawa** "air, wind"	***h***at
ḥ	*S: (not used)*, *T:* **ḥamro** "wine"	*see notes*
i	*S:* **ida**, *T:* **idho** "hand"	h***ea***t
j	*S:* **julle**, *T:* **jule** "clothes"	***j***et
k	*S:* **kukhwa**, *T:* **kukwo** "star"	***k***ick
kh	*S:* **kharita**, *T:* **kharita** "map"	a***ch***, as in German
l	*S:* **lakhma**, *T:* **laḥmo** "bread"	***l***et
m	*S:* **miya**, *T:* **maye** "water"	***m***at
n	*S:* **nashe**, *T:* **noshe** "people"	***n***et
o	*S:* **dokana**, *T:* **dukano** "shop"	c***o***t, as in South British English
p	*S/T:* **paṭaṭa** "potato"	***p***et
q	*S:* **qenṭrun**, *T:* **qunṭrun** "center"	*see notes*
r	*S:* **resha**, *T:* **risho** "head, leader"	***r***at
s	*S:* **sitwa**, *T:* **sathwo** "winter"	***s***it
ṣ	*S:* **ṣni^{c}uta**, *T:* **ṣni^{c}utho** "industry"	*see notes*
sh	*S:* **shqaqa**, *T:* **shqoqo** "street"	***sh***ut
t	*S:* **tar^{c}a**, *T:* **tar^{c}o** "door, gate"	***t***en
ṭ	*S:* **ṭayra**, *T:* **ṭayro** "bird"	*see note*
th	*S:* **methshuqanuta**, *T:* **mezdabnonutho** "marketing"	***th***eory
u	*S:* **khilyuta**, *T:* **ḥalyutho** "dessert"	sh***oo***t
w	*S:* **waraqa**, *T:* **waroqo** "paper"	***w***ing
y	*S:* **yawma**, *T:* **yawmo** "day"	***y***es

z	*S:* **zmirta**, *T:* **zmirto** "song"	zebra
ᶜ	*S:* **ᶜayna**, *T:* **ᶜayno** "eye"	*see notes*
'	*[at the front of any word beginning with a vowel]*	*see notes*

For the alternative consonants **v** and **zh**, see the note on spelling at the end of this section.

Nothing beats listening to a native speaker, but the following notes should help give you some idea of how to pronounce the following letters. Like English, the spoken language has a range of variations in pronunciation that are not reflected in the written language – these are not only from the various villages and towns in the region but also from the various forms of Aramaic spoken elsewhere, including, of course, West and East Syriac. The standard languages presented in this book, however, will enable you to be understood clearly wherever you may be.

—Vowels

1) There is a degree of regional variation in Aramaic vowels which is not reflected in the transliteration used in this book. However, this does not usually affect meaning.
2) The combination **ay** is usually pronounced as in the English word "hay", e.g. *S:* **bayta**, *T:* **bayto** "house", *S:* **zaytone**, *T:* **zayte** "olives".
3) The difference between vowels in Swadaya and Madinkhaya is in reality minimal and easy to identify, if you remember that the main alternation of Swadaya **a** and Turoyo **o** (*S:* **ana** vs. *T:* **ono** – "I") represents the same underlying vowel sound. This is as regular and as simple as the alternative pronunciations (and not reflected in the spelling) in English of the vowel in "John" or "won" (*US:* **"J<u>ah</u>n"** vs. *UK:* **"J<u>oh</u>n"**; *US:* **"w<u>ah</u>n"** vs. *UK:* **"w<u>oh</u>n"**).

—Consonants

kh is the rasping "ch" in Sottish "loch" and German "ach", frequently transcribed in English as "kh". It is also pronounced like the Castilian Spanish "jota" in "jamás". [= Arabic *khā'* خ]

gh — is pronounced like a sort of growl in the back of your throat – like when you're gargling. Frequently transcribed into English as "gh" for other languages that have this sound, the German or Parisian "r" is the easy European equivalent. [= Arabic *ghayn* غ]

ḥ — is a more "emphatic" form of **h**. Take the exhaling sound you make when you've just burnt your mouth after taking a sip of boiling hot soup, push it right back into the very back of your mouth, making sure your tongue goes back too, and that should give a good approximation! [= Arabic *ḥā'* ح]

ᶜ if you follow the same pronunciation rules for **ḥ**, with your tongue and back of mouth all pressed up against the back of your throat, then simply change the hiss of the **ḥ** to a sound using your vocal cords. If you're then sounding like you're being choked, then you've got it. Hint: Rather than think of **ᶜ** as a consonant, think of it as a "vowel modifier", and when listening to a native speaker, note how it changes any vowel in its vicinity, "pharyngealizing" the vowel, sending half the sound up the nose. [= Arabic *ᶜayn* ع]

q is pronounced like a **k**, but right back in your mouth at the throat end, in the same area as **ḥ** and **ᶜ**. Imagine you have a marble in the back of your throat and that you're bouncing it using only your glottis, and make a **k** sound at the same time. [= Arabic ق]

ṣ and **ṭ** are *emphatic* versions of **s** and **t** respectively. You may also hear them referred to as "dark" consonants. As an example, begin making the sound **s** as you normally would with the English word "sir". *Without moving your lips,* move your tongue slightly down and slightly forward towards your teeth, so that the sound changes into something similar to "soar but with a "thicker" sound. Do the same for **t**, using the (invented!) word "tir" to become "tor". At first you may find it easier to do this for consonants at the beginnings of words. [**ṣ** = Arabic *ṣād* ص, **ṭ** = Arabic *ṭā'* ط]

' is what is called the "glottal stop". You simply close the glottis at the very back of mouth/top of your throat, and then release the built up air. The result is a light "uh" sound with a very slight grunt just before it. Although it is not written, it occurs in the conversational speech of nearly all English speakers, being most noticeable in the pronunciation of words like "bottle" as "bo'el" by some Londoners. Although not written in this book because it is always predictable, it occurs at the beginning of every Aramaic word that starts with a vowel. [= Arabic *hamza* ء]

—Notes on spelling

The transliteration used in this book generally reflects the pronunciation of the spoken languages of East Syriac/ Swadaya and West Syriac/Turoyo and not the actual spelling, which is not always predictable and can also be subject to different interpretations by different speakers. Aside from the presence of the more numerous Swadaya speakers with their own differences in pronunciation and grammar, there are personal and regional variations in Turoyo of consonants and vowels. Just as in English, these usually have no effect on meaning, and are easily picked up when you have found your "Assyrian ear."

Changing the sound of certain consonants in the pronunciation of words is a regular feature of some Swadaya sub-dialects, but there is also a marked tendency in conversational Turoyo to do this as well. The most common you will hear are **w** and **v**, **dh** and **z**, **th** and **s**, **ṭ** and **t**, **f** and **p**, and, in loan words from other languages, **j** and **zh**, **ch** and **j**.

Examples are **halwo** "milk" which can be pronounced as **halv̱o**; **qritho** "village", which some dialects pronounce as **qris̱o**; **ṭuro** "mountain", sometimes pronounced as **ṯuro**; **fotho** "face" as **p̱otho**; **didhi** "my" as **diẕi**; **dijmin** "enemy" as **diẕẖmin**. Similarly, the vowels can also be realised in different ways and have both long and short versions associated with them. ■

THE ALPHABET

Modern Aramaic is written in the Assyrian or Syriac alphabet, which is read from right to left. It is a cursive or joined-up script, and is made up of consonants (see the table overleaf). Vowels are sometimes, but rarely, written in the form of smaller signs (called diacritics) above or below these consonants. Note that there are no separate letters for some sounds, such as **gh**, **dh** and **th**.

There are three major variations of the Syriac alphabet. The oldest and classical form of the alphabet is Estrangela or Estrangelo, now used mainly in formal inscriptions or religious texts.

Turoyo, or West Syriac, is usually written in the Western script, known as Serto, and also called Maronite or Jacobite script. The Arabic alphabet was based on a version of this form of Syriac.

Swadaya, or East Syriac, is usually written in the Eastern script, known as Madinkhaya (also used as a name for the dialect). As with the dialect, there are several names for this script, including Assyrian, Chaldean, and Nestorian (the term that is used in the chart on the following page).

You may also come across the term Garshuni or Karshuni. This refers to the forms of Arabic and (rarely) Turkish written in the Aramaic script.

Aramaic script styles

Estrangela	Serto	Nestorian	Names of letters
ܠ	ܠ	ܠ	***l*** *lamadh/ lomadh*
ܡ ܡ	ܡ	ܡ ܡ	***m*** *mim/ mim*
ܢ ܢ	ܢ	ܢ ܢ	***n*** *nun/ nun*
ܣ	ܣ	ܣ	***s*** *simkath/ semkath*
ܥ	ܥ	ܥ	***ʿ*** *ʿe/ ʿe*
ܦ	ܦ	ܦ	***p/f*** *pe/ fe*
ܨ	ܨ	ܨ	***ṣ*** *ṣade/ ṣode*
ܩ	ܩ	ܩ	***q*** *qop/ quf*
ܪ	ܪ	ܪ	***r*** *resh/ rish*
ܫ	ܫ	ܫ	***sh*** *shin/ shin*
ܬ	ܬ	ܬ	***t*** *taw/ taw*

Estrangela	Serto	Nestorian	Names of letters
ܐ	ܐ	ܐ	**’/a** *S: alap/ T:olaf*
ܒ	ܒ	ܒ	***b*** *beth/ beth*
ܓ	ܓ	ܓ	***g*** *gamal/ gomal*
ܕ	ܕ	ܕ	***d*** *dalath/ dolath*
ܗ	ܗ	ܗ	***h*** *he/ he*
ܘ	ܘ	ܘ	***w/u*** *waw/ waw*
ܙ	ܙ	ܙ	***z*** *zayin zayn*
ܚ	ܚ	ܚ	***ḥ*** *kheth/ ḥeth*
ܛ	ܛ	ܛ	***ṭ*** *ṭeth/ ṭeth*
ܝ	ܝ	ܝ	***y*** *yodh/ yuth*
ܟ ܟ	ܟ	ܟ ܟ	***k*** *kap/ kof*

Read from top of right page to bottom of left page! ←

Assyrian/Syriac vowels

Serto vowels

i	e	o	a	u

Nestorian vowels

î	ê	e	â	a	ô/o	û/u

Naming the language...

In English, speakers of Modern Aramaic (also known by linguists as Neo-Aramaic) prefer to call their language Assyrian or Syriac.

As explained elsewhere in this book, Assyrians have many different names to explain their various identities, reflecting the region they come from and the religion they profess. In the same way, speakers of the various dialects also have a variety of names to distinguish the special form of the language they use.

The main language names used in this book — Swadaya ("Spoken [dialect]")* and Turoyo ("Mountain [dialect]")** — are used by the Eastern and Western communities respectively as good identifiers for use by non-Assyrians.

When Assyrians wish to make a special effort to distinguish between the two, Swadaya is called Madinkhaya (or "Madenhoyo" in Turoyo), which means "Eastern (dialect)", and Turoyo is called Ma'erboyo (or "Ma'irwaya" in Swadaya), which means "Western (dialect)". The terms reflect the areas where the dialects were originally spoken (roughly east and west of the Tigris river.

In fact, people who speak Swadaya prefer to call it Suray, Surit, or Sureth. People who speak Turoyo call it Surayt. In both cases, the names mean "Syriac" or "Assyrian".

* **Swada** means "conversation", so **swadaya** literally means "conversational", "spoken" or "vernacular". You may also find it translated as "modern" or "contemporary".
** Note that **turoyo** ultimately means "from/of Tur-Abdin".

ARAMAIC
Dictionary

SWADAYA–ENGLISH
MADINKHAYA–INGLISHAYA

A

aarkhe mill
Ab August
abuba gawaya inner-tube
abub-glulita gun barrel
Adhar March
adhenta handset
adhna ear; **adhnate** ears
ad-lele tonight
adshay dimma blood group
aghogha canal
aha/hadhe this; **ah shawuʿa** this week
akadimyaya/akadimyayta academic *(m/f)*
akara/akarta farmer
akaruta farming
akhida captain; officer
akhidna viper
akhnan we
akhton you *plural*
akhudha clutch
Almanya Germany
alpa thousand
Amerika America
amilla carpet
Amirkaya/Amirkayta American
amnaara artist
amra d-ktana cotton wool
amra wool
amsha marsh
ana I
anaha those
ananas pineapple
ani they
anna these
antibayotiks antibiotics
ap also
apta break; pause
aqla foot; leg; **aqla ṣniʿta** artificial leg; **aqle** feet; legs
shokhlapa season
arbʿa/arbaʿ four
arbobya chalk
arʿa land
ardikhla/ardikhlita architect
Aremnaya/Aremnayta Armenian
Armenia Armenia
armune pomegranate
arnowa rabbit
arya lion; Leo
arzapta; **arzipta** hammer
asakhta copy; photocopy
ashid ṣarukhe rocket-launcher
ashita avalanche
ashpaza guesthouse
asira prisoner; **asira d-qrawa** prisoner-of-war
as-sara decade
asya doctor; **asya d-shinne** dentist
at you *m singular*
ata sign
ate you *f singular*
athta woman; female
atra sharya independent state
Atur Assyria
Aturaya/Aturayta Assyrian
Australia Australia
awa d-awahate patriarch
awaha that
awahata ancestors
awana muziqaya concert hall
awkhar/awkhrath b-shakhra alcoholic
awsaya kyanaya physiotherapy
awyuta coalition
aya shita this year
aya ṭahra aha ramsha this afternoon/evening
ayds AIDS
ayn yes
ayni? which?
Ayrishnaya/Ayrishnayta Irish
Azerbayjan Azerbaijan

B

b- with; in; by; **b-sapra** in the morning; **b-ṭahra** in the afternoon

baba; **babi** father
baʿghal express
bahra noun light; **bahra ramuza** indicator light; **bahra d-ida** flashlight
baluṭe chestnut
bammya okra
banawsha/banawshayta purple
banzin petrol; accelerator
baqala greengrocer
baqta mosquito
bar bar
bar zawga husband
barʿana ram
barda *noun* hail
barmata/bartmata citizen
bart zawga wife
bartakhti slope
baṣa bus; **baṣa zʿora** minibus
bashule to cook
basima fresh
baṭarita battery
baṭṭa duck
bawta d-ʿayna pupil of eye
bayta house
baza falcon; vulture
baziqa hawk
bʿaya to want
bʿildara enemy; opponent
bʿildwawa enemy
bdhara powder; to sow; **bdhara d-shyagha** washing powder; detergent
beʿta egg
bellura crystal
bet house; building
bet-apyuta bakery
bet-arke library
bet-asire prison
bet-bawta hotel
bet-bshala kitchen
bet-ʿorpana bank
bet-dayna namusaya law court
bet-drasha college; academy
bet-drashe sports club
bet-etqe museum
bet-ezgaduta embassy
bet-glakha exhibition
beth-sharire assembly; parliament
bet-khawra theater
bet-khizwane cinema
bet-khmama bathroom
bet-khwushya jail
bet-krihe hospital
bet-maekhla restaurant
bet-mawlada maternity hospital
bet-opera opera house
bet-qasawuta butcher's shop
bet-qore cemetery
bet-samane chemist's; pharmacy
bet-sawba university; **bet-drasha gaysaya** military academy
bet-shiʿya stadium
bet-shulṭana; **bet-sharire** parliament
bet-shyaghta laundry
bet-silya toilet(s)
bet-smakha nightclub
bet-supara barber
bet-ṭawsa airport
bet-tiya tea house
biʿta egg
bikhaya to live
bikhyara to watch
biktawa to write
bildara iloqtronaya e-mail
bildara rqiʿaya air mail
bildara sghila registered mail
binyana building
biqra cattle; herd
birʿasha to wake up
birka knee
birqa lightning
birtha castle; palace
birzarʿe seeds
bista bottle; **bisith miya** water bottle
biṣla onion
bisra meat; **bisra d-sharkha/sharkhe** beef
biyara fallowland
biye eggs; **biye shliqe** boiled eggs
bizqe khilla sand; gravel
bkhira/bkhirta scientist
bkhubukh!/bkhubakh!/bkhub aokhon! cheers!
bnate daughters; children
bnath-gane aubergine/eggplant
bnune children sons; children
bra ide gloves
bramsha in the evening
brata daughter

braya be born
brişim; silk
Briṭania Britain
Briṭnaya/Briṭnayta British
bruna son
bshawuta local
bshila/bshilta cooked
bsir less
bşirot dimma anemia
Btulta Virgo
Budaya/Budayta Buddhist
bukhrana exam; test; to test
bura/burta illiterate
but boots
buṭlana holidays

C

ᶜagholta d-dmakha sleeping car
ᶜagholta d-mukhla dining car
ᶜalᶜala raᶜmaya thunderstorm
ᶜalᶜala storm
ᶜalma world
ᶜalwa envelope; **şanduqa bil-daraya** parcel
ᶜana ewe
ᶜapra soil
ᶜaqara şniᶜaya industrial estate
ᶜaqawaya/ᶜaqawayta/ᶜaqawaye archaeological
ᶜaqirwa scorpion; Scorpio
ᶜaqubra mouse
ᶜArabaya/ᶜArabayta Arab
ᶜarbaᶜsar fourteen
ᶜarawa desert
ᶜarawuta insurance
ᶜarbala sieve
ᶜarbᶜi forty
ᶜArboshiba Wednesday
ᶜarpilla fog/mist
ᶜarpillaya foggy
ᶜarsa roikha double bed
ᶜaşalta muscle
ᶜasqa difficult
ᶜasquta crisis
ᶜasuwa surgeon
ᶜatiqa old
ᶜatira rich
ᶜawa wood; forest
ᶜayba pocket
ᶜayma cloud
ᶜaymana cloudy
ᶜayna eye; **ᶜayna şniᶜta** artificial eye; **ᶜayna *ḍ-miya*** spring of water; **ᶜaynate** eyes
ᶜdana time; **ᶜdana d-khizda** harvest
ᶜelta d-khzuqya reason for travel
ᶜelwa envelope
ᶜenda nightingale
ᶜeqba ankle
ᶜerwa (*plural* **ᶜerwe)** sheep
ᶜerwana charity organisation; **shutas ᶜerwana** charity organisation
ᶜesra/ᶜsar ten
ᶜesri twenty
ᶜetqe ruins
ᶜeṭra perfume; **ᶜeṭra dshkhata** deodorant
ᶜida d-Qyamta Easter
ᶜida Zᶜura Christmas
ᶜinwe grapes
ᶜiqa narrow
ᶜIraq Iraq
ᶜIraqnaya/ᶜIraqnayta Iraqi
ᶜirwe lamb
ᶜisaqta ring
ᶜizza goat
ᶜlayma young
ᶜnupya violence
ᶜodhala d-tuna haystack
ᶜohdana memory
ᶜomra age; church
ᶜopaya funeral
ᶜorwa *noun* crow
ᶜpapa to multiply
ᶜqra root
ᶜrayta breakfast
ᶜRuta Friday
ᶜsar *see* **ᶜesra**
ᶜşara syrup
ᶜşira d-pere fruit juice
ᶜsiraya/ᶜsirayta tenth
ᶜumr age; **Kma le ᶜumrokh/ᶜumrakh?** How old are you *(m/f)*?
ᶜupapa multiplication
ᶜuṭma thigh
ᶜuzaya reinforcements

CH

chaykhana tea house
chercherroka *insect* cricket

D

d- of
dabasha/dabashta/dabashe bee
daʿtid future
daʿwar past
dahwa gold
dakhi? how?
dakhshe razanaye secret police
dakhya clean
dalqiw palkhe anti-personnel
dalqiw rashopyate anti-tank mine
dalqiw taysyate anti-aircraft gun
d-alqobl opposite
dalquw qurme antibiotic
dambuş pin
dan to condemn
dapa d-nişle cupboard
dara century
daraya/darayta modern
darkhe laqit paraye escalator
darra wrestling
darrara guerrilla
darta courtyard
dashna gift
dawe buttermilk; ayran
Dawla Aquarius
dawqa C.D.
dawya unhappy
da-yana referee
dayna debt
dayra monastery; convent
dayurta patrol
dayyana judge
d-bitaya le next
dibba bear
dibbora/dibborta wasp; hornet
didwa fly; **didwe** flies
dijay disc-jockey
dika hen
dikhra male
diktaturaya dictator
diktaturuta dictatorship
dimma blood
dimoqraṭayuta democracy
dipna side of body
diqinta chin
diqna beard
disko disco
diwa wolf
d-la rwakha uncomfortable
dmaeya expensive
dmakha to sleep
dmkhawish to arrest
dokana shop; store; **dokan ʿutade** hardware store; **dokan kerke** stationer's; **dokan krokhya** travel agent; **dokan laqiṭraye** electrical goods store; **dokan makhimle** department store; **dokan msane** shoe shop; **dokan yariquta** vegetable shop; **dokan ktawe** bookshop; **dokan lwushe** clothes shop; **dokan spar zawne** news-stand; **dokana qariwta qa nashe qariwe** a local shop for local people
dollar dollar
draʿa arm; **draʿa şniʿa** artificial arm
Duchnaya/Duchnayta Dutch
dugla to lie
dukat moalada place of birth
durasha discussion; debate
durikta foot
dusha honey
dwara lasṭraya neutral drive
dwiqa/dwiqta reserved
dyuta ink

E

e'n yes
ebbane fruit
ediom today
egarta letter
eka? where?
ekzuz exhaust
elʿa rib; **elʿe** ribs
elpa boat
emama day
emma hundred
Emra Aries
emwate mkhaydate United Nations
enfluwanza flu
England England
Englishaya/Englishnayta English
eshatha fever
eshqat last year
eshta bottom

eshta/shet six
eshtaʿsar sixteen
eshti sixty
esit qa handle
eṣṭla suit
eṭrughaya/eṭrughayta *color* orange
euro euro
Europe Europe
ezgada ambassador
ezla departures

F

faks fax
ferna bakery
Frangaya/Frangayta French

G

gabba suyasaya party political
gabuye voting
gaduda/gadudta teenager
Gadya Capricorn
gaghulta peak
gallawa dagger
galin gallon
galuya/galwayta refugee; **galuye** refugees
galyan paquʿe mine detector
gam la d-grashta tow rope
gamisha buffalo
gamla camel
gannana/gannanta gardener
ganta garden; **ganta d-khaywate** zoo
gare roof
gargurta tractor
garibya north
garma bone; **garma d-shuqala** tibia; **garma d-uṭma** femur
Garmanaya/Garmanayta German
garurta drawer
gashusha spy
gawra man; **gawra/gawirta** brown
gawsa shelter
gaysa army
gaysaya/gaysayta soldier
gazula left-wing
gdanpa balcony
gdhodha hedgehog
gdila woven
ghulyunara/ghulyunarta journalist
gidhʿa trunk of tree
gigarta throat
ghighla tire/tyre; **gighla ʿatida** spare tire
gilaṣe cherry
gilda skin; leather
gilla grass
gipta vine
gishra bridge
gizabra/gizborta cashier
glakh amna art gallery
glapa sculpture
glida ice
glulita gun; pistol
gnawta theft
gnay yawma sunset
gorwe socks
goze walnut
gram gram
grapefrut grapefruit
grasa to grind
grashta to retreat
grista loaf of bread
guba well of water
gubaya election; vote
gubta cheese
guda team; wall; **guda d-mashikne** apartment block
gulla bullet; **gulla d-bahranita** tracer bullet; **gulle la purqiʿe** unexploded ammunition
gupala walking stick
Gurgaya/Gurgayta Georgian
gusha staff
guya ball
gwada pony
gwina eyebrow
gwira/gwirta married
gyade nerve

H

hadam paghra organ *of body*
hadama d-bet-sholṭana member of parliament
hadhe *see* **aha**
hadia leader; guide; guidebook
hadiya now
hae she; it
halkha on foot

harkaa here
hasha just now
haw he/it
hawa air; wind
hawana windy
herga lesson
hgham arʿa landslide
Hindawaya/Hindawayta Indian
Hindaya/Hindayta Hindu
Hindu India
hipkayuta reactionary
HIV HIV
hoki hockey
Holanda the Netherlands
Hoshara/Hosharta Azerbaijani
hpakhta reverse gear
hwaya to be

I

ida hand
idra barn
ika ele?/ika ela/eka lay? where is/are ...?
ikhala meals
ilana; ilanta tree
Ilul September
imama daytime
iman? when?
ina but
iqarta family
Iran Iran
Iranaya/Iranayta Iranian
Ireland Ireland
isara rock; **isare** rocks
isarta rifle
ishṭar ʿarawotha insurance policy
Ishwaṭ February
Israelyaya/Israelyayta Israeli
isure suyasaye diplomatic ties
it tama? is there?/are there?
Iṭalnaya/Iṭalnayta Italian
ituta zawganayta marital status
Iyar May
izla kushe spider

J

jaydan teapot
Jorjiya Georgia
julle clothes
jure urine

K/KH

kababa kebab
kaiwa sick
kalba/kalibta dog
Kaldaya/Kaldayta Chaldean Catholic; Assyrian Catholic
Kaliwta pliers
kamutra pear
Kanada Canada
Kanadaya/Kanadayta Canadian
Kanun Qamaya December
Kanun Tray Yana January
kanuna cooker; stove
kappa palm of hand
karawis celery; parsley
karma orchard; vineyard
karra butter
karsa stomach
karukha/karukhta tourist
karukhuta tourism
Kashshaṭa Saggitarius
kasya hood
katawa/katawta office worker
katpa shoulder; shoulder blade
katuwa/katuwta writer
katuwta d-ida typewriter
kawaza vase
kawda liver
kawe window
kawidna mule
kazbarta coriander
kbar probably
kekhla mascara
kepa rock; **kepe** rocks
kerka d-durasha exercise book
kerka d-zohare notebook
kespa coins; **kespa sharya** loose change
kesta d-dmakha sleeping bag
kha palgaya one-half
kha rwiʿaya one-quarter
kha tlitaya one-third
kha/khda one
khabta d-nawma sleeping pill; **khabe d-nawma** sleeping pills
khabusha apple
khadiʿsar eleven
khadya breast
khakhta plum

khala to eat; vinegar; sand
khalula screw
khalwa milk; **khalwa d-yimma** mother's milk; **khalwa d-ʿeze** goat's milk; **khalwa d-tawiryate** cow's milk; **khalwa ywisha** powdered milk
khalzuna snail
khamesh *see* **khamsha**
khamra wine
khamsha/khamesh five
khamshaʿsar fifteen
khamshi fifty
Khamshoshiba Thursday
khamuṣa/khamuṣta sour
khanuta pub
khaputaya misty
khaqla d-bet-bawte the hotel industry
khaqla d-paquʿe minefield
khaqla d-rwakhanuta the leisure industry
khaqla d-zubana retail industry
kharaya last
kharița map; **kharița d-midta** city map; **kharițta d-Los Angeles** a map of Los Angeles; **kharițta d-urkhate** road map
kharsuma hose
kharwiye maize
khaṣ lettuce
khaṣa back
khasha to go
khashuta calculator; computer
khasna fort
khasya metropolitan
khata/khatda new
khawerta friend; girlfriend
khawla mṣalpana barbed wire
khawri/khwarti friend
khawra friend; boyfriend
khaya alive
khayața/khayațta dressmaker
khaye life
khayla grumanaya nuclear power
khaylawate troops; **khaylawate națure d-shayna** peace-keeping troops
khayyața/khayațta tailor
khazayate glasses; spectacles; **khazayate shimshae** sunglasses
khda *see* **kha**
khegga muziqaya concert
khekhemta wisdom
khel-țawsa airforce
khemra vertebra
kheshlata jewelery
khesra waist
khghira/khghirta disabled
khigga musiqaya concert
khilla sand
khilya/khlita sweet
khilyuta sweets; candy; dessert
khimṣa lemon; lime
khiqla field
khira free
khirba bad; badly
khirdal mustard
khirțmane chickpeas; peas
khiruta freedom
khis aa full moon
khițțe wheat; **khițe shimaye** corn
khizwa view
khlawa to milk an animal
khlita *see* **khilya**
khmara/khmarta donkey
khmața needle; syringe
khmishaya/khmishayta fifth
khnaqa necktie
khnaqta whooping cough
khola rope
Khoshiba Sunday
khrițta map
khruta hip
khṣara siege
khshamita dinner/supper
khshawa to calculate
khtama stamp
khțuța line
khuba love
khukhe peach
khula rope
khulapa exchange
khulmana health
khurara liberation
khushbana calculation
khut under
khuța wire; cable
khutama end
khuțra walking stick
khuwa snake
khuya darkness

khwala corruption
khwara/khwarta white
khyani/khyanti relative
khyuka itching
khzaya to see
Khziran June
khzura pig
kika cake
kilita kidney
kilogram kilogram
kilomiṭra kilometer
kilyata kidneys
kipa stone
kipna famine
kirya short
kisa pocket
kiwa disease
kiya chewing gum
klaya to stop; to stand; **kli!/klay!** stop *(m/f)*!
klayta d-baṣa bus stop
klita kidney
kma; **kma lay?** how many?; **kma qurba?** how near?; **kma rikhqa?** how far?
kmana cumin
kmina ambush
knonta ruler instrument
knoshya assembly; meeting
kobra cobra
kodinta mare
kolf golf
kpina/kpinta hungry
krata thumb
krawa to cultivate; **krawa arʿa** to plow
krukhya travel; tourism
kshara bukhrana to pass an exam
ktana cotton; cotton wool
ktawa book
kteta/ktayate chicken
kukhwa star; **kukhwe** stars
kuma/kumta black
kunash khizda combine harvester
kunash mille dictionary
kunasha sum
kunaya surname
kunikta handkerchief
kupa low
Kurdistan Kurdistan
kurhan kalbuta rabies
kurhana myablana venereal disease
kursya chair; **kursya d-gighle** wheelchair
kushara success
kushk kiosk
kusita hat
kutasha struggle
kutina jacket
kwita iron *for clothing*
kyula d-bahra light meter

L

l- to; for; **l-qodama** forwards; **l-bistar** backwards
la no; **la gwira/la gwirta** single
laakha here
laʿusa jaw
lahana cabbage
lakhma bread
laqiṭ para electricity
laqṭan mille parrot
laweta tiredness
laymuna lemon; lime
layt: layt maʿla no entry; **layt qitra** no problem; **layt tnana** no smoking
lʿel up
Leʿza dialect
lghaw in
libba heart
lile; lilya night; **lilya d-daʿwar** last night
lishana tongue; language
liṭra liter
lkhayta ṭohmanayta ethnic cleansing
lkhepa blanket; quilt
lobye green beans
lori lorry/truck
lowna brick
lukha d-qaysa plank
lukha d-qiryana blackboard
lukha record
lumada conference
Lunan Lebanon
Lunanaya/Lunanayta Lebanese
lwar out; outside
lwushe clothes

M

m'arʿuta reception
ma'asore to take prisoner
mabruye to give birth to
mabṣure to subtract
maʿbar tkhuma passport
maʿirwa west
maʿla entrance
maʿye intestines
madʿure vomiting
madinkha east
Madinkhaya/Madinkhayta Church of the East Christian
maghidla tower
magla sickle
makhara/makharta engineer
makhimla d-radiyate car park; parking lot
makhitwa office; **makhitwa d-pitqe** ticket office
makhizyana television; **makhizyana mziʿana** portable T.V.
makhsa d-bet-ṭawsa airport tax
makhse customs
makhshula d-khimma heat wave
makhube love
makhule khaywa to feed an animal
makhzita mirror
makilyana brake
maktawzawna history
malarya malaria
malka king
malkhot a'ar aviation
mallala speaker; **mallala d-lqara** guest speaker
malpana/malpanta teacher
malukha/malokhta consultant
mamluth arʿa geography
manayuta maths
mani? who?
mapqa exit; **mapqa ʿriṣa** emergency exit
mapqana/mapqanta filmmaker
mapqanuta subtraction
maqip to pursue
maqrana fridge
maqyapta suyasayta political rally
mara spade
marduta culture
marga meadow
maribʿa womb
marira/marirta bitter
markawta d-sosye horse and cart
marmana jack
marmita thought
marmita la mporqiʿta unexploded bomb
marwade earrings
marwakhta fan
marwana telescope
Masata Libra
maṣawta bench
masʿara clinic
mashghan pomma mouthwash
mashikna apartment
mashiqya irrigation
mashkawta bed
mashrita camp; **mashrita d-bawta** hostel; **mashrita d-asire** POW camp; **mashrita d-galuye** refugee camp
mashukhta d-khamimuta thermometer
masilqanita elevator; lift
maṣinʿana/maṣinʿayta factory worker
masipra scissors
masir toqane adapter
masmakh kilsha plaster cast
masran baynat matanaya international operator
masta yogurt
masurqa wrist
matayota citizenship
mathlana/mathlanita actor
mawbla suitcase; **mawble** baggage
mawdhʿanuta information
mawdidh rikhshe insecticide
mawkhrut b-shakhra alcoholism
mawlada birth
mawlode to give birth to
mawlupe to teach
mawta death
mawtba seat
mawtwa seat in assembly; **mawtwa ʿellaya** upper house; **mawtwa takhtaya** lower house; **mawtwa d-sharire** cabinet

mayya water
mazra'ta farm
mazuzṭa lizard
m'adure help
m'aghuda anesthetist
m'arpana/m'arpanta banker
m'artha cave
mdabrana/mdabranita administrator
mdakhe spices
mdakhyana antiseptic; anesthetic
mdarshana/mdarshanta trainer
mdawrana driver
mdawur to drive
mdita town; **mdita 'tiqta** old city
me'ṭapa overcoat
medyara ar'anaya floor; story
megra'ta razor
melya/mlita full
memerta written article
meshkana hostage
meshkha oil; cream; ointment
meshtuta party
mesreqta comb; **mesreqta d-sa'ra** hairbrush
meṭalta umbrella
methshuqanuta marketing
meṭya/mṭeta ripe
mezta a hair
mgawis to take shelter
mgawnana colour
mghalta magazine
mhalukhe to walk
midrashta school; **midrashta d-kahne** seminary; **midrashta gaysayta** military academy
mikanik/mikanikayta mechanic
mikhadh b'eltha protest
mikhulta food
mila mile
milaa flood
milkha salt
milkhana/milkhanta salty
milyon million
mina hair
minara mosque
mishkha oil; cream; **mishkha dalqub shimsha** sunblock cream
mishmishshe apricot
mita dead
miṭra rain; meter
miṭrapoliṭa metropolitan
miya water; **miya qarire** cold water; **miya shakhine** hot water; **miya sipe** mineral water
miyure intestine
mizaṭra/misaṭrana person exile
mkaprana towel; **mkaprane d-zghugha d-radita** windshield wipers
mkapranita eraser; rubber
mkasyanuta to camouflage
mkhalpana transformer
mkharir to free
mkharure to liberate
mkhashwana/makhshwanta accountant
mkhawya binoculars
mkhaya to hit
mkhila weak
mkhira/mkhirta fiancé/fiancée
mkhuta d-libba heat stroke
mkhuta d-shimsha sunstroke
mlita *see* **melya**
mlu'a subject
mmashkhana economist
mna'awle to shoe a horse
mnaya to count
moray sosye horse racing
moṭaya arrivals
mpaqude to command
mparqi' to explode
mqal'ana cannon; **mqal'ana la mporqi'a** unexploded ordnance; **mqal'ane** artillery
mqam before
mqanuwe to conquer
mqarṣana freezing
mqarṭan teprate nail-clippers
mrarta gall bladder
mrawriw wana microscope
mriquta kholmanayta hygiene
msaghlanita tape-recorder
msakhip to destroy
msalip to wound
msane shoes
msapaqta to evacuate

msapiq l-paquʿa to clear a mine
msapranita scissors
msapyanutanaya/msapyanutanayta traditional
msaqolayuta to resist
msarhewana accelerator
msarkhana/msarkhanta criminal
mṣaruye act of surgery
msawte to talk
mṣawyana compass
msayʿana aid worker
mṣayrana/mṣayranta photographer
msharuye start
msharya/msharita paralyzed
msharyuta paralysis; stroke
mshat'asta foundation
mshayin to make peace
Mshikhaya/Mshikhayta Christian *(m/f)*; **Mshikhaya Orthodoksaya/Mshikhayta Orthodoksayta** Orthodox Christian
mshṭakha rishaya main square
mtapinkhana designer
mtaqin shaʿe watchmaker's
mtaqnan radiyate mechanic
mtargimana/mtargimanta translator
mtaslim to surrender
mtawsupe to add
mṭeta *see* **meṭya**
mudi? what?; **mudi ele awaha?** what's that?
mukha brain
munaʿa address
murabba jam
muraya match
Mushilmana/Mushelmanta Muslim
musiqa music; **musiqa klasikayta** classical music
musiqara/musiqarta musician
muza banana
muzagha weather; climate
myata to die
myature to add
myawshan saʿra hairdryer
mzake to win
mzayupe l-gubaya vote-rigging
mziʿana engine
mzighla motorbike

N

naʿuṭa/naʿuṭta tasteless
nahra river; **nahra qrisa** glacier
nakhira nose
nakhla ravine
nakhtuma/nakhtumta baker
namusa law; constitution
naqida thin
naqro caterpillar
naquwa drill
naqwa d-halkha subway
narʿa axe; **narʿa d-glidha** ice axe
nashe people
nasukhta photocopier
nasurta saw
nata ear
naṭir raze/naṭra raze secretary
natyate ears
nawdhana earthquake
nawpa goal
nawrishta candlestick
naya/nayta; raw; uncooked
nʿaṣta bite; **nʿaṣta d-baqa** mosquito bite; **nʿaṣta d-khuwa** snake bite; **nʿaṣta d-rekhshe** insect bite
nghara/ngharta carpenter
nikha slow; gently!
nimra leopard; tiger
Nisan April
nisha objective
nishra eagle
nkhasha copper
nona (*plural* **none**) fish; **none raghye** fresh fish
npala to fall
nqakha smell
nqalta dimma blood transfusion
nsakha to copy
nṣawa to plant
nsoekh copy
nsukh copy
nudhnadha earthquake
nughha dawn
Nuna Pisces
nuqazta station; **nuqazta d-base** bus station; **nuqazta d-qṭara** train station; **nuqazta d-buqare** checkpoint; **nuqazta d-dqaʿye** telephone center; **nuqazta d-mawble** baggage

counter; **nuqaza d-maʿla** check-in counter; **nuqazta d-khayla grumanaya** nuclear power station
nuqnaqa snack
nura fire

O

o; **up** and
opera opera
Orisnaya/Orisnayta Russian
Osṭralaya/Osṭralayta Australian
oxsijin oxygen
ozayla gazelle

P

pager pager
paghra body
pakhalta! excuse me!; sorry!
pakhara pottery
Pakistan Pakistan
Pakistanaya Pakistani
palakha operator; **palakha d-shulṭana/palakhta d-shulṭana** civil servant
palga d-lile midnight
palkhe military personnel
palshat urkhata crossroads
papukhta cap
paqira poor
paquʿa explosive mine; **paquʿe** mines
par rashuta horse riding
para lamb
parda d-nata eardrum
parkhanita butterfly
parkhe cucumber
parmuye understand
parqaʿta bomb; bomblet; **parqaʿta d-ida** grenade; **parqaʿtha sghulayta** cluster bomb
pashuqe to explain
pasolile beans
pasta pasta
pata face; page
paṭikha melon
patkhan khalula screwdriver
patkhan qupse can opener
paturyate mushroom
pawand pound (sterling)
pawda wrong; false
pawga regiment
pawnd pound
payukha cool
pdana plow
peghla radish
pelpel pepper
penisilin penicillin
perka d-shinne toothbrush
perqa cloth
pesme mustache
pesqa flock
peṭaṭe potato
petqa *see* **pitqa**
pezta beer
pghaʿa meet
pila elephant
pilla d-khapupa gas canister/bottle
pilma film
pindiqe hazel nut
pinkha millstone
piqaa frog
piqʿa plain; **piqʿata** plains
pira fruit; **pire raghye** fresh fruit
pirka brush
pirṭana flea; **pirṭane** fleas
pisteqe pistachio
pitqa card; **pitqa bildaraya** postcard; **pitqa dizoputa** credit card; **pitqa d-rkawta** boarding pass
pitsa pizza
pladha steel
plagha to divide
plakha to work
plakhta daqla diarrhea
plasṭik plastic
plug plug
pnita district
poakha shakhina hot wind
pom ma mouth
ponda candle
Portughlaya/Portughlayta Portuguese
prakhdoda bat
prama amputation
Pransa France
praqa finish

pras-kurhana epidemic
prass nawla internet
prezla iron; metal
prista kilim
prizla iron; metal
Pruṭaya/Pruṭayta Protestant
psaᶜ l-paquᶜa to hit a mine
pshina tilokh!/pshina tilak!/ pshina tilokhon! welcome *(m/f/pl)*!
pshiṭa easy
psikha happy
psiquta written abstract
ptaqa hernia
ptikha/ptikhta open
ptukha wide
pulagha division
puma mouth
punaya answer
punda candles
purqaᶜa detonation
putha/puthayta *color* orange

Q

qa: qa mudi? why?
qaᶜya telephone; **qaᶜya d-ida** mobile phone; **qaᶜya dsahra sniᶜaya** satellite phone
qadhma lieutenant; lieutenant-colonel
qadhmaya/qadhmayta first
qadisha saint
qaim present
qala d-qaliluta minority vote
qalil a little bit
qaliluta speed; minority; **qaliluta ṭohmayta** ethnic minority
qalma louse; **qalme** lice
qalula/qalolta light *not heavy*
qalwa military shell
qam in front of
qamaya first
qamista shirt
qamkha flour
qamra belt
qamṣa grasshopper
qanushyate earrings
qanya d-a'wara pencil
qanya pen
qapaṣ constipation
qapla d-radiyate convoy
qarᶜe pumpkin
qarira/qarirta cold; **qarirta** ice-cream
qariwa godfather; nearby
qariwta godmother
qarna summit
qasha priest
qashya/qshita tough
qaṭil khiwle painkiller
qaṭinta minute
qaṭlan baqe insect repellant
qaṭnuta republic
qaṭo/qaṭa cat
Qatoliqaya/Qatoliqayta Catholic
qaṭuba/qaṭubta butcher
qaṭula killer
qawmaya revolution
qawra tomb
qayemta statue; monument
qaysa wood; **qayse d-nura** firewood
qayṭona street
qaza goose
qazbe date
qazik silkworms
qazma pickax
qdala neck
qdila key
qidamta morning; **qidamta d-edio** this morning
qinṭa danger
qinyane livestock
qipla lock
qipniz dragonfly
qiqwana quail
qirqipta skull
qirsa frost
qirṭope potato
qishti maran rainbow
qishya hard
qiṣṣa eyebrow
qiṭa summer
qiṭᶜa d-waraqa sheet of paper
qiṭᶜate shrapnel
qiṭla murder; killing; **qiṭla bliqa** assassination
qiṭmanaya/qiṭmayata; gray
qladha necklace
qlapa military shell
quᶜya bombardment
qmata ᶜaṣwaya bandage
qnuma person
qnumaya personal

qopa monkey
qorbana qadisha holy mass
qrawa war; **qrawa mdinaya** civil war
qrawtana fighter; guerrilla
qraya to read; to study
qrita village
qṣaya to cut
qshita *see* **qashya**
qṭala to kill
qṭapa to reap
qṭara *railway* train
qudme tomorrow; **qudme qedamta** tomorrow morning; **qudme bramsha** tomorrow night; **qudme ṭahra** tomorrow afternoon; **qudme date** the day after tomorrow
qulba bracelet
qunṭrun d-mdita town center
qupsa can
qupta cauliflower; owl
qura cold; head cold
qurba near
Qurdaya/Qurdayta Kurd
qurme germs
qurnasa hatchet
qurnita corner
qursolta elbow
qurtope potato; **qurtope khilye** sweet potato
quya strong

R

raata lung
raba/rabta big
rabana monk
rabanta nun
raᶜma thunder
radio radio
radita car; **radita d-awoshpa/d-ushpa** ambulance; **radita ar-pansayta/zariditha** armored car
radiyator radiator
ragbi rugby
raghla ṣniᶜta artificial leg
raghula valley
rajim diet
rakawa/rakota passenger
rakhsha insect
rakhta butt of rifle
rakikha soft
rama high
ramka herd
ramsha evening; **ramsha d-ediom** tonight
rapa shelf
rapyuta failure
raqada dance; dancing
raqma number; **raqma d-ilanaya** extension number; **raqma d-maᶜbar tkhuma** passport number; **raqma d-maṣṭawta** platform number; **raqma d-tawana** room number
raqmaya digital
rashupta tank
rasosta; rasosyate machine-gun
rasuqta rosary
raṣuṣa shower
rathukhta kettle
raṭiwota humidity
rawba noise; **rawba d-yabrukhe** ketchup
razuqa mercenary
rbiᶜa spring
rᶜulta shivers
reghle feet
rekhsha insect
renya thought
resha head; top; leader; **resh-sharire** prime minister; **resh-gaysa** chief of staff; **resh-tagha** major-general; **resha qarira** cold; head cold
reshana general; **reshana qadhmaya** lieutenant-general
reshmala capitalism
reshquṭna president
rezza rice
rhaṭa run
ridhya d-arbaᶜ gighle 4-wheel drive
rikhana mint
rikhqa far
riqda ᶜammaya folk dancing
risha *see* **resha**
rizza rice
rkhikha/rkhikhta tender
rmay ida signature
rmayta to shoot down
rnaya to think
roba d-shinne toothpaste
ropa/ropita divorced

rpapa second
ruble ruble
ruqe saliva
rusaqa battery
rusha shoulder
Rusya Russia
rwakhana comfortable
rwiʿaya/rwiʿayta fourth
rwisuta pressure; **rwisuta dimma** blood pressure; **rwisuta dimma ʿellaya** high blood pressure; **rwisuta dimma nakhuta** low blood pressure

S/SH/Ṣ

sa para/sa paranta hairdresser
saʿra hair
saʿre barley
saʿuruta to visit
sadita cushion
sadra chest
saggi much; many; very; too; **saggi qura** very cold; **saggi shakhina** very hot
saggi yatir too much/too many
sagiyuta majority
sahda martyr
sahduta d-dwara driver's license
sahra moon; **sahra khata** new moon; **Sahra Smuqa** Red Crescent
ṣalma sculpture
sammana drug; **samma ʿaghuda** narcotic; **sammana dṭlawikhyate bawaye** contact lens solution
samya/smita blind
sandale sandals
sandoq; **sanduqa** box; chest; **sandoq bildara** mailbox; **sanduq glida** ice box; **sanduq radita** trunk/boot
sapiq enough
sapuna soap; **sapuna d-graʿa** shaving cream
saq yawma sunrise
saqulayuta; **saqulaya** opposition
Sarqaya/Sarqayta Arab
sarsiqa sausage
sarṭana cancer; Cancer
ṣarukha missile; rocket; **ṣarukhe** missiles; rockets
ṣarupa/ṣarupta spicy; hot
ṣaruya surgeon
ṣarwa coffee; **ṣarwa ʿm khalwa** coffee with milk
ṣarwaya/ṣarwayta waiter/waitress
sarya/srita stale
sawa/sawta old; old person; elder
sawada accent
ṣawbaya/ṣawbayta university student
sawʿa paint; toe; **sawʿa d-ṭiprate** nail-polish
sawkana steering wheel
ṣawra throat
sayuʿa/sayuʿta aid worker
ṣayurta camera
sebʿate fingers
seghla d-radita car registration/numberplate
sekyate d-yuʿarta tent pegs
selqa beetroot
ṣemda bag; **ṣemda d-khaṣa** backpack
semenire seminary
sepra sparrow
seprayuta literature
Shabta Saturday
shaʿatan hepatitis.
shaʿta clock; time; hour; **shaʿta d-ida** watch; **Shaʿta d-kma la?** What time is it?; **Shaʿta d-eshta la.** It is six o'clock.
shaʿuta/shaʿutta yellow
s-hada to testify
shade almond
shakhina/shakhinta hot
shakhra alcohol
shala scarf; shawl
shalpukhta pancreas
shalqo smallpox
shalwa/shilyuta quiet
shamala candles
shamina/shaminta fertile
shamma mole
shampu shampoo
shamshuma waterfall
shamuʿta dasya stethoscope
shaper ṭarpe spinach
shapira/shapirta beautiful; handsome

shargazza treasury
sharibta clan
sharira minister
shariruta ministry
sharkana d-hadama qṭiʿa stump of limb
sharkha calf
sharuta lunch
sharya independent
sharyuta independence
shata *see* **shita**
shawʿa/shwaʿ seven
shawʿi seventy
shawʿsar seventeen
shawe banknotes
shawra child
shawre children
shawuʿa week; **shawuʿa d-bitaya** next week; **shawuʿa d-daʿwar** last week
shawya cheap; equal
shayna peace; safety
shayudhta artillery
shʿala cough
shdaya to throw
sheba medallion
sheʿya d-ṭablita backgammon
sheʿye drishaye athletics
shelpe d-megraʿta razorblade
shenda torture
shenna tooth; **shenne** teeth
sheryana artery
shet *see* **eshta**
sheṭranj chess
shiberta bracelet
Shiʿaya/Shiʿayta Shi'i
shikar sugar
shikwana ant; **shikwane** ants
shilyuta *see* **shalwa**
shim; shima name
shimsha sun
ship tiya watermelon
shira silk
shirwala trousers; **shirwala d-khuta** underwear; **shirwala ʿiqe** tights
shishelta chain; zipper; **shishelta d-khaṣa** spinal column; spine; **shishelta d-ṭure** mountain range
shishme sesame
shita year; **shita d-atya** next year
shitqa silence
shiwya robbery
shkhinta shrine
shkhira ugly
shlama! hello!
shlita placenta
shmaʿa hear
shmayya sky
shoaala question
shoghla work
sholṭan byata autonomy
shoraya beginning
shorwa soup
shotapaya/shotapayta socialist
shotapayuta socialism
shqala to get; to take; to pick up
shqaqa street
shrara truth
shray mshidta sack
shraya lamp
shrayta accommodation
shṭarmaswa receipt
shtaya to drink
shtitaya/shtitayta sixth
shuʿita novel; **shuʿita Englishayta** a novel in English
shudaʿa advertising
shughla d-ida handicraft
shukhama infection
shukhara delay
shulṭana government
shuqa market
shura wall
shurta navel; umbilical cord
shushbina godfather
shushbinta godmother
shwaya to equal; to loot
shwiʿaya/shwiʿayta seventh
shwita mattress
shwiyate sheet
ṣidra class
ṣihya/ṣ-hita thirsty
sika d-prezla railway
Sikhaya/Sikhayta Sikh
sikra dam
ṣimmala left
simmalta ladder
ṣima silver
simdha bag; **simdha d-midrashta** satchel; **ṣimdha d-ida** handbag
sim-kart sim card
simmala left
simmora squirrel

Ṣin China
sinighra lawyer
sinjaq safety pin
sipa d-nahra river bank
sipa d-ṭure foothills
sipar zero
sipta lip
siqum; **siquma** date; **siqum mawlada** date of birth; **siqum mṭayta** date of arrival; **siqum ṭyasa** date of departure
sirṭana dyama crab
ṣiṣa nail
ṣiṣra cockroach
ṣiṭla bucket
sitwa winter
ṣiwa shrapnel
skhar urkha roadblock
skhaya swimming
skhira shut
skhira/skhirta closed
skinta d-qanya penknife
Ṣkotland Scotland
Ṣkotnaya/Skotnayta Scottish
skwash squash
Sliwa Smuqa Red Cross
smuqa/smuqta red; **smuqa d-spwate** lipstick
smuqe sumac
ṣniʿuta industry
snighra/snighirta lawyer
snunita swallow
soʿa finger
Sonnaya/Sonnayta Sunni
ṣoṣ sauce
sosa horse
ṣoṣla peacock
sosya stallion
spadita pillow
spakha to invade
spakhta d-libba heart attack
spanar spanner; wrench
Spanya Spain
Spanyaya/Spanyayta Spanish
sparigla quince
spar-yama shore
spar-yawma newspaper; **spar-yawme Englishaya** newspaper in English
spenta ferry
spinta boat
spiqa/spiqta empty
spir righla football
spir sala basketball
spira omelette
spongha sponge
spukhya assault; attack; raid; **spukhya rqiʿaya** air-raid
srita *see* **sarya**
sṭar min excluded
sukhapa gaysaya coup d'etat
sumama d-khalta food poisoning
supermarket supermarket
Suraya/Suryayta Syrian
surgada table; timetable
surhawa quick
surkhana crime
Surya Syria
suyaʿa aid; relief aid; **suyaʿa nashaya** humanitarian aid
suyasa politics
suyasara/suyasarta politician; diplomat
Sweden Sweden
Swednaya/Swednayta Swedish
switar sweater; jumper
ṣwyiʿa enamel
ṣyana swamp

T/Ṭ

ta'ame twins; Gemini
ṭabakha/ṭabakhta cook
tabya/tbita deer
taʿbadta ʿaṣuwayta surgical operation
taʿla fox
ṭaʿmana/ṭaʿmanita tasty
taghara businessman
tagharta businesswoman
tagharuta business
taghrumta skeleton
tahniyate! congratulations!
ṭahra noon; afternoon; **ṭahra d-ediom** this afternoon
ṭakhana miller
takhbarta trade union
takhmanta thought
takhrazta computer program
taksi taxi
talga snow
talguta frostbite
ṭaliluta moisture
taluqe to lose
talwashta asyayta *medical* dressing

talwishta uniform
ṭama taste
tama there
Tammuz July
tamre date
tangighla bicycle
tanki d-banzin tank
ṭanna ton
tappa stream
tarba fat
tarbita education
targamta to translate
tarmita mashiknayta housing estate/project
tarnighla cockerel; rooster
tarnighle poultry
ṭarpa leaf
taruqta button
tashᶜita history
tashlita ceasefire; truce
tashrara report
ṭawa/ṭawta good; well
tawana room; **tawan lumada** conference room; **tawana d-taᶜwadtyate** operating theater/room
tawdi! thank you!
tawdita religion
tawhta disaster; **tawhta kyanayta** natural disaster
tawirta cow
tawlᶜa worm
ṭawlita table; desk
tawn arkhe living room
ṭawoᶜta printer
ṭawokha cooker
Tawra Taurus
tawsapta addition
tawsapta more; extra
ṭawsha dirty; rash
tawtawa displaced person; **tawtawe** displaced persons
taya to come
ṭayista airplane
taymna south
ṭayosa/ṭayosnayta pilot
ṭayra bird
ṭayupta helicopter
ṭayusa pilot
ṭᶜama taste
ṭᶜana to carry
tella hill
teltath the year before last
temre eyelids
tenis tennis
ṭepre nail of finger/toe
teshᶜa/tshaᶜ nine
teshᶜi ninety
teshreye autumn
Teshrin Qamaya October
Teshrin Tray Yana November
tetta glue
tiltaᶜsar thirteen
timmal yesterday; **timmal qidamta** yesterday morning; **timmal ṭahra** yesterday afternoon; **timmal bramsha** yesterday night; **timmal d-ᶜwere** the day before yesterday
ṭimra tick
tina fig
tine urine
ṭipya/ṭpita infected
tiqnaye mawdᶜanuta I.T.
tiya tea; **tiya b-khalwa** tea with milk; **tiya ᶜm laymuna** tea with lemon
ṭkhana to grind
tkhet under
tkhube; **tkhuma** frontier
tlata/tlat three; **tla zawnate** three times; **tlata rwiᶜaye** three-quarters
tlati thirty
ṭlawekhta lens
ṭlawikhyate bawaye contact lenses
tlitaya/tlitayata third
Tloshiba Tuesday
ṭlukhe lentils
tmane *see* **tmanya**
tmani eighty
tmaniᶜsar eighteen
tmanya/tmane eight
tminaya/tminayta eighth
tnaya to repeat
ṭokas volte voltage regulator
toma garlic
topaye khtutaye telecommunications
toqan dawqe C.D. player
toqan D.V.D. D.V.D. player
toqan video video-player

tora bull; ox
torgama translation
ṭpita *see* **ṭipya**
trayanaya/trayanayta second
tre tlitaye two-thirds
tre zawnate twice
tre/tarten two
treʿsaraya/tresʿsarayta twentieth
triʿsar twelve
triṣ true; correct; straight
ṭrisa fat
ṭroghe orange
Troshiba Monday
tshaʿ *see* **teshʿa**
tshaʿsar nineteen
tshiʿaya/tshiʿayta ninth
tulmada education
tuna hay
tupaye khṭuṭṭaye telecommunications
tuqan faks fax machine
tuqan marawta projector
ṭura mountain
turas mamla grammar
Turkaya/Turkayta Turk
Turkiya Turkey
ṭurshiye pickle(s)
tuta mulberry; **tuta d-arʿa** strawberry
ṭuwara progress; development
twaʿa to punish
twara to defeat
twarta *noun* defeat

U

Ukhdane Mkhayde d-Amerika USA
umanuta profession
umthayuta nationality
up *see* **o**
upqa horizon
urkha road; **urkha ʿwirta** one-way street; **urkha d-aqla** footpath; **urkha d-ṭurane** mountain pass
Urkhukh ptekhta!/Urkhakh ptekhta!/Urkhukhon ptekhta! bon voyage *(m/f/pl)*!
urqaʿta/urqaʿyata sanitary towels

W

wakilot suyaʿa aid agency
walita baytayta homework
waraqa paper; **waraqe** tissues; **waraqe d-radita** car papers; **waraqe d-khashuwa** file; **waraqe d-silya** toilet paper; **waraqe d-ktawa** writing paper
wardanaya/wardanayta pink
warida vein
warza furrow
wase socks
wasle limbs
Waylz Wales
Welshaya/Welshayta Welsh

Y

Yaban Japan
yabishe raisins
yabrokhe tomato
yaʿita plant
yala boy
yalak waistcoast
yalta girl
yaluda khata newborn child
yalupa/yalupta *school* pupil; student
yamayuta navy
yamina right
yaminaya right-wing
yamta lake
yan or
yanuqa infant
yaqdana fuel *(for fire)*
yaqura/yaqurta heavy
yard yard
yariʿta tent
yarikha tall
yarkha month
yarqana jaundice
yarquta vegetables
yaruqa/yaruqta green
yashṭa trachea; windpipe
yaṣupa/yaṣupta nurse
yatir more; extra
yatra string
yatuma/yatumta orphan
yawma day
yawna pigeon; dove

Yawnan Greece
Yawnaya Greek
yawshana drought
Yawshanuta dehydration
ydhaʿa to know
yhawa to give
Yhudhaya/Yhudhayta Jew; Jewish
yimma; **yimmi** mother
ylapa to learn; **ylapa min lebba** to learn by heart
yrawa to grow
ytawa to sit
ytawta session
yudaʿa the media
yukhla virus
yuqdana burn
Yuridnan Jordan
Yuridnaya/Yuridnayta Jordanian

Z

zagha chick
zahra flash
zakhputa skiing
zakhuta victory
zala straw
zalaṭa salad
zamara/zamarta singer
zamora sandwich
zaqraqude; spider
zarʿone crops
Zardushtaya/Zardushtayta Zoroastrian
zarkha partridge
zarqa/zarqayta blue
zatya olive
zawluth paquʿe mine disposal
zawna time
zayna weapon; **zayne** arms; **zayna d-sitta** mortar weapon
zaytone olive
zbata once
zʿura/zʿurta small
zebda; butter
zghugha dradita windshield/windscreen
zhita dress
ziba condom
zidqe rights; **zidqe mdinaye** civil rights; **zidqe nashaye** human rights
Ziland Khata New Zealand
zimra music; **zimra ʿammaya** folk music; **zimra d-pop** pop music
zinjir; zipper
ziqure ammunition
zkaya to beat; to overcome
zoze currency
zoze shawe banknotes
zqira/zqirta knitted
zraʿ shamra fennel
zraʿa to grow crops; **zraʿ paquʿe** to lay mines
zruʿta agriculture
zubana sales
zul khizwa videotape
zul qala tape (cassette)
zula cassette; film
zunar marwaha fan belt
zunara belt
zuwagha marriage
zwade munitions
zwana shopping
zwla fertilizer; manure

TUROYO–ENGLISH
ṬUROYO–INGLISHOYO

A

abne sons; children
abohotho ancestors
aboroyo pencil
abro son
abshur chalk
abubo tube; **abubo gawonoyo** inner-tube; **abubo di-chifta** gun barrel
abuna priest
aʿlam media
ad-ʿaṣriye this afternoon; this evening
adhno ear; **adhnotho** ears
ad-lalyo tonight
admo blood
adro farm; barn
ad-ṣafrayto this morning
ad-shabtho this week
ad-shato this year
ad-yawma today
afoyo baker
afshotho raisins
aghlabiye majority
aghuno struggle
agire *military* personnel
agiro mercenary
agoṣo plum
aḥidho officer
ahlaydhi relative *(m/f)*
aḥna we
akadimoyo/akadimayto academic *(m/f)*
akhlo hammer
akhul to eat
akoro/akorto farmer
akorutho farming
alfo thousand
algham mines
alkohol alcohol
Almanoyo/Almanayto German
Almanya Germany
Aloho aʿmaykhu! bon voyage *(m/f/pl)!*
ambulans ambulance
Ameriqa America
Ameriqoyo/Ameriqayto American *(m/f)*
amono/amonto artist
ananas pineapple
anfuro report
antibiyotik antibiotic(s)
apartaman apartment
aqalliye minority
aquno strawberry
arbaʿ/arbʿo four
arbaʿsar fourteen
arbʿi forty
arbʿo/arbaʿ four
Arbʿushabo Wednesday
arbubyo chalk
arʿo land; **arʿo bayorto** fallow-land
ardikhlo/ardikhlitho architect
ardoqufo baker
argwonoyo/argwonayto purple
Arimnoyo/Arimnayto Armenian
arkeolojoyo archaeological
Arminya Armenia
arnwo rabbit
arwono calf
aryo lion; Leo
arzaftho hammer
arzon cheap
aṣaḥto copy
asʿaf ambulance
ashitho avalanche
ashkarʿo fennel
asido stork
asiro prisoner; **asiro d-qrobo** prisoner-of-war
askar army
asliḥa arms
asono ammunition; **asono lo mfajro** unexploded ammunition
aspirin aspirin
athari archaeological

athliṭoyutho athletics
athmel yesterday; **athmel ṣafrayto** yesterday morning; **athmel ʿaṣriye** yesterday afternoon; **athmel b-lalyo** yesterday night
athoye arrivals
athroyutho citizenship
athto woman; wife
atqi shawl
Australya Australia
Australyoyo/Australyayto Australian
autobus bus
aw or
awono da-konserat concert hall
awyutho gabayto coalition
aych-ay-vi H.I.V.
aydarbo? how?
aydz AIDS
ayisto plane
ayko? where?; **ayko-yo?/ayko-ne?** where is/are ...?; **Ayko hawat?** born: Where were you *(m/f)* born?
aylo deer
ayna? which?
Azarbayjan Azerbaijan
Azaroyo/Azarayto Azerbaijani
azole departures

B

b- with; by; in; **b-ṣafrayto** in the morning; **b-lalyo** in the evening
babgho parrot
babo father
baʿle d-gayso staff *army*
baʿlo husband
badhinjane komto aubergine/ eggplant
badhinjane semaqto tomato
badle suit
baghlo mule
baghol bag
bahro light; **bahro d-idho** flash-light; **bahro mawdhʿono** indicator light
balki probably
balqon balcony
baluṭ-malko chestnut
bamya okra
banafshoyo/banafshayto purple
banana banana
banch anesthetic
banṭalon trousers
banzin petrol; accelerator
baqolo greengrocer
baqro ox; herd
bar bar; pub
bar-athro/bath-athro citizen
barban d-... next to
bardo hail
barlaman parliament
barqo lightning; flash
barqubʿo water bottle
barquqyo apricot
barrade fridge
bartho girl; daughter
bas but
baṣ bus; **beth-kloyo du-baṣ** bus stop
bashilo/bashilto cooked
basholo cooker
basimo/basimto tasty
baṣlo onion
basmoro nail
basro meat; **basro da-ʿeze** goat meat; **basro da-ʿwone** lamb; **basro da-gyothe** chicken; **basro da-tawre** beef
baṭaṭa potato; **baṭaṭa mqalayto** french fries
bath-athro *see* **bar-athro**
baṭilutho tiredness
bato duck
baṭṭaniye blanket
baṭṭaritho; baṭṭariye battery
baṭṭikh melon
bawṣala compass
bawtho *ḍ-ʿayno* pupil *of eye*
bayro biro
baytayto homework
bayto house; **bayto da-dhayfe** guesthouse; **bayto ʿeloyo** upper house; **bayto taḥtoyo** lower house
bazalya peas
b-ʿaṣriye in the afternoon
bʿeldbobo enemy
bʿoyo to want
bebro tiger
beʿto egg; **beʿe** eggs; **beʿto shliqto** boiled egg
beḥsho pocket

belbuso potato
bele yes
belṭitho termite
benyono building
berulo crystal
besodyo pillow; cushion
besto bottle
beth-arke library
beth-asire prison
beth-busholo kitchen
beth-ᶜetqe museum
beth-ᶜurfono; banqa bank
beth-dino law court
beth-drosho college; academy
beth-durosho sports club
beth-gawso shelter
beth-gazo treasury
beth-gloḥo art gallery; exhibition
beth-ḥbushyo jail
beth-ḥezwe cinema
beth-ḥezwone theater
beth-ḥyofo bathroom
beth-kloyo parking lot
beth-kloyo du-baş bus stop
beth-krihe hospital
beth-makthbo an office
beth-malko palace
beth-mashrye apartment block
beth-mashryo hotel
beth-mawlodo maternity hospital
beth-mayo/bote da-maye toilet(s)
beth-muklo restaurant
beth-osyutho clinic
beth-qafile bar; pub
beth-qawre cemetery
beth-qumoro casino
beth-ṣawbo university; **beth-ṣawbo gaysoyo** military college
beth-shalmo living room
beth-sheᶜyo stadium
beth-shulṭonutho parliament
beth-ṣlutho shrine
beth-smokho nightclub
beth-ṭawso airport
beth-waᶜdo station
bildoro hawoyo air mail
bildoro msaghlo registered mail
bima podium
bira beer
biro well *of water*
bisho bad
bisiklet bicycle
bithir back; behind; **bithir tlotho yawme** three days from now
blanket blanket
bnoth-gane aubergine/eggplant
bnoth-kafe gloves
bnotho children *daughters*
boᶜutho menokh!/boᶜutho menekh!/boᶜutho menaykhu! please *(m/f/pl)*!
bodra powder; **bodra di-mashighonutho** washing powder (detergent)
bomba bomb; **bomba lo mfajarto** unexploded bomb; **bomba mbadronitho** cluster bomb; **bomba naᶜimto** bomblet; **bomba d-idho** grenade
boqo mosquito
boqushe gravel
boya paint
bo-zarᶜe seeds
boziqo falcon
bozo falcon
brayk brake
Briṭanoyo/Briṭanayto British
Briṭanya Britain
britho world
brozo boar
b-shayno w-ba-shlomo! welcome *(m/f/pl)!*
Bthultho Virgo
Budhoyo/Budhayto Buddhist
budro vulture
bughro bullet; **bughro mbadrono** shrapnel; **bughro samuḥo** tracer bullet
buḥrono exam
bulbul nightingale
bumo owl
bundqo hazel nut
burgo tower
burko knee
buro illiterate
busholo cook
buṣoro subtraction
bustono orchard
buṭlono holidays; **buṭlono du-nyoḥo** a break for refreshments

buza *(in Syria)* ice-cream
b-yawmo daytime

C

ʿabo lizard
ʿadasat contact lenses
ʿadase lens
ʿadhale muscle
ʿafro soil
ʿal at; on; **ʿal u-semolo** on the left; **ʿal u-yamino** on the right
ʿalʿolo storm; windy
ʿalʿolo raʿmoyo thunderstorm
ʿalim/ʿalima scientist
ʿalotho; ʿwuro crops
ʿamo people
ʿamro wool
ʿamu?o/ʿamu?to misty
ʿanwe grapes
ʿAqrwo Scorpio
ʿArab *Arab (m/f)*
ʿarbodo pigeon
ʿarbolo sieve
ʿarfelo fog/mist
ʿarfeloyo/ʿarfelayto foggy
ʿarobutho d-gedshe insurance policy
ʿarsho; ʿarshono tooth; **ʿarshone** teeth
ʿarso bed
ʿaryo frost
ʿaṣalto muscle
ʿasir da-fire fruit juice
ʿasqo/ʿasqtho difficult
ʿaṣriye evening
ʿatiqo/ʿatiqto old
ʿatiro rich
ʿaṭmo thigh
ʿawodo mdhinoyo/ʿawodhto mdhinayto civil servant
ʿawsho swamp
ʿaymo cloud
ʿayno eye; spring *of water*; **ʿayno mṣanaʿto** artificial eye; **ʿaynotho** eyes
ʿayosho alive
ʿaywo cloud; cloudy
ʿazbo/ʿazbtho single
ʿidho da-Qyimto; ʿidho Rabo Easter
ʿidho d-Mawlodo; ʿidho Naʿimo Christmas
ʿedono time; moment
ʿeglo calf
ʿeloyo high
ʿeltho du-krukhyo/d-so'urutho reason for travel:
ʿendo nightingale
ʿeqarwo scorpion
ʿeqbo ankle
ʿeqo necklace
ʿeqro root
ʿesri twenty
ʿesrinoyo/ʿesrinayto twentieth
ʿesro/ʿsar ten
ʿeṭmo darkness
ʿeṭro luqbal du-ṣnono deodorant
ʿeṭro perfume
ʿezaqtho ring
ʿezo goat
ʿfofo to multiply
ʿidto church
ʿimare apartment block
ʿiqo narrow
ʿiqutho crisis
ʿIraq Iraq
ʿIraqoyo/ʿIraqayto Iraqi
ʿjiqo/ʿjiqto dirty
ʿlaymo/ʿlaymtho teenager
ʿlobo to beat; to overcome
ʿmij fog/mist
ʿobo wood; forest
ʿobugro mouse; **ʿobugro rabo** rat; **ʿobugro fayoro** bat
ʿoqtho crisis
ʿoṣubayto *surgical* operation
ʿoṣubo/oṣubtho surgeon
ʿrayto lunch
ʿRubto Friday
ʿsar *see* **ʿesro**
ʿsar ishne decade
ʿsiroyo/ʿsirayto tenth
ʿsoro da-fire fruit juice
ʿṣoro syrup
ʿṣowo bandage *medical*
ʿudronayto charity *organisation*
ʿudrono help; **ʿudrono noshoyo** humanitarian aid
ʿudronoyo/ʿudronayto aid worker
ʿufofo multiplication
ʿuhdono memory
ʿulbo can
ʿumro age

ʿurfono coins
ʿurwo crow
ʿuṣobo *act of* surgery
ʿuzoyo to resist
ʿwono (*plural* **ʿwone**) sheep
ʿyodoyo traditional
ʿyosho to live

CH

chaydan kettle
chaye tea; **chaye b-ḥalwo** tea with milk; **chaye b-limon**; **chaye b-laymun** tea with lemon; **chaye komto** black tea; **chaye yaruqto** green tea
chaykhana tea house
chaypas teapot
chewi twins
chifta gun; rifle; **chifta luqbal-ayisyotho** anti-aircraft gun; **chifta makinayto** machine gun; **chifta makinayto naʿimto** submachine gun
chike a little bit

D

dabbaba tank
dabobo fly; **dabobe** flies
dabosho bee
da-ʿbar the past
da-ʿtidh the future
dafno waist; side *of body*
dafo shelf; plank
daḥno corn
daḥshe rozonoye secret police
dahwo gold
daqinto chin
daqno beard
daraj stairs
darbo road; **darbo d-malkho** footpath; **Darbo ftiḥo!** bon voyage *(m/f/pl)!*
dardo vulture
darghe stairs
darmala flock
darmono *medical* drug; **darmono da-ʿarshone** toothpaste; **darmono da-ṭaliḥotho ṭafyotho** contact lens solution
daruktho bicycle
dastur constitution
dawghe buttermilk; ayran
dawlo bucket; Aquarius
dawmo tree
daworo/daworto farmer
dawrutho farming
dawqo captain
dawriye patrol
dawsho honey
dayno debt
dayono judge
dayrayto nun
dayro monastery; convent
dayroyo monk
dboṣo bite; **boṣo da-boqe** mosquito bite; **dboṣo da-raḥshe** insect bite; **dboṣo d-ḥuyo** snake bite
dʿoro *noun* reverse gear; *verb* to retreat
debo bear
deboro wasp
deburitho hornet
dekhro male
deqtho di-mashighonutho washing powder (detergent); **deqtho** powder
dhabiṭ officer
dhaʿifo thin
dhakhire ammunition
diblomasoyo/diblomasayto diplomat
dibo wolf
dijay disc-jockey
dijital *digital*
dijmin enemy
diko cockerel; rooster
diktator dictator
diktatoriye dictatorship
dimoqratutho; **dimoqratiye** democracy
din religion
disko; **diskotek** disco
dividi D.V.D.
dizenṭeria dysentry
dmokho sleep
dnoḥo d-shemsho sunrise
dobar-ḥolule screwdriver
doktor/doktora doctor
dolar dollar
dolmush minibus
dondurma *(in Turkey)* ice-cream
doro century
doyubo luqbal di-shemsho sun-block cream

doyuqtho binoculars
dro'o arm; **dro'o mşana'to** artificial arm
drog drug; narcotic
drosho lesson
drosho to study
droyo fetqe to lay mines
du'tho chewing gum
dudo teapot
dugle lie
dukano shop; store; **dukano dakthowe** bookshop; **dukano da-lbushe/da-jule** clothes shop; **dukano da-mone farzloye** hardware store; **dukano da-msone**; **dukano da-shakale** shoe shop; **dukano da-sfar-zabne** newsstand; **dukano da-sho'e** watchmaker's; **dukano da-tuqone kahroboye** electrical goods store; **dukano da-warde** florist; **dukano da-yarqe** vegetable shop; **dukano rabtho flighayto** department store; **dukano da-mone dukthowo** stationer's; **dukano dukthonoyo la-dukthonoye** a local shop for local people
dukhrono memory
duktho place; **duktho d-mawlodo** place of birth
dukthonoyo/dukthonayto local
dulab cupboard
durakhtho foot
durbin binoculars
durqino peach
durto courtyard
dush shower
dushno gift
dworo to plow
dyutho ink

E

e yes
egartho letter
egartho eleqţrunayto e-mail
ekspres express
ekstra extra
el'o rib; **el'e** ribs
elfo boat
elo but

ema? when?
emo mother
emro ram
Emro Aries
emro lamb
Emwotho Mḥaydotho United Nations
enqelab coup d'etat
eqonomyoyo/eqonomyayto economist
esfiro ball
esfir-raghlo football
esfir-saltho basketball
esfugho sponge
eshotho fever
eshti sixty
eshto bottom; butt *of rifle*
esore diblomasoye diplomatic ties
esoro bandage
Espanya Spain
Espanyoyo/Espanyayto Spanish
esţablo barn
esţlo suit; **esţlo rushmoyo** uniform
eţrugho orange
eţrughoyo/eţrughayto orange

F

fadono plow
faghro body
fago crossroads
fagodho hood
faḥlo stallion
faḥorutho pottery
fako fruit; jaw; **fako ḥatho** fresh fruit
fakoro doorlock
faks fax
falge d-lalyo midnight
falge d-yawmo; ţahro noon/afternoon
falgo one-half
faliji heatstroke
falqe shrapnel
famil family
fanera sweater; jumper
fannan/fannana artist
fanso lamp
faqiro poor
Faransa France

Faransoyo/Faransayto French
fardisqo cupboard
farghuno toothbrush
farḥo cucumber
fariq lieutenant-general
farmo bakery
faro lamb
farṣufoyo personal
farude coins; **farude** coins; loose change
farugo hen
farzlo iron
farzlo hendwoyo steel
faṣuliye beans
faṭeryarkho *patriarch*
fathyo wide
faṭiḥo melon
faṭurto mushroom
fawdo false
fayl *paper/computer* file
feghlo radish
felflo pepper
felqo pickax
femo mouth
fendqo hazel nut
fenqitho notebook
ferno bakery
ferqo cloth
fesqe ḥulmonoye d-kefso sanitary towels
fesqitho bandage
festqo pistachio
fetghomo article; paper
fetqo *noun* card; mine; **fetqo bildoroyo** postcard; **fetqo d-qubolo** receipt; **fetqo d-suloqo** boarding pass; **fetqo du-kredit** credit card; **fetqo luqbal-fulḥe** anti-personnel mine; **fetqo luqbal-roshufotho** anti-tank mine; **mḥoyo fetqo** to hit a mine; **fetqe** mines; **mḥalaqto da-fetqe** mine disposal; **mgalyonitho da-fetqe** mine detector
fhomo to understand
filma film
filo elephant
fircha brush; **fircha du-sawko** hairbrush
fire fruit; **fire ḥathe** fresh fruit
fisha plug; **fisha kahroboyo** electric plug
fistaq pistachio
fizyotherapya physiotherapy
flighutho division
flogho to divide
floḥo to cultivate
fnitho district
foliṭiqi politics
foliṭiqoyo *political* party
foliṭiqoyo/foliṭiqayto politician
folkloroyo traditional
foqudho major-general
forum forum
fotho face; page; **fotho da-gale** sheet
fotokopi photocopier
fotuḥo da-ʿulbe can opener
fqodho to command
fraḥdudo bat
fraḥto bird
fraṭa coins
fredtho gardener
fren brake
fros-ḥezwo television; **fros-ḥezwo meshtanyono** portable T.V.
frosho da-darbone crossroads
froso exhibition; kilim
fros-qolo radio
fshiṭo/fshiṭto easy
fsiḥoyo/fsiḥayto happy
fsiqutho abstract *written*
fsoso du-qloʿo driver's license
ftiḥo open
ftoqo hernia
fṭoro breakfast
fujo melon
fulḥo soldier; fighter; **fulḥe** troops
fulḥone industry; **a-fulḥone sufqonoye** the leisure industry; **a-fulḥone zubonoye** the retail industry
fulḥono profession
fulodho steel
fumo mouth
fundqo hotel
funoyo answer
fuqr-dam anemia
furthaʿno flea; **furthaʿne** fleas
fushfosho tick *insect*
fushoqo to explain
fuṣolo da-sefoqe baggage counter
fuṣolo du-qubolo / di-makhtwonutho check-in counter

fut *measurement* foot
futbol football

G/GH

gabo *political* party
Gadhyo Capricorn
galdho skin; leather
gale bed; **gale mezdawgo** double bed
galon gallon
galwoyo/galwayto exile *person*
gamisho; **gomusho** buffalo
gamiye boat
gamlo camel
ganono/ganonto gardener
gantho garden; park; **gantho d-ḥaywotho** zoo
gantor cupboard
garbyo north
garmo bone; **garmo d-ᶜaṭmo** femur; **garmo d-shoqulo** tibia
garoᶜo barber
gawiro/gawirto married; **Gawir hat?/Gawirto hat?** Are you *(m/f)* married?
gawo stomach
gawre ladies
gawro man; husband
gawsono/gawsonto refugee; **gawsone** refugees
gawzo walnut
gayso army
gazino casino
gbino eyebrow
gᶜoso vomiting
gdhayto chicken
gdhilo/gdhilto woven
gdisho di-kesto haystack
geftho vine
gelo grass
gelyunoro/gelyunorto journalist
gerilla guerrilla
geshro *bridge*
ghallabe many; very; **sagi ḥemo** very hot; **ghallabe quro** very cold
ghamo layto! no problem!
ghas gas
ghlobo to beat; to overcome
gighlo shabolo steering wheel
gir gear
giro nurono rocket
gizoro carrot
glidho ice
gloḥutho di-tagorutho trade fair
gnowo theft
gol goal
golf golf
gomlak shirt
goro roof
goruᶜtho razor
gorusto millstone
goshusho spy
goshusho/goshushto spy
goṣuṣe beans
gram gram
grammatiqi grammar
grapfrut grapefruit
Grikia Greece
griṣtho loaf *of bread*
groso to grind
grufyo d-arᶜo landslide; **grufyo d-talgo** avalanche
Grujiya Georgia
Grujoyo/Grujayto Georgian
gubo well *of water*
guboyo voting; election
gudo regiment
gugi spider
gumruk customs
gunḥo disaster; **gunḥo kyonoyo** natural disaster
gurwe socks
gushmo body
guzᶜo trunk *of tree*
gwayto cheese
gworo marriage
gyodho nerve
gyothe poultry

H/Ḥ

ḥa/ḥdho one
ḥabbothe pills; **ḥabbothe du-dmokho** sleeping pills
ḥabiss jail
ḥabshusho beetle
ḥabtho corn
ḥabusho apple
hadomo organ *of body*; **hadome** limbs
hadomo/hadomto du-mawtbo

d-shulṭono member of parliament
ḥadyo breast
ḥaglo partridge
ḥago party
ḥaḥo plum
ḥakim referee
ḥalo vinegar
ḥaloqo/ḥaloqto hairdresser
ḥalwo milk; **ḥalwo di-emo** mother's milk; **ḥalwo da-ʿeze** goat's milk; **ḥalwo da-tawrotho** cow's milk; **ḥalwo nashifo** powdered milk
ḥalyo/ḥlitho sweet
ḥalyutho sweets/candy; dessert
ḥalzunto snail
hamberger burger
ḥamimo warm
ḥammam bathroom
ḥammish *see* **ḥamsho**
hamnikho necklace
ḥamro wine
ḥamshaʿsar fifteen
ḥamshi fifty
ḥamsho/ḥammish five
Ḥamshushabo Thursday
ḥamṣitho sumac
ḥamuṣo/ḥamuṣto sour
hani these
hanik those
ḥaniqutho whooping cough
hano/hathe this
ḥaqlo field; **ḥaqlo da-fetqe** minefield
har uʿdo just now
ḥarbo bad; badly
ḥardlo mustard
ḥardono lizard
ḥarfo page
ḥarfo ***ḏ-warqo*** sheet *of paper*
ḥarifutho spices
ḥariwo/ḥaruto bad
harke here
ḥaroyo last
ḥarṣaftho hail
ḥarṭumone chickpeas
ḥarwotho ruins
ḥashlotho jewelery
ḥashubthono/ḥashubthonitho accountant
ḥaṣo back
ḥaso lettuce
ḥaṣodo khaliṭo combine harvester
ḥasyo metropolitan
hat/hate you *singular*
hathe *see* **hano**
ḥatho new; modern
hatu you *plural*
havuz pool
hawa air; wind; **hawa shaḥinto** hot wind
hawa weather
hawa ghallabe windy
ḥawbo crime
hawfo gas
ḥawḥo peach
hawino/hawyono: Hawino b-.../Hawyono b-... born: I *(m/f)* was born in ...
hawliye towel
ḥawlo rope; **ḥawlo du-grosho** tow rope
hawo/hayo that
ḥawraydh/ḥwarthaydh friend *(m/f)*
ḥawro *male* riend; boyfriend
hawtho suburb
ḥaye life
hayklo skeleton
ḥaylo power; **ḥaylo fredtonoyo** nuclear power; **ḥaylo hawoyo** airforce; **ḥaylo yamoyo** navy
ḥaylono strong
hayo *see* **hawo**
ḥayo alive
ḥayoṭo/ḥayoṭto tailor; dressmaker
ḥayowo/ḥayowto criminal
ḥazoyotha glasses; spectacles; **ḥazoyotho di-shemsho** sunglasses
ḥbushyo prison
ḥdhaʿsar eleven
ḥdhirutho siege
ḥdho *see* **ḥa**
ḥedhoro to surround
hedi! gently!; **hedi hedi** slow
hefkoyo reactionary *adjective*
ḥefro metal; furrow
ḥekhemtho wisdom
helkho walk
ḥemo hot
ḥemro vertebra
ḥemto fever; rash

Hendu India
Hendwoyo/Hendwayto Indian; Hindu
hergo lesson
ḥerqo necktie
ḥeshukho darkness
ḥeṭe wheat; **ḥeṭe rumoye** maize
ḥewitho lizard
ḥeworo/ḥewarto white
ḥezwo view
ḥfoḥo vomiting
ḥimṣe peas
Hind India
hinne they
ḥiro/ḥirto free
ḥirutho freedom
hiya she; it
hiye he; it
ḥkayiwo sick
ḥlimo well
ḥlitho *see* **ḥalyo**
ḥlowo to milk *an animal*
ḥmiltho carpet
ḥmishoyo/ḥmishayto fifth
ḥmoro donkey
hoki hockey
Holanda the Netherlands
Holandoyo/Holandayto Dutch
ḥolo sand
ḥolulo screw
ḥonutho shop; store
ḥoshubo computer; **ḥoshube** computers
ḥreno next
ḥromo condemn
ḥrutho hip
ḥshimto dinner/supper
ḥshiwo included
ḥshowo to calculate
ḥsirutho minority; **ḥsirutho ṭuhmayto** ethnic minority
ḥṣodo harvest; to reap
ḥṭuṭo line
ḥuṭo kubonoyo barbed wire
ḥubo! *cheers!*
ḥubolo infection
ḥukm dhati autonomy
ḥukume government
ḥuldo mole
ḥulmono health
ḥulmoṭo chameleon
ḥumra lipstick
ḥumtho fever
ḥuroro liberation; to liberate
ḥushabo Sunday
ḥushbono calculation
ḥuṭo string; wire
ḥuṭro walking stick
huwe he; it
ḥuyo snake
ḥuyodho da-tagore trade union
ḥuza ring
ḥwarthaydh *see* **ḥawraydh**
ḥwartho *female* friend; girlfriend
ḥwartho *girlfriend*
ḥwilutho corruption
hwoyo be born
ḥyoko itching
ḥyoro to watch
ḥyoṣo cloth
hyozo arʿonoyo earthquake
ḥziro pig
ḥziron June
ḥzoyo see

I

iʿa'ile family
idari/idariye administrator
idhaʿto know
idho hand; handle
ihobo to give
ihobo fuqdhono to command
ihobo sohdutho to testify
ilofo to learn
ilono tree
Ilul September
imdha signature
imoro to speak
inflawenza flu
Ingiltara England
Inglishoyo/Inglishayto English
internet internet
iqartho family
iqlima weather; climate
iqtiṣadi/iqtiṣadiye economist
Iran Iran
Iranoyo/Iranayto Iranian
Irlanda Ireland
Irlanda Garbyayto Northern Ireland
Irlandoyo/Irlandayto Irish
irowo to grow
iruso mole
isfanj sponge

ishm; ishmo name
ishqadh last year
ishtiraki/ishtirakiye socialist
ishtirakiye socialism
ishto/sheth six
isorto rifle
Israyiloyo/Israyilayto Israeli
isṭadyon stadium
istinsakh photocopier
Iṭaloyo/Iṭalayto Italian
itawto session
itawto to sit
ithutho zuwoghayto marital status:
Iyor May
iyrowo to grow *crops*
izgado/izgadto ambassador
izgadutho embassy

J

jaᶜde street; **jaᶜde d-ḥa darbo** one-way street
jaket jacket
jamiᶜ mosque
jamudo/jamudto cold; freezing
janṭa bag
Japan Japan
jarraḥ/jarraḥa surgeon
jarur drawer
jawaz passport
jaysh army
jaz jazz
jeb pocket
jeneral general
jeyran electricity
jghaliye talk
jibs *medical* plaster cast
jinz jeans
jip 4-wheel drive car
jiyoghrafiya geography
jroḥo to wound
jule clothes; **jule gawonoye** underwear

K/KH

kabab kebab
kabdho liver; hepatitis
kabil cable
kaᶜak cake
kachikat daughters; children
kachikke girl; daughter
kafé-net internet café
Kafinno./Kafinono. I'm hungry.
Kafino-no./Kafinto-no. I'm hungry.
kafno hunger; famine
kafo palm *of hand*
kahraba'; kahrobo electricity
kalbo dog
Kaldoyo/Kaldayto Chaldean Catholic
kalobto pliers
kamyon truck
kanon cannon
kanser cancer
karas cherry
karkdono rhinoceros
karmo vineyard
karokho/karokhto tourist
karokhutho tourism
kart postal postcard
karṭo map; **karṭo da-darbone** road map; **karṭo di-mdhitho** city map; **karṭo d-Los Anjeles** a map of Los Angeles
karyo short
kasher/kashera cashier
Kashoṭo Saggitarius
kashoṭo da-gire nurone rocket-launcher
kathawto *see* **kathowo**
kathfo shoulder; shoulder blade
kathowo/kathawto writer
kawtho window
kayiso good; well
kazko sweater; jumper
kbishutho to conquer
kechap ketchup
kefo rock; stone; **kefe** rocks
kelyon-nuro ceasefire
kelyotho kidneys
kerko notebook; **kerko da-duroshe** exercise book
kesto hay
ketono cotton; cotton wool
kewo disease; **kewo da-kalbe** rabies
khali carpet
khalyo/khlitho empty
khanjar dagger
kharab ruins
khariṭa map
kharṭumo hose
khashino fat

khass lettuce
khaṭ line
khaṭar danger
khayifo express
khayifo quick; light; not heavy
khlitho *see* **khalyo**
khṣoro to lose
khurda coin
khyoro cucumber
killaw kidneys
kilogram kilogram
kilomeṭro kilometer
kilwe kidney
kimme hat
kiso bag; **kiso du-dmokho** sleeping bag
kit?/kito? is there?/are there?
kiyo chewing gum
klach clutch
klash sandals
klay! stop *(m/f)*!
klitho kidney
kloyo to stop; to stand
kmino to ambush
kmo? how many?
kmoyutho sum
kmuno cumin
knushyo assembly; meeting; **knushyo foliṭiqoyo** political rally
kokhushto ferret
kolera cholera
komo/komto black
kompyuter computer; **kompyuterat** computers
konser concert
kontakt lenz contact lenses
Konun Ḥaroyo January
Konun Qamoyo December
konunto ruler *instrument*
krafso celery; **krafso dumyo** parsley
krawo cabbage
kriket cricket
kriza crisis
kroʿo butter
krokho bu-shuqo shopping
krotho thumb
krowo furrow; fallowland
krukhyo travel
kshoro ***buḥrono*** to pass *an exam*
kthowo book; to write; **kthowo di-mhadyonutho** guidebook
kubosho to conquer
kudhanyo mule
kuforo towel
kuḥlo mascara
kuhno priest
kuko cake
kukwo star; **kukwe** stars
kulliye college; academy
kumathro pear
kunosh-mele dictionary
kunosho sum
kunoyo surname
Kurdistan Kurdistan
Kurdoyo/Kurdayto Kurd
kurfo viper
kurhono disease; **kurhono dakalbe** rabies; **kurhono gensonoyo** venereal disease; **kurhono gawonoyo** epidemic
kurikko son; boy; **kurikke** children *sons*
kursyo chair; seat; **kursyo dagighle** wheelchair
kushk kiosk
kushofo blanket
kushoro success
kusitho hat
kuthino shirt
kuthosho debate
kutosho wrestling
kuzbartho coriander
kwosho assault; attack; invasion
kwushyo to attack; to invade
kyaquro heavy

L

lagham *noun* mine
lahana cabbage
laḥayto rubber; eraser
laḥmo bread
lakhalf backwards
lalʿel up
laltaḥt down
lalyo night; **lalyo d-shafiʿ** last night
lamfidho lamp
landkruz 4-wheel drive car
laqiddam forwards
laqlaq stork

larwar out; outside
lawghil in
laymun lemon; lime
layt tenunto no smoking
layto ʿboro no entry
Lebnon Lebanon
Lebnonoyo/Lebnonayto Lebanese
lebo heart
leʿzo; **lahje** dialect
leksiqun dictionary
leshono language; tongue
lewno brick
lfofo envelope
lḥef quilt
limon; **limuno** lemon; lime
liṭro liter; pound
liwaʿ major-general
lo no; **lo ḥshiwo** excluded; **lo ṭimo** cheap
lobya green beans
loqanṭa restaurant
lori lorry; truck
lqoyo to meet
lubosho *medical* dressing
lughmo jaw
luḥo blackboard
luḥo d-qayso plank
luwoyo convoy
luzo almond
lwushe clothes; **lwushe ʿiqe** tights

M

mabṣoro to subtract
maʿbar-tḥume visa
maʿbarto mountain pass
maʿbro entrance; ferry
maʿirbo west
maʿjun da-ʿarshone toothpaste
maʿlyono elevator; lift; jack
maʿṭofo coat
maʿyo intestine
madenḥo east
Madenḥoyo/Madenḥayto Church of the East Christian
madhbro desert
madimkhonitho anesthetic
madimkhono anesthetist
madolo caterpillar
madoqto ʿatiqto cannon
madoqto naʿimto mortar *weapon*
madrashto school; **madrashto di-kuhnutho**; **madrashto kuhnayto** seminary; **madrashto gaysayto** military academy
maflo da-maye waterfall
mafoḥitho fan
mafqo exit; **mafqo di-aliṣutho** emergency exit
maghdlo tower
magirshono tractor
maglo sickle
magraftho spade
magzuno sickle
maḥisto to wake up
maḥoro/maḥorto engineer
maḥrowo to destroy
maḥshulo d-ḥemo heat wave
maḥshwono calculator
maḥzitho mirror
majimdono fridge
makhifono accelerator
makhloyo to evacuate
makhtwo office; **makhtwo dafetqe** ticket office
makhtwono typewriter
makina machine; **makina du-faks** fax machine
maklyono brake
maknishto brush
makrukhto scarf
makso customs; **makso du-beth-ṭawso** airport tax
makthab-zabno history
malarya malaria
malfono/malfonitho teacher
malkho on foot
malko king
malolo speaker; **malolo dhayfo** guest speaker
maluḥo/maluḥto salty
malyo/mlitho enough; full
mameṭyonitho adapter
man? who?
mandhafto ṭuhmayto ethnic cleansing
mandhifone di-zghughitho windshield wipers
mandilo handkerchief; towel; **mandile d-waroqo** tissues
manḥoto to shoot down
manoyo calculator
manoyutho maths

manto coat
manzar view
maqale *written* article
maqarna pasta
maqrono fridge
maqwo drill
marbᶜo womb
mardutho culture
marfiyo/marfayto divorced
margo meadow
mariro/marirto bitter
markawtho di-shorutho; markawtho du-muklo dining car
markawtho du-dmokho sleeping car
marsho cable
maruḥone reinforcements
marwode earrings
marwoḥo fan
Masato Libra
masbaḥ pool
masforo scissors
masfrono scissors; **masfrone da-ṭefre** nail-clippers
masghdho mosque
mashighonitho laundry
mashighono du-femo mouthwash
mashighonutho laundry
Mashilmono/Mashilmonitho Muslim
mashkno tent
mashlomo to surrender
maṣḥonitho photocopier
mashqyo bar; pub
mashqyonutho irrigation
mashritho station; camp; campsite; **mashritho du-qṭoro** train station; **mashritho da-gawsone** refugee camp; **mashritho d-an-asire d-qrobo** POW camp
mashryo du-baṣ bus station; hostel; apartment; **mashryo du-baṣ** bus station
mashtokho pitch
maskara mascara
masmkhono kelshonoyo *medical* plaster cast
masmonutho d-muklo food poisoning
masoro saw
masqono escalator
masṭar ruler *instrument*
maṣṭawtho bench
masto yogurt
masurqo comb
maṣuṣto lizard
mathlono/mathlonitho actor
mathyo to come
maṭlo parachute
matloyo to camouflage
maṭoṭo; maṭṭaṭ rubber
maṭran metropolitan
maṭro rain
maṭyo/mṭitho ripe
mawbalto to take
mawdᶜonutho information
mawkholo ḥaywo to feed an animal
mawlafto teach
mawlodo give birth to
mawlodo birth
mawsfonutho addition
mawtbo d-sharire cabinet
mawtbo d-shulṭono parliament
mawto death
mawtono epidemic
mawzodo to add
maye water; **maye shaḥine** hot water; **maye jamude** cold water; **maye di-ᶜayno** mineral water
maymun monkey
mazlo to go
mazlo d-gawo diarrhea
mazroᶜo farm
mazruqe urine
mᶜadrono/mᶜadronitho aid worker
mᶜarfono/mᶜarfonitho banker
mᶜartho cave
mᶜaryo hostage
mᶜawanto help; **mᶜawanto ᶜudronayto** relief aid
mᶜoye intestines
mdakhyo razorblade
mdakhyono antiseptic
mdarghono escalator
mdarshono/mdarshonitho trainer
mdhitho town; **mdhitho ᶜatiqto** old town
medyoro arᶜonoyo; qaṭ; ṭabaq floor *story*
meḥo brain

melḥo salt
melyun million
menyono number; **menyono di-qelayto** room number; **menyono d-ro?ifto** platform number; **menyono d-saqro** passport number; **menyono mfashaṭto** extension number
meqem: meqem tlotho yawme three days before; **meqem arbᶜo yawme** four days before
meshḥo cream; ointment
meshtawḥronutho delay
meshtawtfonoyo/meshtawtfonitho socialist
meshtawtfonutho socialism
meskino poor
meso main square
mesorto parcel
metalon metal
methᶜamronitho world
methkarkhonutho patrol
methmaṭyonwotho telecommunications
methrazqono mercenary
methṭawronutho development
meṭro meter
mezdabnonutho marketing
mezto a hair
mfajoro to explode
mfajronutho detonation; **mfajronitho lo mfajarto** unexploded ordnance
mfalghono referee
mfarnsono/mfarnsonitho administrator
mfashṭutho extension (number)
mgalyonitho da-fetqe mine detector
mgawno colour
mghaltho magazine
mḥalaqto to throw
mḥalaqto da-fetqe mine disposal
mḥaṭo needle; syringe
mḥawyono microscope
mḥawyonutho address
mḥaylone reinforcements
mḥilo weak
mḥiluth-admo anemia
mḥoyo to hit; **mḥoyo d-ḥemo** heatstroke; **mḥoyo d-shemsho** sunstroke; **mḥoyo fetqo** to hit a mine
mikanikoyo mechanic
mikanikoyo/mikanikayto mechanic
mikrobe germs
mil; milo mile
mimro *written* article
miqqa? how much?; **miqqa qariwo?** how near?; **miqqa raḥuqo?** how far?; **Miqqa-yo ᶜumrokh/ᶜumrekh?** How old are you *(m/f)*?; **... ishne-no**. I *(m/f)* am ... years old.; **Miqqa-yo i-shoᶜtho?** What time is it?
missaḥa rubber; eraser
mitho dead
mkawyonitho iron *(for clothing)*
mkaylono di-shḥuntho thermometer
mkaylono du-bahro light meter
mkhadde pillow; cushion
mkhiro/mkhirto fiancé/fiancée
mlitho *see* **malyo**
mlu'o *written* article
mnashfono du-sawko hairdryer
mnorto candlestick
mnoyo to count
mo hundred
modem modem
mo-ishne century
molukho/molukhto consultant
mosugho syringe
moṭa ***(in Iraq)*** ice-cream
moṭor engine; motorbike
moṭorsiklet motorbike
mqablutho reception
mqadmono lieutenant-colonel
mqalᶜono artillery
mramyo grenade
mrawrwono microscope; **mrawrwono mezdawgo** binoculars; **mrawrwono mqarwono** telescope
mrorto gall bladder
msadronitho *paper/computer* file
msafrono scissors
msaghlonitho: msaghlonitho da-zul-ḥezwe video-player; **msaghlonitho da-zul-qole** tape-recorder; **msaghlonitho**

du-dividi D.V.D. player; **msaghlonitho du-sidi** C.D. player
msargdonitho ruler *instrument*
msarhwo express
msatronitho ma-raḥshe insect repellant
msawyo straight on
mṣaybonitho compass
mṣayrono/mṣayronitho photographer
mshadro/mshadarto ambassador
mshadrutho embassy
mshaḥilfono transformer
mshamnono fertilizer
mshanyo/mshanayto displaced person; **mshanye** displaced persons/people
msharyo/msharyitho paralyzed
msharyutho paralysis; stroke
mshaynono tranquilizer
mshaynutho safety
Mshiḥoyo/Mshiḥayto Christian *(m/f)*
msoko to arrest; **msoko d-asiro** to take prisoner
msone shoes
mṭaksono du-volṭaj voltage regulator
mṭaltho umbrella
mtargmono translator
mtargmonutho translation
mṭʿomo restaurant
mṭitho *see* **maṭyo**
mtonto bladder
mṭoyo to get
muḥami/muḥamiye lawyer
muhandis madani architect
muhandis/muhandisa engineer
muḥasib/muḥasiba accountant
mukhaddar drug; narcotic
mukle meals
muklo food; to eat
mulazim lieutenant
mulkono ṣniʿuthonoyo industrial estate
mumarrid/mumarrida nurse
mun? what?
mun-yo hawo/hayo? what's that?
muqaddim lieutenant-colonel
muqawama to resist
murabba jam/jelly
muroyo da-susye horse racing
mursho carpet
mus razorblade
musaddas pistol
musajjal registered mail
musajjal du-sidi C.D. player
muṣawwar/muṣawwara photographer
musiqa music; **musiqa ʿamayto** pop music; **musiqa folklorayto** folk music; **musiqa klasikayto** classical music
musiqoro/musiqorto musician
mustashar/mustashara consultant
muwadhdhaf madani/muwadhdhafa madaniya civil servant
muzo banana
muzogho weather; climate
myodḥo gawso to take shelter
myodo to pick up
myotho to die
mzighlo motorbike
mzigho combine harvester

N

nabgho spring *of water*
naʿimo/naʿimto child; infant; small; young; **naʿime** children
nadhifo/nadhifto clean
nadi nightclub
nafqo slope; **nafqo (darbo taḥt di-arʿo)** subway
nagoro/nagorto carpenter
nahro river
naḥto dress
naḥtumo baker
najjar/najjara carpenter
namlo ant
naqib captain
naqifo lieutenant
naqifwotho telecommunications
naqqa ḥdo once
naqqawothe twice
nargho ax
nargho du-glidho ice ax
nashifo/nashifto old; stale
nashifutho dehydration; drought
natino/natinto ugly
nawfo goal

nawro mirror
nᶜolo ***susye*** to shoe *a horse*
n-eḥre manure
nemro leopard
neqwo female
neqyo ewe
neṣbo plant
neṣbo makthabzabnoyo monument
neshe gentlemen
neshro eagle; lieutenant-general
neshro meṣroyo vulture
neṣo hawk
nfolo to fall
nḥiro nose
nḥosho copper
nirwo valley
nisho objective
Nison April
nobuzo caterpillar
nodurto waterfall
nomuso ḥulmonoyo hygiene
nomuso law
nonᶜo mint
noqiṣ less
nosho person; **noshe** people
noṭar-kesfo/noṭro-kesfo cashier
noṭer-roze/noṭrath-roze secretary
noṭure d-shlomo peace-keeping troops
noyo raw; uncooked
nqoḥo smell
nsokho troḥo to copy
nṣowo to sow
nṭiro/nṭirto reserved
nuᶜnaᶜ mint
nuno (*plural* **nune**) fish; Pisces; **nune ḥathe** fresh fish
nuqolo d-admo; shuḥlofo d-admo blood transfusion
nuqosho discussion
nuqzo d-buṣoyo checkpoint
nuro fire
nuskha photocopy
nuskho copy
nusoyo to test
Nuzilanda New Zealand

O

Ob August
oda room
Odor March
ofadhno palace
ogzos exhaust
oksijin oxygen
ono I
opera opera
Orthodoksoyo/Orthodoksayto *f* Orthodox Christian
oshufo/oshefto nurse
osyo/ositho doctor; **osyo/ositho da-ᶜarshone** dentist
otho sign
Othur Assyria
Othuroyo/Othurayto Assyrian
oyro euro

P

Pakistan Pakistan
Pakistanoyo/Pakistanayto Pakistani
palto coat
pansiyon hostel
pantur trousers
papuke owl
parashut parachute
pasaport passport
paṭaṭa potato; **paṭaṭa mqalayto** french fries; **paṭaṭa ḥlitho** sweet potato
pawand pound (sterling)
payjer pager
paylot pilot
penisilin penicillin
pire woman; wife
pisṭola gun: *pistol*
pitsa pizza
plaster plaster; Band-Aid
plastik plastic
portaqal orange
Portughaloyo/Portughalayto Portuguese
profisor/profisore academic *(m/f)*
program (computer) program
projektor projector
Pruṭoyo/Pruṭayto Protestant

Q

qadisho/qadishto saint
qaḥwe coffee; **qaḥwe b-ḥalwo** coffee with milk
qalᶜo fort

qalilo/qalilto light; not heavy
qalilutho minority
qalmo louse; **qalme** lice
qaloʿo d-ṭayisto/qaloʿto d-ṭayisto pilot
qaloʿo/qaloʿto driver
qalwo *military* shell
qamera camera
qamḥo flour
qamino stove
qamis shirt
qamoyo/qamayto first
qampa camp
qamro belt; **qamro d-marwoḥo** fan belt
qamṣo grasshopper
Qanada Canada
Qanadoyo/Qanadayto Canadian
qanturro pear
qanyo pen; **qanyo d-lamṭo** felt-tip pen; **qanyo nashifo** ballpoint; **qanyo rṣoṣoyo** pencil; **qanyo semoqo** lipstick
qaqbo kettle
qarʿo pumpkin
qardo tick
qariro/qarirto cool; fresh
qarish belt
qariwaydhi/qariwtaydhi relative *(m/f)*
qariwo/qaruto near
qarnabiṭ cauliflower
qarno d-ṭuro peak; summit
qarno nḥiro rhinoceros
qarqaftho skull
qarqaftho d-ṭuro peak; summit
qarqoso crow
qarṭisoyutho stationer's
qaruto *see* **qariwo**
qaseta cassette
qaseta tape (cassette)
qasho priest
qashyo/qshitho hard; tough
qaṣif bombardment
qaṣluṣo straw
qaṣobutho butcher's
Qatholiqoyo/Qatholiqayto Catholic
qaṭinto minute
qaṭiro yogurt
qaṭlo murder; assassination
qaṭmonoyo/qaṭmonayto gray
qato handle
qaṭo cat
qaṭobo/qaṭobto butcher
qaṭṭab/qaṭṭaba butcher
qawmo revolution
qawro tomb
qawyo! hard!; vigorously!
qay? why?
qayimto monument
qayimto statue
qayso wood; **qayse di-nuro** firewood
qayso qadaḥ rainbow
qayṭo summer
qbath constipation
qdholo neck
qdhoshe earrings
qedimto morning
qelayto room
qenṭo danger
qenṭrun center; station; main square; **qenṭrun di-mdhitho** town center; **qenṭrun d-ḥaylo fredtonoyo** nuclear power station; **qenṭrun du-telefon** telephone center; **qenṭrun ḥulmonoyo** clinic
qenyone livestock
qenyono ṣniʿuthonoyo industrial estate
qeqwono partridge
qerasiya cherry
qerowo alohoy holy mass
qeshte d-moran rainbow
qewitho marsh
qḥiroyo/qḥirayto unhappy
qḥutho coffee
qḥuthonoyo/qḥuthonayto brown
qiluno stallion
qiṭar train
qlab nightclub
qlidho key; **qlidho ṣliḥo** spanner/wrench
qloʿo drive; **qloʿo meṣʿoyo** neutral drive
qlofo *military* shell
qmoro to win
qmoṭo bandage
qobitho pool
qoʿem present
qolo noise; vote; **qolo di-ḥsirutho** minority vote

qomisyon commission
qompas compass
qonser concert
qontorlu telefon telephone center
qonṭrol checkpoint
qonuno law; **qonuno ḥulmonoyo** hygiene; **qonuno shath'esoyo** constitution
qonuq-ewi guesthouse
qoṭulo killer; **qoṭulo du-kewo** painkiller; **qoṭulo da-raḥshe** insecticide
qrabthono soldier; fighter; **qrabthone** troops
qrambo cabbage
qritho village
qrobo war; **qrobo gawonoyo** civil war
qromo enamel
qroyo to read
qrustalus crystal
qṣofo bombardment
qṣoyo to cut
qṭoᶜo to cut
qṭolo to kill
qṭoro train
qubᶜo cap
qudosho alohoyo holy mass
qufdo hedgehog
quflo doorlock; padlock
qufo monkey
qufrin hedgehog
Qufroyo/Qufrayto *f* Cypriot
Qufrus Cyprus
qufso chess
quḥo cauliflower
quklo screw
qukloyo screwdriver
qulbo bracelet
qulobo coup d'etat
qum sand
qum front; in front of
qumash cloth
qunbala bomb; **qunbala lo mfajarto** unexploded bomb
quqo vase
quqoyutho pottery
qurma pistol
qurnitho corner
qurnoso hatchet
quro/qariro cold; cool; **quro d-risho** head cold
qurqoso button
qurṣlo wrist
quṣro castle
quṭnutho republic
quzo squirrel
qwurto funeral
qyomo to stand
qyoṣo men-shelyo d-malkutho coup d'etat

R

rab-ḥaylo general
rabo/rabtho big
raᶜmo thunder
raᶜyo raw; uncooked
radhayto car; **radhayto ᶜa ifto** armored car; **radhayto d-ᶜudrono** ambulance
radyator radiator
ragbi rugby
raghlo foot; leg; **raghle** feet; **raghlo mṣanaᶜto** artificial leg
rahat comfortable
rahatsiz uncomfortable
rahino hostage
raḥoyo miller
raḥsho insect
rahṭo d-karso diarrhea
raḥuqo far
raḥyo mill
ra'is-arkan chief of staff
rajᶜi reactionary *adjective*
rakhiṣ cheap
rakhloyutho chemist's; pharmacy
rakhsho insect
rakhsho ushno stallion
rakikho soft
rakikho/rakikhto tender
rakowo/rakowto passenger
ramḥel tomorrow; **ramḥel ṣafrayto** tomorrow morning; **ramḥel ᶜaṣriye** tomorrow afternoon; **ramḥel b-lalyo** tomorrow night
raqdho dancing; **raqdho ᶜamoyo** folk dancing
raqiqo thin
rashofo lizard
rashomo/rashomto designer
rassam/rassama designer
raṭibutho humidity
rbiᶜo spring

rbiᶜoyo/rbiᶜayto fourth
rᶜultho shivers
rᶜumyo thunder
rdhofo to pursue
rdhoyo ᶜal u-talgo skiing
rebṣo admoyo blood pressure; **rebṣo admoyo ᶜeloyo** high blood pressure; **rebṣo admoyo taḥtoyo** low blood pressure
redyo stream
reḥo perfume
rejim diet
remzo sign
renyo thought
resuqtho rosary
rezo rice
rfofo second
rghumyo bombardment
rḥomo love
rhoṭo run
rish-baᶜle d-gayso chief of staff
rishmeloyutho capitalism
risho head; top; **risho d-sharire** prime minister
rishono/rishonitho leader; general
rish-quṭnoyutho president
rish-wazire prime minister
rkowo da-susye horse riding
rmay-idho signature
rnoyo to think
roghulo stream
romo high
roshufto tank
rotho lung
rṣoṣoyo/rṣoṣayto gray
rubil ruble
ruᶜtho du-ḥloqo shaving cream
rukowo da-qole vote-rigging
rumono pomegranate
ruqᶜe ḥulmonoye d-kefso sanitary towels
ruqe saliva
Rusiya Russia
Rusnoyo/Rusnayto Russian
rusoqo battery
ruwᶜo one-quarter

S/SH/Ṣ

ṣabun soap
saᶜro hair
sadd dam
ṣadro chest
ṣafrayto morning
saftho lip
ṣafuno soap
sagh well
sagi many; very; **ghallabe ḥemo** very hot; **sagi quro** very cold
Ṣahino./Ṣahyono. I'm *(m/f)* thirsty.
sahro moon; **sahro ḥatho** new moon; **sahro kamilo** full moon
Ṣahyo-no./Ṣ-hitho-no. I'm *(m/f)* thirsty.
sakhlo illiterate
sakro
sakro dam; butt *of rifle*; **sakro d-hawa** windshield/windscreen
salaṭa salad
ṣalmo sculpture
ṣalṣa sauce
salway quail
samo drug; narcotic
samsemono/samsemonitho nurse
samsemonutho chemist's; pharmacy
samuro squirrel
samyo/smitho blind
sandole sandals
ṣanduqo box; chest; car boot/trunk; **ṣanduqo d-bildoro** mailbox; **ṣanduqo jamudo** ice box
sandwish sandwich
saqo sack
saqro passport
saqubloyo opponent
saqubloyutho opposition
ṣaquro pickax
saraṭan cancer
ṣarbubtho caterpillar
ṣarbuqo insect
ṣarofo/ṣarofto banker
sarsiqo sausage
ṣarṣuro cockroach
sarṭono crab; Cancer
ṣarufo/ṣarufto spicy (hot)
ṣarukh missile
ṣarwoyo/ṣarwayto waiter/waitress
sathwo winter
sato vine
ṣawarikh missiles

ṣawboyo/ṣawbayto *university* student
sawko hair
ṣawro throat
sawto *see* **sowo**
saybartho snack
sayidna metropolitan
ṣayṭare checkpoint
sbenakh spinach
sᶜore barley
ṣebᶜo finger; toe; **ṣebᶜotho** fingers; toes
sebeltho ladder
sedro class
sefoqe luggage
ṣefro; ṣefruno sparrow; **ṣefro-deqlo** nightingale; **ṣefro kushoyo** parrot
sefroyutho literature
seghlo d-radhayto car registration/numberplate
seke du-mashkno tent pegs
sekreter secretary
sektho pin; **sektho mshayanto** safety pin; **sektho d-farzlo** railway
selqo beetroot
ṣemdo bag; backpack; handbag; satchel; suitcase; **ṣemde** baggage
seminer seminary
semo silver
semolo left
semoloyo/semolayto left-wing
semoqo/semaqto red
seqlo varnish
servis minibus
ṣeṣo nail
sfariglo quince
sfar-mele dictionary
sfar-nahro river bank
sfar-yamo shore
sfar-yawmo newspaper; **sfar-yawmo bu-Inglishoyo** newspaper in English
sfero omelette
sfinto boat
sfinto boat
ṣfoḥo raid; **ṣfoḥo hawoyo** air-raid
ṣfoḥo to attack; to invade
shaboko window
shabtho week; Saturday; **shabtho d-shafiᶜo** last week; **shabtho d-uthyo** next week
shabṭiye watermelon
shaᶜathan hepatitis.
shaᶜṭo viper; **shaᶜṭo meṣroyo** cobra
shaᶜutho/shaᶜuthto yellow
shafiro beautiful; handsome
shafir-ṭarfe spinach
shaflo/shfaltho disabled
shafra razorblade
shagholo/shagholto worker; operator; **shagholo b-maᶜmlo** factory worker; **shagholo tibeloyo** international operator; **shagholo di-banqa** banker; **shagholo b-makhtwo** office worker
shahin falcon
shaḥino/shaḥinto hot
shaḥto/shaḥte disabled
shahwo falcon
shakale shoes
shakar sugar
shakhro alcohol
shakhroyo alcoholic
shakhroyutho alcoholism
shalfuḥtho pancreas
shallal waterfall
shalo shawl
shalwo ravine; mountain pass
shalyo/shlitho quiet
shamᶜo candle; **shamᶜe** candles
shamino/shaminto fertile
shampu shampoo
shamsiye umbrella
sharab syrup
sharbo subject; vase
sharbtho clan
sharfo scarf
shariᶜ d-ḥa darbo one-way street
shariro true; minister
sharirutho ministry
shariṭ videotape
sharkono *ḏ-haḏomo qṯiᶜo* stump *of limb*
sharwolo trousers
sharyo/shritho free; independent
sharyutho freedom; independence
shathqo silence

shato year; **shato ḥreto** the year before last; **shato d-uthyo** next year; **shato ḥreto** the year after next
shatoyo alcoholic
shawbo flu
shawʿi seventy
shawʿo/shwaʿ seven
shawshbino godfather
shawshbintho godmother
shawṭo di-chifta gun barrel
shawyo equal; record
Shbaṭ February
shʿolo cough; **shʿolo ʿam shulhowo** flu
Shebelto Virgo
shebo medallion
sheʿyo di-ṭablitho backgammon
sheghdo almond
shelfo di-chifta bayonet
shemsho sun
shendo torture
sheno tooth; **shene** teeth
shenuro squirrel
sheqlo du-beth-ṭawso airport tax
sheqyo canal; irrigation
shersho root
sheryono artery
sheth *see* **ishto**
shethesto foundation
sheṭḥo plain; plains
sheṭranj chess
shfoyo fetqe to clear a mine
shfule foothills
shgholo work
shghushyo violence
shḥomo/shḥumto brown
Shiʿoyo/Shiʿayto Shi'i
Shin China
shiqqa apartment
shiro silk; bracelet
shishaltho zipper; chain; **shishalto da-ṭure** range/ mountain range; **shishaltho d-ḥaṣo** spinal column; spine
ṣ-hitho *see* **ṣahyo**
shkhintho shrine
shkhiro/shkhirto ugly
shkhiwoyo quail
shlitho placenta; *and see* **shalyo**
shloḥo robbery
shlomo peace; hello
shmayo sky
shmoʿo to hear
shoʿtho hour; time; clock; **shoʿtho d-idho** watch
s-hodo to testify
ṣḥoḥo photocopy
shomuʿto d-osyo stethoscope
shoqitho canal
shoqo trunk *of tree*
shoqulo d-kahrobo electric plug
shorba soup
shoriṭo cassette
shorutho snack
shorwotho meals
shqoqo street; **shqoqo d-ḥa darbo** one-way street
shritho *see* **sharyo**
shroro; **shrolo** truth
shroyo accommodation; to free
shtaʿsar sixteen
shtithoyo/shtithayto sixth
shtoqo d-lebo heart attack
shtoyo drink; **shtoyo d-alkowol** alcoholism
shubqono! excuse me!; sorry!
shuʿo stone
shughlo work; **shughlo d-idho** handicraft
shuḥdo commission
shuḥlofo season
shulfoḥo smallpox
shulfotho smallpox
shulomo end; finish
shulṭonutho government; **shulṭono yothoyo** autonomy
shumoho surname
shuqo market
shuro wall
shuroro insurance
shuroro d-gedshe insurance policy
shuroyo beginning; start
shurto navel; umbilical cord
shushaye bottle; **shushaye damaye** water bottle; **shushaye d-hawfo/d-ghas** gas canister
shushefo towel
shushmo sesame
shushmono ant
shushoṭo progress
shutoso foundation
shuwolo question

shwa' *see* **shaw'o**
shwa'sar seventeen
shwerib mustache
shwi'oyo/shwi'ayto seventh
shwoyo to equal
sibaqa da-susye horse racing
si'to 'udronayto aid agency; **si'to maṭebonitho** charity *organisation*
sidi C.D.
ṣifr zero
sijin jail
Sikh Sikh
sim-kart sim card
simto treasury
Ṣin China
sinama cinema
siqumo date; **siqumo d-mawlodo** date of birth; **siqumo d-mathyo** date of arrival; **siqumo d-mazlo** date of departure
sirka vinegar
ṣiṣro cricket
siṭlo bucket
siyase politics
skaner scanner
skhiro/skhirto closed; shut
skhoro du-darbo roadblock
skhoyo swimming
ski skiing
skino qanyoyo penknife
skwash squash
ṣlibo semoqo Red Cross
slobo to loot
sloqo d-yawmo dawn
smitho *see* **samyo**
ṣni'utho industry
snighro/snighartho lawyer
snunitho swallow
ṣoba stove
so'urutho visit; *surgical* operation
sofrutho literature
sohdo martyr
sohdutho du-qlo'o driver's license
ṣomuḥo da-ṭefre nail-polish
ṣonda hose
ṣoruḥo missile; **ṣoruḥe** missiles
ṣoṣ sauce
sosyalist socialist
sosyalizm socialism
sowo/sawto old; old person; elder
soyumo da-filme/soyumto da-filme filmmaker
Sqotlanda Scotland
Sqotlandoyo/Sqotlandayto Scottish
sqoṭo failure
squt zero
sri' street
ṣrofo exchange
sruftho soup
... ste; ... stene also
ṣuḥafi/ṣuḥafiye journalist
sumaq sumac
Sunnoyo/Sunnayto Sunni
supermarket supermarket
surgodho da-zabne timetable
surhowo speed
Suri/Suriya Syrian
Suriya Syria
Suroyo/Surayto Assyrian
Suryoyo/Suryayto Assyrian
susto mare
susyo horse; **susyo na'imo** pony; **susyo w-'oghaltho** horse and cart
sut suit
suṭmo chain
Swed Sweden
Swedoyo/Swedayto Swedish
swetar sweater; jumper
ṣwo'o paint; **ṣwo'o da-ṭefre** nail-polish
swodo accent
syomo d-shlomo to make peace

T/Ṭ

ṭabbakh/ṭabbakha *noun* cook
ṭabbothe du-dmokho sleeping pills
ṭablitho table; **ṭablitho d-makhtwo** desk
ṭablo d-adhno eardrum
ṭaboḥo/ṭaboḥto *noun* cook
ṭabyo *gazelle*
ta'lo fox
ṭa'mo taste; **d-lo ṭa'mo** tasteless
ṭa'mono tasty
ṭa'no ton
ṭafoyo slope
tafshirto urine
tafyo/tfitho infected

taglitho protest
tagoro/tagorto business person
tagorutho business
tagrumtho skeleton
tahinyotho! congratulations!
taḥrazto (ḥoshubayto) (computer) program
taḥt bed; under
taḥtoye underwear
taḥtoyo/taḥtayto low
tajir/tajira business person
takhtusho match
taksi taxi
talgo snow
talgonitho; talgo sowo glacier
talgutho frostbite
ṭaliḥotho ṭafyotho contact lenses
ṭaliḥto lens
talilutho moisture
ṭalyo/ṭlitho infant
ṭamaṭa tomato
tamo there
tamro date
Tamuz July
tanino dragonfly
tank tank
taqinto fat
ṭaqm suit
tarbitho education
tarbo fat
tarᶜuz cucumber
ṭarfo leaf; **ṭarfo d-warqo** piece of paper
tarmitho housing estate/project
tarnoghlo cockerel; rooster
tarte *see* **tre**
tarte kore twice
tashᶜitho history
tashlitho truce
tashroro report
taslomo to surrender
ṭawᶜo stamp
ṭawᶜonitho printer
tawdi! thank you!
tawditho religion
ṭawfono flood
ṭawla backgammon
tawono room; **tawono dalumode/da-qonferansat** conference room
tawro bull; Taurus
tawrotho cattle
ṭawuso peacock
tayer tire/tyre
tayimno south
ṭayisto airplane
ṭayo/ṭayayto Muslim
ṭayofto helicopter
ṭayostono pilot
ṭayostono/ṭayostonitho pilot
ṭayro bird
ṭayyaran aviation
tᶜishutho tiredness
ṭᶜomo taste
ṭᶜono to carry
ṭebo report
ṭefro nail *of finger/toe*
teknolojia technology; **i-teknolojia di-mawdᶜonutho** I.T.
telefon telephone; **telefon meshtanyono** mobile phone; **telefon sahroyo; qamari** satellite phone
teleks telex
telo hill
ṭelore sandals
telvizyon television; **telvizyon meshtanyono** portable T.V.
temre eyelids
tengighlo bicycle
tenis tennis
teshᶜi ninety
teshᶜo/tshaᶜ nine
Teshrin ḥaroyo November
Teshrin Qamoyo October
teshriyotho; teshritho autumn
teshtᶜinyo di-ṭablitho backgammon
teshwitho mattress
teto glue
tewno straw
tfanga rifle
tfitho *see* **tafyo**
thalbuno pickle(s)
thaṭlushtho infection
thultho one-third
tḥumo border
ṭibbe ball
ṭilayto butterfly
ṭimo expensive
tino fig
tiraḥa carpet
ṭiyare airplane
tiyaṭron theater; **tiyaṭron d-**

opera opera house; **tiyaṭron di-soʿurutho; tawono di-soʿurutho** operating theater/room
tiyo tea
tlawʿo worm
ṭlawḥe lentils
tlethi thirty
ṭlibo/ṭlibto fiancé/fiancée
ṭlitho *see* **ṭalyo**
tlithoyo/tlithayto third
tlonitho butterfly
tlothaʿsar thirteen
tlotho/tloth three; **tlotho-ruwʿe** three-quarters; **tloth kore** three times
Tlothushabo Tuesday
tmanyo/tmone eight
tminoyo/tminayto eighth
tmonaʿsar eighteen
tmone *see* **tmanyo**
tmoni eighty
tnoyo to repeat
Tome Gemini
tome twins
ṭon ton
ṭowo/ṭowto good; well
tqilo heavy
tqilo/tqilto heavy
traʿsar twelve
traktor tractor
trayono/trayonitho second
tre/tarte two; **tre-thulothe** two-thirds
triṣo correct
ṭruno dictator
ṭrunutho dictatorship
Trushabo Monday
tshaʿ *see* **teshʿo**
tshaʿsar nineteen
tshiʿoyo/tshiʿayto ninth
tuberkulozis tuberculosis
ṭuhmo nationality; **ṭuhmo admoyo** blood group
ṭukosoyo uniform
tulʿe du-shiro; tulʿe hendwoye silkworms
tulʿo worm
tumo garlic
tunoyo novel; **tunoye bu-Inglishoyo** novels in English
tuqfo fredtonoyo nuclear power
turgomo to translate
turist tourist
turizm tourism
Turkiya Turkey
Turkoyo/Turkayto Turk
ṭuro mountain; forest
turoṣ-mamlo grammar
ṭurshi pickle(s)
turto cow
tutho mulberry
tuwaylet toilet(s)
ṭuworo development
twirutho *noun* defeat
twoʿo to punish
ṭwoʿo d-yawmo sunset
tworo to defeat

U

uʿdo now
ufno tire/tyre; **ufno zoyudo** spare tire
ufqo horizon
Uḥdone Mḥayde d-Ameriqa USA
uḥdono state; **uḥdono sharyo** independent state
ulqo regiment
ulṣono crisis
umodo conference
umonutho profession
umthoyutho nationality
unqia ounce
urdʿo frog
Urifi Europe
ushmo a little bit
uti iron *(for clothing)*
uyoso aviation

V

van van
varanda veranda
virus virus
vitaminat vitamins
vito veto
viza visa

W

w- and
wakilo du-krukhyo travel agent
wardiye rosary
wardonoyo/wardonayto pink
waridho; warido vein
warido root

warnish varnish
warqo paper; **warqo du-tuwaylet** toilet paper; **waroqe** banknotes; **waroqe du-kthowo** writing paper; **warqe d-radhayto** car papers
Waylz Wales
waziro minister
wazirutho ministry
wazo goose
Welshoyo/Welshayto Welsh
wolitho homework

Y

ya or
yabruḥo tomato
yad-nahro river bank
yad-yamo shore
yahlo team; regiment
yalak waistcoast
yaludo boy; newborn child
yamino right
yaminoyo/yaminayto right-wing
yamtho lake
yaqdhono fuel *(for fire)*
yaquro/yaqurto heavy
yardo yard
yarḥo month
yarikho tall; long
yarqe vegetables
yarqono jaundice
yaruqo/yaruqto green
yashṭo trachea; windpipe
yaṣilo elbow
yatirutho majority
yatumo/yatumto orphan
yawmo day; **yawmo ḥreno** the day after tomorrow; **yawmo ḥreno** the day before yesterday
yawno pigeon; dove
Yawnoyo/Yawnayto Greek
Yawon; **Yawnan** Greece
yoᶜitho plant
yoduᶜthono/yoduᶜthonitho scientist
yolufo/yolufto pupil; student
Yudhoyo/Yudhayto Jew; Jewish
yudoᶜo media
yulfono learn; **yulfono me-lebo** to learn by heart
yuqdhono burn *medical*
Yurdnon Jordan
Yurdnonoyo/Yurdnonayto Jordanian

Z

zabashe watermelon
zabno *space of* time
zagruro throat
zamoro/zamorto singer
zangin rich
zaqoritho spider
zarf envelope
zarqo/zarqtho blue
Zartushtoyo/Zartushtayto Zoroastrian
zawᶜo earthquake
zawlo fertilizer; manure
zayno weapon; **zayne** arms
zayto; **zaytuno** olive
zᶜuro/zᶜurto infant; child; **zᶜure** children
zebdo butter
zedqe rights; **zedqe gawonoye/mdhinoye** civil rights; **zedqe noshoye** human rights
zedqo d-nkoro w-hfukhyo veto
zefe mustache
zghughitho windshield/windscreen
zhinnike woman; wife
zid more
zlam man; husband
zogho/zghono chick
zokhutho victory
zoruᶜutho agriculture
zoyudo/zoyudto/zoyude too much/too many; extra
zqiftho pin; **zqiftho mshayanto** safety pin
zqiro/zqirto knitted
zroᶜo to plant
zubone sales
zul-ḥezwo videotape
zulo film
zulo ṭayfono Band-Aid; plaster
zul-qolo tape (cassette)
zunoro belt
zuyone munitions
zuze currency
zwodo ammunition
zwono shopping

ENGLISH–SWADAYA–TUROYO

INGLISHAYA—MADINKHAYA—ṬUROYO

INGLISHOYO—MADINḤOYO—ṬUROYO

A

abstract *written* *S:* psiquta; *T:* fsiqutho

academic *person* *S:* akadimyaya/akadimyayta; *T:* akadimoyo/akadimayto; profisor/profisore

academy *S:* bet-drasha; *T:* beth-drosho

accelerator *S:* **banzin**; **msarhewana**; *T:* **makhifono**; **banzin**

accent *S:* sawada; *T:* swodo

accommodation *S:* shrayta; *T:* shroyo

accountant *S:* mkhashwana/makhshwanta; *T:* ḥashubthono/ ḥashubthonitho; muḥasib/muḥasiba

actor *S:* mathlana/mathlanita; *T:* mathlono/mathlonitho

adapter *S:* masir toqane; *T:* mameṭyonitho; adapter

add *S:* myature/mtawsupe; *T:* mawzodo

addition *S:* tawsapta; *T:* mawsfonutho

address *S:* muna^{c}a; *T:* mḥawyonutho

administrator *S:* mparsana/mparsanita; *T:* mfarnsono/mfarnsonitho; idari/idariye

advertising *S:* shuda^{c}a; *T:* i-mawd^{c}onutho; i^{c}lanat; de^{c}ayat

afternoon *S:* ṭahra; *T:* ^{c}aṣriye; **in the afternoon** *S:* b-ṭahra; *T:* b-^{c}aṣriye; **this afternoon** *S:* ṭahra d-ediom; *T:* ad-^{c}aṣriye

age *S:* ^{c}omra; *T:* ^{c}umro

agriculture *S:* zru^{c}ta; *T:* zoru^{c}utho

aid worker *S:* msay^{c}ana; sayu^{c}a/sayu^{c}ta; *T:* ^{c}udronoyo/^{c}udronayto; m^{c}adrono/m^{c}adronitho

AIDS *S:* ayds; *T:* aydz

air *S:* hawa; *T:* hawa

air mail *S:* bildara rqi^{c}aya; *T:* bildoro hawoyo

airforce *S:* khel-ṭawsa; *T:* ḥaylo hawoyo

airplane *S:* ṭayista; *T:* ṭayisto; ṭiyare

airport *S:* bet-ṭawsa; *T:* beth-ṭawso; **airport tax** *S:* makhsa d-bet-ṭawsa; *T:* makso du-beth-ṭawso; sheqlo du-beth-ṭawso

air-raid *S:* spukhya rqi^{c}aya; *T:* ṣfoḥo hawoyo

alcohol *S:* shakhra; *T:* shakhro; alkohol

alcoholic *S:* awkhar/awkhrath dshakhra; *T:* shakhroyo; shatoyo

alcoholism *S:* mawkhrut b-shakhra; *T:* shakhroyutho; shtoyo d-alkowol

alive *S:* khaya; *T:* ḥayo/^{c}ayosho

also *S:* ap; *T:* ... ste; ... stene

ambassador *S:* ezgada/ezgadta; *T:* izgado/izgadto; mshadro/mshadarto

ambulance *S:* raditha d-ushpa; *T:* radhayto d-^{c}udrono; ambulans; as^{c}af

ambush *S:* kmina; *T:* kmino

America *S:* Amerika; *T:* Ameriqa

American *(m/f)* S: Amirkaya/ Amirkayta; T: Ameriqoyo/ Ameriqayto
ammunition S: zawde pshange; T: asono; zwodo; dhakhire
amputation S: prama; T: qṭoᶜo; qṣoyo
aid agency S: wakilot suyaᶜa; T: siᶜto ᶜudronayto
ancestors S: awahata; T: abohotho
ancient S: ᶜatiqa; T: ᶜatiqo
and S: o; up; T: w-
anemia S: bṣirot dimma; T: mḥiluth-admo; fuqr-dam
anesthetic S: mdakhyana; T: madimkhonitho; banch
anesthetist S: mᶜaghuda; T: madimkhono
ankle S: ᶜeqba; T: ᶜeqbo
answer S: punaya; T: funoyo
ant S: shikwana/shikwanta/shikwane; T: namlo; shushmono
anti-aircraft gun S: dalqiw taysyate; T: chifta luqbal-ayisyotho
antibiotic S: dalquw qurme; antibayotiks; T: antibiyotik
antiseptic S: mdakhyana; T: mdakhyono; antiseptik
anti-tank S: dalqiw rashopyate; T: fetqo luqbal-roshufotho
apartment S: mashikna; T: mashryo; shiqqa; apartaman
apartment block S: guda d-mashikne; T: beth-mashrye; ᶜimare
apple S: khabusha; T: ḥabusho
apricot S: mishmishshe; barquqya; T: barquqyo
April S: Nisan; T: Nison
Aquarius S: Dawla; T: Dawlo
Arab *(m/f)* S: Sarqaya/ Sarqayta; ᶜArabaya/ᶜArabayta; T:ᶜAraboyo/ᶜArabayto
archaeological S: ᶜaqawaya/ᶜaqawayta/ᶜaqawaye; T: ᶜatiqo; arkeolojoyo; athari
architect S: ardikhla/ardikhlayta; T: ardikhlo/ardikhlitho; muhandis madani
Aries S: Emra; T: Emro
arm S: draᶜna; T: droᶜo
Armenia S: Armenia; T: Arminya
Armenian S: Aremnaya/ Aremnayta; T: Arimnoyo/Arimnayto
armored car S: radita arpansayta; radita zariditha; T: radhayto ᶜa ifto
arms S: zayne; T: zayne; asliḥa
army S: gaysa; T: gayso; askar; jaysh
arrest *verb* S: khwasha; T: msoko
arrivals S: moṭaya; T: athoye
art gallery S: glakh amna; T: beth-gloḥo
artery S: Sheryana; T: sheryono
article *written* S: memerta; T: mlu'o; mimro; maqale
artificial: artificial arm S: draᶜa ṣniᶜta; T: droᶜo mṣanaᶜto; **artificial eye** S: ᶜayna ṣniᶜta; T: ᶜayno mṣanaᶜto; **artificial leg** S: raghla ṣniᶜta; T: raghlo mṣanaᶜto
artillery S: mqalᶜane; shayudhta; T: mqalᶜono
artist S: amnaara; T: amono/ amonto; fannan/fannana
aspirin S: aspirin; T: aspirin
assassination S: qiṭla bliqa; T: qaṭlo
assault; attack S: spukhya; T: kwosho
assembly *meeting* S: knushya; T: knushyo; *parliament* S: beth-sharire; T: knushto
Assyria S: Atur; T: Othur
Assyrian S: Aturaya/Aturayta; T: Othuroyo/Othurayto; Suroyo/Surayto; Suryoyo/ Suryayto
athletics S: sheᶜye drishaye; T: athliṭoyutho
aubergine S: bnath-gane; T: bnoth-gane; badhinjane komto
August S: Ab; T: Ob
Australia S: Australia; T: Australya
Australian S: Osṭralaya/ Osṭralayta; T: Australyoyo/ Australyayto

autonomy *S:* sholṭan byata; *T:* shulṭono yothoyo; ḥukm dhati
autumn *S:* teshreye; *T:* teshriyotho; teshritho
avalanche *S:* ashita; *T:* grufyo d-talgo; ashitho
aviation *S:* malkhot a'ar; *T:* uyoso; ṭayyaran
ax *S:* nar^{c}a; *T:* nargho
Azerbaijan *S:* Azerbayjan; Hushara; *T:* Azarbayjan
Azerbaijani *S:* Hoshara/ Hoshar-ta; *T:* Azaroyo/ Azarayto

B

back *of body S:* khaṣa; *T:* ḥaṣo; *place S:* lbatra; *T:* bithir
backgammon *S:* she^{c}ya d-ṭablita; *T:* tesht^{c}inyo di-ṭablitho; she^{c}yo di-ṭablitho; ṭawla
backpack *S:* ṣemda d-khaṣa; *T:* ṣemdo
backwards *S:* lbistar; *T:* lakhalf
bad *S:* khirba; *T:* ḥarbo/bisho; *spoiled S:* khirba; *T:* ḥarbo; ḥariwo/ḥaruto
badly *S:* khirba; *T:* ḥarbo
bag *S:* ṣemda; simdha; *T:* ṣemdo; kiso; janṭa
baggage *S:* mawble; *T:* sefoqe; ṣemde; **baggage counter** *S:* nuqazta d-mawble; *T:* fuṣolo da-sefoqe
baker *S:* Nakhtuma/ Nakhtumta; *T:* afoyo; ardoqufo; naḥtumo
baker's; bakery *S:* bet-apyuta; nakhtuma; *T:* ferno
balcony *S:* gdanpa; *T:* balqon
ball *S:* guya; *T:* esfiro; ṭibbe
ballpoint *S:* qanya dywashdyuta; *T:* qanyo nashifo
banana *S:* muza; *T:* muzo; banana
bandage cal *S:* qmata ^{c}aṣwaya; *T:* esoro; ^{c}ṣowo; fesqitho; qmoṭo
Band-Aid *S:* ṣmada; *T:* zulo ṭayfono; plaster
bank *S:* bet-^{c}orpana; *T:* beth-^{c}urfono; banqa
banker *S:* m^{c}arpana/m^{c}arpanta; *T:* ṣarofo/ṣarofto; m^{c}arfono/m^{c}arfonitho; shagholo di-banqa/shagholto di-banqa
banknotes *S:* shawe; zoze shawe; *T:* waroqe
bar *S:* bar; *T:* mashqyo; bar
barbed wire *S:* khu'a mṣalpana; *T:* ḥuṭo kubonoyo
barber *S:* bet-supara; *T:* garo^{c}o
barley *S:* sa^{c}re; *T:* s^{c}ore
barn *S:* idra; *T:* adro; esṭablo
basketball *S:* spir sa la; *T:* esfir-saltho
bat *S:* prakhdoda; *T:* fraḥdudo; ^{c}obugro fayoro
bathroom *S:* bet-khmama; *T:* beth-ḥyofo; ḥammam
battery *S:* baṭarita; batri; rusaqa; *T:* baṭṭaritho; rusoqo; baṭṭariye
bayonet *S:* kallawa; *T:* shelfo di-chifta
be *S:* hwaya; *T:* hwoyo; ithutho
beans *S:* pasolile; *T:* faṣuliye; goṣuṣe
bear *S:* dibba; *T:* debo
beard *S:* diqna; *T:* daqno
beat *overcome S:* zkaya; *T:* ^{c}lobo; ghlobo
beautiful *S:* shapir; *T:* shafiro
bed *S:* mashkawta; *T:* gale; ^{c}arso; taḥt
bee *S:* dabasha/dabashta/dabashe; *T:* dabosho
beef *S:* bisra d-sharkha/sharkhe; *T:* basro da-tawre
beer *S:* pezta; *T:* bira
beetle *S:* khawshushta; *T:* ḥabshusho
beetroot *S:* selqa; *T:* selqo
beginning *S:* shoraya; *T:* shuroyo
behind *S:* l-batra; *T:* bithir
belt *S:* zunara; *T:* qamro; zunoro; qarish
bench *S:* maṣ awta; *T:* maṣ awtho
bicycle *S:* tangighla; *T:* daruktho; tengighlo; bisiklet
big *S:* raba/rabta; *T:* rabo/rabtho
binoculars *S:* mkhawya; *T:* doyuqtho; mrawrwono mez-dawgo; durbin
bird *S:* ṭayra; *T:* ṭayro; fraḥto
biro *S:* qanya ywisha; *T:* qanyo; bayro

birth *S:* mawlada; *T:* mawlodo; **to give birth to** *S:* mabruye; mawlode; *T:* mawlodo
bite: This snake bit me. *S:* Aha khuwa qam na^cişli.; *T:* U-ḥuyano dbişşe-li.
bitter *S:* marira/marirta; *T:* mariro / marirto; mayiro/ mayirto
black *S:* kuma/kumta; *T:* komo/komto; **black tea** *S:* tiya kuma; *T:* chaye komto
blackboard *S:* lukha d-qiryana; *T:* luḥo
bladder *S:* mtanta; *T:* mtonto
blanket *S:* lkhepa; *T:* kushofo; baṭṭaniye; blanket
blind *S:* samya/smita; *T:* samyo/smitho
blood *S:* dimma; *T:* admo; **blood group** *S:* adsha d-dimma; *T:* ṭuhmo admoyo; **blood pressure:** *S:* rwisut dimma; *T:* rebşo admoyo; **blood transfusion** *S:* nqalta dimma; *T:* nuqolo d-admo; shuḥlofo d-admo
blue *S:* zarqa/zarqayta; *T:* zarqo/zarqtho
boar *S:* khzura d-dawra/khzurta d-dawra; *T:* brozo
boarding pass *S:* pitqa d-rkawta; *T:* fetqo d-suloqo
boat *S:* spinta; elpa; *T:* sfinto; gamiye; elfo
body *S:* paghra; *T:* faghro; gushmo
boiled egg *S:* bi^cta shliqta; *T:* be^cto shliqto
bomb *S:* parqa^cta; *T:* bomba; qunbala
bombardment *S:* qlu^cya; *T:* rghumyo; qşofo; qaşif
bomber *S:* mparq^canitha; *T:* daroyo/darayto da-bombe
bomblet *S:* parqa^cta; *T:* bomba na^cimto
bon voyage *(m/f/pl)***!** *S:* urkhukh ptekhta!/urkhakh ptekhta!/ urkhukhon ptekhta!; *T:* darbo ftiḥo!; aloho a^cmaykhu!
bone *S:* garma; *T:* garmo
book *S:* ktawa; *T:* kthowo
bookshop *S:* dukan ktawe; *T:* dukano da-kthowe
boot *S:* but; *T:* ?edlo; but; *of car S:* sanduq radita; *T:* şanduqo
border *S:* tkhuma; *T:* tḥumo
born: to be born *S:* braya; *T:* hwoyo; **Where were you** *(m/f)* **born?** *S:* Ika wet birya?/Ika wat brita?; *T:* Ayko hawat?; **I** *(m/f)* **was born in ...** *S:* Ana birya wen go .../Ana brita wan go ...; *T:* Hawino b-.../Hawyono b-...
bottle *S:* basta; *T:* shushaye; besto
bottom *S:* eshta; *T:* eshto
box *S:* sanduqa; *T:* şanduqo
boy *S:* yala; *T:* yaludo; kurikko
boyfriend *S:* khawra; *T:* ḥawro
bracelet *S:* shiberta; qulba; *T:* qulbo; shiro
brain *S:* mukha; *T:* meḥo
brake *S:* makilyana; brayk; *T:* maklyono; fren; brayk
bread *S:* lakhma ^cyadaya; *T:* laḥmo
break for refreshments *S:* apta; *T:* buṭlono du-nyoḥo
breakfast *S:* ^crayta; *T:* fṭoro
breast/chest *S:* khadya/sadra; *T:* ḥadyo/şadro
brick *S:* lowna; *T:* lewno
bridge *S:* gishra le; *T:* geshro
Britain *S:* Briṭania; *T:* Briṭanya
British *S:* Briṭnaya/Briṭnayta; *T:* Briṭanoyo/Briṭanayto
brown *S:* gawra/gawirta; *T:* shḥomo/shḥumto; qḥuthonoyo/qḥuthonayto
brush *S:* pirka; *T:* maknishto; fircha
bucket *S:* şiṭla; *T:* siṭlo; dawlo
Buddhist *S:* Budaya/Budayta; *T:* Budhoyo/Budhayto
buffalo *S:* gamisha; *T:* gamisho; gomusho
bug *insect S:* rekhsha; *T:* rakhsho
building *S:* binyana; *T:* benyono
bull *S:* tora; *T:* tawro
bullet *S:* gulla; *T:* bughro
burger *S:* hambergur; *T:* hamberger

burn *medical* *S:* yuqdana; *T:* yuqdhono
bus *S:* basa; *T:* baş; autobus; **bus station** *S:* nuqazta d-base; *T:* mashryo du-baş; **bus stop** *S:* klayta d-basa; *T:* beth-kloyo du-baş
business *S:* tagharuta; *T:* tagorutho; **businessman/businesswoman** *S:* tghaara/tghaarta; *T:* tagoro/tagorto; tajir/tajira
but *S:* ina; *T:* elo; bas
butcher *S:* qaṭuba/qaṭubta; *T:* qaṭobo/qaṭobto; qaṭṭab/qaṭṭaba
butcher's shop *S:* bet-qasawuta; *T:* qaşobutho
butt *of rifle* *S:* rakhta; *T:* sakro; eshto
butter *S:* karra; zebda; *T:* kroᶜo; zebdo
butterfly *S:* parkhanita; *T:* tlonitho; ṭilayto
buttermilk *ayran* *S:* dawe; *T:* dawghe
button *S:* taruqta; *T:* qurqoso
buy *S:* zwana; *T:* zwono; shqolo

C

cabbage *S:* lahana; *T:* lahana; qrambo; krawo
cabinet *S:* mawtwa d-sharire; *T:* mawtbo d-sharire
cable *S:* khuṭa; *T:* marsho; kabil
cake *S:* kika; *T:* kuko; kaᶜak
calculate *S:* khshawa; *T:* ḥshowo
calculation *S:* khushbana; *T:* ḥushbono
calculator *S:* khashuta; *T:* manoyo; maḥshwono
calf *S:* sharkha; *T:* ᶜeglo; arwono
camel *S:* gamla; *T:* gamlo
camera *S:* şayurta; *T:* qamera
camouflage *S:* mkasyanuta; *T:* matloyo
campsite *S:* mashrita; *T:* mashritho; qampa
can *S:* qupsa; *T:* ᶜulbo; **can opener** *S:* patkhan qupse; *T:* fotuḥo da-ᶜulbe
Canada *S:* Kanada; *T:* Qanada
Canadian *S:* Kanadaya/ Kanadayta; *T:* Qanadoyo/ Qanadayto
canal *S:* aghogha; *T:* shoqitho; sheqyo
Cancer *S:* Sarṭana; *T:* Sarṭono
cancer *S:* sarṭana; *T:* sartono; saratan; kanser
candle *S:* ponda; shamala; *T:* shamᶜo; **candles** *S:* punde; shamale; *T:* shamᶜe
candlestick *S:* nawrishta; *T:* mnorto
candy *S:* khilyuta; *T:* ḥalyutho
cannon *S:* mqalᶜana; *T:* madoqto ᶜatiqto; kanon
cap *S:* papukhta; *T:* qubᶜo
capitalism *S:* reshmala; *T:* rishmeloyutho
Capricorn *S:* Gadya; *T:* Gadhyo
captain *S:* akhida; *T:* dawqo; naqib
car *S:* radita; *T:* radhayto; **car papers** *S:* waraqe d-radida; *T:* warqe d-radhayto; **car registration/numberplate** *S:* seghla d-radita; *T:* seghlo d-radhayto
carpenter *S:* nghara/ngharta; *T:* nagoro/nagorto; najjar/najjara
carpet *S:* amilla; *T:* mursho; ḥmiltho; tiraḥa; khali
carrot *S:* gizara; *T:* gizoro
carry *S:* ṭᶜana; *T:* ṭᶜono
cashier *S:* gizabra/gizabrta; *T:* noṭar-kesfo/noṭro-kesfo; kasher/kashera
casino *S:* casino; *T:* gazino; beth-qumoro
cassette *S:* zula; *T:* shoriṭo; qaseta
castle *S:* apidna; birta; *T:* quşro
cat *S:* qaṭa; qaṭo; *T:* qaṭo
caterpillar *S:* naqro; *T:* şarbubtho; madolo; nobuzo
Catholic *S:* Qatoliqaya/Qatoliqayta; *T:* Qatholiqoyo/Qatholiqayto
cattle *S:* biqra; *T:* tawrotho
cauliflower *S:* qupta; *T:* quḥo; qarnabiṭ
cave *S:* mᶜartha; *T:* mᶜartho
C.D. *S:* dawqa; *T:* sidi
C.D. player *S:* toqan dawqe; *T:* msaghlonitho du-sidi; musajjal du-sidi

ceasefire *S:* tashlita; *T:* kelyon-nuro
celery *S:* karawis; *T:* krafso
cemetery *S:* bet-qore; *T:* beth-qawre
century *S:* dara; *T:* doro; mo-ishne
chain *S:* shishelta; *T:* shishaltho; suṭmo
chair *S:* kursya; *T:* kursyo
Chaldean Catholic *S:* Kaldaya/ Kaldayta; *T:* Kaldoyo/ Kaldayto
chalk *S:* arbobya; *T:* arbubyo; abshur
chameleon *S:* arya d-ar^{c}a; *T:* ḥulmoṭo
charity organisation *S:* ^{c}erwana; *T:* si^{c}to maṭebonitho; ^{c}udron-ayto
cheap *S:* shawya; *T:* lo ṭimo; arzon; rakhiṣ
check-in counter *S:* nuqzta d-ma^{c}la; *T:* fuṣolo du-qubolo; di-makhtwonutho
checkpoint *S:* nuqzata d-buqare; *T:* nuqzo d-buṣoyo; ṣayṭare; qonṭrol
cheers! *S:* b-khubukh!/b-khub-akh!/b-khubaokhon!; *T:* ḥubo!
cheese *S:* gubta; *T:* gwayto
chemist's *S:* bet-samane; *T:* sam-semonutho; rakhloyutho
cherry *S:* gilaṣe; *T:* qerasiya; karas
chess *S:* sheṭranj; *T:* qufso; sheṭranj
chest *box* *S:* sanduqa; *T:* ṣanduqo
chestnut *S:* baluṭe; *T:* baluṭ-malko
chewing gum *S:* kiya; *T:* du^{c}tho; kiyo
chick *S:* zagha; *T:* zogho; zghono
chicken *S:* kteta/ktayate; *T:* basro da-gyothe
chickpeas *S:* khirṭmane; *T:* ḥarṭumone
chief of staff *S:* resh-gaysa; *T:* rish-ba^{c}le d-gayso; ra'is-arkan
child *S:* shawra; *T:* na^{c}imo/ na^{c}imto
children *S:* shawre; *T:* na^{c}ime; z^{c}ure; *sons* *S:* bnune; *T:* abne; kurikke; *daughters* *S:* bnate; *T:* bnotho; kachikat
chin *S:* diqinta; *T:* daqinto
China *S:* ṣin; *T:* ṣin; Shin
cholera *S:* cholira; *T:* kolera
Christian *(m/f)* *S:* Mshikhaya/ Mshikhayta; *T:* Mshiḥoyo/ Mshiḥayto
Christmas *S:* ^{c}ida z^{c}ura; *T:* ^{c}edho d-mawlodo; ^{c}edho na^{c}imo
church *S:* ^{c}omra; *T:* ^{c}idto
Church of the East Christian *S:* Madinkhaya/Madinkhayta; *T:* Madenḥoyo/Madenḥayto
cinema *S:* bet-khizwane; *T:* sina-ma; beth-ḥezwe
citizen *S:* barmata/bartmata; *T:* bar-athro/bath-athro
citizenship *S:* Matayota; *T:* athroyutho
city *S:* midta; *T:* mdhitho
civil rights *S:* zidqe mdinaye; *T:* zedqe gawonoye; zedqe mdhinoye
civil servant *S:* plakha mdhi-naya/palakhta mdhinayta; palakha d-shulṭana/palakhta d-shulṭana; *T:* ^{c}awodo mdhi-noyo/^{c}awodhto mdhinayto; muwadhdhaf madani/muwadh-dhafa madaniya
civil war *S:* qrawa mdinaya; *T:* qrobo gawonoyo
clan *S:* sharibta; *T:* sharbtho
class *S:* ṣidra; *T:* sedro
classical music *S:* musiqa klasikayta; *T:* musiqa klasi-kayto
clean *S:* dakhya; *T:* nadhifo/nad-hifto
clear a mine *S:* msapiq l-paqu^{c}a; *T:* shfoyo fetqe
climate *S:* muzagha; *T:* muzogho; iqlima
clinic *S:* mas^{c}ara; *T:* beth-osyutho; qenṭrun ḥulmonoyo
clock *S:* sha^{c}ta; *T:* sho^{c}tho
closed *S:* skhira/skhirta; *T:* skhiro/skhirto
cloth *S:* perqa; *T:* ferqo; ḥyoṣo; qumash
clothes *S:* lwushe; julle; *T:* lwushe; jule; **clothes shop** *S:* dukan lwushe; *T:* dukano da-lbushe; dukano da-jule

cloud *S:* ᶜayma; *T:* ᶜaymo; ᶜaywo
cloudy *S:* ᶜaymana; *T:* ᶜaywo
cluster bomb *S:* parqaᶜtha sghulayta; *T:* bomba mbadronitho
clutch *of car* *S:* akhudha; *T:* klach
coalition *S:* awyuta; *T:* awyutho gabayto
cobra *S:* kobra; *T:* shaᶜṭo meṣroyo; kobra
cockerel *rooster* *S:* tarnighla; *T:* tarnoghlo; diko
cockroach *S:* ṣiṣra; *T:* ṣarṣuro
coffee *S:* ṣarwa; *T:* qaḥwe; qḥutho; **coffee with milk** *S:* ṣarwa ᶜm khalwa; *T:* qaḥwe b-ḥalwo
coins *S:* kespa; khurda; *T:* farude; ᶜurfono; fraṭa; khurda
cold *adjective* *S:* qarira/qarirta; *T:* jamudo/jamudto; *noun* *S:* qura; *T:* quro; **cold water** *S:* miya qarire; *T:* maye jamude; **head cold** *S:* qura; resha qarira; *T:* quro: quro d-risho
college *S:* bet-drasha; *T:* beth-drosho; kulliye
colour *S:* mgawnana; *T:* mgawno
comb *S:* mesreqta; *T:* masurqo
combine harvester *S:* kunash khizda; *T:* ḥaṣodo khaliṭo; mzigho
come *S:* taya; *T:* mathyo
comfortable *S:* rwakhana; *T:* rahat
command *S:* mpaqude; *T:* fqodho; ihobo fuqdhono
commission *S:* komishon; *T:* shuḥdo; qomisyon
compass *S:* mṣawyana; *T:* mṣaybonitho; bawṣala; qompas
computer *S:* khashuwa; *T:* ḥoshubo; kompyuter; **computers** *S:* khashuwe; *T:* ḥoshube; kompyuterat
concert *S:* khegga muziqaya; *T:* konser; **concert hall** *S:* awana muziqaya; *T:* awono da-konserat
condemn *S:* dyana; makhrume; *T:* ḥromo
condom *S:* mṭaṭa d-khukhomya; *T:* kondom; kabbut
conference *S:* lumada; *T:* umodo; **conference room** *S:* tawan lumada; *T:* tawono dalumode; tawono da-qonferansat
congratulations! *S:* tahniyate!; *T:* tahinyotho!
conquer *S:* kwasha; kwashta; *T:* kubosho; kbishutho
constipation *S:* qapaṣ; *T:* qbath
constitution *S:* namusa; *T:* qonuno shath'esoyo; dastur
consultant *S:* malukha/malokokhta; *T:* molukho/molukhto; mustashar/mustashara
contact lenses *S:* ṭlawikhyate bawaye; *T:* ṭaliḥotho ṭafyotho; ᶜadasat; kontakt lenz; **contact lens solution** *S:* sam mana dṭlawikhyate bawaye; *T:* darmono da-ṭaliḥotho ṭafyotho
convent *S:* dayra; *T:* dayro
convoy *S:* qapla dradiyate; *T:* luwoyo
cook *noun* *S:* ṭabakha/ ṭabakhta; *T:* ṭaboḥo/ṭaboḥto; ṭabbakh/ṭabbakha; *verb* *S:* bashule; *T:* busholo
cooked *S:* bshila/bshilta; *T:* bashilo/bashilto
cooker *S:* ṭawokha/kanuna; *T:* basholo
cool *S:* payukha; *T:* qariro/qarirto
copper *S:* nkhasha; *T:* nḥosho
copy *noun* *S:* nsukh; nsoekh; asakhta; *T:* aṣaḥto; nuskho; *verb* *S:* nsakha; *T:* nsokho troḥo
coriander *S:* kazbarta; *T:* kuzbartho
corn *S:* khiṭe shimaye; *T:* ḥabtho; daḥno
corner *S:* qurnita; *T:* qurnitho
correct *S:* triṣ; *T:* triṣo
corruption *S:* khwala; *T:* ḥwilutho
cotton *S:* ktana; *T:* ketono; **cotton wool** *S:* amra d-ktana; *T:* ketono
cough *S:* shᶜala; *T:* shᶜolo
count *S:* mnaya; *T:* mnoyo
coup d'etat *S:* sukhapa gaysaya; *T:* qulobo; qyoṣo men-shelyo d-malkutho; enqelab

courtyard *S:* darta; *T:* durto
cow *S:* tawirta; *T:* turto; **cow's milk** *S:* khalwa d-tawiryate; *T:* ḥalwo da-tawrotho
crab *S:* sirṭana dyama; *T:* sarṭono
crayon *S:* qanya mgawnana; *T:* qanyo d-shamᶜo mgawno; krayon
cream *ointment* *S:* meshkha; *T:* meshḥo
credit card *S:* pitqa dizoputa; *T:* fetqo du-kredit; kredit kard
cricket *S:* chercherroka; *T:* ṣiṣro
cricket *S:* cricket; *T:* kriket
crime *S:* surkhana; *T:* ḥawbo
criminal *S:* msarkhana/msarkhanta; *T:* ḥayowo/ḥayowto
crisis *S:* ᶜasquta; *T:* ᶜoqtho; ᶜiqutho; ulṣono; kriza
crops *S:* zarᶜone; *T:* ᶜalotho; ᶜwuro
crossroads *S:* palshat urkhate; *T:* fago; frosho da-darbone
crow *S:* ᶜorwa; *T:* ᶜurwo; qarqoso
crystal *S:* bellura; *T:* berulo; qrustalus
cucumber *S:* parkhe; *T:* khyoro; farḥo; tarᶜuz
cultivate *S:* krawa; *T:* floḥo
culture *S:* marduta; *T:* mardutho
cumin *S:* kmana; *T:* kmuno
cupboard *S:* dapa d-niṣle; *T:* fardisqo; gantor; dulab
currency *S:* zoze; *T:* zuze
cushion *S:* sadita; *T:* besodyo; mkhadde
customs *S:* makhse; *T:* makso; gumruk
cut *S:* qṣaya; *T:* qṣoᶜo; qṣoyo
Cypriot *S:* Qubrasaya/Qubrasayta; *T:* Qufroyo/Qufrayto
Cyprus *S:* Qubrus; *T:* Qufrus

D

dagger *S:* gallawa; *T:* khanjar
dam *S:* sikra; *T:* sakro; sadd
dance; **dancing** *S:* raqada; *T:* raqdho
danger *S:* qinṭa; *T:* qenṭo/khaṭar
darkness *S:* khuya; *T:* ᶜeṭmo; ḥeshukho
date *S:* siquma; *T:* siqumo; *fruit* *S:* tamre; qazbe; *T:* tamro; **date of arrival** *S:* siqum mṭayta; *T:* siqumo d-mathyo; **date of departure** *S:* siqum ṭyasa; *T:* siqumo d-mazlo; **date of birth** *S:* siqum mawlada; *T:* siqumo d-mawlodo
daughter *S:* brata; *T:* bartho; kachikke
dawn *S:* nughha; *T:* sloqo d-yawmo
day *S:* yawma; *T:* yawmo
daytime *S:* imama; emama; *T:* b-yawmo
dead *S:* mita; *T:* mitho
death *S:* mawta; *T:* mawto
debate *S:* durasha; *T:* kuthosho
debt *S:* dayna; *T:* dayno
decade *S:* as sara; *T:* ᶜsar ishne
December *S:* Kanun Qamaya; *T:* Konun Qamoyo
deer *S:* tabya/tbita; *T:* aylo
defeat *noun* *S:* twarta; *T:* twirutho; *verb* *S:* twara; *T:* tworo
dehydration *S:* yawshanuta; *T:* nashifutho
delay *S:* shukhara; *T:* meshtawḥronutho
democracy *S:* dimoqraṭayuta; *T:* dimoqratutho; dimoqratiye
dentist *S:* asya dshinne; *T:* osyo/ositho da-ᶜarshone; *T:* osyutho da-ᶜarshone
deodorant *S:* ᶜeṭra dshkhata; *T:* ᶜeṭro luqbal du-ṣnono; deodorant
department store *S:* dokan makhimle; *T:* dukano rabtho flighayto
departures *S:* ezla; *T:* azole
desert *S:* ᶜarawa; *T:* madhbro
designer *S:* mtapinkhana; *T:* rashomo/rashomto; rassam/rassama
desk *S:* ṭawlita; *T:* ṭablitho d-makhtwo
dessert *S:* khilyuta; *T:* ḥalyutho
destroy *S:* msakhip; *T:* maḥrowo
detergent *S:* bdhara dshyagha; *T:* deqtho di-mashighonutho; bodra di-mashighonutho

detonation *S:* purqa^{c}a; *T:* mfajronutho
development *S:* tuwara; *T:* ṭuworo; methṭawronutho
dialect *S:* le^{c}za; *T:* le^{c}zo; lahje
diarrhea *S:* plakhta daqla; *T:* mazlo d-gawo; rahṭo d-karso
dictator *S:* diktaturaya; *T:* ṭruno; diktator
dictatorship *S:* diktaturuta; *T:* ṭrunutho; diktatoriye
dictionary *S:* kunash mille; *T:* sfar-mele; kunosh-mele; leksiqun
die *S:* myata; *T:* myotho
diet *S:* rajim; *T:* rejim
difficult *S:* ^{c}asqa; *T:* ^{c}asqo/^{c}asqtho
digital *S:* raqmaya; dijital; *T:* dijital
dining car *S:* ^{c}agholta d-mukhla; *T:* markawtho di-shorutho; markawtho du-muklo
dinner *S:* khshamita; *T:* ḥshimto
diplomat *S:* suyasara/suyasarta; *T:* diblomasoyo/diblomasayto
diplomatic ties *S:* isure suyasaye; *T:* esore diblomasoye
dirty *S:* ṭawsha; *T:* ^{c}jiqo/^{c}jiqto
disabled *S:* khghira/khghirta; *T:* shaflo/shfaltho; shaḥto/shaḥte
disaster *S:* tawhta; *T:* gunḥo
disc-jockey *S:* dijay; *T:* dijay; disk-joki
disco *S:* disco; *T:* disko; diskotek
discussion *S:* durasha; *T:* nuqosho
disease *S:* kiwa; *T:* kurhono; kewo
displaced person *S:* tawtawa; *T:* mshanyo/mshanayto; **displaced persons/people** *S:* tawtawe; *T:* mshanye
district *S:* pnita; *T:* fnitho
divide *S:* plagha; *T:* flogho
division *S:* pulagha; *T:* flighutho
divorced *S:* rupa/rupita; *T:* marfiyo/marfayto; **I** ***(m/f)*** **am divorced.** *S:* Ropa wen./Ropita wan.; *T:* Marfiyo no./Marfayto no.
doctor *S:* asya; *T:* osyo/ositho; doktor/doktora
dog *S:* kalba/kalibta; *T:* kalbo
dollar *S:* dollar; *T:* dolar
donkey *S:* khmara; *T:* ḥmoro
door *S:* tar^{c}a; *T:* tar^{c}o
doorlock *S:* qipla; *T:* fakoro; quflo
double bed *S:* ^{c}arsa roikha; *T:* gale mezdawgo
dove *S:* yawna; *T:* yawno
down *S:* ltekhet; *T:* laltaḥt
dragonfly *S:* qipniz; *T:* tanino
drawer *S:* garurta; *T:* jarur
dress *S:* zhita; *T:* naḥto
dressing *medical* *S:* ṭalwashta; *T:* lubosho
dressmaker *S:* khayaṭa/khayaṭta; *T:* ḥayoṭo/ḥayoṭto
drill *S:* naquwa; *T:* maqwo
drink *S:* shtaya; *T:* shtoyo
drive *S:* mdawure; *T:* qlo^{c}o
driver *S:* mdawrana/mdawranta; *T:* qalo^{c}o/qalo^{c}to
driver's license *S:* sahduta d-dwara; *T:* sohdutho du-qlo^{c}o; fsoso du-qlo^{c}o
drought *S:* yawshana; *T:* nashifutho
drug *medical* *S:* sammana; *T:* darmono; *narcotic* *S:* samma ^{c}aghuda; *T:* samo; mukhaddar; drog
duck *S:* baṭṭa; *T:* baṭo
Dutch *S:* Duchnaya/Duchnayta; *T:* Holandoyo/Holandayto
D.V.D. *S:* dividi; *T:* dividi
D.V.D. player *S:* toqan dividi; *T:* msaghlonitho du-dividi
dysentry *S:* dizenṭeria; *T:* dizenṭeria

E

eagle *S:* nishra; *T:* neshro
ear *S:* nata; adna; *T:* adhno; *S:* natyate; adnate; *T:* adhnotho
eardrum *S:* parda d-nata; *T:* ṭablo d-adhno
earrings *S:* marwade/qanushyate; *T:* marwode; qdhoshe
earthquake *S:* nawdhana; nudhnadha; *T:* zaw^{c}o; hyozo ar^{c}onoyo

east *S:* madinkha; *T:* madenḥo
Easter *S:* ^{c}ida d-qyamta; *T:* ^{c}edho da-qyimto; ^{c}edho rabo
easy *S:* pshiṭa; *T:* fshiṭo/fshiṭto
eat *S:* khala; *T:* muklo
economist *S:* m mashkhana; *T:* eqonomyoyo/eqonomyayto; iqtiṣadi/iqtiṣadiye
education *S:* Tarbita; Tulmada; *T:* tarbitho
egg *S:* be^{c}ta; bi^{c}i; *T:* be^{c}to; **eggs** *S:* biye; *T:* be^{c}e
eggplant *S:* bnath-gane; *T:* bnoth-gane; badhinjane komto
eight *S:* tmanya/tmane; *T:* tmanyo/tmone
eighteen *S:* tmani^{c}sar; *T:* tmon-a^{c}sar
eighth *S:* tminaya/tminayta; *T:* tminoyo/tminayto
eighty *S:* tmani; *T:* tmoni
elbow *S:* qursolta; *T:* yaṣilo
elder *old person* *S:* sawa/sawta; *T:* sowo/sawto
election *S:* gubaya; *T:* guboyo
electrical goods store *S:* dokan laqiṭraye; *T:* dukano da-tuqone kahroboye
electricity *S:* laqiṭ para; *T:* kahrobo; kahraba'; jeyran
elephant *S:* pila; *T:* filo
elevator *S:* masilqanita; *T:* ma^{c}ly-ono
eleven *S:* khadi^{c}sar; *T:* ḥdha^{c}sar
e-mail *S:* bildara iloqtronaya; "e-mail"; *T:* egartho eleqṭrunayto; "e-mail"
embassy *S:* bet-ezgaduta; *T:* izgadutho; mshadrutho
emergency exit *S:* mapqa ^{c}riṣa; *T:* mafqo di-aliṣutho
empty *S:* spiqa; spiqta; *T:* kha-lyo/khlitho
enamel *S:* ṣwyi^{c}a; *T:* qromo
end *S:* khutama; *T:* shulomo
enemy *S:* b^{c}ildara; b^{c}ildwawa; *T:* b^{c}eldbobo; dijmin
engine *S:* mzi^{c}ana; *T:* moṭor
engineer *S:* mkhara/mkharta; *T:* maḥoro/maḥorto; muhan-dis/muhandisa
England *S:* England; *T:* Ingiltara
English *S:* Englishaya/English-nayta; *T:* Inglishoyo/Inglish-ayto
enough *S:* sapiq; *T:* malyo/mlitho
entrance *S:* ma^{c}la; *T:* ma^{c}bro
envelope *S:* ^{c}elwa; ^{c}alwa; *T:* lfofo; zarf
epidemic *S:* pras-kurhana; *T:* mawtono; kurhono gawonoyo
equal *noun* *S:* shawya; *T:* shawyo; *verb* *S:* shwaya *T:* shwoyo
eraser *S:* mkapranita; *T:* laḥayto; missaḥa
escalator *S:* darkhe laqit parae; *T:* masqono; mdarghono
ethnic cleansing *S:* lkhayta ṭohmanayta; *T:* mandhafto ṭuhmayto
ethnic minority *S:* qaliluta ṭohmayta; *T:* ḥsirutho ṭuhmay-to
euro *S:* euro; *T:* oyro
Europe *S:* Europe; *T:* Urifi
evacuate *S:* msapaqta; *T:* makhloyo
evening *S:* ramsha; *T:* ^{c}aṣriye; **this evening** *S:* aya ṭahra aha ramsha; *T:* ad-^{c}aṣriye; **in the evening** *S:* bramsha; *T:* b-lalyo
ewe *S:* ^{c}ana; *T:* neqyo
exam *S:* bukhrana; *T:* buḥrono
exchange *S:* khulapa; *T:* ṣrofo
excluded *S:* sṭar min; *T:* lo ḥshiwo
excuse me! *S:* pakhalta!; *T:* shubqono!
exercise book *S:* kerka d-durasha; *T:* kerko da-duroshe
exhaust *S:* ekzuz; *T:* ogzos
exhibition *S:* bet-glakha; *T:* beth-gloḥo; froso
exile *person* *S:* mizaṭra/misaṭrana; *T:* galwoyo/gal-wayto
exit *S:* mapqa; *T:* mafqo
expensive *S:* dmaeya; *T:* ṭimo
explain *S:* Pashuqe; *T:* fushoqo
explode *S:* mparqi^c; *T:* mfajoro
express *S:* ba^{c}ghal; *T:* khayifo; msarhwo; ekspres
extension number *S:* raqma dilanaya; *T:* mfashṭutho; menyono mfashaṭto

extra S: yatir/tawsapta; T: zoyudo/zoyudto; ekstra

eye S: ᶜayna; T: ᶜayno; **eyes** S: ᶜaynate; T: ᶜaynotho

eyebrow S: gwina; qiṣṣa; T: gbino

eyeglasses S: khazayate; T: ḥazoyotho

eyelids S: temre; T: temre

F

face S: patta; T: fotho

factory worker S: maṣinᶜana/maṣinᶜayta; T: shagholo b-maᶜmlo/shagholto b-maᶜmlo

failure S: rapyuta; T: sqoṭo

falcon S: baza; T: shahwo; boziqo; bozo; shahin

fall S: npala; T: nfolo

fallowland S: biyara; T: krowo; arᶜo bayorto

false S: pawda; T: fawdo

family S: iqarta; T: iqartho; iqartha; ᶜa'ile; famil

famine S: kipna; T: kafno

fan S: marwakhta; T: marwoḥo; mafoḥitho; **fan belt** S: qamra; zunar marwakhta; T: qamro d-marwoḥo

far S: rikhqa; T: raḥuqo

farm S: mazraᶜta; T: mazroᶜo; adro

farmer S: akara/akarta; T: akoro/akorto; daworo/daworto

farming S: akaruta; T: akorutho; daworutho

fat noun S: tarba; T: tarbo; adjective S: ṭrisa; T: taqinto/khashino

father S: baba; babi; T: babo

fax S: fax; T: faks; **fax machine** S: tuqan faks; T: makina dufaks

February S: ishwaṭ; T: shbaṭ

feed an animal S: makhule khaywa; T: mawkholo ḥaywo

feet S: aqle; reghle; T: raghle

felt-tip pen S: qanya d-sur'a; T: qanyo d-lamṭo

female S: atta; T: neqwo

femur S: garma d-uṭma; T: garmo d-ᶜaṭmo

fennel S: ashlarᶜa; T: ashkarᶜo

ferret S: kakhushta; T: kokhushto

ferry S: spenta; T: maᶜbro

fertile land S: shamina/shaminta; T: shamino/shaminto

fertilizer S: zwla; T: mshamnono; zawlo

fever S: eshatha; T: eshotho; ḥumtho; ḥemto

fiancé/fiancée S: mkhira/mkhirta; T: mkhiro/mkhirto; ṭlibo/ṭlibto

field S: khiqla; T: ḥaqlo

fifteen S: khamshaᶜsar; T: ḥamshaᶜsar

fifth S: khmishaya/khmishayta; T: ḥmishoyo/ḥmishayto

fifty S: khamshi; T: ḥamshi

fig S: tina; T: tino

fighter S: qrawtana; T: qrabthono/qrabthonitho

file paper/computer S: waraqe d-khashuwa; T: msadronitho; fayl

film S: zula; pilma; T: zulo; filma

filmmaker S: mapqana/mapqanta; T: soyumo da-filme/soyumto da-filme

finger S: soᶜa; T: ṣebᶜo; **fingers** S: sebᶜate; T: ṣebᶜotho

finish S: praqa; T: shulomo

fire S: nura; T: nuro

firewood S: qayse d-nura; T: qayse di-nuro

first S: qadhmaya/qadhmayta; qamaya; T: qamoyo/qamayto

fish S: nona (plural none); T: nuno (plural nune)

five S: khamsha/khamesh; T: ḥamsho/ḥammish

flash S: zahra; T: barqo; bahro; flash

flashlight S: bahrad d-ida; T: bahro d-idho

flea S: pirtana; T: furthaᶜno

flea S: pirṭana (plural pirṭane); T: furthaᶜno (plural furthaᶜne)

flies S: didwe; T: dabobe

flock S: pesqa; T: darmala

flood S: milaa; T: ṭawfono

floor story S: medyara arᶜanaya; T: medyoro arᶜonoyo; qaṭ; ṭabaq

florist

florist *s:* wardaya; wardayta; dukan warde; *T:* dukano dawarde
flour *s:* qamkha; *T:* qamḫo
flu *s:* enfluwanza; *T:* shawbo; sh ͨolo ͨam shulhowo; inflawenza
fly *s:* didwa; *T:* dabobo
fog *s:* ͨarpilla; *T:* ͨarfelo; mij
foggy *s:* ͨarpillaya; *T:* ͨarfeloyo/ ͨarfelayto
folk dancing *s:* riqda ͨammaya; *T:* raqdho ͨamoyo; folkloroyo
folk music *s:* zimra ͨammaya; *T:* musiqa folklorayto
food *s:* mikhulta; *T:* muklo
food poisoning *s:* sumama d-khalta; *T:* masmonutho d-muklo
foot *s:* aqla; *T:* raghlo; durakhtho; *measurement s:* durikta; *T:* raghlo; fut; **on foot** *s:* halkha; *T:* malkho
football *s:* spir righla; *T:* esfir-raghlo; futbol
foothills *s:* sipa d-ṭure; *T:* shfule
footpath *s:* urkha d-aqla; *T:* darbo d-malkho
forest *s:* ͨawa; *T:* ṭuro; ͨobo
fort *s:* khasna; *T:* qal ͨo
forty *s:* ͨarb ͨi; *T:* arb ͨi
forum *s:* forum; *T:* forum
forwards *s:* lqodama; *T:* laqid-dam
foundation *s:* mshat'asta; *T:* shutoso; shethesto
four *s:* arb ͨa/arba ͨ; *T:* arb ͨo/arba ͨ
fourteen *s:* ͨara ͨsar; *T:* arba ͨsar
fourth *s:* rwi ͨaya/rwi ͨayta; *T:* rbi ͨoyo/rbi ͨayto
four-wheel drive *s:* ridhya d-arba ͨ gighle; *T:* jip; landkruz
fox *s:* ta ͨla; *T:* ta ͨlo
France *s:* Pransa; *T:* Faransa
free *s:* khira; *T:* ḥiro/ḥirto
free *s:* mkharir; *T:* shroyo
freedom *s:* khiruta; *T:* ḥirutho; sharyutho
freezing *s:* mqarṣana; *T:* jamudo/ jamudto
French *person s:* Frangaya/ Frangayta; *T:* Faransoyo/ Faransayto

french fries *s:* piṭaṭe qilye; *T:* paṭaṭa (*or* baṭaṭa) mqalayto
fresh *s:* raghye; *T:* qariro/qarirto; **fresh fish** *s:* none raghye; *T:* nune ḥathe; **fresh fruit** *s:* pire raghye; *T:* fire ḥathe; fako ḥatho
Friday *s:* ͨRuta; *T:* ͨRubto
fridge *s:* maqrana; *T:* majimdono; maqrono; barrade
friend *s:* khawr/khwart; *T:* ḥawraydh/ḥwarthaydh
friend *s:* khawra; *T:* ḥawro/ḥwartho
frog *s:* piqaa; *T:* urd ͨo
front *s:* lqamta; *T:* qum; **in front of** *s:* qam; *T:* qum
frontier *s:* Tkhube; *T:* tḥumo
frost *s:* qirsa; *T:* ͨaryo
frostbite *s:* talguta; *T:* talgutho
fruit *s:* pira; *T:* firo; fako; **fruit juice** *s:* ͨṣira d-pere; *T:* ͨsoro da-fire; ͨasir da-fire
fuel *petrol s:* banzin; *T:* banzin; *for fire s:* yaqdana; *T:* yaqdhono
full *s:* melya; mlita; *T:* malyo/mlitho; **full moon** *s:* khis aa; *T:* sahro kamilo
funeral *s:* ͨopaya; *T:* qwurto
furrow *s:* warza; *T:* ḥṭuṭo; krowo; ḥefro
future *s:* da ͨtid; *T:* da- ͨtidh

G

gall bladder *s:* mrarta; *T:* mrorto
gallon *s:* galin; *T:* galon
garden *s:* ganta; *T:* gantho
gardener *s:* gannana/gannanta; *T:* ganono/ganonto; fredtho
garlic *s:* toma; *T:* tumo
gas *s:* khapupa; *T:* hawfo; ghas; **gas bottle** *s:* pilla d-khapupa; *T:* shushaye d-hawfo; shushaye d-ghas; **gas canister** *s:* pilla d-khapupa; *T:* shushaye d-hawfo; shushaye d-ghas
gazelle *s:* ozayla; *T:* ṭabyo
gear *s:* gear; *T:* gir
Gemini *s:* T'ame; *T:* Tome
general *s:* reshana; *T:* rab-ḥaylo; rishono; jeneral

gently! *S:* nikha; *T:* hedi!
geography *S:* mamluth ar^{c}a; *T:* jiyoghrafiya
Georgia *S:* Jorjiya; *T:* Grujiya
Georgian *S:* Gurgaya/Gurgayta; *T:* Grujoyo/Grujayto
German *S:* Garmanaya/Garmanayta; *T:* Almanoyo/Almanayto
Germany *S:* Almanya; *T:* Almanya
germs *S:* qurme; *T:* mikrobe
get *S:* shqala; *T:* mṭoyo
gift *S:* dashna; *T:* dushno
girl *S:* yalta; *T:* bartho; kachikke
girlfriend *S:* khawerta; *T:* ḥwartho
give *S:* yhawa; *T:* ihobo
glacier *S:* nahra qrisa; *T:* talgonitho; talgo sowo
glasses *spectacles S:* khazayate; *T:* ḥazoyotha
gloves *S:* braide; *T:* bnoth-kafe
glue *S:* tetta; *T:* teto
go *S:* khasha; sha^{c}ulta *T:* mazlo
goal *S:* nawpa; *T:* nawfo; gol
goat *S:* ^{c}izza; *T:* ^{c}ezo; **goat meat** *S:* bisra d-^{c}izze; *T:* basro da-^{c}eze; **goat's milk** *S:* khalwa d-^{c}eze; *T:* ḥalwo da-^{c}eze
godfather *S:* qariwa; shushbina; *T:* shawshbino
godmother *S:* qariwta; shushbinta; *T:* shawshbintho
gold *S:* dahwa; *T:* dahwo
golf *S:* kolf; *T:* golf
good *S:* ṭawa; ṭawta; *T:* ṭowo/ṭowto; kayiso
goose *S:* qaza; *T:* wazo
government *S:* shulṭana; *T:* shulṭonutho; ḥukume
gram *S:* gram; *T:* gram
grammar *S:* turas mamla; *T:* turoṣ-mamlo; grammatiqi
grapefruit *S:* grapefrut; *T:* grapfrut
grapes *S:* ^{c}inwe; *T:* ^{c}anwe
grass *S:* gilla; *T:* gelo
grasshopper *S:* qamṣa; *T:* qamṣo
gravel *S:* bizqe; *T:* boqushe
gray *S:* qiṭmanaya; qiṭmayata; *T:* qaṭmonoyo/qaṭmonayto; rṣoṣoyo/rṣoṣayto
Greece *S:* Yawnan; *T:* Yawon; Yawnan; Grikia
Greek *S:* Yawnaya; *T:* Yawnoyo/Yawnayto
green beans *S:* lobye; *T:* lobya
green *S:* yaruqa/yaruqta; *T:* yaruqo/yaruqto
green tea *S:* tiya yaruqa; *T:* chaye yaruqto
greengrocer *S:* baqala; *T:* baqolo
grenade *S:* parqa^{c}ta d-ida; *T:* mramyo; bomba d-idho
grind *S:* tkhana/grasa; *T:* groso
grow *S:* yrawa; *T:* irowo; **to grow crops** *S:* zra^{c}a; *T:* iyrowo
guerrilla *S:* dar rara; *T:* gerilla
guest speaker *S:* mala diqara; *T:* malolo dhayfo
guesthouse *S:* ashpaza; *T:* bayto da-dhayfe; qonuq-ewi
guidebook *S:* hadiaa; *T:* kthowo di-mhadyonutho
gun *S:* glulita; *T:* chifta; *pistol S:* glulita; *T:* pis ola; qurma; musaddas; **gun barrel** *S:* abub-glulita; *T:* shaw o di-chifta; abubo di-chifta

H

hail *S:* barda; *T:* bardo; ḥarṣaftho
hair *S:* sa^{c}ra; *T:* sawko; sa^{c}ro; **a hair** *S:* mina; mezta; *T:* mezto
hairbrush *S:* mesriqta d-sa^{c}ra; *T:* fircha du-sawko
hairdresser *S:* sa para/sa paranta; *T:* ḥaloqo/ḥaloqto
hairdryer *S:* myawshan sa^{c}ra; *T:* mnashfono du-sawko
hammer *S:* arzipta; arzapta; *T:* akhlo; arzaftho
hand *S:* ida; *T:* idho; **left hand** *S:* ida d-simmala; *T:* idho d-semolo; **right hand** *S:* ida d-yammina; *T:* idho d-yamino
handbag *S:* ṣimdha d-ida; *T:* ṣemdo
handicraft *S:* shughla d-ida; *T:* shughlo d-idho
handkerchief *S:* kunikta; *T:* mandilo
handle *S:* esit qa; *T:* qato; idho

handset *S:* adhenta; *T:* handset
handsome *S:* shapir; *T:* shafiro
happy *S:* psikha; *T:* fsiḥoyo/fsiḥayto
hard *S:* qishya; *T:* qashyo; **hard!** *vigorously* *S:* quya!; *T:* qawyo!
hardware store *S:* dokan ᶜutade; *T:* dukano da-mone farzloye
harvest *S:* ᶜdana d-khizda; *T:* ḥṣodo
hat *S:* kusita; *T:* kusitho; kimme
hatchet *S:* qurnasa; *T:* qurnoso
have *see page 26.*
hawk *S:* baziqa; *T:* neṣo
hay *S:* tuna; *T:* kesto
haystack *S:* ᶜodhala d-tuna; *T:* gdisho di-kesto
hazel nut *S:* pindiqe; *T:* fendqo; bundqo
he/it *S:* haw; *T:* huwe; hiye
head *S:* risha; *T:* risho
health *S:* khulmana; *T:* ḥulmono
hear *S:* shmaᶜa; *T:* shmoᶜo
heart *S:* libba; *T:* lebo; **heart attack** *S:* spakhta d-libba; *T:* shtoqo d-lebo
heat stroke *S:* mkhuta d-libba; *T:* mḥoyo d-ḥemo; faliji
heat wave *S:* makhshula d-khimma; *T:* maḥshulo d-ḥemo
heavy *S:* yaqura/yaqurta; *T:* yaquro/yaqurto; tqilo/tqilto
hedgehog *S:* gdhodha; *T:* qufdo; qufrin
helicopter *S:* ṭayupta; *T:* ṭayofto
helicopter *S:* ṭayupta; *T:* tayofto
hello! *S:* shlama!; *T:* shlomo!
help *S:* mᶜadure; *T:* mᶜawanto; ᶜudrono
hen *S:* dika; *T:* farugo
hepatitis. *S:* shaᶜatan; *T:* kabdho; shaᶜathan; hepatitis
herd *S:* biqra; ramka; *T:* baqro
here *S:* harkaa; laakha; *T:* harke
hernia *S:* ptaqa; *T:* ftoqo
high *S:* rama; *T:* ᶜeloyo/romo; **high blood pressure** *S:* rwisut dimma ᶜellaya; *T:* rebṣo admoyo ᶜeloyo
hill *S:* tella; *T:* telo
Hindu *S:* Hindaya/Hindayta; *T:* Hendwoyo/Hendwayto
hip *S:* khruta; *T:* ḥrutho
history *S:* tashᶜita; maktawzawna; *T:* makthab-zabno; tashᶜitho
hit *S:* mkhaya; *T:* mḥoyo; **to hit a mine** *S:* psaᶜ l-paquᶜa; *T:* mḥoyo fetqo
H.I.V. *S:* aych-ay-vi; *T:* aych-ay-vi
hockey *S:* hoki; *T:* hoki
holidays *S:* buṭlana; *T:* buṭlono
homework *S:* walita baytayta; *T:* wolitho; baytayto
honey *S:* dusha; *T:* dawsho
hood *S:* kasya; *T:* fagodho
horizon *S:* upqa; *T:* ufqo
hornet *S:* dibbora/dibborta; *T:* deburitho
horse *S:* sosa; susya; *T:* susyo; **horse and cart** *S:* markawta d-sosye; *T:* susyo w-ᶜoghaltho; **horse racing** *S:* moray sosye; *T:* muroyo da-susye; sibaqa da-susye; **horse riding** *S:* par rashuta; *T:* rkowo da-susye
hose *S:* kharṭuma; *T:* kharṭumo; ṣonda
hospital *S:* bet-krihe; *T:* beth-krihe; **maternity hospital** *S:* bet-mawlada; *T:* beth-mawlodo
hostage *S:* meshkana; *T:* rahino; mᶜaryo
hostel *S:* mashrita d-bawta; *T:* mashryo; pansiyon
hot *S:* shakhina; *T:* shaḥino; ḥemo; **hot water** *S:* miya shakhine; *T:* maye shaḥine; **hot wind** *S:* poakha shakhina; *T:* hawa shaḥinto
hotel *S:* bet-bawta; *T:* hotel; beth-mashryo; fundqo; **the hotel industry** *S:* khaqla d-bet-bawte; *T:* i-mashryonutho; a-hotelat
hour *S:* shaᶜta; *T:* shoᶜtho
house *S:* bayta; *T:* bayto
housing estate/project *S:* tarmita mashiknayta; *T:* tarmitho
how? *S:* dakhi?; *T:* aydarbo?; **how near?** *S:* kma qurba?; *T:* miqqa qariwo?; **how far?** *S:* kma rikhqa?; *T:* miqqa raḥuqo?; **how many?** *S:* kma

lay?; *T:* kmo?; **how much?** *S:* kma le?/kma la?/kma lay?; *T:* miqqa?

human rights *S:* zidqe nashaye; *T:* zedqe noshoye

humanitarian aid *S:* suya^{c}a nashaya; *T:* ^{c}udrono noshoyo

humidity *S:* raṭiwota; *T:* raṭibutho

hundred *S:* emma; *T:* mo

hungry: I'm hungry. *S:* Kpina win./Kpinta wan.; *T:* Kafinno./Kafinono.; Kafino-no./Kafinto-no.

husband *S:* bar zawga; *T:* gawro; ba^{c}lo; zlam

hygiene *S:* mriquta kholmanay-ta; *T:* nomuso ḥulmonoyo; qonuno ḥulmonoyo

I

I *S:* ana; *T:* ono

ice *S:* glida; *T:* glidho; **ice box** *S:* ṣanduq qlida; *T:* ṣanduqo jamudo

ice ax *S:* nar^{c}a d-glidha; *T:* nargho du-glidho

ice-cream *S:* qarirta; *T:* *in Syria* buza; *in Turkey* dondurma; *in Iraq* moṭa

illiterate *S:* bura/burta; *T:* buro; sakhlo

in *S:* lghaw; *T:* lawghil

included *S:* ^{c}am ...; *T:* ḥshiwo

independence *S:* sharyuta; *T:* sharyutho

independent *S:* sharya; *T:* sharyo/shritho

independent state *S:* atra sharya; *T:* uḥdono sharyo

India *S:* Hindu; *T:* Hendu; Hind

Indian *S:* Hindawaya/Hindawayta; *T:* Hendwoyo/Hendwayto

indicator light *S:* bahra ramuza; *T:* bahro mawdh^{c}ono

industrial estate *S:* ^{c}aqara ṣni^{c}aya; *T:* mulkono ṣni^{c}u-thonoyo; qenyono ṣni^{c}u-thonoyo

industry *S:* ṣni^{c}uta; *T:* i-ṣni^{c}utho

infant *S:* yanuqa; *T:* ṭalyo/ṭlitho; z^{c}uro/z^{c}urto; na^{c}imo/na^{c}imto

infected *S:* ṭipya/ṭpita; *T:* tafyo/tfitho

infection *S:* shukhama; *T:* ḥubolo; thaṭlushtho

information *S:* mawdh^{c}anuta; *T:* mawd^{c}onutho

ink *S:* dyuta; *T:* dyutho

inner-tube *S:* **abuba gawaya**; *T:* abubo gawonoyo

insect bite *S:* n^{c}aṣta d-rekhshe; *T:* dboṣo da-raḥshe

insect repellant *S:* qaṭlan baqe; *T:* msatronitho ma-raḥshe

insect *S:* rakhsha; *T:* raḥsho; ṣar-buqo

insecticide *S:* mawdidh rikhshe; *T:* qoṭulo da-raḥshe

insurance policy *S:* **akim ^{c}arowota**; *T:* shuroro d-ged-she; ^{c}arobutho d-gedshe

insurance *S:* ^{c}arawuta; *T:* u-shuroro

international operator *S:* mas-ran baynat matanaya; *T:* shagholo tibeloyo/shagholto tibelayto; operator

internet café *S:* "internet café"; *T:* kafé-net

internet *S:* prass nawla; *T:* inter-net

intestine *S:* ma^{c}ye; miyure; *T:* ma^{c}yo; **intestines** *S:* ma^{c}ye; *T:* m^{c}oye

invade *S:* spakha; *T:* kwushyo; ṣfoḥo

Iran *S:* Iran; *T:* Iran

Iran *S:* Iran; *T:* Iran

Iranian *S:* Iranaya/Iranayta; *T:* Iranoyo/Iranayto

Iranian *S:* Iranaya/Iranayta; *T:* Iranoyo/Iranayto

Iraq *S:* ^{c}Iraq; *T:* ^{c}Iraq

Iraqi *S:* ^{c}Iraqnaya/^{c}Iraqnayta; *T:* ^{c}Iraqoyo/^{c}Iraqayto

Ireland *S:* Ireland; *T:* Irlanda

Irish *S:* Ayrishnaya/Ayrish-nayta; *T:* Irlandoyo/Irlandayto

iron *(for clothing)* *S:* kwita; *T:* mkawyonitho; uti

iron *S:* prezla; *T:* farzlo

irrigation *S:* mashiqya; *T:* she-qyo; mashqyonutho

is there?/are there? *S:* it tama?; *T:* kit?/kito?
Israeli *S:* Israelyaya/Israelyayta; *T:* Israyiloyo/Israyilayto
it *see* **he**; **she**
I.T. *S:* tiqnaye mawd^{c}anuta; *T:* i-teknolojia di-mawd^{c}onutho
Italian *S:* Iṭalnaya/Iṭalnayta; *T:* Iṭaloyo/Iṭalayto
itching *S:* khyuka; *T:* ḥyoko

J

jack *S:* marmana; *T:* ma^{c}lyono
jacket *S:* kutina; *T:* jaket
jail *S:* bet-khwushya; *T:* beth-ḥbushyo; ḥabiss; sijin
jam *S:* murabba; rawba; *T:* murabba
January *S:* Kanun Tray Yana; *T:* Konun Ḥaroyo
Japan *S:* Yaban; *T:* Japan
jaundice *S:* yarqana; *T:* yarqono
jaw *S:* la^{c}usa; *T:* fako; lughmo
jazz *S:* jazz; *T:* jaz
jeans *S:* jeans; *T:* jins
Jew; **Jewish** *S:* Yhudhaya/Yhudhayta; *T:* Yudhoyo/Yudhayto
jewelery *S:* kheshlata; *T:* ḥashlotho
Jordan *S:* Yuridnan; *T:* Yurdnon
Jordanian *S:* Yuridnaya/Yuridnayta; *T:* Yurdnonoyo/Yurdnonayto
journalist *S:* ghulyunara/ghulyunarta; *T:* gelyunoro/gelyunorto; ṣuḥafi/ṣuḥafiye
judge *S:* dayyana; *T:* dayono
July *S:* Tammuz; *T:* Tamuz
June *S:* Khziran; *T:* Ḥziron
just now *S:* hasha; *T:* har u^{c}do

K

kebab *S:* kababa; *T:* kabab
ketchup *S:* rawba dyabrukhe; *T:* kechap
kettle *S:* rathukhta; *T:* qaqbo; chaydan
key *S:* qdila; *T:* qlidho
kidney *S:* kilita; *T:* klitho
kidney *S:* klita; *T:* klitho; kilwe; **kidneys** *S:* kilyata; *T:* kelyotho; killaw
kilim *S:* prista; *T:* froso
kill *S:* qṭala; *T:* qṭolo
killer *S:* qaṭula; *T:* qoṭulo
kilogram *S:* kilogram; *T:* kilogram
kilometer *S:* kilomiṭra; *T:* kilomeṭro
king *S:* malka; *T:* malko
kiosk *S:* kushk; *T:* kushk
kitchen *S:* bet-bshala; *T:* beth-busholo
knee *S:* birka; *T:* burko
knitted *S:* zqira; zqirta; *T:* zqiro/zqirto
know *S:* ydha^{c}a; *T:* idha^{c}to
Kurd *S:* Qurdaya/Qurdayta; *T:* Kurdoyo/Kurdayto
Kurdistan *S:* Kurdistan; *T:* Kurdistan

L

ladder *S:* simmalta; *T:* sebeltho
ladies/gents *S:* mayqre/mayqrata; *T:* neshe/gawre
lake *S:* yamta; *T:* yamtho
lamb *S:* para; *T:* faro; emro; **lamb meat** *S:* ^{c}irwe; *T:* basro da-^{c}wone
lamp *S:* shraya; *T:* lamp; fanso; lamfidho
land *S:* ar^{c}a; *T:* ar^{c}o
landslide *S:* hgham ar^{c}a; *T:* grufyo d-ar^{c}o
language *S:* lishana; *T:* leshono
last *S:* kharaya; *T:* ḥaroyo; **last night** *S:* lilya d-da^{c}war; *T:* lalyo d-shafi^c; **last week** *S:* shawu^{c}a d-da^{c}war; *T:* shabtho d-shafi^{c}o; **last year** *S:* eshqat; *T:* ishqadh
laundry *S:* bet-shyagha; bet-shyaghta; *T:* mashighonutho
law *S:* namusa; *T:* nomuso; qonuno
law court *S:* bet-dayna namusaya; *T:* beth-dino
lawyer *S:* snighra/snighirta; *T:* snighro/snighartho; muḥami/muḥamiye
lay mines *S:* zra^c paqu^{c}e; *T:* droyo fetqe

leader *S:* hadia; *T:* rishono/rishonitho
leaf *S:* ṭarpa; *T:* ṭarfo
learn *S:* ylapa; *T:* yulfono; ilofo; **learn by heart** *S:* ylapa min lebba; *T:* yulfono me-lebo
leather *S:* gilda; *T:* galdho
Lebanese *S:* Lunanaya/Lunanayta; *T:* Lebnonoyo/Lebnonayto
Lebanon *S:* Lunan; *T:* Lebnon
left *S:* simmala; ṣimmala; *T:* semolo; **on the left** *S:* l-simalukh shqul; shqoel ṣimala; *T:* ᶜal u-semolo
left-wing *S:* gazula/gazulta; *T:* semoloyo/semolayto
leg *S:* aqla; *T:* raghlo
leisure industry *S:* khaqla d-rwakhanuta; *T:* a-fulḥone sufqonoye
lemon *S:* laymuna; khimṣa; *T:* limon; laymun; limuno
lens *S:* ṭlawekhta; *T:* ṭaliḥto; ᶜadase
lentils *S:* ṭlukhe; *T:* ṭlawḥe
Leo *S:* Arya; *T:* Aryo
leopard *S:* nimra; *T:* nemro
less *S:* bsir; *T:* noqiṣ
lesson *S:* herga; *T:* hergo; drosho
letter *S:* egarta; *T:* egartho
lettuce *S:* khaṣ; *T:* ḥaso; khass
liberate *S:* mkharure; *T:* ḥuroro
liberation *S:* khurara; *T:* ḥuroro
liberty *S:* khiruta; *T:* ḥirutho
Libra *S:* Masata; *T:* Masato
library *S:* bet-arke; *T:* beth-arke
lice *S:* qalme; *T:* qalme
lie *to not tell the truth* *S:* dugla; *T:* dugle
lieutenant *S:* qadhma; *T:* naqifo; mulazim
lieutenant-colonel *S:* qadhma; *T:* mqadmono; muqaddim
lieutenant-general *S:* reshana qadhmaya; *T:* neshro; fariq
life *S:* khaye; *T:* ḥaye
lift *elevator* *S:* masilqanita; *T:* maᶜlyono
light *noun* *S:* bahra; *T:* bahro; **light** *not heavy* *S:* qalula/qalolta; *T:* khayifo/khayifto; qalilo/qalilto; **light meter** *S:* kyula d-bahra; *T:* mkaylono du-bahro
lightning *S:* birqa; *T:* barqo
limbs *S:* wasle; *T:* hadome
lime *S:* laymuna; khimṣa; *T:* limon; laymun; limuno
line *S:* khṭuṭa; *T:* ḥṭuṭo; khaṭ
lion *S:* arya; *T:* aryo
lip *S:* sipta; *T:* saftho
lipstick *S:* smuqa d-spwate; *T:* qanyo semoqo; ḥumra
liter *S:* liṭra; *T:* liṭro
literature *S:* seprayuta; *T:* sofrutho; sefroyutho
little bit *S:* qalil; *T:* ushmo; chike
live *S:* bikhaya; *T:* ᶜyosho
liver *S:* kawda; *T:* kabdho
livestock *S:* qinyane; *T:* qenyone
living room *S:* tawn arkhe; *T:* beth-shalmo
lizard *S:* mazuzṭa; *T:* rashofo; ḥardono; ḥewitho; ᶜabo; maṣuṣto
loaf of bread *S:* grista; *T:* griṣtho
local *S:* bshawuta; *T:* dukthonoyo/dukthonayto
loose change *S:* kespa sharya; *T:* farude
loot *S:* shwaya; *T:* slobo
lorry *S:* lori; *T:* lori
lose *S:* taluqe; *T:* khṣoro
louse (lice) *S:* qalma (qalme); *T:* qalmo (qalme)
love *S:* makhube; *T:* rḥomo
low *S:* kupa; *T:* taḥtoyo/taḥtayto; **low blood pressure** *S:* rwisut dimma nakhuta; *T:* rebṣo admoyo taḥtoyo
lower house *S:* mawtwa takhtaya; *T:* bayto taḥtoyo
luggage *S:* mawble; *T:* sefoqe
lunch *S:* sharuta; *T:* ᶜrayto
lung *S:* raata; *T:* rotho

M

machine *S:* mziᶜana; *T:* makina
machine-gun *S:* rasosta; rasosyate; *T:* chifta makinayto
magazine *S:* mghalta; *T:* mghaltho
mailbox *S:* sandoq bildara; *T:* ṣanduqo d-bildoro

main square *S:* mshṭakha rishaya; *T:* meso; qenṭrun
maize *S:* kharwiye; *T:* ḥeṭe rumoye
major-general *S:* resh tagha; *T:* foqudho; liwaᶜ
majority *S:* sagiyuta; *T:* yatirutho; aghlabiye
make peace *S:* mshayin; *T:* syomo d-shlomo
malaria *S:* malarya; *T:* malarya
male *S:* dikhra; *T:* dekhro
man *S:* gawra; *T:* gawro; zlam
manure *S:* zwla; *T:* n-eḥre; zawlo
many *S:* saggi; *T:* sagi; ghallabe
map *S:* khriṭṭa; *T:* karṭo; khariṭa; **a map of Los Angeles** *S:* khariṭṭa d-Los Angeles; *T:* karṭo d-Los Anjeles
March *S:* Adhar; *T:* Odor
mare *S:* susta; kodinta; *T:* susto
marital status *S:* ituta zawganayta; *T:* ithutho zuwoghayto
market *S:* shuqa; *T:* shuqo
marketing *S:* methshuqanuta; *T:* i-mezdabnonutho
marriage *S:* zuwagha; *T:* gworo
married *S:* gwira/gwirta; *T:* gawiro/gawirto; **Are you** *(m/f)* **married?** *S:* Gwira wet?/Gwirta wat?; *T:* Gawir hat?/Gawirto hat?
marsh *S:* amsha; *T:* qewitho
martyr *S:* sahda; *T:* sohdo
mascara *S:* kekhla; *T:* kuḥlo; maskara
mass *religious service* *S:* qorbana qadisha; *T:* qerowo alohoy; qudosho alohoyo
match *S:* muraya; *T:* takhtusho
maternity hospital *S:* bet-mawlada; *T:* beth-mawlodo
maths *S:* manayuta; *T:* manoyutho
mattress *S:* shwita; *T:* teshwitho
May *S:* Iyar; *T:* Iyor
meadow *S:* marga; *T:* margo
meals *S:* ikhala; mukhilyate; *T:* shorwotho; mukle
meat *S:* bisra; *T:* basro
mechanic *S:* mikanik/mikanikayta; mtaqnan radiyate; *T:* mikanikoyo/ mikanikayto
medallion *S:* sheba; *T:* shebo
media; the media *S:* yudaᶜa; *T:* u-yudoᶜo; an-aᶜlam
meet *S:* pghaᶜa; *T:* lqoyo
meeting *S:* khnoshya; *T:* knushyo
melon *S:* paṭikha; *T:* fujo; faṭiḥo; baṭṭikh
member of parliament *S:* hadama d-bet-sholṭana; *T:* hadomo/hadomto du-mawtbo d-shulṭono
memory *S:* ᶜohdana; *T:* dukhrono; ᶜuhdono
mercenary *S:* razuqa; *T:* methrazqono; agiro
metal *S:* prizla; *T:* ḥefro; metalon
meter *S:* miṭra; *T:* meṭro
metropolitan *S:* khasya; miṭrapoliṭa; *T:* ḥasyo; maṭran; sayidna
microscope *S:* mrawriw wana; *T:* mrawrwono; mḥawyono
midnight *S:* palga d-lile; *T:* falge d-lalyo
mile *S:* mila; *T:* mil; milo
military: military school *S:* midrashta gaysayta; *T:* madrashto gaysayto; **military academy** *S:* bet-sawba gaysaya; *T:* beth-ṣawbo gaysoyo
milk *noun* *S:* khalwa; *T:* ḥalwo; *verb* **to milk an animal** *S:* khlawa; *T:* ḥlowo
mill *S:* aarkhe; *T:* raḥyo
miller *S:* ṭakhana; *T:* raḥoyo
million *S:* milyon; *T:* melyun
millstone *S:* garusta; *T:* gorusto
mine *explosive* *S:* paquᶜa; *T:* fetqo; lagham; **mines** *S:* paquᶜe; *T:* fetqe; algham; **mine detector** *S:* galyan paquᶜe; *T:* mgalyonitho dafetqe; **mine disposal** *S:* zawluth paquᶜe; *T:* mḥalaqto dafetqe; **anti-personnel mine** *S:* dalqiw palkhe; *T:* fetqo luqbal-fulḥe
minefield *S:* khaqla d-paquᶜe; *T:*

ḥaqlo da-fetqe
mineral water *S:* miya d-^{c}ayna; *T:* maye di-^{c}ayno
minibus *S:* baṣa z^{c}ora; *T:* dolmush; servis
minister *S:* sharira; *T:* shariro; waziro
ministry *S:* shariruta; *T:* sharirutho; wazirutho
minority *S:* qaliluta; *T:* ḥsirutho; qalilutho; aqalliye; **minority vote** *S:* qala d-qaliluta; *T:* qolo di-ḥsirutho
mint *S:* rikhana; *T:* nu^{c}na^{c}; non^{c}o
minute *S:* qaṭinta; *T:* qaṭinto
mirror *S:* makhzita; *T:* nawro; maḥzitho
missile *S:* ṣarukha; *T:* ṣoruḥo; ṣarukh; **missiles** *S:* ṣarukhe; *T:* ṣoruḥe; ṣawarikh
mist *S:* ^{c}arpilla; *T:* ^{c}arfelo; mij
misty *S:* khaputaya; *T:* ^{c}amuḥo/ ^{c}amuḥto
mobile phone *S:* qa^{c}ya d-ida; *T:* telefon meshtanyono
modem *S:* modem; *T:* modem
modern *S:* daraya/darayta; *T:* ḥatho
moisture *S:* taliluta; *T:* talilutho
mole *S:* shamma; *T:* ḥuldo; iruso
monastery *S:* dayra; *T:* dayro
Monday *S:* Troshiba; *T:* Trushabo
money *S:* zoze; *T:* zuze
monk *S:* rabana; *T:* dayroyo
monkey *S:* qopa; *T:* qufo; maymun
month *S:* yarkha; *T:* yarḥo
monument *S:* qayemta; *T:* neṣbo makthabzabnoyo; qayimto
moon *S:* sahra; *T:* sahro; **new moon** *S:* sahra khata; *T:* sahro ḥatho
more *S:* yatir; *T:* zid
morning *S:* qidamta; *T:* qedimto; ṣafrayto; **in the morning** *S:* bsapra; *T:* b-ṣafrayto; **this morning** *S:* qidamta d-edio; *T:* ad-ṣafrayto
mortar weapon *S:* zayna dsit ta; *T:* madoqto na^{c}imto
mosque *S:* minara; *T:* masghdho; jami^{c}
mosquito *S:* baqta; *T:* boqo; **mosquito bite** *S:* n^{c}aṣta d-baqa; *T:* dboṣo da-boqe
mother *S:* yimma; yimmi; *T:* emo
motorbike *S:* mzighla; *T:* mzighlo; moṭorsiklet; moṭor
mountain *S:* ṭura; *T:* ṭuro; **mountain pass** *S:* urkha d-ṭurane; *T:* ma^{c}barto; shalwo
mouse *S:* ^{c}aqubra; *T:* ^{c}obugro
mouth *S:* pomma; *T:* fumo
mouthwash *S:* mashghan pomma; *T:* mashighono dufemo
mulberry *S:* tuta; *T:* tutho
mule *S:* kawidna; *T:* baghlo; kudhanyo
multiplication *S:* ^{c}upapa; *T:* ^{c}ufofo
multiply *S:* ^{c}papa; *T:* ^{c}fofo
munitions *S:* zwade; *T:* zuyone
murder *S:* qiṭla; *T:* qaṭlo
muscle *S:* ^{c}aṣalta; *T:* ^{c}aṣalto; ^{c}adhale
museum *S:* bet-etqe; *T:* beth-^{c}etqe
mushroom *S:* paturyate; *T:* faṭurto
musician *S:* musiqara/musiqarta; *T:* musiqoro/ musiqorto
Muslim *S:* Mushilmana/ Mushelmanta; *T:* Mashilmono/Mashilmonitho; Ṭayo/ Ṭayayto
mustache *S:* pesme; *T:* shwerib; zefe
mustard *S:* khirdal; *T:* ḥardlo

N

nail *S:* ṣiṣa; *T:* basmoro; ṣeṣo; *of finger/toe* *S:* ṭepre; *T:* ṭefro; **nail-clippers** *S:* mqarṭan teprate; *T:* masfrone da-ṭefre; **nail-polish** *S:* saw^{c}a d-ṭiprate; *T:* ṣomuḥo da-ṭefre; ṣwo^{c}o da-ṭefre
name *S:* shim; *T:* ishm
narrow *S:* ^{c}iqa; *T:* ^{c}iqo
nationality *S:* matayuta; *T:* umthoyutho; ṭuhmo
natural disaster *S:* tawhta kyanayta; *T:* gunḥo kyonoyo

navel *S:* shurta; *T:* shurto
navy *S:* yamayuta; *T:* ḥaylo yamoyo
near *S:* qurba; *T:* qariwo/qaruto
nearby *S:* qariwa; *T:* qariwo
neck *S:* qdala; *T:* qdholo
necklace *S:* qladha; *T:* ᶜeqo; hamnikho
necktie *S:* khnaqa; *T:* ḥerqo; nektay
needle *S:* khmaṭa; *T:* mḥaṭo
nerve *S:* gyade; *T:* gyodho
Netherlands *S:* Holanda; *T:* Holanda
neutral drive *S:* dwara lasṭraya; *T:* qloᶜo meṣᶜoyo
new *S:* khatda; *T:* ḥatho
New Zealand *S:* Ziland Khata; *T:* Nuzilanda
newborn child *S:* yaluda khata; *T:* yaludo
newspaper *S:* spar yawma; *T:* sfar-yawmo; **newspaper in English** *S:* spar yawme Englishaya; *T:* sfar-yawmo bu-Inglishoyo
newsstand *S:* Dukan spar zawne; *T:* dukano da-sfar-zabne
next *S:* d-bitaya le; *T:* ḥreno; **next week** *S:* shawuᶜa bitaya le; *T:* shabtho d-uthyo; **next week** *S:* shawuᶜa d-bitaya le; *T:* shabtho d-uthyo; **next year** *S:* shita d-atya; *T:* shato d-uthyo
night *S:* lile; lilya; *T:* lalyo
nightclub *S:* bet-smakha; *T:* beth-smokho; nadi; qlab
nightingale *S:* ᶜenda; *T:* ᶜendo; ṣefro-deqlo; bulbul
nine *S:* teshᶜa/tshaᶜ; *T:* teshᶜo/tshaᶜ
nineteen *S:* tshaᶜsar; *T:* tshaᶜsar
ninety *S:* teshᶜi; *T:* teshᶜi
ninth *S:* tshiᶜaya/tshiᶜayta; *T:* tshiᶜoyo/tshiᶜayto
no *S:* la; *T:* lo; **no entry** *S:* layt maᶜla; *T:* layto ᶜboro; **no problem!** *S:* layt qitra!; *T:* ghamo layto!; **no smoking** *S:* layt tnana; *T:* layt tenunto
noise *S:* rawba; *T:* qolo
noon *S:* ṭahra; *T:* falge d-yawmo; ṭahro
north *S:* garibya; *T:* garbyo
Northern Ireland *S:* Irlanda Garbyayta; *T:* Irlanda Garbyayto
nose *S:* nakhira; *T:* nḥiro
notebook *S:* kerka d-zohare; *T:* fenqitho; kerko
novel *S:* shuᶜita; *T:* tunoyo; **novels in English** *S:* shuᶜita Englishayta; *T:* tunoye bu-Inglishoyo
November *S:* Teshrin Tray Yana; *T:* Teshrin ḥaroyo
now *S:* hadiya; *T:* uᶜdo; **just now** *S:* hasha; *T:* har uᶜdo
nuclear: nuclear power *S:* khayla grumanaya; *T:* ḥaylo fredtonoyo; tuqfo fredtonoy; **nuclear power station** *S:* nuqasta d-khayla grumanaya; *T:* qenṭrun d-ḥaylo fredtonoyo
nun *S:* rabanta; *T:* dayrayto
nurse *S:* yasupa/yasupta; *T:* samsemono/samsemonitho; oshufo/oshefto; mumarrid/mumarrida
nut *almond* *S:* shade; *T:* luzo; sheghdo

O

objective *S:* nisha; *T:* nisho
October *S:* Teshrin Qamaya; *T:* Teshrin Qamoyo
office *S:* makhitwa; *T:* makhtwo; beth-makthbo
office worker *S:* katawa/katawta; *T:* shagholo/shagholto b-makhtwo
officer *S:* akhida; *T:* aḥidho; dhabiṭ
oil *S:* meshkha; *T:* meshḥo
ointment *S:* meshkha; *T:* meshḥo
okra *S:* bam mya; *T:* bamya
old *not young* *S:* sawa; *T:* sowo; *not new* *S:* ᶜatiqa; *T:* ᶜatiqo; **old city** *S:* mdita ᶜtiqta; *T:* mdhitho ᶜatiqto; **How old are you *(m/f)*?** *S:* Kma le ᶜumrokh/ᶜumrakh?; *T:* Miqqayo ᶜumrokh/ᶜumrekh?; **I** *(m/f)*

am ... years old. *S:* Ana iwen/iwan ... shine.; *T:* ... ishne-no.
olive *S:* zaytona; *T:* zayto; zaytuno
omelette *S:* spira; *T:* sfero
once *S:* zbata; *T:* naqqa ḥdo
one *S:* kha/khda; *T:* ḥa/ḥdho; *T:* falgo; **one-quarter** *S:* kha rwi^{c}aya; *T:* ruw^{c}o; **one-third** *S:* kha tlitaya; *T:* thultho; **one-half** *S:* kha palgaya;
one-way street *S:* urkha d-akhid shwila; *T:* shqoqo d-ḥa darbo; ja^{c}de d-ḥa darbo; shari^{c} d-ḥa darbo
onion *S:* biṣla; *T:* baṣlo
open *S:* ptikha; *T:* ftiḥo
opera *S:* opera; *T:* opera; **opera house** *S:* bet-opera; *T:* tiyaṭron d-opera
operating theater/room *S:* tawana d-ta^{c}wadtyate; *T:* tiyaṭron di-so^{c}urutho; tawono di-so^{c}urutho
operation *surgical S:* ^{c}aṣuwayta; *T:* so^{c}urutho; ^{c}oṣubayto
operator *S:* palakha; *T:* shagholo/shagholto; operator
opponent *S:* b^{c}eldara; *T:* saqubloyo
opposite *S:* d-alqobl; *T:* mqabel d-...
opposition *S:* saqulayuta; saqulaya; *T:* saqubloyutho
or *S:* yan; *T:* aw; ya
orange *fruit S:* ṭroghe; *T:* eṭrugho; portaqal; *color S:* putha/puthayta; eṭrughaya/eṭrughayta; *T:* eṭrughoyo/eṭrughayto
orchard *S:* karma; *T:* bustono
organ *of body S:* hadam paghra; *T:* hadomo
orphan *S:* yatuma/yatumta; *T:* yatumo/yatumto
Orthodox Christian *S:* Mshikhaya Orthodoksaya/Mshikhayta Orthodoksayta; *T:* Orthodoksoyo/Orthodoksayto
ounce *S:* ounsa; *T:* unqia
out; outside *S:* lwar; *T:* larwar
overcoat *S:* me^{c}ṭapa; *T:* ma^{c}ṭofo; *for women* manto; *for men* palto
owl *S:* qupta; *T:* bumo; papuke
ox *S:* tora; *T:* baqro
oxygen *S:* oxsijin; *T:* oksijin

P

padlock *S:* qipla; *T:* quflo
page *S:* pata; *T:* fotho; ḥarfo
pager *S:* pager; *T:* payjer
painkiller *S:* qaṭil khiwle; *T:* qoṭulo du-kewo
paint *S:* saw^{c}a; *T:* ṣwo^{c}o; boya
Pakistan *S:* Pakistan; *T:* Pakistan
Pakistani *S:* Pakistanaya; *T:* Pakistanoyo/Pakistanayto
palace *S:* birta; *T:* ofadhno; beth-malko
palm *of hand S:* kappa; *T:* kafo
pancreas *S:* shalpukhta; *T:* shalfuḥtho
paper *S:* waraqa/waraqe; *T:* warqo; *article S:* memarta warqayta; *T:* fetghomo; **a piece of paper** *S:* qit^{c}a d-waraqa; *T:* ṭarfo d-warqo
paper *S:* waraqa; waraqe; *T:* warqo
parachute *S:* parashut; *T:* maṭlo; parashut
paralysis *S:* msharyuta; *T:* msharyutho
paralyzed *S:* msharya/msharita; *T:* msharyo/msharyitho
parcel *S:* ^{c}alwa bildaraya; *T:* mesorto
park *S:* makhimla dradiyate; *T:* gantho
parking lot *S:* makhimla d-radiyate; *T:* beth-kloyo
parliament *S:* bet-shultana; bet-sharire; *T:* beth-shulṭonutho; barlaman; mawtbo d-shulṭono
parrot *S:* laqṭan mille; *T:* babgho; ṣefro kushoyo
parsley *S:* karawis; *T:* krafso dumyo
partridge *S:* zarkha; *T:* qeqwono; ḥaglo
party *S:* meshtuta; *T:* ḥago; *political S:* gabba suyasaya; *T:* gabo; foliṭiqoyo

pass an exam *S:* kshara bukhrana; *T:* kshoro buḥrono
passenger *S:* rakawa; rakota; *T:* rakowo/rakowto
passport number *S:* raqma d-maᶜbar tkhuma; *T:* menyono d-saqro
passport *S:* maᶜbar tkhuma; *T:* saqro; jawaz; pasaport
past *S:* daᶜwar; *T:* da-ᶜbar
pasta *S:* pasta; *T:* maqarna
patriarch *S:* awa d-awahate; *T:* faṭeryarkho
patrol *S:* dayurta; *T:* methkarkhonutho; dawriye
peace *S:* shayna; *T:* shlomo; **peace-keeping troops** *S:* khaylawate naṭure d-shayna; *T:* noṭure d-shlomo
peach *S:* khukhe; *T:* ḥawḥo; durqino
peacock *S:* ṣoṣla; *T:* ṭawuso
peak *S:* gaghulta; *T:* qarno d-ṭuro; qarqaftho d-ṭuro
pear *S:* kamutra; *T:* kumathro; qanturro
peas *S:* khirṭmane; *T:* ḥimṣe; bazalya
pen *S:* qanya; *T:* qanyo
pencil *S:* qanya d-awara; *T:* qanyo rṣoṣoyo; aboroyo
penicillin *S:* penisilin; *T:* penisilin
penknife *S:* skinta d-qanya; *T:* skino qanyoyo
people *S:* nashe; *T:* noshe; ᶜamo
pepper *S:* pelpel; *T:* felflo
perfume *S:* ᶜeṭra; *T:* ᶜeṭro; reḥo
person *S:* qnuma; *T:* nosho
personal *S:* qnumaya; *T:* farṣufoyo
personnel *military* *S:* palkhe; *T:* agire
petrol *S:* banzin; *T:* banzin
photocopier *S:* nasukhta; *T:* maṣḥonitho; fotokopi; istinsakh
photocopy *S:* asakhta; *T:* ṣḥoḥo; nuskha
photographer *S:* mṣayrana/mṣayranta; *T:* mṣayrono/mṣayronitho; muṣawwar/muṣawwara
physiotherapy *S:* awsaya kyanaya; *T:* fizyotherapya
pick up *S:* shqala; *T:* myodo
pickax *S:* qazma; *T:* felqo; ṣaquro
pickle(s) *S:* ṭurshiye; *T:* ṭurshi; thalbuno
pig *S:* khzura; *T:* ḥziro
pigeon *S:* yawna; *T:* ᶜarbodo; yawno
pillow *S:* spadita; *T:* besodyo; mkhadde
pilot *S:* ṭayosa/ṭayostanayta; *T:* ṭayostono/ṭayostonitho; qaloᶜo d-ṭayisto / qaloᶜto d-ṭayisto; paylot
pilot *S:* ṭayusa; *T:* ṭayostono
pin *S:* dambuṣ; *T:* sektho; zqiftho
pineapple *S:* ananas; *T:* ananas
pink *S:* wardanaya/wardanayta; *T:* wardonoyo/wardonayto
Pisces *S:* Nuna; *T:* Nune
pistachio *S:* pisteqe; *T:* festqo; fistaq
pistol *S:* glulita; *T:* pisṭola; qurma; musaddas
pitch *football* *S:* mashṭakha d-gilla; *T:* mashtokho
pizza *S:* pitsa; *T:* pitsa
place of birth *S:* dukat moalada; *T:* duktho d-mawlodo
placenta *S:* shlita; *T:* shlitho
plain(s) *S:* piqᶜa; piqᶜata; *T:* sheṭḥo
plane *aviation* *S:* ayasta; *T:* ayisto
plank *S:* lukha d-qaysa; *T:* dafo; luḥo d-qayso
plant *noun* *S:* yaᶜita; *T:* yoᶜitho; neṣbo; *verb* *S:* nṣawa; *T:* zroᶜo
plaster *Band-Aid* *S:* ṣmada; *T:* zulo ṭayfono; plaster; **plaster cast** *medical* *S:* masmakh kilsha; *T:* masmkhono kelshonoyo; jibs
plastic *S:* plasṭik; *T:* plastik
platform number *S:* raqma d-maṣṭawta; *T:* menyono d-ro?ifto
please! *(m/f/pl)* *S:* in basmalokh!/in basmalakh!/in basmalokhon!; *T:* boᶜutho menokh!/boᶜutho menekh!/boᶜutho menaykhu!

pliers *S:* Kaliwta; *T:* kalobto
plow *noun S:* pdana; *T:* fadono; *adjective S:* krawa ar^c^a; *T:* dworo
plug *electric S:* plug; *T:* fisha; shoqulo d-kahrobo
plum *S:* khakhta; *T:* ḥaḥo; agoṣo
pocket *S:* kisa/^c^ayba; *T:* beḥsho; jeb
podium *S:* bima; *T:* bima
political rally *S:* maqyapta suyasayta; mkarzanutha; *T:* knushyo foliṭiqoyo
politician *S:* suyasara; *T:* foliṭiqoyo/foliṭiqayto
politics *S:* suyasa; *T:* foliṭiqi; siyase
pomegranate *S:* armune; *T:* rumono
pony *S:* gwada; *T:* susyo na^c^imo
pool *S:* qawita; *T:* qobitho; havuz; masbaḥ
poor *S:* paqira; *T:* meskino/faqiro
pop music *S:* zimra d-pop; *T:* musiqa ^c^amayto
portable T.V. *S:* makhizyana mzi^c^ana; *T:* fros-ḥezwo meshtanyono; telvizyon meshtanyono
Portuguese *S:* Portughlaya/ Portughlayta; *T:* Portughaloyo/Portughalayto
post office *S:* makhtaw bildara; *T:* makhtwo du-bidoro; makhtwo bildoroyo
postcard *S:* petqa bildaraya; *T:* fetqo bildoroyo; kart postal
potato *S:* qurtope; peṭaṭe; *T:* paṭaṭa; belbuso; baṭaṭa; **sweet potato** *S:* qurtope khilye; *T:* paṭaṭa ḥlitho
pottery *S:* pakhara; *T:* quqoyutho; faḥorutho
poultry *S:* tarnighle; *T:* gyothe
pound *weight S:* pawnd; *T:* liṭro; pawand; *sterling S:* pawand; *T:* pawand
P.O.W. camp *S:* mashrita d-asire; *T:* mashritho d-an-asire d-qrobo
powder *S:* bdhara; *T:* deqtho; bodra
powdered milk *S:* khalwa ywisha; *T:* ḥalwo nashifo
present *now S:* qaim; *T:* qo^c^em; *and see* **gift**
president *S:* reshquṭna; *T:* rishquṭnoyutho
priest *S:* qasha; *T:* qasho; abuna; kuhno
prime minister *S:* resh sharire; *T:* rish-wazire; risho d-sharire
printer *S:* ṭawo^c^ta; *T:* ṭaw^c^onitho
prison *S:* bet-asire; *T:* beth-asire; ḥbushyo
prisoner *S:* asira; *T:* asiro; **prisoner-of-war** *S:* asira dqrawa; *T:* asiro d-qrobo; **to take prisoner** *S:* ma'asore; *T:* msoko d-asiro
probably *S:* kbar; *T:* balki
profession *S:* umanuta; *T:* fulḥono; umonutho
program *computer S:* takhrazta; *T:* taḥrazto (ḥoshubayto); program
progress *S:* ṭuwara; *T:* shushoṭo
projector *S:* tuqana d-marawata; *T:* projektor
protest *S:* mikhadh b^c^eltha; *T:* taglitho
Protestant *S:* Pruṭaya/ Pruṭayta; *T:* Pruṭoyo/Pruṭayto
pub *S:* khanuta; *T:* mashqyo; beth-qafile; bar; pab
pumpkin *S:* qar^c^e; *T:* qar^c^o
punish *S:* twa^c^a; *T:* two^c^o
pupil *S:* yalupa/yalupta; *T:* yolufo/yolufto; *of eye S:* bawta d-^c^ayna; *T:* bawtho d-^c^ayno
purple *S:* banawsha/banawshayta; *T:* argwonoyo/argwonayto; banafshoyo/banafshayto
pursue *S:* maqip; *T:* rdhofo

Q

quail *S:* qiqwana; *T:* salway; shkhiwoyo
question *S:* shoaala; *T:* shuwolo
quick *S:* surhawa; *T:* khayifo
quiet *S:* shalwa/shilyuta; *T:* shalyo/shlitho
quilt *S:* lkhipa; *T:* lḥef
quince *S:* sparigla; *T:* sfariglo

R

rabbit *S:* arnowa; *T:* arnwo
rabies *S:* kurhan kalbuta; *T:* kurhono da-kalbe; kewo da-kalbe
radiator *S:* radiyator; *T:* radyator
radio *S:* radio; *T:* fros-qolo; radio
radish *S:* peghla; *T:* feghlo
raid *S:* spukhya; *T:* şfoḥo
railway *S:* sika d-prezla; *T:* sek-tho d-farzlo
rain *S:* miṭra; *T:* maṭro
rainbow *S:* qishti maran; *T:* qayso qadaḥ; qeshte d-moran
raisins *S:* yabishe; *T:* afshotho
ram *S:* bar^{c}ana; *T:* emro
range: mountain range *S:* shishilta d-ṭure; *T:* shishalto da-ṭure;
rash *S:* ṭawsha; *T:* ḥemṭo
rat *S:* garo; *T:* ^{c}obugro rabo
ravine *S:* nakhla; *T:* shalwo
raw *S:* naya; nayta; *T:* ra^{c}yo; noyo
razor *S:* megra^{c}ta; *T:* goru^{c}tho
razorblade *S:* shelpe d-megra^{c}ta; *T:* mdakhyo; shafra; mus
reactionary *S:* hipkayuta; *T:* hefkoyo; raj^{c}i
read *S:* qraya *T:* qroyo
reap *S:* qṭapa; *T:* ḥşodo
reason: for travel: *S:* ^{c}elta d-khzuqya; *T:* ^{c}eltho du-krukhyo; ^{c}eltho d-so'urutho
receipt *S:* shṭarmaswa; *T:* fetqo d-qubolo
reception *S:* m'ar^{c}uta; *T:* mqablutho
record *S:* lukha; *T:* shawyo
red *S:* smuqa/smuqta; *T:* semo-qo/semaqto
Red Crescent *S:* Sahra Smuqa; *T:* Sahro Semoqo
Red Cross *S:* Sliwa Smuqa; *T:* Ṣlibo Semoqo
referee *S:* da yana; *T:* mfal-ghono; ḥakim
refugee *S:* galuya/galwayta; *T:* gawsono/gawsonto; **refugees** *S:* galuye; *T:* gawsone; **refugee camp** *S:* mashrita d-galuye; *T:* mashritho da-gawsone
regiment *S:* pawga; *T:* ulqo; gudo; yahlo
registered mail *S:* bildara sghila; *T:* bildoro msaghlo; musajjal
reinforcements *S:* ^{c}uzaya; *T:* mḥaylone; maruḥone
relative *(m/f)* *S:* khyani le/ khyanti la; *T:* qariwaydhi/ qariwtaydhi; ahlaydhi
relief aid *S:* suya^{c}a; *T:* m^{c}awanto ^{c}udronayto
religion *S:* tawdita; *T:* tawditho; din
repeat *S:* tnaya; *T:* tnoyo
report *S:* tashrara; *T:* anfuro; tashroro; ṭebo
republic *S:* qaṭnuta; *T:* quṭnutho
reserved *S:* dwiqa/dwiqta; *T:* nṭiro/nṭirto
resist *S:* msaqolayuta; *T:* ^{c}uzoyo; muqawama
restaurant *S:* bet-maekhla; *T:* beth-muklo; mṭ^{c}omo; loqanṭa
retail industry *S:* khaqla d-zubana; *T:* a-fulḥone zubo-noye
retreat *S:* grashta; *T:* d^{c}oro
reverse gear *S:* hpakhta; *T:* d^{c}oro
revolution *S:* gawma; *T:* qawmo
rhinoceros *T:* karkdono; qarno nḥiro
rib *S:* el^{c}a; *T:* el^{c}o; **ribs** *S:* el^{c}e; *T:* el^{c}e
rice *S:* rezza; *T:* rezo
rich *S:* ^{c}atira; *T:* ^{c}atiro; zangin
rifle *S:* isarta; *T:* chifta; tfanga; isorto
right *S:* yamina; *T:* yamino; **on the right** *S:* l-yaminukh shqul; shqoel yamina; *T:* ^{c}al u-yamino
right-wing *S:* yaminaya; *T:* yaminoyo/yaminayto
ring *S:* ^{c}isaqta; *T:* ^{c}ezaqtho; ḥuza
ripe *S:* meṭya; mṭeta; *T:* maṭyo/ mṭitho
river *S:* nahra; *T:* nahro; **river bank** *S:* sipa d-nahra; *T:* sfar-nahro; yad-nahro
road *S:* urkha; *T:* darbo; **road map** *S:* khariṭta d-urkhate; *T:* karṭo da-darbone

roadblock S: skhar urkha; T: skhoro du-darbo
robbery S: shiwya; T: shloḥo
rock S: isara; kepa; T: kefo; **rocks** S: isare; kepe; T: kefe
rocket S: ṣarukha; T: giro nurono; **rocket-launcher** S: ashid ṣarukhe; T: kashoṭo da-gire nurone
roof S: gare; T: goro
room S: tawana; T: qelayto; oda; tawono; **room number** S: raqma d-tawana; T: menyono di-qelayto
rooster S: tarnighla; T: tarnoghlo; diko
root S: ^{c}qra; T: ^{c}eqro; shersho; warido
rope S: khola; T: ḥawlo
rosary S: rasuqta; T: resuqtho; wardiye
rubber S: maṭoṭa; T: maṭoṭo; maṭṭaṭ; *eraser* S: mkapranita; T: laḥayto; missaḥa
ruble S: ruble; T: rubil
rugby S: ragbi; T: ragbi
ruins S: ^{c}etqe; T: ḥarwotho; kharab
ruler *instrument* S: knonta; T: konunto; msargdonitho; masṭar
run S: rhaṭa; T: rhoṭo
Russia S: Rusya; T: Rusiya
Russian S: Orisnaya/Orisnayta; T: Rusnoyo/Rusnayto

S

sack S: shray mshid ta; T: saqo
safety S: shayna; T: mshaynutho; **safety pin** S: sinjaq; T: sektho mshayanto; zqiftho mshayanto
Saggitarius S: Kashshaṭa; T: Kashoṭo
saint S: qadisha; T: qadisho/qadishto
salad S: zalaṭa; T: salaṭa
sales S: zubana; T: a-zubone
saliva S: ruqe; T: ruqe
salt S: milkha; T: melḥo
salty S: milkhana/milkhanta; T: maluḥo/maluḥto
sand S: khaala; khilla; bizqe; baqlushe; T: ḥolo; qum
sandals S: sandale; T: sandole; ṭelore; klash
sandwich S: zamora; T: sandwish
sanitary towels S: urqa^{c}ta/urqa^{c}yata; T: ruq^{c}e ḥulmonoye d-kefso; fesqe ḥulmonoye d-kefso
satchel S: simda d-midrashta; T: ṣemdo
satellite phone S: qa^{c}ya dsahra sni^{c}aya; T: telefon sahroyo; qamari
Saturday S: Shabta; T: Shabtho
sauce S: ṣoṣ; T: ṣoṣ; ṣalṣa
sausage S: sarsiqa; T: sarsiqo
saw S: nasurta; T: masoro
scanner S: scanner; T: skaner
scarf S: shala; T: makrukhto; sharfo
school S: midrashta; T: madrashto
scientist S: bkhira/bkhirta; T: yodu^{c}thono/yodu^{c}thonitho; ^{c}alim/^{c}alima
scissors S: masip ra; msapranita; T: msafrono; masforo
Scorpio; **scorpion** S: ^{c}aqirwa; T: ^{c}eqarwo
Scotland S: ṣkotland; T: Sqotlanda
Scottish S: Skotnaya/Skotnayta; T: Sqotlandoyo/Sqotlandayto
screw S: khalula; T: ḥolulo; quklo
screwdriver S: patkhan khalula; T: dobar-ḥolule; qukloyo
sculpture S: glapa; ṣalma; T: ṣalmo
season S: aqma; T: shuḥlofo
seat S: mawtba; T: kursyo
second *noun* S: rpapa; T: rfofo; *adjective* S: trayanaya/trayanayta; T: trayono/trayonitho
secret police S: dakhshe razanaye; T: daḥshe rozonoye
secretary S: naṭir raze/naṭra raze; T: noṭer-roze/noṭrath-roze; sekreter
see S: khzaya; T: ḥzoyo
seeds S: birzar^{c}e; T: bo-zar^{c}e

seminary *S:* midrashta d-kahne; semenire; *T:* madrashto di-kuhnutho; seminer

September *S:* Ilul; *T:* Ilul

sesame *S:* shishme; *T:* shushmo

session *S:* ytawta; *T:* itawto; **a session chaired by ...** *S:* knusha tkhet mdabranuta d-...; *T:* itawto taḥt i-rishon-utho d-...

seven *S:* shaw^{c}a/shwa^{c}; *T:* shaw^{c}o/shwa^{c}

seventeen *S:* shaw^{c}sar; *T:* shwa^{c}sar

seventh *S:* shwi^{c}aya/shwi^{c}ayta; *T:* shwi^{c}oyo/shwi^{c}ayto

seventy *S:* shaw^{c}i; *T:* shaw^{c}i

shampoo *S:* shampu; *T:* shampu

shaving cream *S:* sapuna d-gra^{c}a; *T:* ru^{c}tho du-ḥloqo

shawl *S:* shala; *T:* shalo; atqi

she *S:* hae; *T:* hiya

sheep *S:* ^{c}erwa; *plural* ^{c}erwe; *T:* ^{c}wono; *plural* ^{c}wone

sheet *S:* shwiyate; *T:* fotho da-gale; *of paper* *S:* qiṭ^{c}a d-waraqa; *T:* ḥarfo d-warqo

shelf *S:* rapa; *T:* dafo

shell *military* *S:* qalwa; qlapa; *T:* qlofo; qalwo

shelter *S:* gawsa; *T:* beth-gawso; **to take shelter** *S:* mgawis; *T:* myodho gawso

Shi'i *S:* Shi^{c}aya/Shi^{c}ayta; *T:* Shi^{c}oyo/Shi^{c}ayto

shirt *S:* qamista; *T:* kuthino; gomlak; qamis

shivers *S:* r^{c}ulta; *T:* r^{c}ultho

shoes *S:* msane; *T:* msone; shakale; **to shoe a horse** *S:* mna^{c}awle; *T:* n^{c}olo susye; **shoe shop** *S:* dokan msane; *T:* dukano da-msone; dukano da-shakale

shoot down *S:* rmayta; *T:* manḥoto

shop *S:* dokana; *T:* dukano; ḥonutho; **a local shop for local people** *S:* dukana qariw-ta qa nashe qariwe; *T:* dukano dukthonoyo la-dukthonoye

shopping *S:* zwana; *T:* krokho bu-shuqo; zwono

shore *S:* spar-yama; *T:* sfar-yamo; yad-yamo

short *S:* kirya; *T:* karyo

shoulder *S:* rusha; katpa; *T:* kathfo; **shoulder blade** *S:* katpa; *T:* kathfo

shower *S:* raṣuṣa; *T:* dush

shrapnel *S:* qiṭ^{c}ate; ṣiwa; *T:* falqe; shrapnel; bughro mbadrono

shrine *S:* shkhinta; *T:* beth-ṣlutho; shkhintho

shut *S:* skhira; *T:* skhiro

sick *S:* kaiwa; *T:* ḥkayiwo

sickle *S:* magla; *T:* magzuno; maglo

side *of body* *S:* Dipna; *T:* dafno

siege *S:* khṣara; *T:* ḥdhirutho

sieve *S:* ^{c}arbala; *T:* ^{c}arbolo

sign *S:* ata; *T:* remzo; otho

signature *S:* rmay ida; *T:* rmay-idho; imdha

Sikh *S:* Sikhaya/Sikhayta; *T:* Sikh

silence *S:* shitqa; *T:* shathqo

silk *S:* shira/ brişim; *T:* shiro

silkworms *S:* qazik; *T:* tul^{c}e du-shiro; tul^{c}e hendwoye

silver *S:* ṣima; *T:* semo

sim card *S:* sim-kart; *T:* sim-kart

singer *S:* zamara/zamarta; *T:* zamoro/zamorto

single *S:* la gwira/la gwirta; *T:* ^{c}azbo/^{c}azbtho

sit *S:* ytawa; *T:* itawto

six *S:* eshta/shet; *T:* ishto/sheth

sixteen *S:* eshta^{c}sar; *T:* shta^{c}sar e

sixth *S:* shtitaya/shtitayta; *T:* shtithoyo/shtithayto

sixty *S:* eshti; *T:* eshti

skeleton *S:* taghrumta; *T:* tagrumtho; hayklo

skiing *S:* zakhputa; *T:* ski; rdhoyo ^{c}al u-talgo

skin *S:* gilda; *T:* galdho

skull *S:* qirqipta; *T:* qarqaftho

sky *S:* shmayya; *T:* shmayo

sleep *S:* dmakha; *T:* dmokho

sleeping: sleeping pills *S:* khabe dnawma; *T:* ḥabbothe du-dmokho; **sleeping bag** *S:* kesta d-dmakha; *T:* kiso du-dmokho; **sleeping car** *S:*

ʿaghulta d-dmakha; T: markawtho du-dmokho

slope S: bartakhti; T: nafqo; ṭafoyo

slow S: nikha; T: hedi hedi

small S: zʿora/zʿorta; T: naʿimo/ naʿimto

smallpox S: shalqo; T: shulfoḥo; shulfotho

smell S: nqakha; T: nqoḥo

snack S: nuqnaqa; T: saybartho; shorutho

snail S: khalzuna; T: ḥalzunto

snake S: khuwa; T: ḥuyo; **snake bite** S: nʿaṣta d-khuwa; T: dboṣo d-ḥuyo

snow S: talga; T: talgo

soap S: sapuna; T: ṣafuno; ṣabun

socialism S: shotapayuta; T: meshtawtfonutho; sosyalizm; ishtirakiye

socialist S: shotapaya/shotapayta; T: meshtawtfonoyo/ meshtawtfonitho; sosyalist; ishtiraki/ishtirakiye

socks S: gorwe/wase; T: gurwe

soft S: rakikha; T: rakikho

soil S: ʿapra; T: ʿafro

soldier S: gaysaya/gaysayta; T: qrabthono/qrabthonitho; fulḥo

son S: bruna; T: abro; kurikko

sorry! S: pakhalta!; T: shubqono!

soup S: shorwa; T: shorba; sruftho

sour S: khamuṣa/khamuṣta; T: ḥamuṣo/ḥamuṣto

south S: taymna; T: tayimno

sow S: bdhara; T: nṣowo

spade S: mara; T: magraftho

Spain S: Spanya; T: Espanya

Spanish S: Spanyaya/Spanyayta; T: Espanyoyo/Espanyayto

spanner S: spanar; T: qlidho ṣliḥo

spare tire S: gighla ʿatida; T: ufno zoyudo

sparrow S: sepra; T: ṣefro; ṣefruno

speak S: msawte; T: imoro

speaker S: mallala; T: malolo

speed S: qaliluta; T: surhowo

spices S: mdakhe; T: ḥarifutho

spicy S: mdakhe; ṣarupa/ṣarupta; T: ṣarufo/ṣarufto

spider S: izla kushe; zaqraqude; T: zaqoritho; gugi

spinach S: shaper ṭarpe; T: shafir-ṭarfe; sbenakh

spinal column; spine S: Shishelta d-Khaṣa; T: shishaltho d-ḥaṣo

sponge S: spongha; T: esfugho; isfanj

sports club S: bet-drashe; T: beth-durosho

spring *season* S: rbiʿa; T: rbiʿo; *of water* S: ʿayna d-miya; T: ʿayno; nabgho

spy S: gashusha; T: goshusho

squash S: skwash; T: skwash

squirrel S: simmora; T: samuro; shenuro; quzo

stadium S: bet-sheʿya; T: isṭadyon; beth-sheʿyo

staff army S: gusha; T: baʿle d-gayso

stairs S: darghe; daraje; palakane; T: darghe; daraj

stale S: sarya/srita; T: ʿatiqo/ ʿatiqto; nashifo/nashifto

stallion S: sosya; T: qiluno; faḥlo; rakhsho ushno

stamp S: khtama; T: ṭawʿo

stand S: klaya; T: kloyo; qyomo

star S: kukhwa; T: kukwo; **stars** S: kukhwe; T: kukwe

start S: msharuye; T: shuroyo

station S: nuqazta; T: mashryo; mashritho; beth-waʿdo

stationer's; stationery shop S: dokan kerke; T: qarṭisoyutho; dukano da-mone du-kthowo

statue S: qaymita; T: qayimto

steel S: pladha; T: fulodho; farz-lo hendwoyo

steering wheel S: sawkana; T: gighlo shabolo

stethoscope S: shamuʿta dasya; T: shomuʿto d-osyo; stethoskop

stomach S: karsa; T: gawo

stone S: kipa; T: kefo; shuʿo

stop S: klaya; T: kloyo; **stop** *(m/f)*! S: kli!/klay!; T: klay!

store *shop* S: dokana; T: dukano; ḥonutho

stork S: laqlaq; T: asido; laqlaq

storm *S:* ^{c}al^{c}ala; *T:* ^{c}al^{c}olo
stove *S:* kanuna; *T:* qamino; ṣoba
straight on *S:* triṣ; *T:* msawyo
straw *S:* zala; *T:* tewno; qaṣluṣo
strawberry *S:* tuta d-ar^{c}a; *T:* aquno
stream *S:* tappa; *T:* roghulo; redyo
street *S:* qayṭona; shqaqa; *T:* shqoqo; ja^{c}de; sri^c
string *S:* yatra; *T:* ḥuṭo
stroke *S:* msharyuta; *T:* msharyutho
strong *S:* quya; *T:* ḥaylono
struggle *S:* kutasha; *T:* aghuno
student *S:* *school* yalupa/yalupta; *university* ṣawbaya/ ṣawbayta; *T:* *school* yolufo/ yolufto; *university* ṣawboyo/ ṣawbayto
study *S:* qraya; *T:* drosho
stump *of limb* *S:* sharkana d-hadama qṭi^{c}a; *T:* sharkono d-hadomo qṭi^{c}o
subject *S:* mlu'a; *T:* sharbo
submachine gun *S:* rasosta; *T:* chifta mikanikayto na^{c}imto
subtract *S:* mabṣure; *T:* mabṣoro
subtraction *S:* mapqanuta; *T:* buṣoro
suburb *S:* wawtala; *T:* hawtho
subway *S:* naqwa d-halkha; *T:* nafqo (darbo taḥt di-ar^{c}o)
success *S:* kushara; *T:* kushoro
sugar *S:* shikar; *T:* shakar
suit *S:* eṣṭla; *T:* esṭlo; ṭaqm; badle; sut
suitcase *S:* mawbla; ṣimda; *T:* ṣemdo; janṭa; baghol
sum *S:* kunasha; *T:* kunosho; kmoyutho
sumac *S:* smuqe; *T:* ḥamṣitho; sumaq
summer *S:* qiṭa; *T:* qayṭo
summit *S:* qarna; *T:* qarno d-ṭuro; qarqaftho d-ṭuro
sun *S:* shimsha; *T:* shemsho
sunblock cream *S:* mishkha dalqub shimsha; *T:* doyubo luqbal di-shemsho
Sunday *S:* Khoshiba; *T:* ḥushabo
sunglasses *S:* khazayate shimshaye; *T:* ḥazoyotho di-shemsho
Sunni *S:* Sonnaya/Sonnayta; *T:* Sunnoyo/Sunnayto
sunrise *S:* saq yawma; *T:* dnoḥo d-shemsho
sunset *S:* gnay yawma; *T:* ṭwo^{c}o d-yawmo
sunstroke *S:* mkhuta d-shimsha; *T:* mḥoyo d-shemsho
supermarket *S:* supermarket; *T:* supermarket
supper *S:* khshamita; *T:* ḥshimto
surgeon *S:* ^{c}asuwa; ṣaruya; *T:* ^{c}osubo/^{c}osubtho; jarraḥ/jarraḥa
surgery *operation* *S:* mṣaruye; *T:* ^{c}uṣobo
surname *S:* kunaya; *T:* kunoyo; shumoho
surrender *S:* mtaslim; *T:* mashlomo; taslomo
surround *S:* mkarikh; *T:* ḥedhoro
swallow *S:* snunita; *T:* snunitho
swamp *S:* ṣyana; *T:* ^{c}awsho
sweater *S:* switar; *T:* kazko; fanera; swetar
Sweden *S:* Sweden; *T:* Swed
Swedish *S:* Swednaya/ Swednayta; *T:* Swedoyo/Swedayto
sweet *S:* khilya/khlita; *T:* ḥalyo/ḥlitho; **sweets** *S:* khilyuta; *T:* ḥalyutho
sweet potato *S:* qurtope khilye; *T:* paṭaṭa ḥlitho
swimming *S:* skhaya; *T:* skhoyo
Syria *S:* Surya; *T:* Suriya
Syrian *S:* Suraya/Suryayta; *T:* Suri/Suriya
syringe *S:* khmaṭa; *T:* mḥaṭo; mosugho
syrup *S:* ^{c}ṣara; *T:* ^{c}ṣoro; sharab

T

table *S:* ṭawlita; *T:* ṭablitho; masa
tailor *S:* khayyaṭa/khayaṭṭa; *T:* ḥayoṭo/ḥayoṭṭo
take *S:* shqala; *T:* mawbalto
talk *S:* msawte; *T:* jghaliye
tall *S:* yarikha; *T:* yarikho
tampon *S:* urqa^{c}ta qaṭinta; *T:* tampon
tank *military* *S:* rashupta; *T:* roshufto; dabbaba; tank; *of*

car *S:* tanki d-banzin; *T:* tank

tape (cassette) *S:* zul qala; *T:* zul-qolo; qaseta; **tape-recorder** *S:* msaghlanita; *T:* msaghlonitho da-zul-qole

taste *S:* ṭᶜama; *T:* ṭᶜomo

tasteless *S:* naᶜuṭa/naᶜuṭṭa; *T:* d-lo ṭaᶜmo

tasty *S:* ṭaᶜmana/ṭaᶜmanita; *T:* basimo/basimto; ṭaᶜmono

Taurus *S:* Tawra; *T:* Tawro

taxi *S:* taksi; *T:* taksi

tea house *S:* bet-tiya; chaykhana; *T:* chaykhana

tea *S:* tiya; *T:* chaye; tiyo; **tea with lemon** *S:* tiya ᶜm laymuna; *T:* chaye b-limon; chaye b-laymun; **tea with milk** *S:* tiya b-khalwa; *T:* chaye b-ḥalwo

teach *S:* mawlupe; *T:* mawlafto

teacher *S:* malpana/malpanta; *T:* malfono/malfonitho

teacher *S:* malpana/malpanta; *T:* malfono/malfonitho

team *S:* guda; *T:* yahlo

teapot *S:* jaydan; *T:* dudo; chaypas

teenager *S:* gaduda/gadudta; *T:* ᶜlaymo/ᶜlaymtho

teeth *S:* shenne; *T:* ᶜarshone; shene

telecommunications *S:* topaye khtutaye; *T:* naqifwotho; methmaṭyonutho

telephone *S:* qaᶜya; *T:* telefon; **telephone center** *S:* nuqazta d-dqaᶜye; *T:* qenṭrun du-telefon; qontorlu telefon

telescope *S:* marwana; *T:* mrawrwono mqarwono; teleskop

television *S:* makhizyana; *T:* fros-ḥezwo; telvizyon

telex *S:* khṭuṭa barqiᶜa; *T:* t eleks

ten *S:* ᶜesra/csar; *T:* ᶜesro/ᶜsar

tender *S:* rkhikha; rkhikhta; *T:* rakikho/rakikhto

tennis *S:* tenis; *T:* tenis

tent *S:* yariᶜta; *T:* mashkno; **tent pegs** *S:* Sekyate d Yuᶜarta; *T:* seke du-mashkno

tenth *S:* ᶜsiraya/ᶜsirayta; *T:* ᶜsiroyo/ᶜsirayto

termite *S:* shikwana khwara; *T:* belṭitho

test *S:* bukhrana; *T:* nusoyo

testify *S:* s-hada; *T:* s-hodo; ihobo sohdutho

thank you! *S:* tawdi!; *T:* tawdi!

that *S:* awaha; *T:* hawo/hayo

theater *S:* bet-khawra; *T:* beth-ḥezwone; tiyaṭron

theft *S:* gnawta; *T:* gnowo

there *S:* tama; *T:* tamo

thermometer *S:* mashukhta d-khamimut; *T:* mkaylono di-shḥuntho; thermometer

these *S:* anna; *T:* hani

they *S:* ani; *T:* hinne

thigh *S:* ᶜuṭma; *T:* ᶜaṭmo

thin *S:* naqida; *T:* dhaᶜifo; raqiqo

think *S:* rnaya; *T:* rnoyo

third *S:* tlitaya/tlitayata; *T:* tlithoyo/tlithayto

thirsty: I'm *(m/f)* **thirsty.** *S:* Ṣihya win./Ṣ-hita wan.; *T:* Ṣahino./Ṣahyono.; Ṣahyo-no./Ṣ-hitho-no.

thirteen *S:* tiltaᶜsar; *T:* tlothaᶜsar

thirty *S:* tlati; *T:* tlethi

this *S:* aha/hadhe; *T:* hano/hathe; **this week** *S:* ah shawuᶜa; *T:* ad-shabtho; **this year** *S:* aya shita; *T:* ad-shato

those *S:* anaha; *T:* hanik

thought *S:* marmita; renya; takhmanta; *T:* renyo

thousand *S:* alpa; *T:* alfo

three *S:* tlata/tlat; *T:* tlotho/tloth; **three times** *S:* tla zawnate; *T:* tloth kore; **three-quarters** *S:* tlata rwiᶜaye; *T:* tlotho-ruwᶜe

throat *S:* gigarta; ṣawra; *T:* ṣawro; zagruro

throw *S:* shdaya; *T:* mḥalaqto

thumb *S:* krata; *T:* krotho

thunder *S:* raᶜma; *T:* raᶜmo; rᶜumyo

thunderstorm *S:* ᶜalᶜala raᶜmaya; *T:* ᶜalᶜolo raᶜmoyo

Thursday *S:* Khamshoshiba; *T:* Ḥamshushabo

tibia *S:* garma d-shuqala; *T:* garmo d-shoqulo

tick *S:* ṭimra; *T:* qardo; fushfosho

ticket office *S:* makhitwa d-pitqe; *T:* makhtwo da-fetqe
tiger *S:* nimra; *T:* bebro
tights *S:* shirwale ^{c}iqe; *T:* lwushe ^{c}iqe
time *S:* sha^{c}ta; *space of time* zawna; *moment in time* ^{c}dana; *T:* sho^{c}tho; *space of time* zabno; *moment in time* ^{c}edono; **What time is it?** *S:* Sha^{c}ta d-kma la?; *T:* Miqqa-yo i-sho^{c}tho?; I-sho^{c}tho kmo-yo?; **It is six o'clock.** *S:* Sha^{c}ta d-eshta la.; *T:* Sheth-yo.
timetable *S:* surgada; *T:* surgod-ho da-zabne
tire *of car S:* gighla; *T:* ufno; tayer
tiredness *S:* laweta; *T:* baṭilutho; t^{c}ishutho
tissues *S:* shushipa; *T:* mandile d-waroqo
today *S:* ediom; *T:* ad-yawma
toe *S:* saw^{c}a; *T:* ṣeb^{c}o
toilet(s) *S:* bet-silya; *T:* beth-mayo/bote da-maye; tuwaylet; **toilet paper** *S:* waraqe d-silya; *T:* warqo du-tuwaylet
tomato *S:* yabrokhe; *T:* ṭamaṭa; yabruḥo; badhinjane semaqto
tomb *S:* qawra; *T:* qawro
tomorrow *S:* qudme; *T:* ramḥel; **tomorrow morning** *S:* qudme qedamta; *T:* ramḥel ṣafrayto; **tomorrow afternoon** *S:* qudme ṭahra; *T:* ramḥel ^{c}aṣriye; **tomorrow night** *S:* qudme bramsha; *T:* ramḥel b-lalyo; **the day after tomorrow** *S:* qudme date; *T:* yawmo ḥreno
ton *S:* ṭanna; *T:* ṭa^{c}no; ṭon
tongue *S:* lishana; *T:* leshono
tonight *S:* ad-lele; ramsha ediom; *T:* ad-lalyo
too: too much/too many *S:* saggi yatir; *T:* zoyudo/zoyud-to/zoyude
tooth *S:* shenna; *T:* sheno; ^{c}arsho; ^{c}arshono; **teeth** *S:* shenne; *T:* ^{c}arshone; shene
toothbrush *S:* perka d-shinne; *T:* farghuno
toothpaste *S:* roba d-shinne; *T:* darmono da-^{c}arshone; ma^{c}jun da-^{c}arshone
top *S:* resha; *T:* risho
torture *S:* shenda; *T:* shendo
tough *S:* qashya/qshita; *T:* qashyo/qshitho
tourism *S:* karukhuta; krukhya; *T:* karokhutho; turizm
tourist *S:* karukha/karukhta; *T:* karokho/karokhto; turist
tow rope *S:* gam la d-grashta; *T:* ḥawlo du-grosho
towel *S:* mkaprana; *T:* hawliye; kuforo; shushefo; mandilo
tower *S:* maghidla; *T:* burgo; maghdlo
town center *S:* qunṭrun d-mdita; *T:* qenṭrun di-mdhitho
town *S:* mdita; *T:* mdhitho
tracer bullet *S:* gulla d-bahrani-ta; *T:* bughro samuḥo
trachea *S:* yashṭa; *T:* yashṭo
tractor *S:* gargurta; *T:* magir-shono; traktor
trade fair *S:* glikhut tagharuta; *T:* gloḥutho di-tagorutho
trade union *S:* takhbarta; *T:* ḥuyodho da-tagore
traditional *S:* msapyanutanaya; *T:* ^{c}yodoyo; folkloroyo
train *S:* qṭara; *T:* qṭoro; qiṭar; **train station** *S:* nuqazta d-qṭara; *T:* mashritho du-qṭoro
trainer *S:* mdarshana/mdarshanta; *T:* mdarshono/mdarshonitho
tranquilizer *S:* mshlyana; *T:* mshaynono
transformer *S:* mkhalpana; *T:* mshaḥilfono
translate *S:* turgamta; *T:* turgo-mo
translation *S:* torgama; *T:* mtargmonutho
translator *S:* mtargimana/mtargimanta; *T:* mtargmono
travel *S:* krukhya; *T:* krukhyo; **travel agent** *S:* dokan krokhya; *T:* wakilo du-krukhyo
treasury *S:* shargazza; *T:* beth-gazo; simto

tree *S:* ilana; ilanta; *T:* dawmo; ilono
troops *S:* khaylawate; *T:* qrabthone; fulḥe
trousers *S:* shirwala; *T:* sharwolo; pantur; banṭalon
truce *S:* tashlita; *T:* tashlitho
truck *S:* shaqulta; *T:* kamyon
true *S:* tris; *T:* shariro
trunk *of tree S:* gidh^{c}a; *T:* shoqo; guz^{c}o; *of car S:* sanduq radita; *T:* ṣanduqo
truth *S:* shrara; *T:* shroro; shrolo
tuberculosis *S:* ṭuberculosis; *T:* tuberkulozis
Tuesday *S:* Tloshiba; *T:* Tlothushabo
Turk *S:* Turkaya/Turkayta; *T:* Turkoyo/Turkayto
turkey *S:* dika rumaya; *T:* ^{c}ali-^{c}alo; tarnoghlo daqnono; tarnoghlo rumoyo; ^{c}ali-shish
Turkey *S:* Turkiya; *T:* Turkiya
twelve *S:* tri^{c}sar; *T:* tra^{c}sar
twentieth *S:* tre^{c}saraya/ tres^{c}sarayta; *T:* ^{c}esrinoyo/ ^{c}esrinayto
twenty *S:* ^{c}esri; *T:* ^{c}esri
twice *S:* tre zawnate; *T:* tarte kore; naqqawothe
twins *S:* ta'ame; *T:* tome; chewi
two *S:* tre/tarten; *T:* tre/tarte; **two-thirds** *S:* tre tlitaye; *T:* tre-thulothe
typewriter *S:* katuwta d-ida; *T:* makhtwono
tyre *S:* gighla; *T:* ufno; tayer

U

ugly *S:* shkhira; *T:* natino/natinto; shkhiro/shkhirto
umbilical cord *S:* shurta; *T:* shurto
umbrella *S:* meṭalta; *T:* mṭaltho; shamsiye
uncomfortable *S:* dla rwakha; *T:* rahatsiz
uncooked *S:* naya; nayta; *T:* ra^{c}yo; noyo
under *S:* tkhet; khut; *T:* taḥt
understand *S:* parmuye; *T:* fhomo
underwear *S:* shirwala d-khuta; *T:* jule gawonoye; taḥtoye
unexploded: unexploded ammunition *S:* gulle la purqi^{c}e; *T:* asono lo mfajro; **unexploded bomb** *S:* marmita la mporqi^{c}ta; *T:* bomba lo mfajarto; qunbala lo mfajarto; **unexploded ordnance** *S:* mqal^{c}ana la mporqi^{c}a; *T:* mfajronitho lo mfajarto
unhappy *S:* dawya; *T:* qḥiroyo/ qḥirayto
uniform *S:* talwishta; *T:* esṭlo rushmoyo; ṭukosoyo
United Nations *S:* Emwate Mkhaydate; *T:* Emwotho Mḥaydotho
university *S:* bet-sawba; *T:* beth-ṣawbo
up *S:* l^{c}el; *T:* lal^{c}el
upper house *parliament S:* mawtwa ^{c}ellaya; *T:* bayto ^{c}eloyo
urine *S:* jure; tine; *T:* mazruqe; tafshirto
USA *S:* Ukhdane Mkhayde d-Amerika; *T:* Uḥdone Mḥayde d-Ameriqa

V

valley *S:* raghula; *T:* nirwo
van *S:* van; *T:* van
varnish *S:* varnish; *T:* seqlo; warnish
vase *S:* kawaza; zawirta; *T:* quqo; sharbo
vegetable shop *S:* dokan yariquta; *T:* dukano da-yarqe
vegetables *S:* yarquta; *T:* yarqe
vein *S:* warida; *T:* waridho
venereal disease *S:* kurhana myablana; *T:* kurhono gensonoyo; kewo gensonoyo
vertebra *S:* khemra; *T:* ḥemro
very *S:* saggi; *T:* sagi; ghallabe; **very hot** *S:* saggi shakhina; *T:* sagi ḥemo; ghallabe ḥemo; **very cold** *S:* saggi qura; *T:* sagi quro; ghallabe quro
veto *S:* veto; *T:* vito; zedqo d-nkoro w-hfukhyo

victory S: zakhuta; T: zokhutho
video-player S: toqan video; T: msaghlonitho da-zul-ḥezwe
videotape S: zul khizwa; T: zul-ḥezwo; sharit̩
view S: khizwa; T: ḥezwo; manzar
village S: qrita; T: qritho
vine S: gipta; T: sato; geftho
vinegar S: khala; T: ḥalo; sirka
vineyard S: karma; T: karmo
violence S: ^{c}nupya; T: shghushyo
viper S: akhidna; T: sha^{c}t̩o; kurfo
Virgo S: Btulta; T: Shebelto; Bthultho
virus S: yukhla; virus; T: virus
visa S: visa; T: ma^{c}bar-tḥume; viza
visit S: sa^{c}uruta; T: so^{c}urutho
vitamins S: vitamin; T: vitaminat
voltage regulator S: t̩okas volte; T: mt̩aksono du-volt̩aj
vomiting S: mad^{c}ure; T: ḥfoḥo; g^{c}oso
vote S: gubaya; T: qolo
vote-rigging S: mzayupe l-gubaya; T: rukowo da-qole
voting S: gabuye; T: guboyo
vulture S: baza; T: dardo; budro; neshro meṣroyo

W

waist S: khesra; T: dafno
waistcoast S: yalak; T: yalak
waiter/waitress S: ṣarwaya/ṣarwayta; T: ṣarwoyo/ṣarwayto
wake up S: bir^{c}asha; T: maḥisto
Wales S: Waylz; T: Waylz
walk S: mhalukhe; T: helkho
walking stick S: khut̩ra; gupala; T: ḥut̩ro
wall S: guda; shura; T: shuro
walnut S: goze; T: gawzo
want S: b^{c}aya; T: b^{c}oyo
war S: qrawa; T: qrobo
warm S: shakhina; T: shaḥino; ḥamimo
washing powder S: bdhara dshyagha; T: deqtho di-mashighonutho; bodra di-mashighonutho
wasp S: dibbora; T: deboro
watch *noun* S: sha^{c}ta d-ida; T: sho^{c}tho d-idho; *verb* S: bikhyara T: ḥyoro
watchmaker's S: mtaqin sha^{c}e; T: dukano da-sho^{c}e
water S: mayya; miya; T: maye; **water bottle** S: basta d-miya; T: shushaye da-maye; bar-qub^{c}o
waterfall S: shamshuma; T: nodurto; maflo da-maye; shallal
watermelon S: ship tiya; T: zabashe; shabt̩iye
we S: akhnan; T: aḥna
weak S: mkhila; T: mḥilo
weapon S: zayna; T: zayno
weather S: muzagha; T: muzogho; hawa
Wednesday S: ^{c}Arboshiba; T: Arb^{c}ushabo
week S: shawu^{c}a; T: shabtho; showu^{c}o
welcome *(m/f/pl)*! S: pshina tilokh!/pshina tilak!/pshina tilokhon!; T: b-shayno w-ba-shlomo!
well *adjective* S: t̩awa; T: t̩owo; kayiso; ḥlimo; sagh; *noun: of water* S: guba; T: gubo; biro
Welsh S: Welshaya/Welshayta; T: Welshoyo/Welshayto
west S: ma^{c}irwa; T: ma^{c}irbo
what? S: mudi?; T: mun?; **what's that?** S: mudi ele awaha?; T: mun-yo hawo/hayo?
wheat S: khit̩t̩e; T: ḥet̩e
wheelchair S: kursiya d-gighle; T: kursyo da-gighle
when? S: iman?; T: ema?
where? S: eka?; T: ayko?; **where is/are ...?** S: ika ele?/ika ela/eka lay?; T: ayko-yo?/ayko-ne?
which? S: ayni?; T: ayna?
white S: khwara/khwarta; T: ḥeworo/ḥewarto
who? S: mani?; T: man?
whooping cough S: khnaqta; T: ḥaniqutho
why? S: qa mudi?; T: qay?
wide S: ptukha; T: fathyo

wife *S:* bart zawga; *T:* athto; zhinnike; pire
win *S:* mzake; *T:* qmoro
wind *S:* hawa; *T:* hawa
window *S:* kawe; *T:* kawtho; shaboko
windpipe *S:* yashṭa; *T:* yashṭo
windshield; **windscreen** *S:* zghugha d-radita; *T:* zghughitho; sakro d-hawa; **windshield wipers** *S:* mkaprane d-zghugha d-radita; *T:* mandhifone di-zghughitho
windy *S:* hawana; *T:* hawa ghallabe; ^{c}al^{c}olo
wine *S:* khamra; *T:* ḥamro
winter *S:* sitwa; *T:* sathwo
wire *S:* khuṭa; *T:* ḥuṭo
wisdom *S:* khekhemta; *T:* ḥekhemtho
wolf *S:* diwa; *T:* dibo
woman *S:* athta; *T:* athto; zhinnike; pire
womb *S:* marib^{c}a; *T:* marb^{c}o
wood *S:* qaysa; *T:* qayso
wood *S:* qayse; *T:* qayse; **a wood** *S:* ^{c}awa; *T:* ^{c}obo
wool *S:* amra; *T:* ^{c}amro
work *noun S:* plakha; *T:* shgholo; *verb S:* shoghla; *T:* shughlo
world *S:* ^{c}alma; *T:* britho; meth^{c}amronitho
worm *S:* tawl^{c}a; *T:* tul^{c}o; tlaw^{c}o
wound *S:* msalip; *T:* jroḥo
woven *S:* gdila; *T:* gdhilo
wrench *S:* spanar; *T:* qlidho ṣliḥo
wrestling *S:* darra; *T:* kutosho
wrist *S:* masurqa; *T:* qurṣlo
write *S:* biktawa *T:* kthowo
writer *S:* katuwa/katuwta; *T:* kathowo/kathawto
writing paper *S:* waraqe d-ktawa; dappe d-ktawa; *T:* waroqe du-kthowo
wrong *S:* pawda; *T:* fawdo

Y

yard *distance S:* yard; *T:* yardo
year *S:* shata; *T:* shato; **the year after next** *S:* shita d-bar hay d atya; *T:* shato ḥreto; **the year before last** *S:* teltath; *T:* shato ḥreto
yellow *S:* sha^{c}uta/sha^{c}utta; *T:* sha^{c}utho/sha^{c}uthto
yes *S:* ayn; e'n; *T:* e; bele
yesterday *S:* timmal; *T:* athmel; **yesterday morning** *S:* tim mal qidamta; *T:* athmel ṣafrayto; **yesterday afternoon** *S:* tim mal ṭahra; *T:* athmel ^{c}aṣriye; **yesterday night** *S:* tim mal bramsha; *T:* athmel b-lalyo; **the day before yesterday** *S:* timmal d-^{c}were; *T:* yawmo ḥreno
yogurt *S:* masta; *T:* qaṭiro; masto
you *m singular S:* at; *T:* hat; *f singular S:* ate; *T:* hate; *plural S:* akhton; *T:* hatu
young *S:* ^{c}layma; *T:* na^{c}imo

Z

zero *S:* sipar; *T:* ṣifr; squt
zipper *S:* shishilta; zinjir; *T:* shishaltho
zoo *S:* ganta d-khaywate; *T:* gantho d-ḥaywotho
Zoroastrian *S:* Zardushtaya/ Zardushtayta; *T:* Zartushtoyo/ Zartushtayto

ARAMAIC
Phrasebook

ܐ ܒ ܓ ܕ ܗ ܘ ܙ ܚ ܛ ܝ ܟ ܠ ܡ ܢ ܣ ܥ ܦ ܨ ܩ ܪ ܫ ܬ

ܐ ܒ ܓ ܕ ܗ ܘ ܙ ܚ ܛ ܝ ܟ ܠ ܡ ܢ ܣ ܥ ܦ ܨ ܩ ܪ ܫ ܬ

ܐ ܒ ܓ ܕ ܗ ܘ ܙ ܚ ܛ ܝ ܟ ܠ ܡ ܢ ܣ ܥ ܦ ܨ ܩ ܪ ܫ ܬ

ܐ ܒ ܓ ܕ ܗ ܘ ܙ ܚ ܛ ܝ ܟ ܠ ܡ ܢ ܣ ܥ ܦ ܨ ܩ ܪ ܫ ܬ

1. ETIQUETTE

Hello!
S: **Shlama!**
T: **Shlomo!**

How are you *(m/f/pl)*?
S: **Dakhi wit?/Dakhi wat?/Dakhi ton?**
T: **Aydarbo hat?**

I'm *(m/f)* fine, thanks!
S: **Ṭawa win tawdi/Ṭawta wan tawdi**
T: **Ṭowo-no, tawdi!/Ṭowto-no, tawdi!** *or* **Kayiso-no, tawdi!/Kayisto-no, tawdi!**

I'm *(m/f)* not bad!
S: **Lawin khirba!/Lewan khirba!**
T: **Latno ḥarbo!** *(m/f)*

What's up?
S: **Mu it mu layt?**
T: **Mun kit mun layt?**

Pleased to meet you *(m/f/pl)*!
S: **Khdili b-khzitukh!/b-khzitakh!/ b-khzitokhon!**
T: *said by a male:* **Fṣiḥno bi-ḥzaytaydhokh!/ bi-ḥzaytaydhekh!/bi-ḥzaytathkhu!**; *said by a female:* **Fṣiḥono bi-ḥzaytaydhokh!/ bi-ḥzaytaydhekh!/bi-ḥzaytathkhu!**

Good morning!
S: **Brikh ṣapra**
T: **Brikh-ṣafro!** *or* **Ṣafro ṭobo!**

Good afternoon/evening!
S: **Brikh ṭahra!/Brikh ramsha!**
T: **Brikh-ṭahro!**

Good night!
S: **Lilya ṭawa**
—*Response:* **Ap lilyokh/lilyakh/lilyaokhon!**
T: **Brikh-ramsho!** *or* **Lalyo ṭobo!**
—*Response:* **Brikh-ṭobo!** *or* **Aᶜlokh ste!/Aᶜlekh ste!**

Goodbye *(sing/pl)*!
S: **Posh b-shlama!/Poshon b-shlama!**
—*Response: S:* **Bshayna!**
T: **Fush ba-shlomo!/Fushu ba-shlomo!**
—*Response:* **Zel b-shayno!** *or* **Zel ba-shlomo!** *or* **Aloho aᶜmaykhu!**

See you later *(m/f/pl)*!
S: **B-khazinokh kharta!/B-khazinakh kharta!/B-khazinokhon kharta!**
T: said by a male: **G-ḥozenokh bithir-kene!/G-ḥozenekh bithir-kene!/G-ḥozenolkhu bithir-kene!**; *said by a female:* **G-ḥuzyonokh bithir-kene!/G-ḥuzyonekh bithir-kene/G-ḥuzy-onolkhu bithir-kene!**

See you *(m/f/pl)* tomorrow!
S: said by a male: **Bkhazinokh ramkhil!/Bkhazinakh ramkhil!/Bkhazinokhon ramkhil!**; *said by a female:* **Bkhazyanukh ramkhil!/Bkhazyanakh ramkhil!/Bkhazyanaokhon ramkhil!**
T: said by a male: **G-ḥozenokh ramḥel!/G-ḥozenekh ramḥel!/G-ḥozenolkhu ramḥel!**; *said by a female:* **G-ḥuzyonokh ramḥel!/G-ḥuzyonekh ramḥel!/G-ḥuzyankhu ramḥel!**

Please *(m/f/pl)*!
S: **In basmalokh!/In basmalakh!/In basmalokhon!**
T: **Boᶜutho menokh!/Boᶜutho menekh!/Boᶜutho menaykhu!**

Thank you!
S: **Tawdi!**
T: **Tawdi!**

Thank you very much!
S: **Tawdi saggi!**
T: **Tawdi sagi!** *or* **Tawdi ghallabe!**

Not at all!
S: **La middim!**
T: **Lo medem!**

Excuse me!; Sorry!
S: **Pakhalta!**
T: **Shubqono!**

Cheers! *(m/f/pl)*
S: **B-khubukh!/B-khubakh!/B-khubaokhon!**
T: **ḥubo!**

Congratulations!
S: **Tahniyate!**
T: **Tahinyotho!**

Welcome *(m/f/pl)*!
S: **Pshina tilokh!/Pshina tilak!/Pshina tilokhon!**
T: **B-shayno w-ba-shlomo!**

Bon voyage *(m/f/pl)*!
S: **Urkhukh ptekhta!/Urkhakh ptekhta!/Urkhukhon ptekhta!**
T: **Darbo fti?o!** *or* **Aloho aᶜmaykhu!**

Please eat *(m/f)*!
S: **ᶜUwod ṭaybo okhul/okhuel!**
T: **Boᶜutho menokh/menekh, khal!**

Please sit down *(m/f)*!
S: **Paqid w ytu!/Paqid w ytaw!**
T: **Boᶜutho menokh/menekh, iytaw!**

2. QUICK REFERENCE

yes	*S:* **ayn**; *T:* **e; bele***
no	*S:* **la**; *T:* **lo**
I	*S:* **ana**; *T:* **ono**
you *m singular*	*S:* **at**; *T:* **hat**
you *f singular*	*S:* **ate**; *T:* **hate**
he/it	*S:* **haw**; *T:* **huwe; hiye**
she/it	*S:* **hae**; *T:* **hiya**
we	*S:* **akhnan**; *T:* **aḥna**
you *plural*	*S:* **akhton**; *T:* **hatu**
they	*S:* **ani**; *T:* **hinne**
this	*S:* **aha/hadhe**; *T:* **hano/hathe**
these	*S:* **anna**; *T:* **hani**
that	*S:* **awaha**; *T:* **hawo/hayo**
those	*S:* **anaha**; *T:* **hanik**
here	*S:* **laakha**; *T:* **harke**
there	*S:* **tama**; *T:* **tamo**
is there?/are there?	*S:* **it tama?**; *T:* **kit?/kito?**
where is/are ...?	*S:* **ika ele?/ika ela/eka lay?**; *T:* **ayko-yo?/ayko-ne?**
where?	*S:* **eka?**; *T:* **ayko?**
who?	*S:* **mani?**; *T:* **man?**
what?	*S:* **mudi?**; *T:* **mun?**
when?	*S:* **iman?**; *T:* **ema?**
which?	*S:* **ayni?**; *T:* **ayna?**
how?	*S:* **dakhi?**; *T:* **aydarbo?**
why?	*S:* **qa mudi?**; *T:* **qay?**
how far?	*S:* **kma rikhqa?**; *T:* **miqqa raḥuqo?**
how near?	*S:* **kma qurba?**; *T:* **miqqa qariwo?**
how much?	*S:* **kma le?/kma la?/kma lay?**; *T:* **miqqa?**
how many?	*S:* **kma lay?**; *T:* **kmo?**
what's that?	*S:* **mudi ele awaha?**; *T:* **mun-yo hawo/hayo?**

* Bele means "yes" when replying to negative statements or questions, e.g. "You're not going are you?" "Yes (of course, I am)!"

QUICK REFERENCE

very — *S:* **saggi**; *T:* **sagi; ghallabe**
and — *S:* **o; up**; *T:* **w-**
or — *S:* **yan**; *T:* **aw; ya**
but — *S:* **ina**; *T:* **elo; bas**

I *(m/f)* like ...
S: **Ana makhbin .../Ana makhban ...**
T: **G-roḥamno .../G-ruḥmono ...**

I *(m/f)* don't like ...
S: **Ana le makhbin .../Ana le makhiban ...**
T: **Lo g-roḥamno .../Lo g-ruḥmono ...**

I *(m/f)* want ...
S: **Ana bayin .../Ana bayan ...**
T: **K-oba^{c}no .../K-ub^{c}ono ...**

I *(m/f)* don't want ...
S: **Ana le bayin .../Ana le bayan ...**
T: **Lo k-oba^{c}no .../Lo k-ub^{c}ono ...**

I *(m/f)* know.
S: **Ana yad^{c}in./Ana yad^{c}an.**
T: **K-odha^{c}no./K-udh^{c}ono.**

I *(m/f)* don't know.
S: **Ana le yad^{c}in./Ana le yad^{c}an.**
T: **Lo k-odha^{c}no./Lo k-udh^{c}ono.**

Do you *(m/f)* understand?
S: **Prama wet?/Prama wat?**
T: **Ko-fuhmat?**

I *(m/f)* understand.
S: **Ana prama wen./Ana prama wan.**
T: **Ko-fohamno./Ko-fuhmono.**

I *(m/f)* don't understand.
S: **Ana le wen prama./Ana le wan prama.**
T: **Lo k-fohamno./Lo k-fuhmono.**

I am sorry *(to hear that).*
S: **Twikhli bi-shmi^{c}ta.**
T: **Yaqidh lebi.** *(literally: "my heart aches")*

I *(m/f)* am grateful.
S: **Ṭaʿnana d-minta wen./Ṭaʿnanta d-minta wan.**
T: **Kit-li quboltaybutho.** *or* **Mashkarno./Mashkrono.**

It's important!
S: **Alṣaya le!**
T: **Ulṣoyo-yo!** *or* **Muhem-yo!**

It doesn't matter.
S: **Layt la kham.**
T: **Latyo qeṭro.**

No problem!
S: **Layt qitra!**
T: **Ghamo layto!**

more or less
S: **yatir khasir**
T: **hawkha mede** *or* **taqriban**

Here is *(m/f)* ...
S: **Ha hole .../Ha hola ...**
T: **Kale .../Kala ...**

Here are ...
S: **Ha holae ...**
T: **Kalen ...**

Is everything OK?
S: **Kul mindi ṭawa le?**
T: **Kul mede tamam-yo?**

Danger!
S: **Qinṭa!**
T: **Qenṭo!** *or* **Khatar!**

How do you *(m/f)* spell that?
S: **Dakhi yhagitla?/Dakhi yhagyatla?**
T: **Aydarbo ko-hogat-le?**

I am cold.
S: **Ana qarti la.**
T: **Ko-qorashli.**

I am hot.
S: **Ana khimmi le.**
T: **Ḥemo-yo aᶜli.**

I am sleepy.
S: **Shinti la.**
T: **Kothe-li shantho.**

I *(m/f)* am hungry.
S: **Kpina wen./Kpinta wan.**
T: **Kafinno/kafinono.** *or* **Kafino-no./Kafinto-no.**

I *(m/f)* am thirsty.
S: **Ṣiya wen./ṣita wan.**
T: **Ṣahino./Ṣahyono.** *or* **Ṣahyo-no/Ṣ-hitho-no .**

I *(m/f)* am angry.
S: **Kriba wen./Kribta wan.**
T: **Khbinoyo-no./Khbinayto-no.**

I *(m/f)* am happy.
S: **Khidya wen./Khdita wan.**
T: **Fṣiḥoyo-no./Fṣiḥayto-no.**

I *(m/f)* am sad.
S: **Khishana wen./Khishanta wan.**
T: **Qḥiroyo-no./Qḥirayto-no.**

I *(m/f)* am tired.
S: **La'ya win./L'ayta wan.**
or **Shurshiya win./Shurshita wan.**
T: **Baṭilo-no./Baṭilto-no.**

I *(m/f)* am well.
S: **Ana ṭawa wen./Ana ṭawta wan.**
T: **Ṭowo-no./Ṭowto-no.**

3. INTRODUCTIONS

What is your *(m/f)* name?
S: **Mudi le shimokh/shimakh?**
T: **Mun-yo ishmokh/ishmekh?**

My name is ...
S: **Shimi ile.**
T: **Ishmi ... yo.**

This *(m/f)* is ...
S: **Aha/Hadhi...**
T: **Hano/Hathe ... yo.**

... my friend *(m/f)* *S:* **khawri le/khwarti la**
T: **ḥawraydhi/ḥwarthaydhi**

... my colleague *(m/f)* *S:* **luyi le/luwiti la**
T: **ḥawraydhi du-shughlo/ ḥwarthaydhi du-shughlo**

... my companion *(m/f)* *S:* **knati le/knati la**
T: **lewyaydhi/lewithaydhi**

...my neighbor *(m/f)* *S:* **shwawi/shwawti**
T: **shbobaydhi/shbobtaydhi; jiranaydhi**

... my relative *(m/f)* *S:* **khyani le/khyanti la**
T: **qariwaydhi/qariwtaydhi; ahlaydhi**

—Nationality

Assyria *S:* **Atur**; *T:* **Othur**
—Assyrian *S:* **Aturaya/Aturayta;**
T: **Othuroyo/Othurayto; Suroyo/ Surayto; Suryoyo/Suryayto**

Where are you *(m/f)* from?
S: **Meka wet/wat?**
T: **Mayko hat?**

I *(m/f)* am from ...	*S:* **Ana i wen/wan min ...** *T:* **Men ... no.**
America	*S:* **Amerika**; *T:* **Ameriqa**
Australia	*S:* **Australya**; *T:* **Australya**
Britain	*S:* **Briṭanya**; *T:* **Briṭanya**
Canada	*S:* **Kanada**; *T:* **Qanada**
China	*S:* **Ṣin**; *T:* **Ṣin**; **Shin**
Cyprus	*S:* **Qubrus**; *T:* **Qufrus**
England	*S:* **Ingland**; *T:* **Ingiltara**
Europe	*S:* **Europe**; *T:* **Urifi**
France	*S:* **Pransa**; *T:* **Faransa**
Germany	*S:* **Almanya**; *T:* **Almanya**
Greece	*S:* **Yawnan**; *T:* **Yawon**; **Yawnan**; **Grikia**
India	*S:* **Hindu**; *T:* **Hendu**; **Hind**
Iran	*S:* **Iran**; *T:* **Iran**
Ireland	*S:* **Ireland**; *T:* **Irlanda**
Japan	*S:* **Yaban**; *T:* **Japan**
the Netherlands	*S:* **Holanda**; *T:* **Holanda**
New Zealand	*S:* **Ziland Khata**; *T:* **Nuzilanda**
Northern Ireland	*S:* **Irlanda Garbyayta**; *T:* **Irlanda Garbyayto**
Pakistan	*S:* **Pakistan**; *T:* **Pakistan**
Scotland	*S:* **Ṣkotland**; *T:* **Sqotlanda**
Spain	*S:* **Spanya**; *T:* **Espanya**
Sweden	*S:* **Sweden**; *T:* **Swed**
the USA	*S:* **Ukhdane Mkhayde d-Amerika**; *T:* **Uḥdone Mḥayde d-Ameriqa**
Wales	*S:* **Waylz**; *T:* **Waylz**

I *(m/f)* am ...	*S:* **Ana ... wen/wan.**; *T:* **... no.**
American *(m/f)*	*S:* **Amirkaya/Amirkayta**; *T:* **Ameriqoyo/Ameriqayto**
Australian	*S:* **Osṭralaya/Osṭralayta**; *T:* **Australyoyo/Australyayto**
British	*S:* **Briṭnaya/Briṭnayta**; *T:* **Briṭanoyo/Briṭanayto**
Canadian	*S:* **Kanadaya/Kanadayta**; *T:* **Qanadoyo/Qanadayto**

Cypriot	*S:* **Qubrasaya/Qubrasayta;** *T:* **Qufroyo/Qufrayto** *f*
Dutch	*S:* **Duchnaya/Duchnayta;** *T:* **Holandoyo/Holandayto**
English	*S:* **Englishaya/Englishnayta;** *T:* **Inglishoyo/Inglishayto**
French	*S:* **Frangaya/Frangayta;** *T:* **Faransoyo/Faransayto**
German	*S:* **Garmanaya/Garmanayta;** *T:* **Almanoyo/Almanayto**
Greek	*S:* **Yawnaya/Yawnayta;** *T:* **Yawnoyo/Yawnayto**
Indian	*S:* **Hindawaya/Hindawayta;** *T:* **Hendwoyo/Hendwayto**
Iranian	*S:* **Iranaya/Iranayta;** *T:* **Iranoyo/Iranayto**
Irish	*S:* **Ayrishnaya/Ayrishnayta;** *T:* **Irlandoyo/Irlandayto**
Israeli	*S:* **Israelyaya/Israelyayta;** *T:* **Israyiloyo/Israyilayto**
Italian	*S:* **Iṭalnaya/Iṭalnayta;** *T:* **Iṭaloyo/Iṭalayto**
Pakistani	*S:* **PakistanayaPakistanayta;** *T:* **Pakistanoyo/Pakistanayto**
Portuguese	*S:* **Portughlaya/Portughlayta;** *T:* **Portughaloyo/Portughalayto**
Scottish	*S:* **Skotnaya/Skotnayta;** *T:* **Sqotlandoyo/Sqotlandayto**
Spanish	*S:* **Spanyaya/Spanyayta;** *T:* **Espanyoyo/Espanyayto**
Swedish	*S:* **Swednaya/Swednayta;** *T:* **Swedoyo/Swedayto**
Welsh	*S:* **Welshaya/Welshayta;** *T:* **Welshoyo/Welshayto**

Where were you *(m/f)* born?
S: **Ika wet birya?/Ika wat brita?**
T: **Ayko hawat?**

I *(m/f)* was born in ...
S: **Ana birya wen go .../Ana brita wan go ...**
T: **Hawino b-.../Hawyono b-...**

Where is your *(m/f)* family from?
S: **Mika ela iqartokh/Mika ela iqartakh?**
T: **Mayko-yo iqarthaydhokh?/Mayko-yo iqarthaydhekh?** ***or*** **Mayko-yo ʿal'ilayd-hokh?/Mayko-yo ʿal'ilaydhekh?**

My family is from ...
S: **Iqarti ela min ...**
T: **Iqarthaydhi me-yo ...** *or* **ʿA'ilaydhi me-yo ...**

—Regional nationalities

—Arab *(m/f)*	*S:* **Sarqaya/ Sarqayta** *or* **ʿArabaya/ʿArabayta;** *T:* **ʿAraboyo/ʿArabayto**
Armenia	*S:* **Armenia;** *T:* **Arminya**
—Armenian	*S:* **Aremnaya/Aremnayta;** *T:* **Arimnoyo/Arimnayto**
Azerbaijan	*S:* **Azerbayjan;** *T:* **Azarbayjan**
—Azerbaijani	*S:* **Hoshara/Hosharta;** *T:* **Azaroyo/Azarayto**
Georgia	*S:* **Jorjiya;** *T:* **Grujiya**
—Georgian	*S:* **Gurgaya/Gurgayta;** *T:* **Grujoyo/Grujayto**
Iraq	*S:* **ʿIraq;** *T:* **ʿIraq**
—Iraqi	*S:* **ʿIraqnaya/ʿIraqnayta;** *T:* **ʿIraqoyo/ʿIraqayto**
Iran	*S:* **Iran;** *T:* **Iran**
—Iranian	*S:* **Iranaya/Iranayta;** *T:* **Iranoyo/Iranayto**
—Jew	*S:* **Yhudhaya/Yhudhayta;** *T:* **Yudhoyo/Yudhayto**
Jordan	*S:* **Yuridnan;** *T:* **Yurdnon**
—Jordanian	*S:* **Yuridnaya/Yuridnayta;** *T:* **Yurdnonoyo/Yurdnonayto**
Kurdistan	*S:* **Kurdistan;** *T:* **Kurdistan**
—Kurd	*S:* **Qurdaya/Qurdayta;** *T:* **Kurdoyo/Kurdayto**
Lebanon	*S:* **Lunan;** *T:* **Lebnon**
—Lebanese	*S:* **Lunanaya/Lunanayta;** *T:* **Lebnonoyo/Lebnonayto**
Russia	*S:* **Rusya;** *T:* **Rusiya**

—Russian	*S:* **Orisnaya/Orisnayta;** *T:* **Rusnoyo/Rusnayto**
Syria	*S:* **Surya;** *T:* **Suriya**
—Syrian	*S:* **Suraya/Suryayta;** *T:* **Suri/Suriya**
Turkey	*S:* **Turkiya;** *T:* **Turkiya**
—Turk	*S:* **Turkaya/Turkayta;** *T:* **Turkoyo/Turkayto**

—Occupations

What do you *(m/f)* do?
S: **Mudi ypalkhit?/Mudi ypalkhat?**
T: **Mun ko-shuglat?**

I *(m/f)* am a/an ...
S: **Ana iwin .../Ana iwan ...**
T: **Ano ... no.**

academic *(m/f)*	*S:* **akadimyaya/akadimyayta;** *T:* **akadimoyo/akadimayto; profisor/profisore**
accountant	*S:* **mkhashwana/makhshwanta;** *T:* **ḥashubthono/ḥashubthonitho; muḥasib/muḥasiba**
actor	*S:* **mathlana/mathlanita;** *T:* **mathlono/mathlonitho**
administrator	*S:* **mparnisana/mparnsayta;** *T:* **mfarnsono/mfarnsonitho; idari/idariye**
aid worker	*S:* **sayu^{c}a/sayu^{c}ta;** *T:* **m^{c}adrono/m^{c}adronitho**
architect	*S:* **ardikhla/ardikhlayta;** *T:* **ardikhlo/ardikhlitho; muhandis madani**
artist	*S:* **amnara/amnarta;** *T:* **amono/amonto; fannan/fannana**
baker	*S:* **nakhtuma/nakhtumta;** *T:* **afoyo; ardoqufo; naḥtumo**
banker	*S:* **m^{c}arpana/m^{c}arpanta;** *T:* **ṣarofo/ṣarofto; m^{c}arfono/m^{c}arfonitho; shagholo di-banqa/shagholto di-banqa**

business person *S:* **tghaara/tghaarta**; *T:* **tagoro/tagorto; tajir/tajira**

butcher *S:* **qaṭuba/ qaṭubta**; *T:* **qaṭobo/qaṭobto; qaṭṭab/qaṭṭaba**

carpenter *S:* **nghara/ngharta**; *T:* **nagoro/nagorto; najjar/najjara**

civil servant *S:* **palakha d-shulṭaana/palakhta d-shulṭana**; *T:* **ᶜawodo mdhinoyo/ᶜawodhto mdhinayto; muwadhdhaf madani/muwadhdhafa madaniya**

consultant *S:* **malukha/malokokhta**; *T:* **molukho/molukhto; mustashar/mustashara**

cook *S:* **ṭabakha/ ṭabakhta**; *T:* **ṭaboḥo/ṭaboḥto; ṭabbakh/ṭabbakha**

dentist *S:* **asya d-shine**; *T:* **osyo da-ᶜarshone/ositho da-ᶜarshone**

designer *S:* **mtapinkhana**; *T:* **rashomo/rashomto; rassam/rassama**

diplomat *S:* **suyasara/suyasarta**; *T:* **diblomasoyo/diblomasayto**

doctor *S:* **asya**; *T:* **osyo/ositho; doktor/doktora**

economist *S:* **mmashkhana**; *T:* **eqonomyoyo/eqonomyayto; iqtiṣadi/iqtiṣadiye**

engineer *S:* **makhara/makharta**; *T:* **maḥoro/maḥorto; muhandis/muhandisa**

factory worker *S:* **maṣinᶜana/maṣinᶜayta**; *T:* **shagholo b-maᶜmlo/shagholto b-maᶜmlo**

farmer *S:* **akara/akarta**; *T:* **akoro/akorto; daworo/daworto**

filmmaker *S:* **mapqana/mapqanta**; *T:* **soyumo da-filme/soyumto da-filme**

gardner *S:* **gannana/gannanta**; *T:* **ganono/ganonto**

journalist *S:* **ghulyunara/ghulyunarta**; *T:* **gelyunoro/gelyunorto; ṣuḥafi/ṣuḥafiye**

lawyer *S:* **snighra/snighirta**; *T:* **snighro/snighartho; muḥami/muḥamiye**

mechanic	*S:* **mikanik/mikanikayta**; *T:* **mikanikoyo/mikanikayto**
musician	*S:* **musiqara/musiqarta**; *T:* **musiqoro/musiqorto**
nurse	*S:* **yaṣupa/yaṣupta**; *T:* **samsemono/samsemonitho; mumarrid/mumarrida**
office worker	*S:* **katawa/katawta**; *T:* **shagholo/shagholto b-makhtwo**
photographer	*S:* **mṣayrana/mṣayranta**; *T:* **mṣayrono/mṣayronitho; muṣawwar/muṣawwara**
pilot	*S:* **ṭayosa/ṭayosnayta**; *T:* **ṭayostono/ṭayostonitho; qaloᶜo d-ṭayisto/qaloᶜto d-ṭayisto; paylot**
scientist	*S:* **bkhira/bkhirta**; *T:* **yoduᶜthono/yoduᶜthonitho; ᶜalim/ᶜalima**
secretary	*S:* **naṭir raze/naṭra raze**; *T:* **noṭer-roze/noṭrath-roze; sekreter**
singer	*S:* **zamara/zamarta**; *T:* **zamoro/zamorto**
soldier	*S:* **gaysaya/gaysayta**; *T:* **qrabthono/qrabthonitho; fulḥo**
student	*S:* *school:* **yalupa/yalupta**; *university:* **ṣawbaya/ṣawbayta**; *T:* *school:* **yolufo/yolufto**; *university:* **ṣawboyo/ṣawbayto**
surgeon	*S:* **ᶜasuwa**; *T:* **ᶜosubo/ᶜosubtho; jarraḥ/jarraḥa**
tailor	*S:* **khayyaṭa/khayaṭta**; *T:* **ḥayoṭo/ḥayoṭto**
teacher	*S:* **malpana/malpanta**; *T:* **malfono/malfonitho**
tourist	*S:* **karukha/karukhta**; *T:* **karokho/karokhto; turist**
trainer	*S:* **mdarshana/mdarshanta**; *T:* **mdarshono/mdarshonitho**
waiter/waitress	*S:* **ṣarwaya/ṣarwayta**; *T:* **ṣarwoyo/ṣarwayto**
writer	*S:* **katuwa/katuwta**; *T:* **kathowo/kathawto**

I *(m/f)* work in ...
S: **Ana ypalkhin/ypalkhan go...**
T: **Ko-shoghalno/shughlono b-...**

advertising	*S:* **shudaʿa**; *T:* **i-mawdʿonutho**; **iʿlanat; deʿayat**
an aid agency	*S:* **wakilot suyaʿa;** *T:* **siʿto ʿudronayto**
computers	*S:* **khashuwe**; *T:* **a-ḥoshube; a-kompyuterat**
industry	*S:* **ṣniʿuta**; *T:* **i-ṣniʿutho**
insurance	*S:* **ʿarawuta**; *T:* **u-shuroro**
I.T.	*S:* **tiqnaye mawdʿanuta;** *T:* **i-teknolojia di-mawdʿonutho**
the leisure industry	*S:* **khaqla d-rwakhanuta;** *T:* **a-fulḥone sufqonoye**
marketing	*S:* **methshuqanuta;** *T:* **i-mezdabnonutho**
the media	*S:* **yudaʿa**; *T:* **u-yudoʿo; an-aʿlam**
an office	*S:* **makhitwa**; *T:* **makhtwo; beth-makthbo**
the retail industry	*S:* **khaqla d-zubana;** *T:* **a-fulḥone zubonoye**
sales	*S:* **zubana**; *T:* **a-zubone**
a shop	*S:* **dokana**; *T:* **dukano; ḥonutho**
telecommunications	*S:* **topaye khtutaye;** *T:* **a-naqifwotho; i-methmaṭyonutho**
tourism	*S:* **karukhuta**; *T:* **i-karokhutho; u-turizm**
the hotel industry	*S:* **khaqla d-bet-bawte;** *T:* **i-mashryonutho; a-hotelat**

—Age

How old are you *(m/f)*?
S: **Kma le ʿumrokh/ʿumrakh?**
T: **Miqqa-yo ʿumrokh/ʿumrekh?**

I *(m/f)* am ... years old.
S: **Ana iwen/iwan ... shine.**
T: **... ishne-no.**

—Family

Are you *(m/f)* married?
S: **Gwira wet?/Gwirta wat?**
T: **Gawiro hat?/Gawirto hat?**

I *(m/f)* am not married.
S: **La dla gwara wen./La dla gwara wan.**
T: **Lat-no gawiro./Lat-no gawirto.**

I *(m/f)* am married.
S: **Gwira wen./Gwirta wan.**
T: **Gawiro no./Gawirto no.**

I *(m/f)* am divorced.
S: **Ropa wen./Ropita wan.**
T: **Marfiyo no./Marfayto no.**

I *(m/f)* am widowed.
S: **Arimla wen./Armilta wan.**
T: **Armlo no./Armaltho no.**

Do you *(m/f)* have a boyfriend?
S: **Itlakh khawra?**
T: **Kit-lekh ḥawro?**

Do you *(m/f)* have a girlfriend?
S: **Itlokh khawerta**
T: **Kit-lokh ḥwartho?**

What is his/her name?
S: **Mudi le shim me/ma?**
T: **Mun-yo ishme/ishma?**

How many children do you*(m/f)* have?
S: **Kma yale itlokh/itlakh?**
T: **Kmo naᶜime kit-lokh/kit-lekh?**

I don't have any children.
S: **Lit li sakh yale.**
T: **Lat-li naᶜime.**

I have a daughter.
S: **Itli khda brata**
T: **Kit-li bartho (*or* kachikke).**

I have a son.
S: **Itli kha bruna.**
T: **Kit-li abro (*or* kurikko).**

How many sisters do you *(m/f)* have?
S: **Kma khatwate itlokh/itlakh?**
T: **Kmo aḥwotho kit-lokh/kit-lekh?**

How many brothers do you *(m/f)* have?
S: **Kma khonawate itlokh/itlakh?**
T: **Kmo aḥunone kit-lokh/kit-lekh?**

child	s: Shawra; t: na^{c}imo/na^{c}imto
children	*S:* **shawre**; *T:* **na^{c}ime; z^{c}ure**
children *sons*	*S:* **bnune**; *T:* **abne; kurikke**
children *daughters*	*S:* **bnate**; *T:* **bnotho; kachikat**
daughter	*S:* **brata**; *T:* **bartho; kachikke**
son	*S:* **bruna**; *T:* **abro; kurikko**
twins	*S:* **ta'ame**; *T:* **tome; chewi**
mother	*S:* **yimma; yimmi**; *T:* **emo**
father	*S:* **baba; babi**; *T:* **babo**
husband	*S:* **bar zawga**; *T:* **gawro; ba^{c}lo; zlam**
wife	*S:* **bart zawga**; *T:* **athto; zhinnike; pire**
fiancé/fiancée	*S:* **mkhira/mkhirta**; *T:* **mkhiro/ mkhirto; ṭlibo/ṭlibto**
family	*S:* **iqarta**; *T:* **iqartho; 'a'ile; famil**
man	*S:* **gawra**; *T:* **gawro; zlam**
woman	*S:* **at ta**; *T:* **athto; zhinnike; pire**
boy	*S:* **yala**; *T:* **yaludo; kurikko**
girl	*S:* **yalta**; *T:* **bartho; kachikke**
teenager	*S:* **gaduda/gadudta**; *T:* **'laymo/ 'laymtho**
orphan	*S:* **yatuma/yatumta**; *T:* **yatumo/ yatumto**
person	*S:* **qnuma**; *T:* **nosho**
people	*S:* **nashe**; *T:* **noshe**
elder *old person*	*S:* **sawa/sawta**; *T:* **sowo/sawto**
clan	*S:* **sharibta**; *T:* **sharbtho**
ancestors	*S:* **awahata**; *T:* **abohotho**
godfather	*S:* **qariwa; shushbina**; *T:* **shawshbino**

godmother *S:* **qariwta; shushbinta;** *T:* **shawshbintho**

More on family...

Assyrians have a wide range of specialized words for family members. Some of the more common are:

aunt *mother's sister* *S:* **khalta; khalti;** *T:* **ḥulto**
aunt *father's sister* *S:* **dadta; dadti;** *T:* **ʿamtho; dado**
brother *S:* **khona; khoni;** *T:* **aḥuno**
brother-in-law *S:* **barikhmaya;** *T:* **barḥmo**
brother-in-law *married to wife's sister* *S:* **yayisa;** *T:* **ʿadilo**
brother-in-law *sister's husband* *S:* **khitna;** *T:* **yabmo**
father-in-law *S:* **khimyana;** *T:* **ḥemyono**
granddaughter *S:* **nawigta;** *T:* **barbartho; navikke**
grandfather *S:* **sawa; sawi;** *T:* **jiddo**
grandmother *S:* **qashta;** *T:* **qashto**
grandson *S:* **nawigga;** *T:* **barbro; navikko**
mother-in-law *S:* **khmata;** *T:* **ḥmotho**
nephew *brother's son* *S:* **bruna d-khona/khoni;** *T:* **abro d-aḥuno; brasi**
nephew *sister's son* *S:* **bruna d-khati; khwarzayi;** *T:* **abro d-ḥotho; khwarz**
niece *brother's daughter* *S:* **brata d-khona/brata d-khoni;** *T:* **bartho d-aḥuno**
niece *sister's daughter* *S:* **khwarzayti;** *T:* **bartho d-ḥotho**
parents *S:* **awahe;** *T:* **abohe**
sister *S:* **khata/khati;** *T:* **ḥotho**
sister-in-law *brother's sister* *S:* **barikhmayta;** *T:* **barḥmayto**
sister-in-law *wife's sister* *S:* **yayisti;** *T:* **yibemtho**
uncle *mother's brother* *S:* **khala;** *T:* **ḥolo**
uncle *father's brother* *S:* **dada; mama;** *T:* **ʿammo; dodo**

—Religion

What is your *(m/f)* religion?
S: **Mudi la tawditukh/Mudi la tawditakh?**
T: **Mun-yo i-tawdithaydhukh?/Mun-yo i-tawdithaydhekh?**

I *(m/f)* am (a) ... *S:* **Ana ewin/ewan ...**; *T:* **... no.**

Christian *(m/f)* *S:* **Mshikhaya/Mshikhayta**; *T:* **Mshiḥoyo/mshiḥayto**
Orthodox Christian *S:* **Mshikhaya Orthodoksaya/Mshikhayta Orthodoksayta**; *T:* **Orthodoksoyo/Orthodoksayto**
Chaldean Catholic *S:* **Kaldaya/Kaldayta**; *T:* **Kaldoyo/Kaldayto**
Church of the East Christian *S:* **Madinkhaya/Madinkhayta**; *T:* **Madenḥoyo/Madenḥayto**
Catholic *S:* **Qatoliqaya/Qatoliqayta**; *T:* **Qatholiqoyo/Qatholiqayto**
Protestant *S:* **Pruṭaya/ Pruṭayta**; *T:* **Pruṭoyo/Pruṭayto**
Buddhist *S:* **Budaya/Budayta**; *T:* **Budhoyo/Budhayto**
Hindu *S:* **Hindaya/Hindayta**; *T:* **Hendwoyo/Hendwayto**
Jewish *S:* **Yhudhaya/Yhudhayta**; *T:* **Yudhoyo/Yudhayto**
Muslim *S:* **Mushilmana/Mushelmanta**; *T:* **Mashilmono/Mashilmonitho**; **Ṭayo/Ṭayayto**
Sunni *S:* **Sonnaya/Sonnayta**; *T:* **Sunnoyo/Sunnayto**
Shi'i *S:* **Shiᶜaya/Shiᶜayta**; *T:* **Shiᶜoyo/Shiᶜayto**
Sikh *S:* **Sikhaya/Sikhayta**; *T:* **Sikh**
Zoroastrian *S:* **Zardushtaya/Zardushtayta**; *T:* **Zartushtoyo/Zartushtayto**

I *(m/f)* am not religious.
S: **Ana la win mhumna./Ana la wan mhuminta.**
T: **Lat-no tawdithonoyo./Lat-no tawdithonayto.**

4. LANGUAGE

Throughout Mesopotamia, most Assyrians will speak Arabic. Many will also know at least one or more European languages like English or French, while some may also know German. In addition, you will find many speakers of local languages such as Turkish, Kurdish, Farsi (Persian) and Armenian.

Do you *(m/f)* speak English?
S: **Msawtit/Msawtat lishana Englishaya?**
T: **Kibokh/Kibekh mijgholat Inglishoyo?**

Do you speak Assyrian?
S: **Msawtit/Msawtat lishana Aturaya?**
T: **Kibokh/Kibekh mijgholat Surayt (*or* Suryoyo)?**

Do you speak Arabic?
S: **Msawtit/Msawtat lishana ᶜArabaya?**
T: **Kibokh/Kibekh mijgholat ᶜAraboyo?**

Do you speak Armenian?
S: **Msawtit/Msawtat lishana Aremnaya?**
T: **Kibokh/Kibekh mijgholat Arimnoyo?**

Do you speak Azeri?
S: **Msawtit/Msawtat lishana Azari?**
T: **Kibokh/Kibekh mijgholat Azaroyo (*or* Azari)?**

Do you speak Danish?
S: **Msawtit/Msawtat lishana Denmarkaya?**
T: **Kibokh/Kibekh mijgholat Denmarkayo?**

Do you speak Dutch?
S: **Msawtit/Msawtat lishana Holandaya?**
T: **Kibokh/Kibekh mijgholat Holandoyo?**

Do you speak Farsi (Persian)?
S: **Msawtit/Msawtat lishana Parsaya?**
T: **Kibokh/Kibekh mijgholat Forsoyo?**

Do you speak French?
S: **Msawtit/Msawtat lishana Fransaya?**
T: **Kibokh/Kibekh mijgholat Faransoyo?**

Do you speak Georgian?
S: **Msawtit/Msawtat lishana Gorgaya?**
T: **Kibokh/Kibekh mijgholat Grujoyo?**

Do you speak German?
S: **Msawtit/Msawtat lishana Almanaya?**
T: **Kibokh/Kibekh mijgholat Almanoyo?**

Do you speak Greek?
S: **Msaotit/Msawtat lishana Yawnaya?**
T: **Kibokh/Kibekh mijgholat Yawnoyo?**

Do you speak Italian?
S: **Msawtit/Msawtat lishana Iṭalnaya?**
T: **Kibokh/Kibekh mijgholat Iṭaloyo?**

Do you speak Kurdish?
S: **Msawtit/Msawtat lishana Qurdaya?**
T: **Kibokh/Kibekh mijgholat Kurdoyo (*or* Kurmanji)?**

Do you speak Russian?
S: **Msawtit/Msawtat lishana Rusnaya?**
T: **Kibokh/Kibekh mijgholat Rusnoyo**

Do you speak Spanish?
S: **Msawtit/Msawtat lishana Spanyaya?**
T: **Kibokh/Kibekh mijgholat Espanoyo?**

Do you speak Swedish?
S: **Msawtit/Msawtat lishana Swidaya?**
T: **Kibokh/Kibekh mijgholat Swedoyo?**

Do you speak Turkish?
S: **Msawtit/Msawtat lishana ṭurkaya?**
T: **Kibokh/Kibekh mijgholat Turkoyo?**

Does anyone *(m/f)* speak English?
S: **Et kha dmsawit lishana Inglishaya?/Et khda dmsawta lishana Inglishaya?**
T: **Kit ḥa d-kibe mijghil Inglishoyo?**

Does anyone *(m/f)* speak Assyrian?
S: **Et kha dmsawit lishana Aturaya?/Et khda dmsawta lishana Aturaya?**
T: **Kit ḥa d-kibe mijghil Surayt (*or* Suryoyo)?**

I *(m/f)* speak a little ...
S: **Ana msawtin qalil .../Ana msawtan qalil ...**
T: **Kibi mijghalno/mijgholono ushmo (*or* chike) ...**

I *(m/f)* don't speak ...
S: **Ana la yadhin msawtin .../Ana la yadhan masawtan ...**
T: **Laybi mijghalno/k-mijgholono ...**

I *(m/f)* understand.
S: **Ana yparmiyin./Ana yparmiyan.**
T: **Ko-fohamno./Ko-fuhmono.**

I *(m/f)* don't understand.
S: **Ana la yparmiyin./Ana la yparmiyan.**
T: **Lo k-fohamno./Lo k-fuhmono.**

Could you *(m/f)* speak more slowly, please?
S: **Masit msawtit yatir nikha in mbasmalukh?/Masyat msawtat yatir nikha in mbasmalakh?**
T: **Boᶜutho menokh, kibokh mijgholat hedi hedi?/Boᶜutho menekh, kibekh mijgholat hedi hedi?**

Could you *(m/f)* repeat that?
S: **Masit tanitla medre?/Masyat tanyatla medre?**
T: **Kibokh/Kibekh tonat-la (*or* mᶜaydat-la)? *or* Kibokh/Kibekh d-immat-la naqqa ḥreto?**

How do you say ... in Assyrian?
S: **Dakhi y amri ... b-lishana Aturaya?**
T: **Aydarbo kimmutu ... b-Surayt (*or* bu-Suryoyo)?**

What does ... mean?
S: **Mudi le sukala d-...?**
T: **Mun-yo u-sukolo d-...? *or* Mun-yo i-maᶜnaye d-...?**

How do you *(m/f)* pronounce this word?
S: **Dakhi yratmitla/yratmatla hadhe melta?**
T: **Aydarbo ko-rutmutu u-khabrano?**

Please point *(m/f)* to the word in the book.
S: **In mbasmalukh rmoz l-melta go ktawa./In**

mbasmalakh rmoez l-melta go ktawa.
T: **Boʿutho menokh/menekh, maḥway-li u-khabro b-u-kthowo.**

Please wait *(m/f)* while I look up the word.
s: said by a male: **ʿWod/ʿWoed ṭaybo ontur hal d-khazinna melta.**; *said by a female:*
ʿWod/ʿWoed ṭaybo ontur hal d-khazyanna melta.
T: said by a male: **Boʿutho menokh/menekh, nṭar hul d-ḥozeno i-meltho** (*or* **u-khabro**).; *said by a female:* **Boʿutho menokh/menekh, nṭar hul d-ḥuzyono i-meltho** (*or* **u-khabro**).

I *(m/f)* speak ...
s: **Ana msawtin/Ana msawtan lishana ...**
T: **Kibi mijghalno/mijgholono ...**

English	*s:* **Englishaya**; *T:* **Inglishoyo**
Assyrian	*s:* **Aturaya**; *T:* **Surayt; Suryoyo**
Arabic	*s:* **ʿArabaya**; *T:* **ʿAraboyo**
Armenian	*s:* **Aremnaya**; *T:* **Arimnoyo**
Azeri	*s:* **Azaraya**; *T:* **Azaroyo; Azari**
Danish	*s:* **Denmarkaya**; *T:* **Danmarkoyo**
Dutch	*s:* **Holandaya**; *T:* **Holandoyo**
Farsi	*s:* **Parsaya**; *T:* **Forsoyo**
French	*s:* **Fransaya**; *T:* **Faransoyo**
Georgian	*s:* **Gorgaya**; *T:* **Grujoyo**
German	*s:* **Almanaya**; *T:* **Almanoyo**
Greek	*s:* **Yawnaya**; *T:* **Yawnoyo**
Hindi	*s:* **Hindawaya**; *T:* **Hendwoyo; Hindi**
Italian	*s:* **Iṭalyaya**; *T:* **Iṭaloyo**
Japanese	*s:* **Yabanaya**; *T:* **Japanoyo**
Kurdish	*s:* **Qurdaya**; *T:* **Kurdoyo; Kurmanji**
Russian	*s:* **Orisnaya**; *T:* **Rusoyo**
Spanish	*s:* **Spanyaya**; *T:* **Espanoyo**
Swedish	*s:* **Swidaya**; *T:* **Swedoyo**
Turkish	*s:* **ṭurkaya**; *T:* **Turkoyo**
language	s: **lishana**; t: **leshono**
dialect	*s:* **leʿza**; *T:* **leʿzo; lahje**
accent	*s:* **sawada**; *T:* **swodo**

5. BUREAUCRACY

Note that many of these terms are for reference only since you will not encounter any civil administrative documents written in Aramaic. There is no Assyrian administrative body and Aramaic is not recognized at official levels. Any forms you encounter will be written in Turkish, Arabic, Persian, Kurdish, or English.

name	*S:* **shima**; *T:* **ishmo**
surname	*S:* **kunaya**; *T:* **kunoyo; shumoho**
address	*S:* **munaʿa**; *T:* **mḥawyonutho**
date of birth	*S:* **siqum mawlada**; *T:* **siqumo d-mawlodo**
place of birth	*S:* **dukat moalada**; *T:* **duktho d-mawlodo**
nationality	*S:* **matayuta**; *T:* **umthoyutho; ṭuhmo**
citizenship	*S:* **matayota**; *T:* **athroyutho**
age	*S:* **ʿomra**; *T:* **ʿumro**
sex: male	*S:* **dikhra**; *T:* **dekhro**
female	*S:* **atta**; *T:* **neqwo**
religion	*S:* **tawdita**; *T:* **tawditho; din**
reason for travel:	*S:* **ʿelta d-khzuqya**; *T:* **ʿeltho du-krukhyo; ʿeltho d-so'urutho**
business	*S:* **tagharuta**; *T:* **tagorutho**
tourism	*S:* **krukhya**; *T:* **karokhutho; turizm**
work	*S:* **shoghla**; *T:* **shughlo**
personal	*S:* **qnumaya**; *T:* **farṣufoyo**
visit	*S:* **saʿuruta**; *T:* **soʿurutho**
profession	*S:* **umanuta**; *T:* **fulḥono; umonutho**
marital status:	*S:* **ituta zawganayta**; *T:* **ithutho zuwoghayto**
single	*S:* **la gwira/la gwirta**; *T:* **ʿazbo/ʿazbtho**
married	*S:* **gwira/gwirta**; *T:* **gawiro/gawirto**

divorced	*S:* **rupa/rupita**; *T:* **marfiyo/ marfayto**
date	*S:* **siquma**; *T:* **siqumo**
date of arrival	*S:* **siqum mṭayta**; *T:* **siqumo d-mathyo**
date of departure	*S:* **siqum ṭyasa**; *T:* **siqumo d-mazlo**
passport	*S:* **maᶜbar tkhuma**; *T:* **saqro; jawaz; pasaport**
passport number	*S:* **raqma d-maᶜbar tkhuma**; *T:* **menyono d-saqro**
visa	*S:* **visa**; *T:* **maᶜbar-tḥume; viza**
currency	*S:* **zoze**; *T:* **zuze**

—Getting around

What does this *(m/f)* mean?
S: **Mudi le sukala d-aha/hadhe?**
T: **Mun-yo u-sukolo d-hano/hathe?**

Where is ...'s office?
S: **Ika le makhitwa d-...?**
T: **Ayko-yo makhtwo d-...?**

Which floor is it on?
S: **ᶜAl mud medhyara**
T: **ᶜAl ayna medyoro (*or* ṭabaq *or* qaṭ) yo?**

Does the elevator work?
S: **Masqana plakha le?**
T: **U-maᶜlyono (*or* asansur) k-shoghil?**

Is Mr./Mrs./Miss ... in?
S: **Mayqra ... lakha le?/Myoqarta... lakha la?**
T: **Myaqro/Myaqartho ... harke-yo?**

Please *(m/f)* tell him/her that ...
S: **In basmalukh, mure/mura d-...**
T: **Boᶜutho menokh, mar-le/mar-la .../Boᶜutho menekh, mar-le/mar-la d-...**

... I *(m/f)* have arrived.
S: **... ana miṭya win./... ana mṭita wan**
T: **... maṭino./... maṭyono.**

... I *(m/f)* am here.
S: **... ana lakha win/wan.**
T: **... harke-no.**

I *(m/f)* can't wait, I *(m/f)* have an appointment.
S: **Ana le masin saprin itli kha shudaya./Ana le masyan sapran itli kha shudaya.**
T: **Laybi noṭarno/nuṭrono, kitli wa^{c}do (*or* maw^{c}ad).**

Tell him/her that I was here.
S: said by a male: **Mure/Mura d-ana lakha winwa.**; *said by a female:* **Mure/Mura d-ana lakha ewanwa.**
T: **Mar-le/Mar-la d-harke-we-no.** *or* **Mar-le/Mar-la d-kit-wi harke.**

6. TRAVEL

PUBLIC TRANSPORT – The most practical way to get around is via the numerous privately run shared taxis or minibuses (called *S:* **raghiyaṭ aghra**, *T:* **servis**) which stop at pre-determined pick-up points. You either pay the driver or his assistant (if he has one) after alighting. Individual taxis are also a good way to get around, though they are costlier. Longer distance travel out of town offers you the usual variety of means. In Turkey and Syria, there are now car rental firms, offering you vehicles with or without drivers. You may also hire a driver privately. Rates vary. Buses are reliable and leave from specially designated areas. Throughout Mesopotamia travel by rail is rare, except in Iraq. Note that all public announcements are made in the country's offical language (e.g. Arabic, Persian, Kurdish or Turkish). Bicycles and motorbikes are easier to find in Syria, though in the rugged Tur-Abdin terrain they can often be impractical.

What time does ... leave?
S: **B-mud shaʿta b-aza/b-azil?**
T: **B-ayna shoʿtho ... gid-othe/gid-uthyo?**

What time does ... arrive?
S: **B-mud shaʿta bmaṭya/bmaṭe?**
T: **B-ayna shoʿtho ... gid-azze/gid-azza?**

the airplane	s: **ṭayasta**; t: **i-ṭayisto**; **i-ṭiyare**
the boat	*S:* **spinta**; *T:* **i-sfinto**; **i-gamiye**; **u-elfo**
the bus	*S:* **basa**; *T:* **u-baṣ**; **u-autobus**
the train	*S:* **qṭara**; *T:* **u-qṭoro**; **u-qiṭar**

The plane is delayed.
S: **Ṭayasta mshukharta la.**
T: **I-ṭayisto meshtawḥarto-yo.**

The plane is canceled.
S: **ʿṬi la ṭayasta.**
T: **I-ṭayisto mbaṭela.**

The train is delayed.
S: **Qṭara mshukhira le.**
T: **U-qṭoro meshtawḥro-yo.**

The train is canceled.
S: **ʿṬi le qṭara.**
T: **U-qṭoro mbaṭele.**

How long will it be delayed?
S: **Kma b-mshawkhir/b-mshawkhira?**
T: **Miqqa gid-meshtawḥar/gid-meshtawḥro?**

There is a delay of ... minutes.
S: **Et shukhara d-qatinyate ...**
T: **Kit meshtawḥronutho d-... qaṭinyotho.**

There is a delay of ... hours.
S: **Et shukhara d-shaʿe ...**
T: **Kit meshtawḥronutho d-... shoʿe (*or* saʿat).**

Excuse me, where is the ticket office?
S: **Pakhalta ika le/la makhitwa d-pitqe?**
T: **Shubqono, ayko-yo u-makhtwo da-fetqe?**

Where can I *(m/f)* buy a ticket?
S: **Ika masin zawnin l-khda pitqa?/Ika masyan d-zawnan l-khda pitqa?**
T: **Ayko kibi zowanno/zownono fetqo?**

I *(m/f)* want to go to ...
S: **Bayin azin l-.../Bayan d-azan l-...**
T: **K-obaʿno/K-ubʿono d-azzino l-...**

I want a ticket to ...
S: **Bayin/Bayan khda pitqa qa ...**
T: **K-obaʿno/K-ubʿono fetqo l-...**

I *(m/f)* would like ...
S: **Bayin .../Bayan ...**
T: **K-obaʿno .../K-ubʿono ...**

a one-way ticket *S:* **pitqa d-zalta balkhud**; *T:* **fetqo d-mazlo balḥud**
a return ticket *S:* **pitqa d-zalta o d-ʿarta**; *T:* **fetqo du-dʿoro (mazlo w-mathyo)**
first class *S:* **sidra qamaya**; *T:* **dargho qamoyo**
second class *S:* **sidra traeyana**; *T:* **dargho trayono**

Can I *(m/f)* pay in dollars?
S: **Masin parin b-dolare?/Masyan pariyan b-dolare?**
T: **Kibi mdafaᶜno/mdafᶜono b-dolare?**

You *(m/f)* must pay in dollars.
S: **Wale d-parit/d-pariyat b-dolare.**
T: **K-lozim mdafᶜat b-dolare.**

You *(m/f)* can pay in dollars.
S: **Masit parit b-dolare./Masyat pariyat b-dolare.**
T: **Kibokh/kibekh mdafᶜat b-dolare.**

Can I *(m/f)* reserve a place?
S: **Masin duqini dukta?/Masyan duqani dukta?**
T: **Kibi mḥajazno/mḥajzono duktho?**

How long does the trip take?
S: **Kma b-garsha orkha?**
T: **U-krukhyo miqqa ko-goresh?**

Is it a direct route?
S: **Orkha trista la?**
T: **Kit darbo msawyo (***or* **direkt)?**

—By air

Is there a flight to ...?
S: **Et tawsa qa ...**
T: **Kit fyoro l-...?**

When is the next flight to ...?
S: **Iman bhawe ṭawsa qamaya qa ...?**
T: **Ema-yo u-fyoro ḥreno l-...?**

How long is the flight?
S: **Kma bgarish ṭawsa?**
T: **Miqqa ko-goresh u-fyoro?**

What is the flight number?
S: **Mudi le raqma d-ṭawsa?**
T: **Mun-yo u-menyono (***or* **raqmo) du-fyoro?**

You *(m/f)* must check in at ...
S: **Wale d-ᶜawrit m-gaw ...**
T: **K-lozim mikothwat ruḥokh/ruḥekh b-...**

Is the flight delayed?
S: **Ṭawsa mshukhira le?**
T: **U-fyoro meshtawḥro-yo?**

How long is the flight delayed?
S: **Ṭawsa qa kma le mshukhira?**
T: **Miqqa gid-meshtawḥar u-fyoro?**

Is this the flight for ...?
S: **Aha le haw tawsa d-qa ...?**
T: **U-fyoro l-... hano-yo?**

When is the London flight arriving?
S: **Eman maṭe tawsa d-min London?**
T: **Ema gid-othe u-fyoro d-Londra?**

Is it on time?
S: **Mṭaya le bʿdana?**
T: **Bu-zabnaydhe-yo?**

Is it late?
S: **Mshukhira le?**
T: **Meshtawḥro-yo?**

Do I *(m/f)* have to change planes?
S: **Wale d-mshakhlipin l-ṭayastyate?**
T: **K-lozim mshaḥlafno/mshaḥilfono ṭayisyotho?**

Has the plane left Los Angeles yet?
S: **Sṭita la ṭayasta min Los Angeles?**
T: **I-ṭayisto hesh lo qayimo me Los Angeles?**

What time does the plane take off?
S: **B-mud shaʿta b-parkha ṭayasta?**
T: **B-ayna shoʿtho gid-qaymo i-ṭayisto?**

What time do we arrive in Baghdad?
S: **B-mud shaʿta b-matikh l-Baghdad?**
T: **B-ayna shoʿtho g-moṭina l-Boghdod?**

excess baggage *S:* **mawble laʿube**; *T:* **sefoqe zoyude**
international flight *S:* **ṭawsa baynat matanaya**; *T:* **fyoro tibeloyo**
internal/domestic flight *S:* **ṭawsa gawaya**; *T:* **fyoro gawonoyo**

—By bus

bus stop	*S:* **klayta d-basa;** *T:* **beth-kloyo du-baṣ**
bus station	*S:* **nuqazta d-base;** *T:* **mashryo du-baṣ**

Where is the bus stop/station?
S: **Ika ela klayta d-basa/nuqazta d-base?**
T: **Ayko-yo u-beth-kloyo/mashryo du-baṣ?**

Take me to the bus station.
S: **Labil li l-nuqazta d-base.**
T: **Mawbeli lu-mashryo du-baṣ.**

Which bus goes to ...?
S: **Ayni basa eyazil l-...**
T: **Ayna baṣ k-izze l-...?**

Does this bus go to ...?
S: **Aha basa yazil l-...**
T: **U-baṣ-ano k-izze l-...?**

How often do buses leave?
S: **Kud kma base y-pashṭi?**
T: **Kul kmo k-izzin a-baṣe?**

What time is the ... bus?
S: **Ṣ-haᶜta d-kma bate basa ...?**
T: **U-baṣ ... b-ayna shoᶜtho gid-othe?**

next	*S:* **d-bitaya le;** *T:* **ḥreno**
first	*S:* **qamaya;** *T:* **qamoyo**
last	*S:* **kharaya;** *T:* **ḥaroyo**

Will you *(m/f)* let me know when we get to ...?
S: **Masit maditli/Masyat madiyatli eman d-maṭikh ...?**
T: **Kibokh/Kibekh mawdhᶜatli ema d-moṭina l-...?**

Stop, I *(m/f)* want to get off!
S: **Kli bayin d-nakhtin!/Kli bayan d-nakhtan!**
T: **Klay, k-obaᶜno noḥatno!/Klay, k-ubᶜono nuḥtono!**

Where can I *(m/f)* get a bus to ...?
S: **Ika masin shaqlin basa qa ...?/Ika masyan shaqlaan basa qa...?**
T: **Ayko kibi moyadno/maydono baṣ d-k-izze l-...?**

When is the first bus to ...?
S: **Iman b-ate basa qamaya qa ...?**
T: **U-baṣ qamoyo d-k-izze l-... ema-yo?**

When is the last bus to ...?
S: **Iman bate basa kharaya qa ...**
T: **U-baṣ ḥaroyo d-k-izze l-... ema-yo?**

When is the next bus to ...?
S: **Baṣa d-aᶜqip eman bate...**
T: **U-baṣ ḥreno d-k-izze l-... ema-yo?**

Do I *(m/f)* have to change buses?
S: **Wale d-shakhlipin l-base?**
T: **K-lozim mshaḥlafno/mshaḥilfono baṣṣat?**

How long is the journey?
S: **Kma y garsha urkha?**
T: **U-krukhyo miqqa ko-goresh?**

What is the fare?
S: **Kma le dmaeya durkha?**
T: **Miqqa-yo u-aghro?**

I *(m/f)* want to get off at ...
S: **Bayin nakhtin go.../Bayan nakhtan go...**
T: **K-obaᶜno noḥatno b-.../K-ubᶜono nuḥtono b-...**

Please *(m/f)* let me off at the next stop.
S: **In mbasmalukh/mbasmalakh, mankhitli ᶜal klayta d-bitaya la.**
T: **Boᶜutho menokh/menekh, manḥat-li ᶜal u-beth-kloyo ḥreno.**

Please *(m/f)* let me off here.
S: **In mbasmalukh/mbasmalakh, mankhitli lakha.**
T: **Boᶜutho menokh/menekh, manḥat-li harke.**

I need my luggage, please *(m/f)* .
S: —said by a male: **In mbasmalukh/mbasmalakh, bayin wa lmawbli.**; *—said by a female:* **In mbasmalukh/mbasmalakh, bayan wa lmawbli.**
T: **Boᶜutho menokh/menekh, a-sefoqaydhi g-luzmi-li.**

That's my bag.
S: **Hadhe ṣimdhi la.**
T: **Ṣemdaydhi-yo (*or* jantaydhi-yo) hayo.**

—By rail

Passengers must ...
S: **Rakawe wale ...**
T: **A-ḥozuqe k-lozim ...**

... change trains.
S: **... d-shakhlipi l-qṭare.**
T: **... mshaḥilfi qṭore.**

... change platforms.
S: **... d-shakhlipi l-maṣṭawta.**
T: **... mshaḥilfi roṣifotho (*or* raṣif).**

Is there a timetable?
S: **It surgada d-ᶜdanate**
T: **Kit surgodho da-zabne?**

Is this the right platform for ...?
S: **Hadhe maṣṭawta trista la qa ...?**
T: **Hathe-yo i-raṣifto d-...?**

The train leaves from platform ...
S: **Qṭara ypaliṭ min maṣṭawta ...**
T: **... gid-izze u-qṭoro mi-roṣifto.**

Take me to the railway station.
S: **Labil li l-nuqazta d-qṭare.**
T: **Mawbeli lu-beth-qṭoro.**

Where can I *(m/f)* buy tickets?
S: **M-ika masin zonin l-pitqe?/M-ika masyan zonan l-pitqe?**
T: **M-ayko kibi zowanno/zownono fetqe?**

Which platform should I *(m/f)* go to?
S: **L-ayni maṣṭawta wale d-azin/d-azan?**
T: **ᶜAl ayna roṣifto k-lozim azzino?**

platform one/platform two
S: **maṣṭawta d-kha; maṣṭawta d-tre**
T: **roṣifto qamayto; roṣifto trayonitho**

You *(m/f)* must change trains at ...
S: **Wale d-mshakhlipit l-qṭare gaw .../Wale mshakhlipat l-qṭare gaw ...**
T: **K-lozim mshaḥilfat qṭore b-...**

Will the train leave on time?
S: **Qṭara pshaṭa le b-daᶜne?**
T: **U-qṭoro bu-zabnayde gid-izze?**

There will be a delay of ... minutes.
S: **Bhawe shukhara dkma ... qaṭinyate.**
T: **Gid-huyo meshtawḥronutho d-... qaṭinyotho.**

There will be a delay of ... hours.
S: **Bhawe shukhara d-kma ... shaᶜe.**
T: **Gid-huyo meshtawḥronutho d-... shoᶜe.**

—By taxi

Some taxis are marked, while others are not. To avoid unpleasant surprises, agree to fares in advance. It is useful to be able to tell the driver your destination in Aramaic, Turkish, Arabic, Persian or Kurdish (or have it written down on a piece of paper). Be warned, however, that some drivers may have as little idea as you as the precise whereabouts of your destination.

Taxi! *S:* **Taksi!**; *T:* **Taksi!**

Where can I *(m/f)* get a taxi?
S: **M-ika masin dawqin taksi?/M-ika masyan dawqin taksi?**
T: **M-ayko kibi moyadno/maydono taksi?**

Please could you *(m/f)* get me a taxi?
S: **In mbasmalukh, masit dawqitli kha taksi?/In mbasmalakh, masyat dawqitli kha taksi?**
T: **Boᶜutho menokh, kibokh maydat-li taksi?/ Boᶜutho menekh, kibekh maydat-li taksi?**

Can you *(m/f)* take me to ...?
S: **Masit lablitli l-...?/Masyat lablat li l-...?**
T: **Kibokh/Kibekh mawblat-li l-...?**

How much will it cost to ...?
S: **Kma le d-maeya l-...?**
T: **Miqqa ko-mosek m-arke hul ...?**

To this address, please *(m/f)*.
S: **ʿAl aha munaʿa, in mbasmalukh/mbasmalakh.**
T: **ʿAl i-mḥawyonuth-athe, boʿutho menokh/menekh.**

Turn *(m/f)* left.
S: **Ptul/Ptoel l-simala.**
T: **Bram lu-semolo.**

Turn *(m/f)* right.
S: **Ptul/Ptoel l-yamina**
T: **Bram lu-yamino.**

Go *(m/f)* straight ahead.
S: **Ṣi tris./Ṣe tris.**
T: **Zokh msawyo./Zekh msawyo.**

Here is fine, thank you *(m/f)* .
S: **Lakhkha ṭawta ela, tawdi.**
T: **Harke tamam-yo, tawdi.**

The next corner, please.
S: **L-qurnita d-bitaya la in mbasmalukh/mbasmalakh.**
T: **I-qurnitho ḥreto, boʿutho menokh/menekh.**

The next street to the left.
S: **Qayṭona d-bitaya le l-ṣimala.**
T: **U-shqoqo hreno ʿal u-semolo.**

The next street to the right.
S: **Qayṭona d-bitaya le l-yamina.**
T: **U-shqoqo hreno ʿal u-yamino.**

Stop *(m/f)*!
S: **Kli!/Klay!**; *T:* **Klay!**

Don't stop *(m/f)*!
S: **La kalit!/La kalyat!**; *T:* **Lo kolat!**

I'm *(m/f)* in a hurry.
S: **Msarhuwe wen./Msarhuwe wan.**
T: **Ko-malizno./Ko-malizono.**

Please *(m/f)* drive slowly!
S: **In mbasmalukh, rdi b-nikhuta!/In mbas-malakh, rde b-nikhuta!**
T: **Kedi hedi qlaᶜ boᶜutho menokh/menekh!**

Stop *(m/f)* here!
S: **Kli lakha!/Kle lakha!**
T: **Klay harke!**

Stop *(m/f)* the car, I want to get out.
S: *—said by a male:* **Makli/Makle l-radita bayin nakhtin./***—said by a female:* **Makli/Makle l-radita bayan nakhtan.**
T: *—said by a male:* **Maklay i-radhayto, k-obaᶜno nofaqno./***—said by a female:* **Maklay i-radhay-to, k-ubᶜono nufqono.**

Please wait *(m/f)* here.
S: **Nṭor lakha, in mbasmalukh./Nṭoer lakha, in mbasmalakh.**
T: **Boᶜutho menokh/menekh, nṭar harke.**

Please *(m/f)* take me to the airport.
S: **ᶜWod/ᶜWoed tawta labilli lbet-tawsa.**
T: **Boᶜutho menokh/menekh, mawbeli lu-beth-ṭawso.**

—General phrases

I *(m/f)* want to get off at ...
S: **Bayin nakhtin go .../Bayan nakhtan go ...**
T: **K-obaᶜno noḥatno b-.../K-ubᶜono nuḥtono b-...**

Excuse me!
S: **Pakhalta!**
T: **Shubqono!**

Excuse me, may I *(m/f)* get by?
S: **Pakhalta, masin ᶜawrin?/Pakhalta, masyan ᶜawraan?**
T: **Shubqono, kibi shofaᶜno/shufᶜono?**

I *(m/f)* want to get out of the bus.
S: **Bayin nakhtin min baṣa./Bayan nakhtan min baṣa.**
T: **K-obaʿno nofaqno min baṣa./K-ubʿono nufqono min baṣa.**

These are my bags.
S: **An na ṣimdhi laye.**
T: **As-sefoq-ani didhi-ne.**

Please *(m/f)* put them there.
S: **In mbasmalukh/mbasmalakh, matu lay lakha.**
T: **Boʿutho menokh/menekh, maḥeten tamo.**

Is this seat free?
S: **Aha kursiya spiqa le?**
T: **U-kursi-ano khalyo-yo?**

I *(m/f)* think that's my seat.
S: **Bikhsha win aha kursiyi le./Bikhshawa wan aha kursiyi le.**
T: **Ko-ḥoshawno/Ko-ḥushwono u-kursi-awo didhi-yo.**

—Travel words

airport tax	*S:* **makhsa d-bet-ṭawsa**; *T:* **makso du-beth-ṭawso; sheqlo du-beth-ṭawso**
airport	*S:* **bet-ṭawsa**; *T:* **beth-ṭawso**
ambulance	*S:* **radita d-awoshpa**; *T:* **radhayto d-ʿudrono**
arrivals	*S:* **moṭaya**; *T:* **athoye**
bag	*S:* **ṣemda**; *T:* **ṣemdo; janṭa**
baggage counter	*S:* **nuqazta d-mawble**; *T:* **fuṣolo da-sefoqe**
baggage	*S:* **mawble**; *T:* **sefoqe; ṣemde**
bicycle	*S:* **tangighla**; *T:* **daruktho; tengighlo; bisiklet**
boarding pass	*S:* **pitqa d-rkawta**; *T:* **fetqo d-suloqo**
boat	*S:* **elpa**; *T:* **elfo; sfinto**
border	*S:* **tkhuma**; *T:* **tḥumo**
bus stop	*S:* **klayta d-baṣa**; *T:* **beth-kloyo du-baṣ**
camel	*S:* **gamla**; *T:* **gamlo**
car	*S:* **radita**; *T:* **radhayto**

check-in counter	*S:* **nuqzta d-ma^{c}la**; *T:* **fuṣolo du-qubolo; di-makhtwonutho**
closed	*S:* **skhira/skhirta**; *T:* **skhiro/skhirto**
customs	*S:* **makhse**; *T:* **makso; gumruk**
delay	*S:* **shukhara**; *T:* **meshtawḥronutho**
departures	*S:* **ezla**; *T:* **azole**
dining car	*S:* **^{c}agholta d-mukhla**; *T:* **markawtho di-shorutho; markawtho du-muklo**
donkey	*S:* **khmara**; *T:* **ḥmoro**
emergency exit	*S:* **mapqa ^{c}riṣa**; *T:* **mafqo di-aliṣutho**
entrance	*S:* **ma^{c}la**; *T:* **ma^{c}bro**
exit	*S:* **mapqa**; *T:* **mafqo**
express	*S:* **ba^{c}ghal**; *T:* **khayifo; msarhwo; ekspres**
ferry	*S:* **spenta**; *T:* **ma^{c}bro**
foot: on foot	*S:* **halkha**; *T:* **malkho**
4-wheel drive	*S:* **ridhya d-arba^c gighle**; *T:* **jip; landkruz**
frontier	*S:* **tkhube**; *T:* **tḥumo**
helicopter	*S:* **ṭayupta**; *T:* **ṭayofto**
horse and cart	*S:* **markawta d-sosye**; *T:* **susyo w-^{c}oghaltho**
horse	*S:* **susya**; *T:* **susyo**
information	*S:* **mawdh^{c}anuta**; *T:* **mawd^{c}onutho**
ladies/gents	*S:* **mayqre/mayqrata**; *T:* **neshe/gawre**
local	*S:* **bshawuta**; *T:* **dukthonoyo/dukthonayto**
lorry/truck	*S:* **lori**; *T:* **lori**
luggage	*S:* **mawble**; *T:* **sefoqe**
minibus	*S:* **baṣa z^{c}ora**; *T:* **dolmush; servis**
motorbike	*S:* **mzighla**; *T:* **mzighlo; moṭorsiklet; moṭor**
mule	*S:* **kawidna**; *T:* **baghlo; kudhanyo**
no entry	*S:* **layt ma^{c}la**; *T:* **layto ^{c}boro**
no smoking	*S:* **layt tnana**; *T:* **layt tenunto**
open	*S:* **ptikha/ptikhta**; *T:* **ftiḥo**
platform number	*S:* **raqma d-maṣṭawta**; *T:* **menyono d-roṭifto**

railway	*S:* **sika d-prezla**; *T:* **sektho d-farzlo**
reserved	*S:* **dwiqa/dwiqta**; *T:* **nṭiro/nṭirto**
road	*S:* **urkha**; *T:* **darbo**
sign	*S:* **ata**; *T:* **remzo**; **otho**
sleeping car	*S:* **ʿaghulta d-dmakha**; *T:* **markawtho du-dmokho**
station	*S:* **nuqazta**; *T:* **mashryo** *or* **mashritho**; **beth-waʿdo**
subway	*S:* **naqwa d-halkha**; *T:* **nafqo (darbo taḥt di-arʿo)**
ticket office	*S:* **makhitwa d-pitqe**; *T:* **makhtwo da-fetqe**
timetable	*S:* **surgada**; *T:* **surgodho da-zabne**
toilet(s)	*S:* **bet-silya**; *T:* **beth-mayo/bote da-maye**; **tuwaylet**
town center	*S:* **qunṭrun d-mdita**; *T:* **qenṭrun di-mdhitho**
train station	*S:* **nuqazta d-qṭara**; *T:* **mashritho du-qṭoro**
travel	*S:* **krukhya**; *T:* **krukhyo**
truck	*S:* **shaqulta**; *T:* **kamyon**
van	*S:* **van**; *T:* **van**

—Disabilities

wheelchair	*S:* **kursiya d-gighle**; *T:* **kursyo da-gighle**
disabled	*S:* **khghira/khghirta**; *T:* **shaflo/shfaltho**; **shaḥto/shaḥte**

Do you *(m/f/pl)* have seats for the disabled?
S: **Etlokh/Etlakh/Etlokhon mawtwe qa khghire?**
T: **Kitkhu kursye lajan da-shafle?**

Do you *(m/f/pl)* have access for the disabled?
S: **Etlokh/Etlakh/Etlokhon urkha qa khghire?**
T: **Kitkhu ʿboro fshiṭo lajan da-shafle?**

Do you *(m/f/pl)* have facilities for the disabled?
S: **Etlokh/Etlakh/Etlokhon suyaʿe qa khghire?**
T: **Kitkhu fshiqwotho lajan da-shafle?**

7. ACCOMMODATION

The hotel and guesthouse network in Turkey and Syria is rapidly being developed, and is steadily being rebuilt in Iraq. Should adequate accommodation be found away from the major towns, you will find that room service is not available, and breakfast or other meals will have to be negotiated and paid for separately. An excellent option in more rural areas is to have your accommodation arranged at a monastery or private house, where traditional hospitality will guarantee that you are well looked after and, as always for Assyrians, well-fed. In these cases a modest contribution or donation is expected. A few places in Turkey offer details of their services and location on the internet.

I *(m/f)* am looking for a ...
S: **Ṭawuye win bar.../Ṭawuye wan bar...**
T: **Ko-korakhno l-.../Ko-kurkhono l-...**

guesthouse	*S:* **ashpaza**; *T:* **bayto da-dhayfe; qonuq-ewi**
hotel	*S:* **bet-bawta**; *T:* **hotel; beth-mashryo; fundqo**
hostel	*S:* **mashrita d-bawta**; *T:* **mashryo; pansiyon**

Is there anywhere I *(m/f)* can stay for the night?
S: **Et dokta d-pyashta qa lilya?**
T: **Kit duktho d-foyashno/d-fayshono u-lalyano?**

Where is a ... hotel?
S: **Ika it kha bet-bawta ...?**
T: **Ayko kit hotel ...?**

cheap	*S:* **shawya**; *T:* **lo ṭimo; arzon; rakhis**
good	*S:* **ṭawa**; *T:* **ṭowo**
nearby	*S:* **qariwa**; *T:* **qariwo**

accommodation *S:* **shrayta**; *T:* **shroyo**

What is the address?
S: **Mudi le munaʿa?**
T: **Mun-yo i-mḥawyonutho?**

Could you *(m/f)* write the address please?
S: **Masit katwit le munaᶜa, in mbasmalokh?/Masyat katwat le munaᶜa, in mbasmalakh?**
T: **Boᶜutho menokh kibokh kuthwat i-mḥawyonutho?/Boᶜutho menekh kibekh kuthwat i-mḥawyonutho?**

—At the hotel

Do you *(pl)* have any rooms free?
S: **Itlokhon tawane spiqe?**
T: **Kitkhu qlayotho (*or* odat) khalye?**

I *(m/f)* would like ...
S: **Bayin .../Bayan ...**
T: **K-obaᶜno .../K-ubᶜono ...**

... a single room *S:* **... khda tawana zᶜorta**; *T:* **... qelayto ḥdonayto**
... a double room *S:* **... khda tawana rabta**; *T:* **... qelayto mezdawagto**

We'd like a room.
S: **Bayikh khda tawana.**
T: **K-ubᶜina qelayto (*or* oda) ḥdho.**

We'd like two rooms.
S: **Bayikh tre tawane.**
T: **K-ubᶜina tarte qlayotho (*or* tarte odat).**

I *(m/f)* want a room with ...
S: **Bayin/Bayan khda tawana d-hawila...**
T: **K-obaᶜno/K-ubᶜono qelayto ᶜam ...**

a bathroom	*S:* **bet-khmama**; *T:* **beth-ḥyofo; ḥammam**
a shower	*S:* **raṣuṣa**; *T:* **dush**
a television	*S:* **makhizyana**; *T:* **frus-ḥezwo; telvizyon**
a window	*S:* **kawe**; *T:* **kawtho; shaboko**
a double bed	*S:* **ᶜarsa roikha**; *T:* **gale mezdawgo**
a balcony	*S:* **gdanpa**; *T:* **balqon**
a view	*S:* **khizwa**; *T:* **ḥezwo; manzar**

I *(m/f)* want a room that's quiet.
S: **Ana bayin/bayan khda tawana d-hawya shlita.**
T: **K-obaʿno/K-ubʿono qelayto (***or* **oda) shlitho.**

How long will you *(m/f/pl)* be staying?
S: said to one person: **Qa kma bayit payshet?/ Qa kma bayat payshat?/***said to more than one person:* **Qa kma bayitun payshitun?**
T: said to one person: **Miqqa g-fayshat?/***said to more than one person:* **Miqqa g-fayshitu?**

How many nights?
S: **Kma lelawate?**
T: **Kmo lalye?**

I'm *(m/f)* going to stay for ...
S: **Ana bed payshin/payshan qa ...**
T: **G-foyashno .../G-fayshono ...**

... one day	*S:* **... kha yuma**; *T:* **... yawmo**
... two days	*S:* **... tre yume**; *T:* **... tre yawme**
... one week	*S:* **... kha shawoʿa**; *T:* **... shabtho**

Do you *(m/f)* have any I.D.?
S: **Etlokh/Etlakh hyayuta?**
T: **Kitlokh/Kitlekh fetqo d-hiyoyutho mede?**

Sorry, we're full.
S: **Pakhalta litlan dokta pyasha.**
T: **Shubqono, lat-lan duktho.**

I *(m/f)* have a reservation.
S: **Ana itli nṭiruta.**
T: **Kit-li nṭirutho (***or* **ḥajiz).**

We have a reservation.
S: **Itlan Nṭiruta**
T: **Kit-lan nṭirutho (***or* **ḥajiz).**

I *(m/f)* have to meet someone here.
S: **Wale d-tapqin/d-tapqan ʿam kha nasha lakh.**
T: **K-lozim loqeno/luqyono b-nosho harke.**

ACCOMMODATION

My name is ...
S: **Shimi ile.**
T: **Ishmi ... yo.**

May I *(m/f)* speak to the manager, please?
S: **Masyin msawtin msoatan ʿam mdabrana, in mbasmalokh/mbasmalakh?/Masyin masyan msoatan ʿam mdabrana, in mbasmalokh/ mbasmalakh?**
T: **Boʿutho menaykhu, kibi mijghalno ʿam u-mdabrono/i-mdabronitho?/Boʿutho menaykhu, kibi mijgholono ʿam u-mdabrono/ i-mdabronitho?**

How much is it per night?
S: **Kma le d-maeya d-kol lale?**
T: **U-lalyo b-miqqa-yo?**

How much is it per person?
S: **Kma le d-maeya d-kul qnuma?**
T: **B-miqqa-yo l-kul farṣufo (***or* **shakhs** *or* **nafar)?**

How much is it per week?
S: **Kma le d-maeya kul shawoʿa?**
T: **I-shabtho b-miqqa-yo?**

It's ... per night.
S: **Kul lale ile ...**
T: **Kul lalyo b-... yo.**

It's ... per person.
S: **Kul qnuma ile ...**
T: **Kul farṣufo b-... yo.**

It's ... per week.
S: **Ṣ-hawoʿa ile ...**
T: **Kul shabtho b-... yo.**

Can I see it *(m/f)*?
S: said by a male: **Masin khazine/khazina?**/*said by a female:* **Masyan khazyane/khazyana?**
T: said by a male: **Kibi ḥozeno-le/ḥozeno-la?**/*said by a female:* **Kibi ḥuzyalle/ḥuzyalla?**

Are there any others?
S: **Itlokhon khine?**
T: **Kito ḥrene?**

Is there ...?
S: **Itin ...?**
T: **Kit ...?**

air-conditioning	*S:* **mqalmana;** *T:* **maqilmono; mukayyaf**
a telephone	*S:* **qaᶜya;** *T:* **telefon**
a bar	*S:* **bar; bet shiqya;** *T:* **mashqyo; bar**
hot water	*S:* **miya shakhine;** *T:* **maye shaḥine**
laundry service	*S:* **tishmishta d-shyagha;** *T:* **teshmeshto di-mashighonutho; khidmat-ghasal; quru-temizli**
room service	*S:* **tishmishta l-tawana;** *T:* **teshmeshto tawonayto**

No, I *(m/f)* don't like it.
S: **La, ana le bayin./La, ana le bayan.**
T: **Lo, lo k-obaᶜne./Lo, lo k-ubᶜone.**

It's too ...
S: **Raba le ...**
T: **Sagi ... yo.** *or* **Ghallabe ... yo.**

cold	*S:* **qarta;** *T:* **qariro/qarirto**
hot	*S:* **khimma;** *T:* **ḥamimo/ḥamimto**
small	*S:* **zᶜora/zᶜorta;** *T:* **naᶜimo/naᶜimto**
big	*S:* **gura/gurta;** *T:* **rabo/rabtho**
dark	*S:* **khishkana/khishkanta;** *T:* **ḥeshukho/ḥeshukhto or ᶜeṭmo**
noisy	*S:* **rawba/rawbana/rawbanta;** *T:* **qolo ᶜeloyo**
dirty	*S:* **ṭawsha;** *T:* **ᶜjiqo/ᶜjiqto**

It's fine, I'll *(m/f)* take it.
S: **Ṭawta la, b-shaqlina/tawta la b-shaqlan na.**
T: **Ṭowo-yo, g-moyadne/g-maydalle.**

Where is the bathroom?
S: **Ika la bet-khmama?**
T: **Ayko-yo u-beth-mayo?**

Is there hot water all day?
S: **Et miya shakhina b-kule yuma?**
T: **Kito maye shaḥine u-yawmo kule?**

Do you *(pl)* have a safe?
S: **Etlokhon bet-gaza?**
T: **Kitkhu khazno (*or* khazina)?**

Is there anywhere to wash clothes?
S: **Et dokta d-shayghta d-lwushe?**
T: **Kit duktho d-mashighno/d-mashighono a-lbushaydhi?**

Can I *(m/f)* use the telephone?
S: **Masin maplikhin l-qaʿya?/Masyan maplikhan l-qaʿya?**
T: **Kibi mistaʿmalno/mistaʿmlono u-telefon?**

—Needs

I *(m/f)* need ...
S: **Sniqa win l-.../Sniqta wan l-...**
T: **Ko-lozam-li .../Ko-luzmo-li ...**

candles	*S:* **ponde**; *T:* **shamʿe**
toilet paper	*S:* **shushipa d-bet-silya**; *T:* **warqo du-beth-mayo; warqo du-tuwaylet**
soap	*S:* **ṣapuna**; *T:* **ṣafuno; ṣabun**
clean sheets	*S:* **malape khate**; *T:* **fothotho da-gale nadhife**
an extra blanket	*S:* **kha lkhipa khina**; *T:* **kushofo zoyudo; baṭṭaniye zoyudto**
drinking water	*S:* **miya d-shtaya**; *T:* **maye d-shtoyo**
a light bulb	*S:* **zghughita d-bahra; dalqa**; *T:* **dalqo**
a mosquito net	*S:* **tila d-baqyate**; *T:* **ʿafuro da-boqe**
mosquito repellent	*S:* **qaṭlan baqe**; *T:* **msatronitho ma-boqe**

Please *(pl)* change the sheets.
S: **In mbasmalukh, mshakhlip l-malape.**
T: **Boʿutho menkhayu, mshaḥlefu a-fothotho da-gale.**

Can I *(m/f)* have the key to my room?
S: **Masin shaqlin l-qdile d-tawani?/Masyan shaqlan l-qdile d-tawani?**
T: **Kibokh/Kibekh d-obatli u-qlidho di-qelaytaydhi?**

I *(m/f)* can't close ...
S: **Len msaya d-sakhrin .../Len msaya d-sakhran ...**
T: **Laybi sokharno/sukhrono ...**

I *(m/f)* can't open ...
S: **Len msaya d-patkhin .../Len msaya d-patkhan ...**
T: **Laybi fotaḥno/futḥono ...**
... the window. *S:* **... l-kawe.**; *T:* **... i-kawtho.**; **... u-shaboko.**
... the door. *S:* **... l-tarʿa.**; *T:* **u-tarʿo.**

I *(m/f)* have lost my key.
S: **Tulqa win l-qdili./Tuliqta wan l-qdili.**
T: **Msakar-li u-qlidhaydhi.**

The shower won't work.
S: **Bet-khmama khriwa le.**
T: **U-dush lo ko-shoghil.**

How do I *(m/f)* get hot water?
S: **Dakhi maplikhin/maplikhan l-miya shakhine?**
T: **Aydarbo k-othin am-maye shaḥine?**

The toilet won't flush.
S: **Bet-silya la le zlaʿa.**
T: **U-tuwaylet lo ko-shogil.**

The water has been cut off.
S: **Miya qṭilon.**
T: **Am-maye qṭiʿi.**

The electricity has been cut off.
S: **Liqṭara qṭile.**
T: **U-kahrobo (*or* u-kahraba' *or* u-jeyran) qṭiʿ.**

The gas has been cut off.
S: **Khapupa qṭile.**
T: **U-hawfo (*or* ghas) qṭiʿ.**

The heating has been cut off.
S: **Shkhunta qṭita ela.**
T: **U-mashiḥnono (*or* shofaj) qṭi^{c}.**

The heater doesn't work.
S: **Mashkhinanta la la plakha.**
T: **U-mashiḥnono (*or* shofaj) lo k-shoghil.**

The air-conditioning doesn't work.
S: **Mqalmana la le plakha.**
T: **U-maqilmono (*or* mukayyaf) lo ko-shoghil.**

The phone doesn't work.
S: **Qa^{c}ya la le plakha.**
T: **U-telefon lo k-shoghil.**

I *(m/f)* can't flush the toilet.
S: **La win msaya dzal^{c}in l-bet-silya./La wan msaya dzal^{c}an l-bet-silya.**
T: **Maye du-tuwaylet lo ko-nuḥti.**

The toilet is blocked.
S: **Dwiq le bet-silya.**
T: **U-tuwaylet skhiro-yo.**

I *(m/f)* can't switch off the tap.
S: **La win msaya d-sakhrin l-abuba d-miya./La wan msaya d-sakhran l-abuba d-miya.**
T: **Laybi sokharno/sukhrono u-fethyuno (*or* i-ḥanafiye).**

I *(m/f)* need a plug for the bath.
S: **Sniqa win/Sniqta wan kha plug qa bet-khmama.**
T: **K-lozam-li sokhuro lajan u-banyo.**

Where is the plug socket?
S: **Ika la dokta d-plug?**
T: **Ayko-yo i-neqbo da-fishat?**

There are strange insects in my room.
S: **It rikhshe shnize gaw tawani.**
T: **Kit raḥshe nukhroye bi-qelaytaydhi.**

There's an animal in my room.
S: **It kha khaywa gaw tawani.**
T: **Kito ḥaywo (*or* ḥaywan) bi-qelaytaydhi.**

wake-up call *S:* **qᶜayta d-ᶜiruta;**
T: **qroyo d-maḥisutho**

Could you *(m/f)* wake me up at ... o'clock?
S: **Masit maᶜiritli qa shaᶜta ...?/Masyat maᶜiratli qa shaᶜta ...?**
T: **Kibokh/Kibekh maḥisat-li ba-...?**

I *(m/f)* am leaving now.
S: **Ana bizala win/wan hadiya.**
T: **G-izzino/G-izzono uᶜdo.**

We are leaving now.
S: **Akhnan bizala wikh hadiya.**
T: **G-izzano uᶜdo.**

May I *(m/f)* pay the bill now?
S: **Masin pariyin l-takhshawta hadiya?/Masyan pariyan l-takhshawta hadiya?**
T: **Kibi mdafaᶜno/mdafᶜono u-shṭoro (*or* i-fatura) uᶜdo?**

—Useful words

bathroom	*S:* **bet-khmama;** *T:* **beth-ḥyofo; ḥammam**
bed	*S:* **mashkawta;** *T:* **gale; ᶜarso; taḥt**
blanket	*S:* **lkhepa;** *T:* **kushofo; baṭṭaniye; blanket**
candle	*S:* **ponda; shamala;** *T:* **shamᶜo**
candles	*S:* **ponde; shamale;** *T:* **shamᶜe**
chair	*S:* **kursya;** *T:* **kursyo**
cold water	*S:* **miya qarire;** *T:* **maye jamude**
courtyard	*S:* **darta;** *T:* **durto**
cupboard	*S:* **dapa d-niṣle;** *T:* **fardisqo; gantor; dulab**
door lock	*S:* **qipla;** *T:* **fakoro; quflo**
electricity	*S:* **laqiṭ para;** *T:* **kahrobo; kahraba'; jeyran**

excluded	*S:* **sṭar min**; *T:* **lo ḥshiwo**
extra	*S:* **yatir/tawsapta**; *T:* **zoyudo/ zoyudto; ekstra**
floor *story*	*S:* **medyara arᶜanaya**; *T:* **medyoro arᶜonoyo; qaṭ; ṭabaq**
fridge	*S:* **maqrana**; *T:* **majimdono; maqrono; barrade**
hot water	*S:* **miya shakhine**; *T:* **maye shaḥine**
included	*S:* **ᶜam ...**; *T:* **ḥshiwo**
key	*S:* **qdila**; *T:* **qlidho**
kitchen	*S:* **bet-bshala**; *T:* **beth-busholo**
lamp	*S:* **shraya**; *T:* **lamp; fanso; lamfidho**
laundry	*S:* **bet-shyaghta**; *T:* **mashighonitho**
light *electric*	*S:* **bahra**; *T:* **bahro**
living room	*S:* **tawn arkhe**; *T:* **beth-shalmo**
mattress	*S:* **shwita**; *T:* **teshwitho**
meals	*S:* **ikhala**; *T:* **shorwotho; mukle**
mirror	*S:* **makhzita**; *T:* **nawro; maḥzitho**
name	*S:* **shimma**; *T:* **ishmo**
noise	*S:* **rawba**; *T:* **qolo**
padlock	*S:* **qipla**; *T:* **quflo**
pillow	*S:* **spadita**; *T:* **besodyo; mkhadde**
plug *electric*	*S:* **plug**; *T:* **fisha; kahroboyo**
pool	*S:* **qawita**; *T:* **qobitho; havuz; masbaḥ**
quiet	*S:* **shalwa/shilyuta**; *T:* **shalyo/ shlitho**
quilt	*S:* **lkhipa**; *T:* **lḥef**
reception	*S:* **m'arᶜuta**; *T:* **mqablutho**
roof	*S:* **gare**; *T:* **goro**
room number	*S:* **raqma d-tawana**; *T:* **menyono di-qelayto**
room	*S:* **tawana**; *T:* **qelayto; oda; tawono**
sheet	*S:* **shwiyate**; *T:* **fotho da-gale**
shelf	*S:* **rapa**; *T:* **dafo**
shower	*S:* **raṣuṣa**; *T:* **dush**
stairs	*S:* **darghe**; *T:* **darghe; daraj**
suitcase	*S:* **mawbla**; *T:* **ṣemdo; janṭa; baghol**

surname	*S:* **kunaya**; *T:* **kunoyo**
table	*S:* **ṭawlita**; *T:* **ṭablitho**
towel	*S:* **mkaprana**; *T:* **hawliye**; **kuforo**; **shushefo**; **mandilo**
veranda	*S:* **varanda**; *T:* **varanda**
wall	*S:* **guda**; **shura**; *T:* **shuro**
water	*S:* **miya**; *T:* **maye**
window	*S:* **kawe**; *T:* **kawtho**; **shaboko**

Holidays and festivals . . .

There are a wide variety of traditional festivals celebrated in every village and area that strongly reflect Assyrian culture and history. Major Assyrian holidays commemorate both religious and historical events. Besides Christmas (*S:* **^{c}Ida Z^{c}ura**, *T:* **^{c}Edho Na^{c}imo**; December 25 or January 7), and Easter (*S:* **^{c}Ida Gura**, *T:* **^{c}Edho Rabo**; March/April), the most important holidays are *S:* **Akitu** or **Kha b-Nisan**, *T:* **Ḥa b-Nison**, which celebrates the Assyrian New Year and the coming of spring, and, Remembrance Day (*S:* **Yoma d-Sahde**, *T:* **Yawmo da-Suhde**; August 7), which commemorates all the Assyrians who have died in past genocides and massacres, especially in 1915 and 1933.

OTHER FESTIVALS – The most important saints' days celebrated by the Assyrians of Tur-Abdin are those of the Dormition of the Mother of God (August 15), St. Gabriel (August 31), St. Malke (September 1), and St. Simon of the Olives. The Eastern Assyrians venerate other significant saints, such as St. Zaia, St. Bhishu, St. Sawa, and the Holy Cross (all celebrated on September 13), St. George (September 23), St. Cyriacus (September 15), St. Simon Bar-Sabbaye (September 14), and St. Shmuni. Other festivities include **Noosardel** in the summer, on which people sprinkle water on one another, and Ascension Day, popularly known as **Kalu Sulaqa**, on which young girls dress as brides and hold parties. A similar festivity is held in Tur-Abdin called **Hano Qritho**.

8. FOOD & DRINK

Food plays a key role in Assyrian life, and important events in all aspects of life and the year are marked with a feast of one form or another. Food is a part of hospitality – it is both the host's duty to make sure his guests are eating and the guest's duty to partake of what is offered. Assyrian cuisine varies and in normal times, at homes or in the very few Assyrian-owned restaurants, you will be offered a dazzling variety of dishes, delicacies and drinks, which vary from area to area and from season to season. Any menu you may encounter may be written in Arabic, Turkish, Persian or English – but rarely Aramaic.

breakfast	*S:* **ʿrayta**; *T:* **fṭoro**
lunch	*S:* **sharuta**; *T:* **ʿrayto**
snack	*S:* **nuqnaqa**; *T:* **saybartho; shorutho**
dinner/supper	*S:* **khshamita**; *T:* **ḥshimto**
dessert	*S:* **khilyuta**; *T:* **ḥalyutho**

I'm hungry.
S: **Kpina win./Kpinta wan.**
T: **Kafinno./Kafinono.** *or* **Kafino-no./Kafinto-no.**

I'm *(m/f)* thirsty.
S: **Ṣihya win./Ṣ-hita wan.**
T: **Ṣahino./Ṣahyono.** *or* **Ṣahyo-no./Ṣ-hitho-no.**

Do you *(m/f)* know a good restaurant?
S: **Yaṭid/Yaṭad/Yaṭitun kha bet-mawkhla ṭawa?**
T: **K-odhʿat beth-muklo (***or* **maṭʿomo** *or* **loqanṭa) ṭowo?**

Do you *(m/f)* have a table, please?
S: **In mbasmalukh/mbasmalakh, itlokh/itlakh khda ṭawlita spiqta?**
T: **Boʿutho menokh/menekh, kitkhu ṭablitho?**

I would like a table for ... people, please *(m/f)*.
S: *—said by a male:* **In mbasmalokh/mbasmalakh, bayin khda ṭawlita qa ...qnume./***—said by a female:* **In mbasmalokh/mbasmalakh, bayan khda ṭawlita qa ...qnume.**

T: —*said by a male:* **Boᶜutho menokh/menekh, k-obaᶜno ṭablitho lajan ... noshe** (*or* **far?ufe** *or* **shakhsat).**/—*said by a female:* **Boᶜutho menokh/menekh, k-ubᶜono ṭablitho lajan ... noshe** (*or* **farṣufe** *or* **shakhsat).**

Can I *(m/f)* see the menu please?
S: **In mbasmalokh, masin khazina lukhita?/In mbasmalakh, masyan khazyana lukhita?**
T: **Boᶜutho menokh, kibi ḥozeno sedro du-muklo?/Boᶜutho menekh, kibi ḥuzyono sedro du-muklo?**

I'm *(m/f)* still looking at the menu.
S: **Lᶜadmesh khyara win b-lukhita./Lᶜadmesh khyara wan b-lukhita.**
T: **Hesh ko-ḥoyarno/ko-ḥayrono bu-sedro d-muklo.**

I *(m/f)* would like to order now.
S: **Mṭaywa win d-ṭalbin hadiya./Mṭayota wan d-ṭalban hadiya.**
T: **Uᶜdo k-obaᶜno ṭolabno./Uᶜdo k-ubᶜono ṭulbono.**

What would you *(m/f)* recommend?
S: **At mud mara?**
T: **Hat mun k-immat?**

What's this?
S: **Mudi le aha?/Mudi la hadhe?**
T: **Mun-yo hano/hathe?**

Is it spicy?
S: **B-mdakhe le?/B-mdakhe la?**
T: **ḥarufo-yo?/ḥarufto-yo?**

Does it have meat in it?
S: **It gawe bisra?**
T: **Kit basro ebe/eba?**

There is no meat in it.
S: **Lit bisra gawe.**
T: **Layt basro ebe/eba.**

Does it have alcohol in it?
S: **It gawe shakhra;**
T: **Kit shakhro (*or* alkohol) ebe/eba?**

Do you *(m/f/pl)* have ...?
S: **It lokh/lakh/lokhon ...?**
T: **Kitkhu ...?**

We don't have ...
S: **Litlan ...**
T: **Latlan ...**

Do you *(m/f/pl)* want ...?
S: **Bayit/Bayat/Bayitun ...?**
T: **K-ob^{c}at ...?**

Can I *(m/f)* order some more ...?
S: **Masin ṭalbin yatir ...?/Masyan ṭalban yatir ...?**
T: **Kibi ṭolabno/ṭulbono ... hesh?**

That's all, thank you.
S: **La medem khina, tawdi.** *or* **Sapiq, tawdi.**
T: **Tawdi, bas-yo.**

That's enough, thanks.
S: **Ṣapiq hana, tawdi.**
T: **Bas-yo, tawdi.**

I *(m/f)* haven't finished yet.
S: **La win priqa/ La wan priqta**
T: **Hesh lo makhlaṣ-li.**

I *(m/f)* am still eating.
S: **Hala bikhala win./Hala bikhala wan.**
T: **Hesh k-okhalno./Hesh k-ukhlono.**

I have finished eating.
S: **Preqli mkhalta.**
T: **Makhlaṣ-li mu-muklo.**

I *(m/f)* am full up!
S: **Ṣaggi swi^{c}li!**
T: **Sawe^{c}no!/Saw^{c}ono!**

I *(m/f)* am a vegetarian.
S: **Ya^{c}itanaya win./Ya^{c}itanayta wan.**
T: **Yarqonoyo-no./Yarqonayto-no.**

I *(m/f)* don't eat meat.
S: **Le yakhlin/yakhlan bisra.**
T: **Lo k-okhalno/k-ukhlono basro.**

I *(m/f)* don't eat pork.
S: **Le yakhlin/yakhlan khzura.**
T: **Lo k-okhalno/k-ukhlono basro da-broze.**

I *(m/f)* don't eat chicken or fish.
S: **Le yakhlin/yakhlan la kteta o la nuna.**
T: **Lo k-okhalno/k-ukhlono basro da-gyothe aw da-nune.**

I *(m/f)* don't drink alcohol.
S: **Le yshatin/yshatyan shakhra.**
T: **Lo k-shoteno/k-shutyono shakhro (***or* **alkohol).**

I *(m/f)* don't smoke.
S: **La mtanennen tenenta/ la mtanennan tenenta.**
T: **Lo ko-shoteno tenunto./Lo ko-shutyono tenunto.** *or* **Lo ko-mtantanno./Lo ko-mtantinono.**

—Needs

I *(m/f)* would like ...
S: **Bayin .../Bayan ...**
T: **K-obaʿno .../K-ubʿono ...**

an ashtray *S:* **kha man qiṭma;** *T:* **mono d-qaṭmo**
the bill *S:* **l-takhshawta;** *T:* **u-shṭoro**
the menu *S:* **l-lukhita;** *T:* **sedro du-muklo**
a glass of water *S:* **kasa d-miya;** *T:* **koso d-maye**
a bottle of water *S:* **basta d-miya;** *T:* **shushaye d-maye; qinnina d-maye**
a bottle of wine *S:* **lina d-khamra;** *T:* **shushaye d-ḥamro**
a bottle of beer *S:* **basta d-pizta;** *T:* **shushaye d-bira**
another bottle (of ...) *S:* **basta khita (d-...);** *T:* **shushaye ḥreto (d-...)**
a bottle-opener *S:* **patkhana;** *T:* **fatoḥo da-shushayat**

dessert	*S:* **khilyuta**; *T:* **ḥalyutho**
a drink	*S:* **shtita**; *T:* **shtoyo**
another chair	*S:* **kursya khina**; *T:* **kursyo ḥreno**
another plate	*S:* **mana khina**; *T:* **mono ḥreno**
another glass	*S:* **kasa khina**; *T:* **koso ḥreno**
another cup	*S:* **niṣla khina**; *T:* **qaqunto ḥreto**
a glass	*S:* **kasa**; *T:* **koso**
a jug	*S:* **quqma**; *T:* **quqmo; agono; jak**
a knife	*S:* **skinta**; *T:* **skino; shalfo**
a fork	*S:* **mashilyona**; *T:* **mashilyono**
a spoon	*S:* **tarwada**; *T:* **tarwodo**
a teaspoon	*S:* **tarwada d-tiya**; *T:* **tarwodo di-chaye**
a plate	*S:* **mana**; *T:* **mono; sfoqo**
a dish	*S:* **qedra**; *T:* **qedro**
a bowl	*S:* **laqna**; *T:* **laqno**
a table	*S:* **ṭablita**; *T:* **ṭablitho**
a napkin	*S:* **yalikhta; shushipa**; *T:* **mandilo**
a toothpick	*S:* **qisa d-shinne**; *T:* **ḥoṣuyo; qaysuno da-ʿarshone**
a tablecloth	*S:* **Ksaya d-tablita**; *T:* **ksoyo d-ṭablitho**
the sugar bowl	*S:* **laqna d shikar**; *T:* **mono d-shakar**
a washbowl	*S:* **mshaghta**; *T:* **mshoghto; maghsal**
too much	*S:* **saggi yatir**; *T:* **zoyudo/zoyudto/zoyude**
too little	*S:* **saggi bṣir**; *T:* **noquṣo/noquṣto/noquṣe**
not enough	*S:* **la sapiq**; *T:* **lo-ko-makfe/lo-ko-makfyo/lo-ko-makfin; lo-bas-yo**

—Tastes

fresh fruit	*S:* **pire raghye**; *T:* **fire ḥathe; fako ḥatho**
fresh fish	*S:* **none raghye**; *T:* **nune ḥathe**
raw; uncooked	*S:* **naya;nayta**; *T:* **raʿyo; noyo**
cooked	*S:* **bshila/bshilta**; *T:* **bashilo/bashilto**

ripe	*S:* **meṭya;mṭeta**; *T:* **maṭyo/mṭitho**
tender	*S:* **rkhikha;rkhikhta**; *T:* **rakikho/ rakikhto**
tough	*S:* **qashya;qshita**; *T:* **qashyo/ qshitho**
spicy (hot)	*S:* **mdakhe; ṣarupa/ṣarupta**; *T:* **ṣarufo/ṣarufto**
stale	*S:* **sarya/srita**; *T:* **ᶜatiqo/ᶜatiqto; nashifo/nashifto**
sour	*S:* **khamuṣa/khamuṣta**; *T:* **ḥamuṣo/ḥamuṣto**
sweet	*S:* **khilya/khlita**; *T:* **ḥalyo/ḥlitho**
bitter	*S:* **marira/marirta**; *T:* **mariro/ marirto; mayiro/mayirto**
hot	*S:* **shakhina/shakhinta**; *T:* **shaḥino/ shaḥinto**
cold	*S:* **qarira/qarirta**; *T:* **jamudo/ jamudto**
salty	*S:* **milkhana/milkhanta**; *T:* **maluḥo/ maluḥto**
taste	*S:* **ṭama**; *T:* **ṭaᶜmo**
tasteless	*S:* **naᶜuṭa/naᶜuṭta**; *T:* **d-lo ṭaᶜmo**
bad; spoiled	*S:* **khirba**; *T:* **ḥarbo; ḥariwo/ ḥaruto**
tasty	*S:* **ṭaᶜmana/ṭaᶜmanita**; *T:* **basimo/ basimto; ṭaᶜmono**
empty	*S:* **spiqa;spiqta**; *T:* **khalyo/ khlitho**
full	*S:* **melya;mlita**; *T:* **malyo/mlitho**
good	*S:* **ṭawa;ṭawta**; *T:* **ṭowo/ṭowto**

—Food

bread	*S:* **lakhma ᶜyadaya**; *T:* **laḥmo**
burger	*S:* **hambergur**; *T:* **hamberger**
butter	*S:* **karra;zebda**; *T:* **kroᶜo; zebdo**
cake	*S:* **kika**; *T:* **kuko; kaᶜak**
candy	*S:* **khilyuta**; *T:* **ḥalyutho**
celery	*S:* **karawis**; *T:* **krafso**
cheese	*S:* **gubta**; *T:* **gwayto**
chewing gum	*S:* **kiya**; *T:* **duᶜtho; kiyo**
coriander	*S:* **kazbarta**; *T:* **kuzbartho**

cumin	*S:* **kmana**; *T:* **kmuno**
egg	*S:* **be^{c}ta; bi^{c}i**; *T:* **be^{c}to**
eggs	*S:* **biye**; *T:* **be^{c}e**
boiled egg	*S:* **biye shliqe**; *T:* **be^{c}to shliqto**
fat *animal*	*S:* **tarba**; *T:* **tarbo**
fennel	*S:* **ashlar^{c}a**; *T:* **ashkar^{c}o**
flour	*S:* **qamkha**; *T:* **qamḥo**
food	*S:* **mikhulta**; *T:* **muklo**
french fries	*S:* **"chips" shakhina**; *T:* **paṭaṭa** (*or* **baṭaṭa) mqalayto**
garlic	*S:* **toma**; *T:* **tumo**
honey	*S:* **dusha**; *T:* **dawsho**
ice-cream	*S:* **qarirta**; *T:* **buza** *(in Syria)*; **dondurma** *(in Turkey)*; **moṭa** *(in Iraq)*
jam/jelly	*S:* **murabba/rawba**; *T:* **murabba**
ketchup	*S:* **rawba dyabrukhe**; *T:* **kechap**
loaf *of bread*	*S:* **grista**; *T:* **griṣtho**
mint	*S:* **rikhana**; *T:* **nu^{c}na^{c}; non^{c}o**
mustard	*S:* **khirdal**; *T:* **ḥardlo**
oil	*S:* **mishkha**; *T:* **meshḥo**
omelette	*S:* **spira**; *T:* **sfero**
parsley	*S:* **karawis**; *T:* **krafso dumyo**
pasta	*S:* **pasta**; *T:* **maqarna**
pepper	*S:* **pelpel**; *T:* **felflo**
pickle(s)	*S:* **ṭurshiye**; *T:* **ṭurshi; thalbuno**
pizza	*S:* **pitsa**; *T:* **pitsa**
rice	*S:* **rezza**; *T:* **rezo**
salad	*S:* **zalaṭa**; *T:* **salaṭa**
salt	*S:* **milkha**; *T:* **melḥo**
sandwich	*S:* **zamora**; *T:* **sandwish**
sauce	*S:* **ṣoṣ**; *T:* **ṣoṣ; ṣalṣa**
sesame	*S:* **shishme**; *T:* **shushmo**
shopping	*S:* **zwana**; *T:* **krokho bu-shuqo; zwono**
soup	*S:* **shorwa**; *T:* **shorba; sruftho**
spices	*S:* **mdakhe**; *T:* **ḥarifutho**
sugar	*S:* **shikar**; *T:* **shakar**
sumac	*S:* **smuqe**; *T:* **ḥamṣitho; sumaq**
sweets	*S:* **khilyuta**; *T:* **ḥalyutho**
teapot	*S:* **jaydan; rathukhta**; *T:* **dudo; chaypas**

vinegar	*S:* **khala**; *T:* **ḥalo; sirka**
yogurt	*S:* **masta**; *T:* **qaṭiro; masto**

—Vegetables & fruit

apple	*S:* **khabusha**; *T:* **ḥabusho**
apricot	*S:* **mishmishshe**; *T:* **barquqyo**
aubergine/eggplant	*S:* **bnath-gane**; *T:* **bnoth-gane; badhinjane komto**
banana	*S:* **muza**; *T:* **muzo; banana**
beans	*S:* **pasolile**; *T:* **faṣuliye; goṣuṣe**
green beans	*S:* **lobye**; *T:* **lobya**
beetroot	*S:* **selqa**; *T:* **selqo**
cabbage	*S:* **lahana**; *T:* **lahana; qrambo; krawo**
carrot	*S:* **gizara**; *T:* **gizoro**
cauliflower	*S:* **qupta**; *T:* **quḥo; qarnabiṭ**
cherry	*S:* **gilaṣe**; *T:* **qerasiya; karas**
chestnut	*S:* **baluṭe**; *T:* **baluṭ-malko**
chickpeas	*S:* **khirṭmane**; *T:* **ḥarṭumone**
cucumber	*S:* **parkhe**; *T:* **khyoro; farḥo; tarʿuz**
date	*S:* **tamre/ qazbe**; *T:* **tamro**
fig	*S:* **tina**; *T:* **tino**
fruit	*S:* **pira**; *T:* **firo; fako**
grapes	*S:* **ʿinwe**; *T:* **ʿanwe**
grapefruit	*S:* **grapefrut**; *T:* **grapfrut**
hazel nut	*S:* **pindiqe**; *T:* **fendqo; bundqo**
lemon; lime	*S:* **laymuna/khimṣa**; *T:* **limon; laymun; limuno**
lentils	*S:* **ṭlukhe**; *T:* **ṭlawḥe**
lettuce	*S:* **khaṣ**; *T:* **ḥaso; khass**
melon	*S:* **paṭikha**; *T:* **fujo; faṭiḥo; baṭṭikh**
mulberry	*S:* **tuta**; *T:* **tutho**
mushroom	*S:* **paturyate**; *T:* **faṭurto**
nut: almond	*S:* **shade**; *T:* **luzo; sheghdo**
okra	*S:* **bam mya**; *T:* **bamya**
olive	*S:* **zayta; zaytona**; *T:* **zayto; zaytuno**
onion	*S:* **biṣla**; *T:* **baṣlo**
orange	*S:* **ṭroghe**; *T:* **eṭrugho; portaqal**
peach	*S:* **khukhe**; *T:* **ḥawḥo; durqino**

pear	*S:* **kamutra**; *T:* **kumathro; qanturro**
peas	*S:* **khirṭmane**; *T:* **ḥimṣe; bazalya**
pineapple	*S:* **ananas**; *T:* **ananas**
pistachio	*S:* **pisteqe**; *T:* **festqo; fistaq**
plum	*S:* **khakhta**; *T:* **ḥaḥo; agoṣo**
pomegranate	*S:* **armune**; *T:* **rumono**
potato	*S:* **qurtope; peṭaṭe**; *T:* **paṭaṭa; belbuso; baṭaṭa**
pumpkin	*S:* **qarᶜe**; *T:* **qarᶜo**
quince	*S:* **sparigla**; *T:* **sfariglo**
radish	*S:* **peghla**; *T:* **feghlo**
raisins	*S:* **yabishe**; *T:* **afshotho**
spinach	*S:* **shaper ṭarpe**; *T:* **shafir-ṭarfe; sbenakh**
strawberry	*S:* **tuta d-arᶜa**; *T:* **aquno**
sweet potato	*S:* **qurtope khilye**; *T:* **paṭaṭa ḥlitho**
tomato	*S:* **yabrokhe**; *T:* **ṭamaṭa; yabruḥo; badhinjane semaqto**
vegetables	*S:* **yarquta**; *T:* **yarqe**
walnut	*S:* **goze**; *T:* **gawzo**
watermelon	*S:* **ship tiya**; *T:* **zabashe; shabṭiye**

—Meat & fish

beef	*S:* **bisra d-sharkha/sharkhe**; *T:* **basro da-tawre**
chicken	*S:* **kteta/ktayate**; *T:* **basro da-gyothe**
fat	*S:* **tarba**; *T:* **tarbo**
fish	*S:* **nona/none**; *T:* **nune**
goat meat	*S:* **bisra d-ᶜizze**; *T:* **basro da-ᶜeze**
kebab	*S:* **kababa**; *T:* **kabab**
lamb	*S:* **ᶜirwe**; *T:* **basro da-ᶜwone**
meat	*S:* **bisra**; *T:* **basro**
sausage	*S:* **sarsiqa**; *T:* **sarsiqo**
turkey	*S:* **bisra d-dika romaya**; *T:* **basro da-ᶜalokat**

—Drinks

Remember to ask for modern soft drinks by brand name.

alcohol	*S:* **shakhra**; *T:* **shakhro; alkohol**
beer	*S:* **pezta**; *T:* **bira**
black tea	*S:* **tiya kuma**; *T:* **chaye komto**
bottle	*S:* **basta**; *T:* **shushaye; besto**
buttermilk (ayran)	*S:* **dawe**; *T:* **dawghe**
can	*S:* **qupsa**; *T:* **ʿulbo**
coffee	*S:* **ṣarwa**; *T:* **qaḥwe; qḥutho**
coffee with milk	*S:* **ṣarwa ʿm khalwa**; *T:* **qaḥwe b-ḥalwo**
fruit juice	*S:* **ʿṣira d-pere**; *T:* **ʿsoro da-fire; ʿasir da-fire**
ice	*S:* **glida**; *T:* **glidho**
milk	*S:* **khalwa**; *T:* **ḥalwo**
mineral water	*S:* **miya d-ʿayna**; *T:* **maye di-ʿayno**
No sugar, please.	*S:* **D-la shikar in mbasmalokh/ in mbasmalakh**; *T:* **Boʿutho menokh/menekh, d-lo shakar.**
tea with lemon	*S:* **tiya ʿm laymuna**; *T:* **chaye b-limon; chaye b-laymun**
tea with milk	*S:* **tiya b-khalwa**; *T:* **chaye b-ḥalwo**
green tea	*S:* **tiya yaruqa**; *T:* **chaye yaruqto**
tea	*S:* **tiya**; *T:* **chaye; tiyo**
water	*S:* **mayya; miya**; *T:* **maye**
wine	*S:* **khamra**; *T:* **ḥamro**

More on food & drink...

Assyrian cuisine worldwide is an incredibly varied range of tastes and styles. The main Assyrian centres will always have a large number of cafés and restaurants everywhere, but weddings are the best opportunity to enjoy a feast. The many barbecue restaurants in the cities and larger towns are to be recommended, but the best is always a feast prepared in a private home the traditional way. Assyrians place a great emphasis on lamb which is served in a variety of ways, either grilled or in soups and stews. Hors d'oeuvres are usually served at meal times and can include a wide range of foods such as hot peppers, vine leaves stuffed with meat and rice, pickled vegetables, olives, cheese, bread and cured meats. Some common specialties include:

S: **tikka**; *T:* **tikka** or **kushbashi** – grilled lamb served with flat bread.
S: **dolma**; *T:* **aprakh** – meat and rice wrapped in vine, cabbage leaves, aubergines, pepper and tomatoes, often served with yoghurt and garlic.
S: **kipte**; *T:* **kufte** – ground beef with onion, green pepper, garlic and salt.
S: **chig-kufte**; *T:* **chig-kufte** – balls of ground raw meat, spiced with onions and hot peppers.
S: **kubbe-neye**; *T:* **kibbi** – raw meat served in different varieties and with various spices.
S: **kubbe**; *T:* **kutle** – boiled pockets of ground wheat packed with spiced meat.
S/T: **kabab** – grilled spiced ground meat.
S/T: **harisa** – wheat and chicken dish traditionally eaten on religious holidays.
S/T: **basṭurma** – dried slices of lean beef soaked in spicy marinade.
S: **rizza**; *T:* **rezo** – rice. Often served with...
S: **shorwa**; *T:* **shorba** – classic Assyrian soup or casserole (ingredients vary).
S: **gurgur**; **burghul**; **pirda**; *T:* **birghil** – cracked wheat.
S: **kutle d-awke**; *T:* **labaniye** – kufte balls cooked in a yoghurt based soup.
S/T: **rishta** – egg noodles served in a soup of spinach and lentils.
S/T: **shaykh maḥshi** – stuffed and baked aubergine served with yoghurt and mint sauce.
S/T: **mjaddara** – soup of lentils cooked with either cracked wheat or rice.

FOOD & DRINK

There are many different types of fish in the rivers in Iraq, Syria and Iran and those that that surround Tur-Abdin, especially the Tigris, Euphrates, Khabur, Upper and Lower Zab and Maye Hewore (Beyazsu). Assyrian cuisine is also rich in seasonal vegetable dishes, including lentils, beans, eggplants and salads, which may be served with nuts, mint or yoghurt (*S:* **qaṭira**, *T:* **qaṭiro**, e.g. *S/T:* **jajik**, yoghurt with cucumbers). Yoghurts are also used in soups and drinks as well as in side dishes that depend from season to season. Other side dishes include *S:* **ṭurshiye**, *T:* **ṭurshi** (mixed pickles), *S:* **gubta**, *T:* **gwayto** (cheese) and pizzas.

— Bread is always on the Assyrian table, and the two traditional types of bread in the region are *S:* **girdayya**, *T:* **ṣammun** and *S:* **lawasha** *or* **raqqa**, *T:* **lawash**. The wafer-thin oven-baked **lawasha/lawash** is a particular favourite – it is sometimes used to wrap cheese or meat spiced with onions and salads, and marinated before barbecuing or baking in a clay oven (*S:* **tanura**, *T:* **tanuro**).

— Desserts can include various filos, strudels and cakes as well as the ever-popular dried apricots, or grapes dried into flat sheets (*S/T:* **qamardin**). Depending on the season there will always be fruit such as apricots, peaches, apples, pears, cherries, mulberries, pomegranates, figs, strawberries, watermelons and rockmelons. In winter you will find many of these offered as delicious compotes or sweet preserved (*S/T:* **murabba**), including slightly more unusual offerings such as walnuts and rose petals. Sometimes you will be given these, or dates, as an accompaniment to tea.

— Assyrians are proud of their many wells and natural springs, which provide their villages and homes with pure water. They are not bottled. Served strong and black in small cups, coffee marks the end of every Assyrian meal. It is usually served with a delicious assortment of sweet pastries and cakes such as *S/T:* **baqlawa** (flaky layers of nut-filled pastry), *S:* **kilije**, *T:* **klicha** and *S:* **kika**, *T:* **ᶜrebiye**. Tea is a gentler alternative. Assyrians are proud of the wines, sherries and other alcoholic beverages they produce locally. *S/T:* **araq** is a very strong spirit distilled from raisins and flavoured with anise, and which should be approached with care! Those being entertained in Assyrian homes should be warned that Assyrian hospitality could often involve a ready supply of alcohol.

9. DIRECTIONS

Where is ...?
S: **Ika le/la ...?**
T: **Ayko-yo ...?**

the academy *S:* **bet-drasha**; *T:* **u-beth-drosho; i-akadimya**
the airport *S:* **bet-ṭawsa**; *T:* **u-beth-ṭawso**
the art gallery *S:* **bet-glakha d-amna**; *T:* **u-beth-gloṭo**
a bank *S:* **banka; beth ʿurpana**; *T:* **u-beth-ʿurfono; i-banqa**
the cathedral *S:* **ʿomra**; *archbishopric* **khasyuta**; *patriarchate* **paṭriyarkuta**; *T: archbishopric* **i-ḥasyutho** *or* **i-maṭraniye**; *patriarchate T:* **i-fateryarkhutho; i-baṭrakiye**
the church *S:* **ʿidta**; *T:* **i-ʿidto**
the city center *S:* **leba d-mita**; *T:* **qenṭrun d-mdhitho**
the consulate *S:* **mshadranutha**; *T:* **i-mshadrutho**
the ... embassy *S:* **ezgaduta d-...**; *T:* **i-izgadutho ...**
the ... faculty *S:* **purnasa d..**; *T:* **i-fakulta d-...**
my hotel *S:* **bet-bawti**; *T:* **u-hotelaydhi**
the information bureau *S:* **makhitwa d-mawdʿanwata**; *T:* **u-makhtwo di-mawdʿonutho**
the internet café *S:* **bet-ṣarwa d-nawla**; *T:* **u-kafe-net**
the main square *S:* **mishṭakha gawanaya**; *T:* **u-meso; u-qenṭrun**
the market *S:* **shuqa**; *T:* **u-shuqo**
the ministry of ... *S:* **shariruta d-**; *T:* **i-sharirutho d-...; wazirutho d-...**
the monastery *S:* **dayra**; *T:* **i-dayro**
the mosque *S:* **minara**; *T:* **u-masghdho; u-jamiʿ**

the museum	*S:* **bet-ʿetqe**; *T:* **u-beth-ʿetqe**
parliament	*S:* **bet-sharire**; *T:* **mawtbo d-shulṭono; barlaman**
the police station	*S:* **nuqazta d-dakhshe**; *T:* **mashryo (qenṭrun) da-daḥshe**
the post office	*S:* **bet-bildara**; *T:* **u-makhtwo d-bildoro**
the station	*S:* **mashrita**; *T:* **u-mashryo; i-mashritho**
the telephone center	*S:* **nuqazta d-qaʿye**; *T:* **qenṭrun du-telefon**
a toilet	*S:* **bet-silya**; *T:* **beth-maye**
the university	*S:* **bet-sawba**; *T:* **u-beth-ṣawbo**

Which ... is this?
S: **Aha/Hadhe mud ... (e)le/(e)la?**
T: **Hano/Hathe ayna ... yo?**

bridge	*S:* **gishra (le)**; *T:* **geshro**
town	*S:* **mdita (la)**; *T:* **mdhitho**
building	*S:* **binyana (le)**; *T:* **benyono**
district	*S:* **pnita (la)**; *T:* **fnitho**
river	*S:* **nahra (le)**; *T:* **nahro**
road	*S:* **urkha (la)**; *T:* **darbo**
street	*S:* **qayṭona (la)**; *T:* **shqoqo; jaʿde; shariʿ**
suburb	*S:* **shwawta (la)**; *T:* **shawtho**
village	*S:* **qrita (la)**; *T:* **qritho**

What is this building?
S: **Mudi le aha benyana?**
T: **Mun-yo u-benyon-ano?**

What is that building?
S: **Mudi le awah binyana?**
T: **Mun-yo u-benyon-awo?**

What time does it open?
S: **B-shaʿta d-kma ypatikh/ypatkha?**
T: **B-ayna shoʿto ko-fotaḥ/ko-futḥo?**

What time does it close?
S: **B-shaʿta d-kma ysakhir/ysakhra?**
T: **B-ayna shoʿto ko-sokhar/ko-sukhro?**

Are we on the right road for ...?
S: **B-urkha trista wikh qa ...?**
T: **U-darbo d-... hano-yo?**

How many kilometers/miles is it to ...?
S: **Kma kilometre/mayile ila qa ...?**
T: **Kmo kilometre-yo/mile-yo m-arke hul ...?**

It is ... kilometers/miles away.
S: **... kilometre/mayile ila.**
T: **... kilometer/mile raḥuqo-yo/raḥuqto-yo.**

How far is the next town?
S: **Kma la rikhqa qrita da-qpa?**
T: **I-qritho ḥreto miqqa raḥuqto-yo m-arke?**

Where can I *(m/f)* find this address?
S: **Dakhi masin khazin ne/masyan khazyan ne aha munaʿa?**
T: **Ayko kibi ḥozeno/ḥuzyono i-mḥawyonuth-athe?**

Can you *(m/f)* show me on the map?
S: **Masit makhzitli l-kharița?/Masyat makhzatli l-kharița?**
T: **Kibokh/Kibekh maḥwat-li ʿal u-karṭo (*or* kharița)?**

How do I *(m/f)* get to ...?
S: **Dakhi azin/azan l-...**
T: **Aydarbo kibi moṭeno/mu?yono l-...**

I *(m/f)* want to go to ...
S: **Bayin azin l-.../Bayan azan l-...**
T: **K-obaʿno d-izzino l-.../K-ubʿono d-izzino l-...**

Can I *(m/f)* walk there?
S: **Masin mhalkhin l-tama?/Masyan mhalkhan l-tama?**
T: **Kibi malakhno/malkhono l-tamo?**

Can I *(m/f)* park here?
S: **Masin maklin l-raditi lakha?/Masyan maklan l-raditi lakha?**
T: **Kibi koleno/kulyono harke?**

Is it far?
S: **Rikhqa le?/Rikhqa la?**
T: **Raḥuqo-yo?/Raḥuqto-yo?**

Is it near?
S: **Qurba le?/Qurba la?**
T: **Qariwo-yo?/Qaruto-yo?**

Is it far from here?
S: **Rikhqa le/la m-lakha?**
T: **Raḥuqo-yo/Raḥuqto-yo m-arke?**

Is it near here?
S: **Qurba le/la m-lakha**
T: **Qariwo-yo/Qaruto-yo m-arke?**

It is not far.
S: **La le rikhqa./La la rikhqa.**
T: **Latyo raḥuqo/Latyo raḥuqto.**

Go *(m/f)* straight ahead.
S: **Zal triṣ.**
T: **Zokh/Zekh msawyo.**

Turn *(m/f)* left.
S: **Shqul/shqoel l-ṣimala.**
T: **Bram lu-semolo.**

Turn *(m/f)* right.
S: **Shqul/shqoel l-yamina.**
T: **Bram lu-yamino.**

at the next corner *S:* **l-qurnita da-qpa;**
T: **ʿal i-qurnitho ḥreto**
at the traffic lights *S:* **ʿal bahre;**
T: **ʿal a-bahre du-shfoʿo**
(*or* **du-murur)**

–Directions

behind	*S:* **l-batra**; *T:* **bithir**
corner	*S:* **qurnita**; *T:* **qurnitho**
crossroads	*S:* **palshat urkhate**; *T:* **fago; frosho da-darbone**
far	*S:* **rikhqa**; *T:* **raḥuqo**
in front of	*S:* **qam**; *T:* **qum**
left	*S:* **ṣim mala**; *T:* **semolo**
on the left	*S:* **l-simalukh shqul; shqoel ṣimala**; *T:* **ᶜal u-semolo**
near	*S:* **qurba**; *T:* **qariwo/qaruto**
one-way street	*S:* **urkha d-akhid shwila**; *T:* **shqoqo d-ḥa darbo; jaᶜde d-ḥa darbo; shariᶜ d-ḥa darbo**
opposite	*S:* **d-alqobl**; *T:* **barban d-...**
outside	*S:* **lwar**; *T:* **larwar**
right	*S:* **yamina**; *T:* **yamino**
on the right	*S:* **l-yaminukh shqul; shqoel yamina**; *T:* **ᶜal u-yamino**
straight on	*S:* **triṣ**; *T:* **msawyo**
under	*S:* **tkhet; khut**; *T:* **taḥt**
north	*S:* **garibya**; *T:* **garbyo**
south	*S:* **taymna**; *T:* **tayimno**
east	*S:* **madinkha**; *T:* **madenḥo**
west	*S:* **maᶜirwa**; *T:* **maᶜirbo**

10. SHOPPING

WHEN TO SHOP – Shops open after 8 am in Iraq, Syria and Turkey, and close before 7 pm. Most private shops break for lunch around 2 to 3 pm in Iraq, 12 to 2 pm in Turkey, or 2 to 4 pm in Syria. Some shops don't close for lunch and open also on official rest days. Markets are open every day except for Fridays (in Iraq and Syria), Sundays (in Turkey), and major holidays.

HOW TO PAY – Everything is best paid for in cash. Credit cards are acceptable in the larger cities of the Middle East and traveler's checks can be difficult to cash. Shops may have price tags attached to items but in most places you will have to ask and haggle.

FOOD & WINE – As well as the main streets of stores in the town centers, every street seems to have its own small produce kiosk or store. There is also a growing number of specialty shops, including supermarkets where you can buy western products.

MARKETS – For fresh produce go to a *S:* **shuqa**, *T:* **shuqo** or bazaar – a big market. Prices and availability of goods are seasonal. As a foreigner, you may occasionally find yourself paying a little more here – but not much! The best time is early morning when everything is at its freshest, particularly for meat and fish. Many local delicacies can be found here, including smoked and dried meats, and a veritable plethora of spices nuts and berries. Qamishli has one of the best of these markets, where you can buy all the usual produce and consumer products at a bargain, from cigarettes to C.D.-players, from clothing to pirate D.V.D.s.

Where can I *(m/f)* find a ...?
S: **Ika masin khazin kha ...?/Ika masyan khazan kha ...?**
T: **Ayko kibi ḥozeno/ḥuzyono ...?**

Where can I *(m/f)* buy ...?
S: **Ika masin zawnin ...?/Ika masyan zawnan** ...?
T: **Ayko kibi zowanno/zuwnono ...?**

Where is the market?
S: **Ika le shuqa**?
T: **U-shuqo ayko-yo?**

Where is the nearest ...?
S: **Ika le haw ... qurba?/Ika la hay ... qurba?**
T: **Ayko kit ... qariwo/qaruto?**

Can you *(m/f)* help me?
S: **Masit mᶜadritli?/Masyat mᶜadratli?**
T: **Kibokh/Kibekh mᶜawnat-li?**

Can I *(m/f)* help you?
S: **Masin mᶜadrinukh/mᶜadrinakh?/Masyan mᶜadranukh/mᶜadranakh?**
T: **Kibi mᶜawannolokh/mᶜawannolekh?/Kibi mᶜawnalokh/mᶜawnalekh?**

I'm *(m/f)* just looking.
S: **Balkhud bikhyara win./Balkhud bikhyara wan.**
T: **Bas ko-ḥoyarno./Bas ko-ḥayrono.**

I'd *(m/f)* like to buy ...
S: **Bayin zawnin .../Bayan zawnan ...**
T: **K-obaᶜno zowanno .../K-ubᶜono zuwnono ...**

Could you *(m/f)* show me some ...?
S: **Masit makhzitli kha kma ...?/Masyat makhzatli kha kma ...?**
T: **Kibokh/Kibekh maḥwat-li ushmo (*or* chike) m-...?**

Can I *(m/f)* look at it *(m/f)*?
S: **Masin khirin be/bah?/Masyan khayran be/bah?**
T: *said by a male:* **Kibi ḥozene/ḥozena?**; *said by a female:* **Kibi ḥuzyalle/ḥuzyalla?**

Do you *(pl)* have any ...?
S: **Itlokhon ...?**
T: **Kitkhu m-...?**

This.
S: **Hana./Hadhe.**
T: **Hano./Hathe.**

That.
S: **Haw./Hay.**
T: **Hawo./Hayo.**

I don't like it *(m/f)*.
S: —said by a male: **La win makhobe./La win makhoba.**/*—said by a female:* **La wan makhobe./La wan makhobah.**
T: —said by a male: **Lo k-roḥamne./Lo k-roḥamna.**/*—said by a female:* **Lo k-ruḥmalle./Lo k-ruḥmalla.**

I like it *(m/f)*.
S: **Makhubin./Makhuben.**
T: —said by a male: **Ko-roḥamne./Ko-roḥamna.**/*—said by a female:* **Ko-ruḥmalle./Ko-ruḥmalla.**

Do you *(pl)* have anything else?
S: **Itlokh sṭar min aha?**
T: **Kitkhu mede ḥreno?**

cheaper	*S:* **shawya**; *T:* **arzan-tir**; **rakhis-tir**
better	*S:* **ṭaw yatir**; *T:* **sh-ṭow-tir**
larger	*S:* **ṭaw rab**; *T:* **rab**; **rab-tir**
smaller	*S:* **ṭaw zʿor**; *T:* **naʿim**; **naʿim-tir**

Sorry, this is the only one.
S: **Pakhalta balkhudh hana/hadhe etli.**
T: **Shubqono, bas hano-yo/hathe-yo.**

I'll take it *(m/f)*.
S: said by a male: **Bzawnine/bzawnina.**; *said by a female:* **Bzawnane/bzawnana.**
T: said by a male: **G-moyadne/G-moyadna.**; *said by a female:* **G-maydalle./G-maydalla.**

How much/many do you *(m/f)* want?
S: **Kma bayit?/Kma bayat**?
T: **Miqqa k-obʿat?** *or* **Kmo k-obʿat?**

How much is it *(m/f)*?
S: **Kma le dmaeye/dmaeyah?**
T: **B-miqqa yo?**

Can you *(m/f)* write down the price?
S: **Masit katwit le l-dmaeya?/Masyat katwat le l-dmaeya**?
T: **Kibokh/Kibekh kuthwat u-ṭimo?**

Can you *(m/f)* lower the price?
S: **Masit mshawit l-dmaeya?/Masyat mshawyat l-dmaeya?**
T: **Kibokh/Kibekh manḥtat u-ṭimo?**

I don't have much money.
S: **Lit le saggi zoze.**
T: **Lat-li zuze (*or* kallat) ghallabe.**

Do you *(pl)* take credit cards?
S: **Yqablitun pitqe diziputa?**
T: **Ko-maqiblutu fetqe (*or* kartat) du-kredit?**

Would you *(m/f)* like it *(m/f)* wrapped?
S: **Bayit/Bayat le krikha?/Bayit/Bayat la krikhta?**
T: **K-ubᶜat-le b-kurokho?/K-ubᶜat-la b-kurokho?**

Will that be all?
S: **Sapiq an na?**
T: **K-ubᶜat mede ḥreno?**

Thank you *(m/f)*, goodbye.
S: **Tawdi push pshina./Tawdi poesh pshina.**
T: **Tawdi, fushu ba-shlomo.**

I want to return this *(m/f)* .
S: said by a male: **Bayin madᶜirin l-aha/l-hadhe.**; *said by a female:* **Bayan madᶜaran l-aha/l-hadhe.**
T: said by a male: **K-obaᶜno madᶜarno hano/hathe.**; *said by a female:* **K-ubᶜono madiᶜrono hano/hathe.**

—Outlets

baker's — *S:* **bet-apyuta**; *T:* **ferno**
bank — *S:* **bet-ᶜorpana**; *T:* **beth-ᶜurfono**; **banqa**
barber — *S:* **bet-supara**; *T:* **garoᶜo**
I'd *(m/f)* like a haircut. *S:* **Bayin d-msaprin l-saᶜri./Bayan d-msapran l-saᶜri** *T:* **K-obaᶜno qoyaṣno sawki./K-ubᶜono qayṣono sawki .**
bookshop — *S:* **dukan ktawe**; *T:* **dukano da-kthowe**

butcher's — *S:* **bet-qasawuta**; *T:* **qaṣobutho**
chemist's — *S:* **bet-samane**; *T:* **samsemonutho; rakhloyutho**
clothes shop — *S:* **dukan lwushe**; *T:* **dukano da-lbushe; dukano da-jule**
dentist — *S:* **asya d-shinne**; *T:* **osyutho da-ʿarshone**
department store — *S:* **dokan makhimle**; *T:* **dukano rabtho flighayto**
dressmaker — *S:* **khayaṭa/khayaṭṭa**; *T:* **ḥayoṭo/ḥayoṭṭo**
electrical goods store — *S:* **dokan laqiṭraye**; *T:* **dukano da-tuqone kahroboye**
florist — *S:* **wardaya; wardayta** *or* **duka warde**; *T:* **dukano da-warde**
greengrocer — *S:* **baqala**; *T:* **baqolo**
hairdresser — *S:* **sapara/saparanta**; *T:* **ḥaloqo/ḥaloqto**
hardware store — *S:* **dokan ʿutade**; *T:* **dukano da-mone farzloye**
hospital — *S:* **bet-krihe**; *T:* **beth-krihe**
kiosk — *S:* **kushk**; *T:* **kushk**
laundry — *S:* **bet-shyagha**; *T:* **mashighonutho**
market — *S:* **shuqa**; *T:* **shuqo**
newsstand — *S:* **dukan spar zawne**; *T:* **dukano da-sfar-zabne**
shoe shop — *S:* **dokan msane**; *T:* **dukano da-msone; dukano da-shakale**
shop — *S:* **dokana**; *T:* **dukano; ḥonutho**
  a local shop for local people *S:* **dukana qariwta qa nashe qariwe**; *T:* **dukano dukthonoyo la-dukthonoye**
stationer's — *S:* **dokan kerke**; *T:* **qarṭisoyutho; dukano da-mone du-kthowo**
supermarket — *S:* **supermarket**; *T:* **supermarket**
travel agent — *S:* **dokan krokhya**; *T:* **wakilo du-krukhyo**
vegetable shop — *S:* **dokan yariquta**; *T:* **dukano da-yarqe**
watchmaker's — *S:* **mtaqin shaʿe**; *T:* **dukano da-shoʿe**

–Gifts

ARTS & CRAFTS – Assyrians boast numerous artists of varying quality, though antique shops are rare. Check to see if there are restrictions on what you can take out of the country. The best places still to buy gifts, souvenirs and carpets are the *S:* **shuqas** or bazaars, *T:* **bazaars** or market districts of the larger towns and cities. Assyrians are well known for their fine silver filigree work and they own many jewelery stores in the bazaars. The best places to buy authentic Assyrian silver or antiques are Mosul or Nineveh in Iraq, Qamishli in Syria, and in Turkey the Dortyol area in central Midyat.

ANTIQUES – Depending on what you have bought, it is illegal to take certain antiques out of any country, unless accompanied by the relevant paperwork. Check with the dealer beforehand.

box; chest	*S:* **sanduqa**; *T:* **ṣanduqo**
bracelet	*S:* **shiberta; qulba**; *T:* **qulbo; shiro**
candlestick	*S:* **nawrishta**; *T:* **mnorto**
carpet	*S:* **amilla**; *T:* **mursho; ḥmiltho; tiraḥa; khali**
chain	*S:* **shishelta**; *T:* **shishaltho; suṭmo**
clock	*S:* **shaᶜta**; *T:* **shoᶜtho**
copper	*S:* **nkhasha**; *T:* **nḥosho**
crystal	*S:* **bellura**; *T:* **berulo; qrustalus**
cushion	*S:* **sadita**; *T:* **besodyo; mkhadde**
earrings	*S:* **marwade/qanushyate**; *T:* **marwode; qdhoshe**
enamel	*S:* **ṣwyiᶜa**; *T:* **qromo**
gift	*S:* **dashna**; *T:* **dushno**
gold	*S:* **dahwa**; *T:* **dahwo**
handicraft	*S:* **shughla d-ida**; *T:* **shughlo d-idho**
iron	*S:* **prezla**; *T:* **farzlo**
jewelery	*S:* **kheshlata**; *T:* **ḥashlotho**
kilim	*S:* **prista**; *T:* **froso**
knitted	*S:* **zqira;zqirta**; *T:* **zqiro/zqirto**
leather	*S:* **gilda**; *T:* **galdho**
medallion	*S:* **sheba**; *T:* **shebo**
metal	*S:* **prizla**; *T:* **ḥefro; metalon**
modern	*S:* **daraya/darayta**; *T:* **ḥatho**
necklace	*S:* **qladha**; *T:* **ᶜeqo; hamnikho**

pottery	*S:* **pakhara**; *T:* **quqoyutho; faṭorutho**
ring	*S:* **ʿisaqta**; *T:* **ʿezaqtho; ḥuza**
rosary	*S:* **rasuqta**; *T:* **resuqtho; wardiye**
silver	*S:* **ṣima**; *T:* **semo**
steel	*S:* **pladha**; *T:* **fulodho; farzlo hendwoyo**
stone	*S:* **kipa**; *T:* **kefo**
traditional	*S:* **msapyanutanaya/msapyanu-tanayta**; *T:* **ʿyodoyo; folkloroyo**
vase	*S:* **kawaza;zawirta**; *T:* **quqo; sharbo**
watch	*S:* **shaʿta d-ida**; *T:* **shoʿtho d-idho**
wood	*S:* **qaysa**; *T:* **qayso**
woven	*S:* **gdila**; *T:* **gdhilo/gdhilto**

—Clothes

bag	*S:* **simdha**; *T:* **kiso**
belt	*S:* **zunara**; *T:* **qamro; zunoro; qarish**
boots	*S:* **but**; *T:* **?edlo; but**
button	*S:* **taruqta**; *T:* **qurqoso**
cap	*S:* **papukhta**; *T:* **qubʿo**
cloth	*S:* **perqa**; *T:* **ferqo; ḥyoṣo; qumash**
clothes	*S:* **lwushe; julle**; *T:* **lwushe; jule**
cotton	*S:* **ktana**; *T:* **ketono**
dress	*S:* **zhita**; *T:* **naḥto**
gloves	*S:* **bra ide**; *T:* **bnoth-kafe**
handbag	*S:* **ṣimdha d-ida**; *T:* **ṣemdo**
handkerchief	*S:* **kunikta**; *T:* **mandilo**
hat	*S:* **kusita**; *T:* **kusitho; kimme**
jacket	*S:* **kutina**; *T:* **jaket**
jeans	*S:* **jinz**; *T:* **jinz**
leather	*S:* **gilda**; *T:* **galdho**
necktie	*S:* **khnaqa**; *T:* **ḥerqo; nektay**
overcoat	*S:* **meʿṭapa**; *T:* **maʿṭofo;** *for women* **manto;** *for men* **palto**
pin	*S:* **dambuṣ**; *T:* **sektho; zqiftho**
pocket	*S:* **kisa/ʿayba**; *T:* **beḥsho; jeb**
sandals	*S:* **sandale**; *T:* **sandole; ṭelore; klash**

scarf	*S:* **shala**; *T:* **makrukhto; sharfo**
shawl	*S:* **shala**; *T:* **shalo; atqi**
shirt	*S:* **qamista**; *T:* **kuthino; gomlak; qamis**
shoes	*S:* **msane**; *T:* **msone; shakale**
silk	*S:* **shira/ brişim**; *T:* **shiro**
socks	*S:* **gorwe/wase**; *T:* **gurwe**
suit	*S:* **eṣṭla**; *T:* **esṭlo; ṭaqm; badle; sut**
sweater; jumper	*S:* **switar**; *T:* **kazko; fanera; swetar**
tights	*S:* **shirwale ʿiqe**; *T:* **lwushe ʿiqe**
trousers	*S:* **shirwala**; *T:* **sharwolo; pantur; banṭalon**
umbrella	*S:* **meṭalta**; *T:* **mṭaltho; shamsiye**
underwear	*S:* **shirwala d-khuta**; *T:* **jule gawonoye; taḥtoye**
uniform	*S:* **talwishta**; *T:* **esṭlo rushmoyo; ṭukosoyo**
waistcoast	*S:* **yalak**; *T:* **yalak**
walking stick	*S:* **khuṭra/ gupala**; *T:* **ḥuṭro**
wool	*S:* **amra**; *T:* **ʿamro**
zipper	*S:* **shishilta/ zinjir**; *T:* **shishaltho**

—Toiletries

aspirin	*S:* **aspirin**; *T:* **aspirin**
brush	*S:* **parukhta**; *T:* **maknishto; fircha**
comb	*S:* **mesreqta**; *T:* **masurqo**
condom	*S:* **mṭaṭa d-khukhomya**; *T:* **kondom; kabbut**
cotton wool	*S:* **amra d-ktana**; *T:* **ketono**
deodorant	*S:* **ʿeṭra dshkhata**; *T:* **ʿeṭro luqbal du-ṣnono; deodorant**
hairbrush	*S:* **mesriqta d-saʿra**; *T:* **fircha du-sawko**
insect repellant	*S:* **qaṭlan baqe**; *T:* **msatronitho ma-raḥshe**
lipstick	*S:* **smuqa d-spwate**; *T:* **qanyo semoqo; ḥumra**
mascara	*S:* **kekhla**; *T:* **kuḥlo; maskara**
mouthwash	*S:* **mashghan pomma**; *T:* **mashighono du-femo**

nail-clippers *S:* **mqarṭan teprate**; *T:* **masfrone da-ṭefre**
nail-polish *S:* **sawʿa d-ṭiprate**; *T:* **ṣomuḥo da-ṭefre; ṣwoʿo da-ṭefre**
perfume *S:* **ʿeṭra**; *T:* **ʿeṭro; reḥo**
powder *S:* **bdhara**; *T:* **deqtho; bodra**
razor *S:* **megraʿta**; *T:* **goruʿtho**
razorblade *S:* **shelpe d-megraʿta**; *T:* **mdakhyo; shafra; mus**
safety pin *S:* **sinjaq**; *T:* **sektho mshayanto; zqiftho mshayanto**
sanitary towels *S:* **urqaʿta/urqaʿyata**; *T:* **ruqʿe ḥulmonoye d-kefso; fesqe ḥulmonoye d-kefso**
shampoo *S:* **shampu**; *T:* **shampu**
shaving cream *S:* **sapuna d-graʿa**; *T:* **ruʿtho du-ḥloqo**
sleeping pills *S:* **khabe d-nawma**; *T:* **ḥabbothe du-dmokho**
soap *S:* **sapuna**; *T:* **ṣafuno; ṣabun**
sponge *S:* **spongha**; *T:* **esfugho; isfanj**
sunblock cream *S:* **mishkha dalqub shimsha**; *T:* **doyubo luqbal di-shemsho**
tampon *S:* **urqaʿta qaṭinta**; *T:* **tampon**
tissues *S:* **shushipa**; *T:* **mandile d-waroqo**
toilet paper *S:* **shushipa d-silya**; *T:* **warqo du-tuwaylet**
toothbrush *S:* **perka d-shinne**; *T:* **farghuno**
toothpaste *S:* **roba d-shinne**; *T:* **darmono da-ʿarshone; maʿjun da-ʿarshone**
washing powder (detergent) *S:* **bdhara dshyagha**; *T:* **deqtho di-mashighonutho; bodra di-mashighonutho**

—Stationery

ballpoint *S:* **qanya dywashdyuta**; *T:* **qanyo nashifo**
book *S:* **ktawa**; *T:* **kthowo**
dictionary *S:* **kunash mille**; *T:* **sfar-mele; kunosh-mele; leksiqun**
envelope *S:* **ʿelwa**; *T:* **lfofo; zarf**

guidebook *S:* **hadiaa;** *T:* **kthowo di-mhadyonutho**
ink *S:* **dyuta;** *T:* **dyutho**
magazine *S:* **mghalta;** *T:* **mghaltho**
map *S:* **khriṭta;** *T:* **karṭo** *or* **khariṭa**
a map of Los Angeles *S:* **khariṭta d-Los Angeles;** *T:* **karṭo d-Los Anjeles**
road map *S:* **khariṭta d-urkhate;** *T:* **karṭo da-darbone**
newspaper *S:* **spar yawma;** *T:* **sfar-yawmo**
newspaper in English *S:* **spar yawme Englishaya;** *T:* **sfar-yawmo bu-Inglishoyo**
notebook *S:* **kerka d-zohare;** *T:* **fenqitho; kerko**
novel *S:* **shuᶜita;** *T:* **tunoyo**
novels in English *S:* **shuᶜita Englishayta;** *T:* **tunoye bu-Inglishoyo**
(piece of) paper *S:* **(qitᶜa d-) waraqa;** *T:* **(ṭarfo d-) warqo**
pen *S:* **qanya;** *T:* **qanyo**
pencil *S:* **qanya d-a'wara;** *T:* **qanyo rṣoṣoyo; aboroyo**
postcard *S:* **pitqa bildaraya;** *T:* **fetqo bildoroyo; kart postal**
scissors *S:* **masipra;** *T:* **msafrono; masforo**
writing paper *S:* **waraqe/ dappe d-ktawa;** *T:* **waroqe du-kthowo**

Do you *(pl)* have any foreign publications?
S: **Itlokho prase nukhraye**
T: **Kitkhu mghale aw kthowe nukhroye?**

—Photography

How much is it to process this film?
S: **Kma le dmaeya nupaqa d-aha pilma?**
T: **D-mashighat u-zul-ano (***or* **u-film-ano) b-miqqa-yo?**

When will it be ready?
S: **Eman bhawe mṭaywa?**
T: **Ema gid-owe ḥadhiro?**

I'd *(m/f)* like film for this camera.
S: **Bayin kha pilma qa hadhe ṣayurta.**
T: **K-obaᶜno/kubᶜono zulo (*or* filma) lajan di-qamerathe.**

B&W (film)	*S:* **kuma o khwara (pilma);** *T:* **komo w-ḥeworo (zulo)**
camera	*S:* **ṣayurta;** *T:* **qamera**
colour (film)	*S:* **mgawnana (pilma);** *T:* **mgawno (zulo)**
film	*S:* **zula;pilma;** *T:* **zulo; filma**
flash	*S:* **zahra;** *T:* **barqo; bahro; flash**
lens	*S:* **ṭlawekhta;** *T:* **ṭaliḥto; ᶜadase**
light meter	*S:* **kyula d-bahra;** *T:* **mkaylono du-bahro**

—Electrical equipment

BUYING TIP – For high-tech stuff like cassettes, videos/video-players or transformers, C.D.-players and D.V.D. you mare more likely to be understood if you use the English terms.

adapter	*S:* **masir toqane;** *T:* **mameṭyonitho; adapter**
battery	*S:* **baṭarita;** *T:* **baṭṭaritho; rusoqo; baṭṭariye**
cassette	*S:* **zula;** *T:* **shoriṭo; qaseta**
C.D.	*S:* **dawqa;** *T:* **sidi**
C.D. player	*S:* **toqan dawqe;** *T:* **msaghlonitho du-sidi; musajjal du-sidi**
D.V.D.	*S:* **dividi;** *T:* **dividi**
D.V.D. player	*S:* **toqan dividi;** *T:* **msaghlonitho du-dividi**
fan	*S:* **marwakhta;** *T:* **marwoḥo; mafoḥitho**
hairdryer	*S:* **myawshan saᶜra;** *T:* **mnashfono du-sawko**
iron *(for clothing)*	*S:* **kwita;** *T:* **mkawyonitho; uti**
kettle	*S:* **rathukhta;** *T:* **qaqbo; chaydan**
plug	*S:* **plug;** *T:* **fisha; shoqulo d-kahrobo**

portable T.V. — *S:* **makhizyana mziᶜana;** *T:* **fros-ḥezwo meshtanyono; telvizyon meshtanyono**
radio — *S:* **radio;** *T:* **fros-qolo; radio**
record — *S:* **lukha;** *T:* **shawyo**
tape (cassette) — *S:* **zul qala;** *T:* **zul-qolo; qaseta**
tape-recorder — *S:* **msaghlanita;** *T:* **msaghlonitho da-zul-qole**
television — *S:* **makhizyana;** *T:* **fros-ḥezwo; telvizyon**
transformer — *S:* **mkhalpana;** *T:* **mshaḥilfono**
video-player — *S:* **toqan video;** *T:* **msaghlonitho da-zul-ḥezwe**
videotape — *S:* **zul khizwa;** *T:* **zul-ḥezwo; sharit̩**
voltage regulator — *S:* **t̩okas volte;** *T:* **mt̩aksono du-volt̩aj**

—Sizes

small — *S:* **zᶜura/zᶜurta;** *T:* **naᶜimo/naᶜimto**
big — *S:* **raba/rabta;** *T:* **rabo/rabtho**
heavy — *S:* **yaqura/yaqurta;** *T:* **yaquro/yaqurto; tqilo/tqilto**
light — *S:* **qalula/qalolta;** *T:* **khayifo/khayifto; qalilo/qalilto**
more — *S:* **yatir;** *T:* **zid**
less — *S:* **bsir;** *T:* **noqiṣ**
many — *S:* **saggi;** *T:* **sagi; ghallabe**
too much/too many — *S:* **saggi yatir;** *T:* **zoyudo/zoyudto/zoyude**
enough — *S:* **sapiq;** *T:* **malyo/mlitho**
that's enough! — *S:* **sapiq aha!;** *T:* **bas-yo!**
also — *S:* **ap;** *T:* **... ste; ... stene**
a little bit — *S:* **qalil;** *T:* **ushmo; chike**

I'd *(m/f)* like a carrier bag to carry these things in.
S: **Baᶜin khda kista d-t̩aᶜnin an na./Baᶜyan khda kista d-t̩aᶜnan an na.**
T: **K-obaᶜno ṣemdo du-t̩ᶜono lajan d-t̩oᶜanno a-medon-ani eba./K-ubᶜono ṣemdo du-t̩ᶜono lajan d-t̩uᶜnono a-medon-ani eba.**

—Colors

black	*S:* **kuma/kumta**; *T:* **komo/komto**
pink	*S:* **wardanaya/wardanayta**; *T:* **wardonoyo/wardonayto**
blue	*S:* **zarqa/zarqayta**; *T:* **zarqo/zarqtho**
purple	*S:* **banawsha/banawshayta**; *T:* **argwonoyo/argwonayto**; **banafshoyo/banafshayto**
brown	*S:* **gawra/gawirta**; *T:* **shḥomo/shḥumto**; **qḥuthonoyo/qḥuthonayto**
red	*S:* **smuqa/smuqta**; *T:* **semoqo/semaqto**
gray	*S:* **qiṭmanaya**; **qiṭmayata**; *T:* **qaṭmonoyo/qaṭmonayto**; **rṣoṣoyo/rṣoṣayto**
green	*S:* **yaruqa/yaruqta**; *T:* **yaruqo/yaruqto**
white	*S:* **khwara/khwarta**; *T:* **ḥeworo/ḥewarto**
orange	*S:* **putha/puthayta**; **eṭrughaya/eṭrughayta**; *T:* **eṭrughoyo/eṭrughayto**
yellow	*S:* **shaʿuta/shaʿutta**; *T:* **shaʿutho/shaʿuthto**

11. WHAT'S TO SEE

Do you *(m/f)* have a guidebook?
S: **Etlokh/Etlakh hadiaa?**
T: **Kitlokh/Kitlekh kthowo di-mhadyonutho (*or* dalil)?**

Do you *(m/f)* have a local map?
S: **Etlokh/Etlakh kharițta d-aha dokta?**
T: **Kitlokh/Kitlekh karțo (*or* kharița) di-fnith-athe?**

Is there a guide *(m/f)* who speaks English?
S: **Et kha mhadyana d-msawit lishana Inglishaya?/Et khda mhadyanta d-msawta lis-hana Inglishaya?**
T: **Kit mhadyono d-ko-mijghil Inglishoyo?/Kit mhadyonitho d-ko-mijgholo Inglishoyo?**

What are the main attractions?
S: **Mudi na dokani rishaye d-țoyala?**
T: **Mun-ne a-medone magirshone harke?**

What is that *(m/f)*?
S: **Mudi le aha?/Mudi la hadhe?**
T: **Mun-yo hawo/hayo?**

How old is it *(m/f)*?
S: **Kma le ʿomre?/Kma le ʿomra?**
T: **Miqqa ʿatiqo-yo?**

What animal is that?
S: **Ma khaywa le aha?**
T: **Mun ḥaywo-yo hawo?**

What fish is that?
S: **Ma nona le aha?**
T: **Mun nuno-yo hawo?**

What insect is that?
S: **Ma rakhsha le aha?**
T: **Mun raḥsho-yo hawo?**

May I *(m/f)* take a photograph?
S: **Masin shaqlin ṣurta?**
T: **Kibi gorashno/gurshono ṣurto?**

What time does it open?
S: **Eman ypatikh?**
T: **B-ayna shoᶜtho ko-fotaḥ?**

What time does it close?
S: **Eman ysakhir?**
T: **B-ayna shoᶜtho ko-sokhar?**

What does that say?
S: **Mudi le sukala d-aha?**
T: **Hawo mun k-omar?**

Who is that statue of?
S: **Hadhe qayimta d-mani la?**
T: **I-qayimtathe d-man yo?**

Is there an entrance fee?
S: **Maᶜla bzoze le?**
T: **Kit aghro du-ᶜboro?**

How much?
S: **Kma?**
T: **Miqqa-yo?**

What's there to do in the evening?
S: **mudi it l-ᶜwada b-ramsha?**
T: **ᶜAṣriye ḥa mun kibe soyem?**

Are there any nightclubs/discos?
S: **Et bet-smakhe/disko lakha?**
T: **Kito beth-smokhe/diskowat?**

Is there a concert?
S: **it khigga musiqaya?**
T: **Kito qonser?**

What time does it begin?
S: **Iman b-mshare?**
T: **B-ayna shoᶜtho gi-mshore?**

How much does it cost to get in?
S: **Kma le d-maeya d-maᶜla?** *or* **Kma la ᶜworta?**
T: **B-miqqa-yo u-ᶜboro?**

When is the wedding?
S: **Eman ile burakha** (*ceremony*)/**khlola** (*reception*)?
T: **Ema-yo u-klilo** (*ceremony*)/**i-meshtutho** (*reception*)?

bridegroom	*S:* **khitna**; *T:* **ḥathno**
bride	*S:* **kalu**; *T:* **kaltho**
invitation	*S:* **zminuta/ jyadta**; *T:* **zminutho**; **daʿwe**

Can we swim here?
S: **Masikh sakhikh lakha?**
T: **Kiban soḥina harke?**

—Activities

classical music	*S:* **musiqa klasikayta**; *T:* **musiqa klasikayto**
concert	*S:* **khigga musiqaya**; *T:* **qonser**
dancing	*S:* **raqada**; *T:* **raqdho**
disc-jockey	*S:* **dijay**; *T:* **dijay**; **disk-joki**
disco	*S:* **disco**; *T:* **disko**; **diskotek**
elevator; lift	*S:* **masilqanita**; *T:* **maʿlyono**
escalator	*S:* **darkhe laqit parae**; *T:* **masqono**; **mdarghono**
exhibition	*S:* **bet-glakha**; *T:* **beth-gloḥo**; **froso**
folk dancing	*S:* **riqda ʿammaya**; *T:* **raqdho ʿamoyo**; **folkloroyo**
folk music	*S:* **zimra ʿammaya**; *T:* **musiqa folklorayto**
jazz	*S:* **jazz**; *T:* **jaz**
nightclub	*S:* **bet-smakha**; *T:* **beth-smokho**; **nadi**; **qlab**
opera	*S:* **opera**; *T:* **opera**
party	*S:* **meshtuta**; *T:* **ḥago**
pop music	*S:* **zimra d-pop**; *T:* **musiqa ʿamayto**
pub	*S:* **khanuta**; *T:* **mashqyo**; **beth-qafile**; **bar**; **pab**
trade fair	*S:* **glikhut tagharuta**; *T:* **gloḥutho di-tagorutho**

WHAT'S TO SEE

—Places

academy	*S:* **bet-drasha**; *T:* **beth-drosho**
apartment	*S:* **mashikna**; *T:* **mashryo; shiqqa; apartaman**
apartment block	*S:* **guda d-mashikne**; *T:* **beth-mashrye; ᶜimare**
archaeological	*S:* **ᶜaqawaya/ᶜaqawayta/ᶜaqawaye**; *T:* **ᶜatiqo; arkeolojoyo; athari**
art gallery	*S:* **glakh amna**; *T:* **beth-gloḥo**
bakery	*S:* **nakhtuma**; *T:* **ferno; farmo**
bar	*S:* **bar**; *T:* **mashqyo; bar**
building	*S:* **binyana**; *T:* **benyono**
casino	*S:* **casino**; *T:* **gazino; beth-qumoro**
castle	*S:* **apidna**; *T:* **quṣro**
cemetery	*S:* **bet-qore**; *T:* **beth-qawre**
church	*S:* **ᶜomra**; *T:* **ᶜidto**
cinema	*S:* **bet-khizwane**; *T:* **sinama; beth-ḥezwe**
city map	*S:* **kharita d-midta**; *T:* **karṭo di-mdhitho**
college	*S:* **bet-drasha**; *T:* **beth-drosho; kulliye**
concert	*S:* **khegga muziqaya**; *T:* **konser**
concert hall	*S:* **awana muziqaya**; *T:* **awono da-konserat**
convent	*S:* **dayra**; *T:* **dayro**
embassy	*S:* bet-**ezgaduta**; *T:* **izgadutho**
fort	*S:* **khasna**; *T:* **qalᶜo**
foundation	*S:* **mshat'asta**; *T:* **shutoso; shethesto**
hospital	*S:* **bet-krihe**; *T:* **beth-krihe**
house	*S:* **bayta**; *T:* **bayto**
housing estate/project	*S:* **tarmita mashiknayta**; *T:* **tarmitho**
industrial estate	*S:* **ᶜaqara ṣniᶜaya**; *T:* **mulkono ṣniᶜuthonoyo; qenyono ṣniᶜuthonoyo**
library	*S:* **bet-arke**; *T:* **beth-arke**
main square	*S:* **mshṭakha rishaya**; *T:* **meso; qenṭrun**
market	*S:* **shuqa**; *T:* **shuqo**

monastery	*S:* **dayra**; *T:* **dayro**
monument	*S:* **qayemta**; *T:* **neṣbo makthabzabnoyo**; **qayimto**
mosque	*S:* **minara**; *T:* **masghdho**; **jamiʿ**
museum	*S:* **bet-etqe**; *T:* **beth-ʿetqe**
old city	*S:* **mdita ʿtiqta**; *T:* **mdhitho ʿatiqto**
opera house	*S:* **bet-opera**; *T:* **tiyaṭron d-opera**
palace	*S:* **apidna**; *T:* **ofadhno**; **beth-malko**
park	*S:* **makhimla dradiyate**; *T:* **gantho**
parliament	*S:* **bet-shultanaor bet-sharire**; *T:* **beth-shulṭonutho**; **barlaman**
restaurant	*S:* **bet-maekhla**; *T:* **beth-muklo**; **mṭʿomo**; **loqanṭa**
ruins	*S:* **ʿetqe**; *T:* **ḥarwotho**; **kharab**
school	*S:* **midrashta**; *T:* **madrashto**
sculpture	*S:* **glapa** *or* **ṣalma**; *T:* **ṣalmo**
seminary	*S:* **midrashta d-kahne**; *T:* **madrashto kuhnayto**; **seminer**
shop; store	*S:* **dok ana**; *T:* **dukano**; **ḥonutho**
shrine	*S:* **shkhinta**; *T:* **beth-ṣlutho**; **shkhintho**
sports club	*S:* **bet-drashe**; *T:* **beth-durosho**
stadium	*S:* **bet-shiʿya**; *T:* **isṭadyon**; **beth-sheʿyo**
statue	*S:* **qaymita**; *T:* **qayimto**
street	*S:* **qayṭuna**; **shqaqa**; *T:* **shquqo**
tea house	*S:* **bet- tiya**; **chaykhana**; *T:* **chaykhana**
theater	*S:* **bet-khawra**; *T:* **beth-ḥezwone**; **tiyaṭron**
tomb	*S:* **qawra**; *T:* **qawro**
tower	*S:* **maghidla**; *T:* **burgo**; **maghdlo**
university	*S:* **bet-sawba**; *T:* **beth-ṣawbo**
zoo	*S:* **ganta d-khaywate**; *T:* **gantho d-ḥaywotho**

—Occasions

birth	*S:* **mawlada**; *T:* **mawlodo**
death	*S:* **mawta**; *T:* **mawto**
funeral	*S:* **ʿopaya**; *T:* **qwurto**
marriage	*S:* **zuwagha**; *T:* **gworo**

—Religious culture

patriarch	*S:* **awa d-awahate**; *T:* **faṭeryarkho**
metropolitan	*S:* **khasya or miṭrapoliṭa**; *T:* **ḥasyo; maṭran; sayidna**
priest	*S:* **qasha**; *T:* **qasho; abuna; kuhno**
monk	*S:* **rabana**; *T:* **dayroyo**
nun	*S:* **rabanta** *or* **dayrayta**; *T:* **dayrayto**
saint	*S:* **qadisha**; *T:* **qadisho/qadishto**
holy mass	*S:* **qorbana qadisha**; *T:* **qerowo alohoyo; qudosho alohoyo**
Easter	*S:* **ʿIda d-Qyamta**; *T:* **ʿEdho da-Qyimto; ʿEdho Rabo**
Christmas	*S:* **ʿIda Zʿura**; *T:* **ʿEdho d-Mawlodo; ʿEdho Naʿimo**

Religious Heritage...

Christianity has played a fundamental role in the formation of the Assyrian identity. The Assyrians were the first people to adopt Christianity, guided by the apostle St. Thaddeus who converted the Assyrian king of Edessa, Abgar the Black, in the mid-first century A.D. Other apostles known to have evangelized the Assyrians are St. Thomas, St. Bartholemew and St. Peter. One of the founding fathers of the Syriac Church, St. Ephrem (d. 373), a monk, theologian and poet who directed the theological universities of Nisibis and later Edessa and helped to establish the golden age of Syriac literature.

Christianity has played a fundamental role in the formation of the Assyrian identity. The Assyrians were the first people to adopt Christianity, guided by the apostle St. Thaddeus who converted the Assyrian king of Edessa, Abgar the Black, in the mid first century A.D. Other apostles known to have evangelized the Assyrians are St. Thomas, St. Bartholemew and St. Peter. One of the founding fathers of the Syriac Church, St. Ephrem (d. 373), a monk, theologian and poet who directed the theological universities of Nisibis and later Edessa and helped to establish the golden age of Syriac literature.

The Assyrian/Syriac Church has since developed independently from the other Christian Churches, and is today divided into two main spheres: East and West. The Eastern Assyrians (i.e. speakers of Swadaya/Madinkhaya) are mostly members of the Church of the East and its Catholic counterpart the Chaldean Church, while the Western Assyrians (i.e. speakers of Turoyo) are mostly members of the Syriac Orthodox Church of Antioch, but also the Syriac Catholic Church. All Assyrian Churches act as custodians of the nation's culture and form an essential part of the growing Diaspora.

The head of the Syriac Orthodox Church is referred to as the Patriarch of Antioch and All the East. His seat is in the Syrian capital Damascus. There is also a minority of Syriac Catholics with a patriarch in Beirut, Lebanon. The head of the Church of the East is referred to as the Catholicos-Patriarch of the East. There are presently two: one with his seat in Chicago and another in Baghdad. The Patriarch of the Chaldean Catholics also resides in Baghdad. There are also smaller Protestant Assyrian communities. Residing in the same region as the Assyrians are large numbers of Muslim Kurds, Arabs and Turks.

The longstanding history of Assyrians and Christianity means that wherever you are you'll never be far from one of their splendid churches. Mardin in Turkey was the seat of the Syriac Orthodox and Catholic Patriarchs until the1920s and is still the center of a diocese. It is therefore here that you can see the nearby Saffron Monastery (Dayro d-Kurkmo), founded in the sixth century. The monasteries of St. Matthew (Syriac Orthodox) and St. Behnam (Syriac Catholic) in northern Iraq are also important historically and artistically, as well as the monastery of Rabban Hurmizd near the town of Alqosh, which served as the seat of the Church of the East and later Chaldean Patriarchs.

The next most important monasteries are those of St. Gabriel, the center of the diocese of Tur-Adbin founded in the fourth century and the fifth-century monastery of St James the Recluse at Salah (Baristepe), which was the seat of the Patriarchs of Tur-Abdin during a 500-year church split.

Others include the first-century monastery of the Mother of God in Hah (Anitli), the fourth-century monasteries, all very well preserved, of St. Malke and St. Eugene in the Izlo mountains and the fourth-century church of St. James in Nisibis. The most famous Assyrian churches in Iran are the first century church of the Virgin Mary in the city of Urmia and the fifth century monastery of Sts. Sergius and Bacchus at Mar Sargis, also worth a visit.

12. FINANCE

CURRENCIES – Everything is best paid for in cash. Credit cards are acceptable in Turkey's cities as are traveler's checks, which are best purchased in U.S. dollars. In Syria, Iraq and Iran (at present) these are less acceptable. The Turkish currency is the lira, the Syrian currency is the pound (lira), the Iraqi currency is the dinar and the Iranian currency is the riyal (or toman), all of which come in bills and coins of various denominations. However, U.S. dollars are used throughout Iraq and in varying degrees in Syria and Turkey. Euros are also accepted in some places, especially in Turkey. Bills may be reused if they are crease, torn, old or simply a low denomination. Be prepared to accept change in the local currency. Also, if you are paying with the local currency, avoid taking large bills as you might have difficulty in getting them changed while out shopping.

CHANGING MONEY – Banks in Turkey are open from 8.30am to noon and from 1.30pm to 5pm every day from Monday to Friday. In Syria they are open between 9am and 12.30pm or 2pm every day from Saturday to Thursday. In Iraq times vary. It is often better to change money at exchange offices, which are open until late in the evening seven days a week. The cashiers may know a European language or two, and almost all will show the workings of the exchange on a calculator for you and give you a receipt. Many shops and kiosks will be happy to change money for you but the best rates are offered at jewelry stores (many of which are Assyrian-owned).

TIPPING – If you're happy with the service you receive in restaurants then 10 percent of the check is the norm (but always double check with local friends!). If you're only having a coffee in a café simply round up the total. Other services are also carried out with a view to being tipped – everything from having your luggage carried to having doors opened for you come into this category.

I *(m/f)* want to change some dollars.
S: **Bayin shakhlipin dolare./Bayan shakhlipan dolare.**
T: **K-obaᶜno mṣarafno kmo dolare./K-ubᶜono mṣarfono kmo dolare.**

I *(m/f)* want to change some euros.
S: **Bayin shakhlipin euroz./Bayan shakhlipan euroz.**

T: **K-obaᶜno mṣarafno kmo oyro./K-ubᶜono mṣarfono kmo oyro.**

I *(m/f)* want to change some pounds.
S: **Bayin shakhlipin pawande./Bayan shakhlipan pawande.**
T: **K-obaᶜno mṣarafno kmo pawande./***T:* **K-ubᶜono mṣarfono kmo pawande.**

Where can I *(m/f)* change some money?
S: **Ika masin shakhlipin zoze?/Ika masyan shakhlipan zoze?**
T: **Ayko kibi mṣarafno zuze (***or* **kallat)?; Ayko kibi mṣarfono zuze (***or* **kallat)?**

What is the exchange rate?
S: **Mudi ele shawya d-shakhlapta?**
T: **Miqqa-yo ṭimo du-ṣrofo?**

What is the commission?
S: **Mudi ele hinyana or comishin.**
T: **U-shuḥdo (***or* **U-qomisyon) miqqa-yo?**

Could you *(m/f)* please check that again?
S: **En mbasmalukh/mbasmalakh m-akid medre?**
T: **Boᶜutho menokh, kibokh ḥayrat b-uwe naqla ḥreto?/***T:* **Boᶜutho menekh, kibekh ḥayrat b-uwe naqla ḥreto?**

Could you *(m/f)* please write that down for me?
S: **En mbasmalokh, masit katwetle qati?**
T: **Boᶜutho menokh, kibokh kothwat-li-yo?/Boᶜutho menekh, kibekh kothwat-li-yo?**

Do you *(m/f)* have a calculator?
S: **Etlokh/Etlakh khashuta?**
T: **Kit-lokh/Kit-lekh manoyo (***or* **maḥshwono)?**

—International currencies

dollar	*S:* **dollar**; *T:* **dolar**
euro	*S:* **euro**; *T:* **oyro**
ruble	*S:* **ruble**; *T:* **rubil**
pound (sterling)	*S:* **pawand**; *T:* **pawand**

FINANCE

banknotes	*S:* **shawe; zoze shawe**; *T:* **waroqe**
calculator	*S:* **khashuta**; *T:* **manoyo; maḥshwono**
cashier	*S:* **gizabra/gizabrta**; *T:* **noṭar-kesfo/noṭro-kesfo; kasher/kashera**
coins	*S:* **kespa**; *T:* **farude; ʿurfono; fraṭa; khurda**
credit card	*S:* **pitqa dizoputa**; *T:* **fetqo du-kredit; kredit kard**
commission	*S:* **commission**; *T:* **shuḥdo; qomisyon**
exchange	*S:* **khulapa**; *T:* **ṣrofo**
loose change	*S:* **kespa sharya**; *T:* **farude**
receipt	*S:* **shṭarmaswa**; *T:* **fetqo d-qubolo**
signature	*S:* **rmay ida**; *T:* **rmay-idho; imdha**

13. COMMUNICATIONS

—Post

Where is the post office?
S: **Ika le bet-bildara?**
T: **Ayko-yo u-makhtwo d-bildoro?**

What time does the post office open?
S: **Shaᶜta dkma ypatikh bet-bildara?**
T: **B-ayna shoᶜtho gid-fotaḥ u-makhtwo d-bildoro?**

What time does the post office close?
S: **shaᶜta dkma ysakhir bet-bildar?**
T: **B-ayna shoᶜtho gid-sokhar u-makhtwo d-bildoro?**

Where is the mail box?
S: **Ika le sanduqa d-bildara?**
T: **U-ṣanduqo d-bildoro ayko-yo?**

Is there any mail for me?
S: **It bildara qati?**
T: **Kit egaryotho lajani?**

How long will it take for this *(m/f)* to get there?
S: **Kma bgarsha d-aha maṭe l-tama?/Kma bgarsha d-hadhe matya l-tama?**
T: **Miqqa gid-goresh hano hul d-moṭe l-tamo?/Miqqa gid-gursho hathe hul d-moṭe l-tamo?**

How much does it cost to send this *(m/f)* to ...?
S: **Kma b-dqra shadarta d-aha/d-hadhe l-...?**
T: **B-miqqa-yo d-mshadarno hano l-...?/B-miqqa-yo d-mshadrono hathe l-...?**

I *(m/f)* would like some stamps.
S: **Bayin/Bayan qalil khtamae.**
T: **K-obaᶜno zowanno kmo ṭawᶜe./K-ubᶜono zuwnono kmo ṭawᶜe.**

I *(m/f)* would like to send this to ...
S: **Bayin shadrin aha/hadhe l-.../Bayan shadran aha/hadhe l-...**
T: **K-obaʿno mshadarno ano/hathe l-.../K-ubʿono mshadrono hano/hathe l-...**

air mail	*S:* **bildara rqiʿaya**; *T:* **bildoro hawoyo**
envelope	*S:* **ʿalwa**; *T:* **lfofo; zarf**
letter	*S:* **egarta**; *T:* **egartho**
mailbox	*S:* **sandoq bildara**; *T:* **ṣanduqo d-bildoro**
parcel	*S:* **ʿalwa bildaraya**; *T:* **mesorto**
postcard	*S:* **petqa bildaraya**; *T:* **fetqo bildoroyo; kart postal**
registered mail	*S:* **bildara sghila**; *T:* **bildoro msaghlo; musajjal**
stamp	*S:* **khtama**; *T:* **ṭawʿo**

—Tele-etiquette

I *(m/f)* would like to make a phone call.
S: **Bayin maplikhin l-qaʿya./Bayan maplikhan l-qaʿya.**
T: **K-obaʿno mtalfanno./K-ubʿono mtalfinono.**

I *(m/f)* would like to send a fax.
S: **Bayin shadrin faks./Bayan shadran faks.**
T: **K-obaʿno mshadarno faks./K-ubʿono mshadrono faks.**

I *(m/f)* would like to fax this letter.
S: **Bayin ʿawdin fax/ Bayan ʿawdan fax l- aha/hade.**
T: **K-obaʿno mshadarno i-egarthathe bu-faks./ K-ubʿono mshadrono i-egarthathe bu-faks.**

Where is the telephone?
S: **Ika le qaʿya?**
T: **U-telefon ayko-yo?**

May I *(m/f)* use your phone?
S: **Masin maplikhin l-qaʿya?/Masyan maplikhan l-qaʿya?**

T: **Kibi mista^c^malno/mista^c^mlono u-telefonathkhu?**

Can I *(m/f)* telephone from here?
S: **Masin qaren b-qa^c^ya min lakha?/Masyan qaryan b-qa^c^ya min lakha?**
T: **Kibi mtalfanno/mtalfinono m-arke?**

Can you *(m/f)* help me *(m/f)* find this number?
S: **Masit m^c^adretli d-machkhin/d-machkhan l-aha raqma?/Masyat d-m^c^adratli d-machkhin/d-machkhan l-aha raqma?**
T: **Kibokh m^c^awnat-li ko-korakhno/ko-kurkhono ^c^al u-menyon-ano?/Kibekh m^c^awnat-li ko-korakhno/ko-kurkhono ^c^al u-menyon-ano.**

Can I *(m/f)* dial direct?
S: **Masin qaren tresait?/Masyan qaryan tresait?**
T: **Kibi doyaqno/dayqono msawyo (*or* direkt)?**

May I (m/f) speak to Mr. ...?
S: **Masin/Masyan msawtin ^c^am myaqra...?**
T: **Kibi mijghalno/mijgholono ^c^am myaqro ...?**

May I *(m/f)* speak to Mrs./Miss ...?
S: **Masin/Masyan msawtin ^c^am myaqarta...?**
T: **Kibi mijghalno/mijgholono ^c^am myaqartho ...?**

Can I *(m/f)* leave a message?
S: **Masit amritle?/Masyat amritla?**
T: **Kibi ṭoreno/ṭuryono egartho?**

Who *(m/f)* is calling, please?
S: **En mbasmalokh/mbasmalakh mani le biqraya?**
T: **Man ko-mijghil/ko-mijgholo, bo^c^utho menaykhu?**

Who *(m/f)* are you calling?
S: **Qa mani wit/wat biqraya?**
T: **L-man ko-mtalfinat?**

What is your *(m/f)* name?
S: **Mudi le shimokh/shimakh?**
T: **Mun-yo ishmokh/ishmekh?**

Which number are you *(m/f)* dialing?
S: **L-mud raqma qraya wit/wat?**
T: **Ayna menyono (*or* raqmo) ko-dayqat?**

He/She is not here.
S: **Haw la le lakha./Hay la lah lakha.**
T: **La-tyarke.**

Would you *(m/f)* like to leave a message?
S: **Bayit shuqit egarta/ bayat shuqat eqarta**
T: **K-obᶜat ṭorat egartho?**

This *(m/f)* is not ...
S: **Aha la le .../Hadhe la lah ...**
T: **La-tyo ... hano.**

You *(m/f)* are mistaken.
S: **At ᶜwidlokh pawda./Ate ᶜwidlakh pawda.**
T: **Mghalaṭlokh./Mghalaṭlekh.** *or* **Ghaliṭat.**

This is the office of ...
S: **Aha makhitwa d-...**
T: **Hano u-makhtwo d-... yo.**

Hello, I *(m/f)* need to speak to ...
S: **Shlama, bayin msawtin ᶜam .../Shlama, bayan msawtan ᶜam ...**
T: **Shlomo, k-lozim mijghalno/mijgholono ᶜam ...**

I'm *(m/f)* calling this number.
S: **Qrayawin l-aha raqma/ qrayewan l-aha raqma.**
T: **U-menyon-ano ko-doyaqno/ko-dayqono.**

Sorry wrong number.
S: **Shubqana, raqma pawda le.**
T: **Shubqono, u-menyono ghalṭo-yo.**

Please phone *(m/f)* me.
S: **ᶜwud ṭawta w-qrili/ ᶜwued ṭawta w-qrehli.**
T: **Mtalfan-li, boᶜutho menokh/menekh.**

Send *(m/f)* me a text message.
S: **shadirli eqarta d text.**
T: **Mshayaᶜ-li egartho du-tekst.**

I *(m/f)* want to call ...
S: **Bayin qarin .../Bayan qaryan ...**
T: **K-obaʿno mtalfanno/mtalfinono l-...**

What is the code for ...?
S: **Mudi le qdila d-...?**
T: **Mun-yo u-qlidho d-...?**

What is the international dialing code?
S: **Mudi le qdila tiwilaya ...?**
T: **Mun-yo u-qlidho du-dyoqo tibeloyo?**

What do I *(m/f)* dial for an outside line?
S: **Mudi le raqma d-naswan khṭuṭa bar raya?**
T: **Mun k-lozim doyaqno/dayqono lajan ḥṭuṭo (*or* khaṭ) baroyo?**

The number is ...
S: **Raqma ele ...**
T: **U-menyono ... yo.**

The extension is ...
S: **Raqma dilanaya ele ...**
T: **I-mfashṭutho ... yo.**

It's engaged.
S: **Shghima le.**
T: **Shagholo yo.** *or* **Mashgul yo.**

The line has been cut off.
S: **Qiṭyale raqma.**
T: **U-ḥṭuṭo qṭiʿ.**

Where is the nearest public phone?
S: **Ika le haw qaʿya gawanaya?**
T: **Ayko kit telefon qariwo?**

—Phone words

digital — *S:* **raqmaya/digital**; *T:* **dijital**
e-mail — *S:* **bildara iloqtronaya/'email'**; *T:* **egartho eleqṭrunayto; 'e-mail'**
extension (number) — *S:* **raqma dilanaya**; *T:* **mfashṭutho; menyono mfashaṭto**
fax machine — *S:* **tuqan faks**; *T:* **makina du-faks**
fax — *S:* **faks**; *T:* **faks**

handset — *S:* **adhenta**; *T:* **handset**
international operator — *S:* **masran baynat matanaya**; *T:* **shagholo tibeloyo/ shagholto tibelayto; operator**
internet café — *S:* **internet cafe**; *T:* **kafé-net**
internet — *S:* **prass nawla**; *T:* **internet**
line — *S:* **khṭuṭa**; *T:* **ḥṭuṭo; khaṭ**
mobile phone — *S:* **qaᶜya d-ida**; *T:* **telefon meshtanyono**
modem — *S:* **modem**; *T:* **modem**
operator — *S:* **palakha**; *T:* **shagholo/shagholto; operator**
pager — *S:* **peyjer**; *T:* **peyjer**
satellite phone — *S:* **qaᶜya dsahra sniᶜaya**; *T:* **telefon sahroyo; qamari**
sim card — *S:* **sim-kart**; *T:* **sim-kart**

Where can I *(m/f)* buy a sim card for my mobile phone?
S: **Meka masin zawnin sim-kart qa mitziᶜani?/ Meka masyan zawnan sim-kart qa mitziᶜani?**
T: **Mayko kibi shoqlano/shuqlono sim-kart l-u-mobilaydhi?**

telecommunications — *S:* **tupaye khṭuṭṭaye**; *T:* **naqifwotho; methmaṭyonwotho**
telephone center — *S:* **nuqazta d-dqaᶜye**; *T:* **qenṭrun du-telefon; qontorlu telefon**
telex — *S:* **khtuta barqiᶜa**; *T:* **teleks**

More on tele-etiquette...

T: When answering the phone, you say *S:* **shlama!**, *T:* **alo!** And if the caller knows you, they will generally respond with *S:* **b-shayna!**, *T:* **shlomo!** or **shlomo aᶜlaykhu!**, prompting your response *S:* **b-shayna w-bi-shlama!**, *T:* **b-shayno w-ba-shlomo!**, then *S:* **dakhiton?**, *T:* **aydarbo hat?** Now you are ready to start the conversation.

—Faxing & e-mailing

Where can I *(m/f)* send a fax from?
S: **M-ika masin shadrin faks?/M-ika masyan shadran faks?**
T: **M-ayko kibi mshadarno/mshadrono faks?**

Can I *(m/f)* fax from here?
S: **Masin ʿawdin faks m-lakha?/masyan ʿawdan faks m-lakha?**
T: **Kibi mshadarno/mshadrono faks m-arke?**

How much is it to fax?
S: **Kma le dmaeya d-faks?**
T: **B-miqqa-yo mshadarto d-faks?**

Where can I *(m/f)* find a place to e-mail from?
S: **Ika it dokta d-masin ʿawdin "e-mail"?/Ika it dokta d-masyan ʿawdan "e-mail"?**
T: **Ayko kibi ḥozeno duktho d-mshadarno "e-mail" me-tamo?/Ayko kibi ḥuzyono duktho d-mshadrono "e-mail" me-tamo?**

Is there an internet café near here?
S: **It bet-sarwa d-pras nawla qurba min lakha?**
T: **Kito kafé-net qariwo l-arke?**

Can I *(m/f)* e-mail from here?
S: **Masin ʿawdin "e-mail" min lakha?/Masyan ʿawdan "e-mail" min lakha?**
T: **Kibi mshadarno/mshadrono "e-mail" m-arke?**

How much is it to use a computer?
S: **Kma le dmaeya d-maplakhta d-khashuwa?**
T: **B-miqqa-yo mistaʿmolo d-ḥoshubo (*or* kompyuter)?**

How do you turn on this computer?
S: **Makhi ypalikh aha khashuwa?**
T: **Aydarbo ko-maṭfat u-ḥoshub-ano (*or* u-kompyuter-ano)?**

The computer has crashed.
S: **Khashuwa glidle.**
T: **Kali u-ḥoshubo.**

I *(m/f)* need help with this computer.
S: **bayin ʿudrana b-aha khashuwa/ bayan ʿudrana b-aha khashuwa.**
T: **K-luzmo-li mʿadronutho (*or* K-lozam-li mʿawanto) bu-ḥoshubano (*or* u-kompyuter-ano).**

I *(m/f)* don't know how to use this program.
S: **La yaṭin maplikhin l-aha takhrazta./La yaṭan maplikhan l-aha takhrazta.**
T: **Lo k-odhaʿno mistaʿmalno i-taḥraztathe (*or* u-program-ano)./Lo k-udhʿono mistaʿmlono i-taḥraztathe (*or* u-program-ano).**

I *(m/f)* know how to use this program.
S: **Ana yaṭin maplikhin l-aha takhrazta./Ana yaṭan maplikhan l-aha takhrazta.**
T: **K-odhaʿno mistaʿmalno i-taḥraztathe (*or* u-program-ano)./K-udhʿono mistaʿmlono i-taḥraztathe (*or* u-program-ano).**

I *(m/f)* want to print.
S: **Bayin ṭawʿin/bayan ṭawʿan.**
T: **K-obaʿno ṭowaʿno./K-ubʿono ṭawʿono.**

14. THE OFFICE

chair	*S:* **kursya**; *T:* **kursyo**
computer	*S:* **khashuwa**; *T:* **ḥoshubo; kompyuter**
desk	*S:* **ṭawlita**; *T:* **ṭablitho d-makhtwo**
drawer	*S:* **garurta**; *T:* **jarur**
fax	*S:* **fax**; *T:* **faks**
file *paper/computer*	*S:* **waraqe d-khashuwa**; *T:* **msadronitho; fayl**
meeting	*S:* **khnoshya**; *T:* **knushyo**
office	*S:* **makhitwa**; *T:* **makhtwo**
paper	*S:* **waraqa/waraqe**; *T:* **warqo**
pen	*S:* **qanya**; *T:* **qanyo**
pencil	*S:* **qanya d-awara**; *T:* **qanyo rṣoṣoyo; aboroyo**
photocopier	*S:* **nasukhta**; *T:* **maṣḥonitho; fotokopi; istinsakh**
photocopy	*S:* **asakhta**; *T:* **ṣḥoḥo; nuskha**
printer	*S:* **ṭawoᶜta**; *T:* **ṭawᶜonitho**
(computer) program	*S:* **takhrazta**; *T:* **taḥrazto (ḥoshubayto); program**
report	*S:* **tashrara**; *T:* **anfuro; tashroro; ṭebo**
ruler	*S:* **knunta**; *T:* **konunto; msargdonitho; masṭar**
scanner	*S:* **scanner**; *T:* **skaner**
telephone	*S:* **qaᶜya**; *T:* **telefon**
telex	*S:* **khṭuṭa barqiᶜa**; *T:* **teleks**
typewriter	*S:* **katuwta d-ida**; *T:* **makhtwono**

15. THE CONFERENCE

abstract *written* *S:* **psiquta**; *T:* **fsiqutho**
article *written* *S:* **memerta**; *T:* **mlu'o; mimro; maqale**
a break for refreshments *S:* **apta**; *T:* **buṭlono du-nyoḥo**
conference room *S:* **tawan lumada**; *T:* **tawono da-lumode; tawono da-qonferansat**
conference *S:* **lumada**; *T:* **umodo**
copy *S:* **nsukh; nsoekh; asakhta**; *T:* **aṣaḥto; nuskho**
discussion *S:* **durasha**; *T:* **nuqosho**
forum *S:* **forum**; *T:* **forum**
guest speaker *S:* **mala diqara**; *T:* **malolo dhayfo**
paper *article* *S:* **memarta warqayta**; *T:* **fetghomo**
podium *S:* **bima**; *T:* **bima**
projector *S:* **tuqana d-marawata**; *T:* **projektor**
session *S:* **ytawta**; *T:* **itawto**
a session chaired by ... *S:* **knusha tkhet mdabranuta d-...**; *T:* **itawto taḥt i-rishonutho d-...**
speaker *S:* **mallala**; *T:* **malolo**
subject *S:* **mlu'a**; *T:* **sharbo**
to translate *S:* **turgamta**; *T:* **turgomo**
translation *S:* **torgama**; *T:* **mtargmonutho**
translator *(m/f)* *S:* **mtargimana/mtargimanta**; *T:* **mtargmono/mtargimontho**

16. EDUCATION

addition	*S:* **tawsapta**; *T:* **mawsfonutho**
bench	*S:* **maṣ awta**; *T:* **maṣ awtho**
biro	*S:* **qanya ywisha**; *T:* **qanyo; bayro**
blackboard	*S:* **lukha d-qiryana**; *T:* **luḥo**
book	*S:* **ktawa**; *T:* **kthowo**
calculation	*S:* **khushbana**; *T:* **ḥushbono**
chalk	*S:* **arbobya**; *T:* **arbubyo; abshur**
class	*S:* **ṣidra**; *T:* **sedro**
correct	*S:* **triṣ**; *T:* **triṣo**
crayon	*S:* **qanya mgawnana**; *T:* **qanyo d-shamᶜo mgawno; krayon**
culture	*S:* **marduta**; *T:* **mardutho**
difficult	*S:* **ᶜasqa**; *T:* **ᶜasqo; ᶜasqtho**
division	*S:* **pulagha**; *T:* **flighutho**
easy	*S:* **pshiṭa**; *T:* **fshiṭo/fshiṭto**
education	*S:* **tarbita** *or* **tulmada**; *T:* **tarbitho**
equal	*S:* **shawya**; *T:* **shawyo**
eraser	*S:* **mkapranita**; *T:* **laḥayto; missaḥa**
exam	*S:* **bukhrana**; *T:* **buḥrono**
exercise book	*S:* **kerka d-durasha**; *T:* **kerko da-duroshe**
felt-tip pen	*S:* **qanya d-sur'a**; *T:* **qanyo d-lamṭo**
geography	*S:* **mamluth arᶜa**; *T:* **jiyoghrafiya**
glue	*S:* **tetta**; *T:* **teto**
grammar	*S:* **turas mamla**; *T:* **turoṣ-mamlo; grammatiqi**
history	*S:* **tashᶜita; maktawzawna**; *T:* **makthab-zabno; tashᶜitho**
holidays	*S:* **buṭlana**; *T:* **buṭlono**
homework	*S:* **walita baytayta**; *T:* **wolitho; baytayto**
illiterate	*S:* **bura/burta**; *T:* **buro; sakhlo**
language	*S:* **lishana**; *T:* **leshono**
lesson	*S:* **herga**; *T:* **hergo; drosho**

EDUCATION

library	*S:* **bet-arke**; *T:* **beth-arke**
literature	*S:* **seprayuta**; *T:* **sofrutho**; **sefroyutho**
maths	*S:* **manayuta**; *T:* **manoyutho**
memory	*S:* **ʿohdana**; *T:* **dukhrono**; **ʿuḥdono**
multiplication	*S:* **ʿupapa**; *T:* **ʿufofo**
notebook	*S:* **kerka d-zuhare**; *T:* **fenqitho**
page	*S:* **pata**; *T:* **fotho**; **ḥarfo**
paper	*S:* **waraqa**; **waraqe**; *T:* **warqo**
pen	*S:* **qanya**; *T:* **qanyo**
pencil	*S:* **qanya d-awara**; *T:* **qanyo rṣoṣoyo**; **aboroyo**
progress	*S:* **ṭuwara**; *T:* **shushoṭo**
pupil	*S:* **yalupa/yalupta**; *T:* **yolufo/yolufto**
rubber *eraser*	*S:* **mkapranita**; *T:* **laḥayto**; **missaḥa**
ruler *instrument*	*S:* **knonta**; *T:* **konunto**; **msargdonitho**; **masṭar**
satchel	*S:* **simda d-midrashta**; *T:* **ṣemdo**
school	*S:* **midrashta**; *T:* **madrashto**
seminary	*S:* **midrashta d-kahne** *or* **semenire**; *T:* **madrashto di-kuhnutho**; **seminer**
sheet *of paper*	*S:* **qiṭʿa *ḍ-waraqa***; *T:* **ḥarfo *ḍ-warqo***
student *university*	*S:* **ṣawbaya/ṣawbayta**; *T:* **ṣawboyo/ṣawbayto**
subtraction	*S:* **mapqanuta**; *T:* **buṣoro**
sum	*S:* **kunasha**; *T:* **kunosho**; **kmoyutho**
table	*S:* **surgada**; *T:* **ṭablitho**
teacher	*S:* **malpana/malpanta**; *T:* **malfono/malfonitho**
thought	*S:* **marmita**; **renya**; **takhmanta**; *T:* **renyo**
time	*S:* **shaʿta**; **zawna**; **ʿdana**; *T:* **shoʿtho** *(hour)*; **zabno** *(space of time)*; **ʿedono** *(moment in time)*

to add	*S:* **myature/mtawsupe;** *T:* **mawzodo**
to calculate	*S:* **khshawa;** *T:* **ḥshowo**
to copy	*S:* **nsakha;** *T:* **nsokho; troṣo**
to count	*S:* **mnaya;** *T:* **mnoyo**
to divide	*S:* **plagha/ploegh;** *T:* **flogho**
to equal	*S:* **Shwaya;** *T:* **shwoyo**
to explain	*S:* **Pashuqe;** *T:* **fushoqo**
to learn by heart	*S:* **ylapa min lebba;** *T:* **yulfono me-lebo**
to multiply	*S:* **ᶜpapa;** *T:* **ᶜfofo**
to pass *an exam*	*S:* **kshara bukhrana;** *T:* **kshoro buḥrono**
to punish	*S:* **twaᶜa;** *T:* **twoᶜo**
to read	*S:* **qraya;** *T:* **qroyo**
to repeat	*S:* **tnaya;** *T:* **tnoyo**
to study	*S:* **qraya;** *T:* **drosho**
to subtract	*S:* **mabṣure;** *T:* **mabṣoro**
to test *academic*	*S:* **bukhrana;** *T:* **nusoyo**
to think	*S:* **rnaya;** *T:* **rnoyo**
wisdom	*S:* **khekhemta;** *T:* **ḥekhemtho**
wrong	*S:* **pawda;** *T:* **fawdo; ghalṭo**

17. AGRICULTURE

agriculture	*S:* **zru^{c}ta**; *T:* **zoru^{c}utho**
barley	*S:* **sa^{c}re**; *T:* **s^{c}ore**
barn	*S:* **idra**; *T:* **adro; esṭablo**
canal	*S:* **shaqita**; *T:* **shoqitho; sheqyo**
cattle	*S:* **biqra**; *T:* **tawrotho**
combine harvester	*S:* **kunash khizda**; *T:* **ḥaṣodo khaliṭo; mzigho**
corn	*S:* **khiṭe shimaye**; *T:* **ḥabtho; daḥno**
cotton	*S:* **ktana**; *T:* **ketono**
crops	*S:* **zar^{c}one**; *T:* **^{c}alotho; ^{c}wuro**
fallowland	*S:* **biyara**; *T:* **krowo; ar^{c}o bayorto**
farm	*S:* **mazra^{c}ta**; *T:* **mazro^{c}o; adro**
farmer	*S:* **akara/akarta**; *T:* **akoro/akorto; daworo/daworto**
farming	*S:* **akaruta**; *T:* **akorutho; dawørutho**
fertilizer	*S:* **zwla**; *T:* **mshamnono; zawlo**
field	*S:* **khiqla**; *T:* **ḥaqlo**
fruit	*S:* **eb bane**; *T:* **fire; fako**
furrow	*S:* **warza**; *T:* **ḥṭuṭo; krowo; ḥefro**
garden	*S:* **ganta**; *T:* **gantho**
gardener	*S:* **gannana/gannanta**; *T:* **ganono/ganonto; fredtho**
grass	*S:* **gilla**; *T:* **gelo**
harvest	*S:* **^{c}dana d-khizda**; *T:* **ḥṣodo**
hay	*S:* **tuna**; *T:* **kesto**
haystack	*S:* **^{c}odhala d-tuna**; *T:* **gdisho di-kesto**
irrigation	*S:* **mashiqya**; *T:* **sheqyo; mashqyonutho**
land	*S:* **ar^{c}a**; *T:* **ar^{c}o**
leaf	*S:* **ṭarpa**; *T:* **ṭarfo**
livestock	*S:* **qinyane**; *T:* **qenyone**
maize	*S:* **kharwiye**; *T:* **ḥeṭe rumoye**

manure	*S:* **zwla**; *T:* **neḥre; zawlo**
marsh	*S:* **amsha**; *T:* **qewitho**
meadow	*S:* **marga**; *T:* **margo**
mill	*S:* **aarkhe**; *T:* **raḥyo**
miller	*S:* **ṭakhana**; *T:* **raḥoyo**
millstone	*S:* **pinkha**; *T:* **gorusto**
orchard	*S:* **karma**; *T:* **bustono**
plow	*S:* **pdana**; *T:* **fadono**
potato	*S:* **qirṭope**; *T:* **baṭaṭa**
poultry	*S:* **tarnighle**; *T:* **gyothe**
rice	*S:* **rizza**; *T:* **rezo**
root	*S:* **^{c}qra**; *T:* **^{c}eqro; shersho; warido**
season	*S:* **aqma**; *T:* **shuḥlofo**
seeds	*S:* **birzar^{c}e**; *T:* **bo-zar^{c}e**
sickle	*S:* **magla**; *T:* **magzuno; maglo**
silkworms	*S:* **qazik**; *T:* **tul^{c}e du-shiro; tul^{c}e hendwoye**
soil	*S:* **^{c}apra**; *T:* **^{c}afro**
straw	*S:* **zala**; *T:* **tewno; qaṣluṣo**
to cultivate	*S:* **krawa**; *T:* **floḥo**
to feed an animal	*S:* **makhule khaywa**; *T:* **mawkholo ḥaywo**
to grind	*S:* **tkhana/grasa**; *T:* **groso**
to grow *crops*	*S:* **zra^{c}a**; *T:* **iyrowo**
to milk *an animal*	*S:* **khlawa**; *T:* **ḥlowo**
to plant	*S:* **nṣawa**; *T:* **zro^{c}o**
to plow	*S:* **krawa ar^{c}a**; *T:* **dworo**
to reap	*S:* **qṭapa**; *T:* **ḥṣodo**
to shoe *a horse*	*S:* **mna^{c}awle**; *T:* **n^{c}olo *susye***
to sow	*S:* **bdhara**; *T:* **nṣowo**
tractor	*S:* **gargurta**; *T:* **magirshono; traktor**
tree	*S:* **ilana; ilanta**; *T:* **dawmo; ilono**
trunk *of tree*	*S:* **gidh^{c}a**; *T:* **shoqo; guz^{c}o**
vine	*S:* **gipta**; *T:* **sato; geftho**
vineyard	*S:* **Karma**; *T:* **karmo**
well *of water*	*S:* **guba**; *T:* **gubo; biro**
wheat	*S:* **khiṭṭe**; *T:* **ḥeṭe**

18. ANIMALS

—Mammals

bat	*S:* **prakhdoda**; *T:* **fraḩdudo; ᶜobugro fayoro**
bear	*S:* **dibba**; *T:* **debo**
boar	*S:* **khzura d-dawra/ khzurta d-dawra**; *T:* **brozo**
buffalo	*S:* **gamisha**; *T:* **gamisho; gomusho**
bull	*S:* **tora**; *T:* **tawro**
calf	*S:* **sharkha**; *T:* **ᶜeglo; arwono**
camel	*S:* **kumla**; *T:* **gamlo**
cat	*S:* **qaṭa; qaṭo**; *T:* **qaṭo**
cow	*S:* **tawirta**; *T:* **turto**
deer	*S:* **tabya/tbita**; *T:* **aylo**
dog	*S:* **kalba/kalibta**; *T:* **kalbo**
donkey	*S:* **khmara/khmarta**; *T:* **ḥmoro**
elephant	*S:* **pila**; *T:* **filo**
ewe	*S:* **ᶜana**; *T:* **neqyo**
ferret	*S:* **kakhusht(a)**; *T:* **kokhushto**
flock	*S:* **pesqa**; *T:* **darmala**
fox	*S:* **taᶜla**; *T:* **taᶜlo**
gazelle	*S:* **ozayla**; *T:* **ṭabyo**
goat	*S:* **ᶜizza**; *T:* **ᶜezo**
herd	*S:* **biqra; ramka**; *T:* **baqro**
horse	*S:* **sosa**; *T:* **susyo**
lamb	*S:* **para**; *T:* **faro; emro**
leopard	*S:* **nimra**; *T:* **nemro**
lion	*S:* **arya**; *T:* **aryo**
mare	*S:* **kodinta**; *T:* **susto**
mole	*S:* **shamma**; *T:* **ḥuldo; iruso**
monkey	*S:* **qopa**; *T:* **qufo; maymun**
mouse	*S:* **ᶜaqubra**; *T:* **ᶜobugro**
mule	*S:* **kawidna**; *T:* **baghlo; kudhanyo**
ox	*S:* **tora**; *T:* **baqro**
pig	*S:* **khzura**; *T:* **ḥziro**
pony	*S:* **gwada**; *T:* **susyo naᶜimo**
rabbit	*S:* **arnowa**; *T:* **arnwo**
ram	*S:* **barᶜana**; *T:* **emro**

rat	*S:* **garo**; *T:* **ᶜobugro rabo**
rhinoceros	*T:* **karkdono; qarno nḥiro**
sheep	*S:* **ᶜerwa** (*plural* **ᶜerwe**); *T:* **ᶜwono** (*plural* **ᶜwone**)
squirrel	*S:* **simmora**; *T:* **samuro; shenuro; quzo**
stallion	*S:* **sosya**; *T:* **qiluno; faḥlo**
tiger	*S:* **nimra**; *T:* **bebro**
wolf	*S:* **diwa**; *T:* **dibo**

—Birds

bird	*S:* **ṭayra**; *T:* **ṭayro; fraḥto**
chick	*S:* **zagha**; *T:* **zogho; zghono**
chicken (hen)	*S:* **kteta (dika)**; *T:* **gdhayto (farugo)**
cockerel; rooster	*S:* **tarnighla**; *T:* **tarnoghlo; diko**
crow	*S:* **ᶜorwa**; *T:* **ᶜurwo; qarqoso**
dove	*S:* **yawna**; *T:* **yawno**
duck	*S:* **baṭṭa**; *T:* **baṭo**
eagle	*S:* **nishra**; *T:* **neshro**
falcon	*S:* **baza**; *T:* **shahwo; boziqo; bozo; shahin**
goose	*S:* **qaza**; *T:* **wazo**
hawk	*S:* **baziqa**; *T:* **neṣo**
nightingale	*S:* **ᶜenda**; *T:* **ᶜendo; ṣefro-deqlo; bulbul**
owl	*S:* **qupta**; *T:* **bumo; papuke**
parrot	*S:* **laqṭan mille**; *T:* **babgho; ṣefro kushoyo**
partridge	*S:* **zarkha**; *T:* **qeqwono; ḥaglo**
peacock	*S:* **ṣoṣla**; *T:* **ṭawuso**
pigeon	*S:* **yawna**; *T:* **ᶜarbodo; yawno**
quail	*S:* **qiqwana**; *T:* **salway; shkhiwoyo**
sparrow	*S:* **sepra**; *T:* **ṣefro; ṣefruno**
stork	*S:* **laqlaq**; *T:* **asido; laqlaq**
swallow	*S:* **snunita**; *T:* **snunitho**
turkey	*S:* **dika rumaya**; *T:* **ᶜali-ᶜalo; tarnoghlo daqnono; tarnoghlo rumoyo; ᶜali-shish**
vulture	*S:* **baza**; *T:* **dardo; budro; neshro meṣroyo**

ANIMALS

—Insects & amphibians

ant	*S:* **shikwana**; *T:* **namlo**; **shushmono**
bee	*S:* **dabasha**; *T:* **dabosho**
beetle	*S:* **khashushta**; *T:* **ḥabshusho**
butterfly	*S:* **parkhanita**; *T:* **tlonitho**; **ṭilayto**
caterpillar	*S:* **naqro**; *T:* **ṣarbubtho**; **madolo**; **nobuzo**
chameleon	*S:* **arya d-ar^{c}a**; *T:* **ḥulmoṭo**
cobra	*S:* **kobra**; *T:* **sha^{c}ṭo meṣroyo**; **kobra**
cockroach	*S:* **ṣiṣra**; *T:* **ṣarṣuro**
crab	*S:* **sirṭana dyama**; *T:* **sarṭono**
cricket	*S:* **chercherroka**; *T:* **ṣiṣro**
dragonfly	*S:* **qipniz**; *T:* **tanino**
fish	*S:* **none**; *T:* **nuno**
flea(s)	*S:* **pirṭana** (*plural* **pirṭane**); *T:* **furtha^{c}no** (*plural* **furtha^{c}ne**)
fly	*S:* **didwa**; *T:* **dabobo**
flies	*S:* **didwe**; *T:* **dabobe**
frog	*S:* **piqaa**; *T:* **urd^{c}o**
grasshopper	*S:* **qamṣa**; *T:* **qamṣo**
hedgehog	*S:* **gdhodha**; *T:* **qufdo**; **qufrin**
hornet	*S:* **dibbora/dibborta**; *T:* **deburitho**
insect	*S:* **rakhsha**; *T:* **raḥsho**; **ṣarbuqo**
lizard	*S:* **mazuzṭa**; *T:* **rashofo**; **ḥardono**; **ḥewitho**; **^{c}abo**; **maṣuṣto**
louse (lice)	*S:* **qalma (qalme)**; *T:* **qalmo (qalme)**
mosquito	*S:* **baqta**; *T:* **boqo**
scorpion	*S:* **^{c}aqirwa**; *T:* **^{c}eqarwo**
snail	*S:* **khalzuna**; *T:* **ḥalzunto**
snake	*S:* **khuwa**; *T:* **ḥuyo**
spider	*S:* **izla kushe**; **zaqraqude**; *T:* **zaqoritho**; **gugi**
termite	*S:* **shikwana khawara**; *T:* **belṭitho**
tick	*S:* **ṭimra**; *T:* **qardo**; **fushfosho**
viper	*S:* **akhidna**; *T:* **sha^{c}ṭo**; **kurfo**
wasp	*S:* **dibbora**; *T:* **deboro**
worm	*S:* **tawl^{c}a**; *T:* **tul^{c}o**; **tlaw^{c}o**

19. THE COUNTRYSIDE

avalanche	*S:* **ashita**; *T:* **grufyo d-talgo; ashitho**
canal	*S:* **aghogha**; *T:* **shoqitho; sheqyo**
cave	*S:* **mᶜartha**; *T:* **mᶜartho**
dam	*S:* **sikra**; *T:* **sakro; sadd**
desert	*S:* **ᶜarawa**; *T:* **madhbro**
earthquake	*S:* **nawdhana**; *T:* **zawᶜo; hyozo arᶜonoyo**
fire	*S:* **nura**; *T:* **nuro**
flood	*S:* **milaa**; *T:* **ṭawfono**
foothills	*S:* **sipa d-ṭure**; *T:* **shfule**
footpath	*S:* **urkha d-aqla**; *T:* **darbo d-malkho**
forest	*S:* **ᶜawa**; *T:* **ṭuro; ᶜobo**
glacier	*S:* **nahra qrisa**; *T:* **talgonitho; talgo sowo**
hill	*S:* **tella**; *T:* **telo**
lake	*S:* **yamta**; *T:* **yamtho**
landslide	*S:* **hgham arᶜa**; *T:* **grufyo d-arᶜo**
mountain	*S:* **ṭura**; *T:* **ṭuro**
mountain pass	*S:* **urkha d-ṭurane**; *T:* **maᶜbarto; shalwo**
peak	*S:* **gaghulta**; *T:* **qarno d-ṭuro; qarqaftho d-ṭuro**
plain/plains	*S:* **piqᶜa/piqᶜata**; *T:* **sheṭḥo**
plant	*S:* **yaᶜita**; *T:* **yoᶜitho; neṣbo**
range/mountain range	*S:* **shishilta d-ṭure**; *T:* **shishalto da-ṭure**
ravine	*S:* **nakhla**; *T:* **shalwo**
river	*S:* **nahra**; *T:* **nahro**
river bank	*S:* **sipa d-nahra**; *T:* **sfar-nahro; yad-nahro**
rock	*S:* **isara; kepa**; *T:* **kefo**
sand	*S:* **khilla**; *T:* **ḥolo**
shore	*S:* **spar-yama**; *T:* **sfar-yamo; yad-yamo**
slope	*S:* **bartakhti**; *T:* **nafqo; ṭafoyo**

soil	*S:* **ʿapra**; *T:* **ʿafro**
spring *of water*	*S:* **ʿayna d-miya**; *T:* **ʿayno**; **nabgho**
stone	*S:* **kipa**; *T:* **shuʿo**; **sheno**
stream	*S:* **tappa**; *T:* **roghulo**; **redyo**
summit	*S:* **qarna**; *T:* **qarno d-ṭuro**; **qarqaftho d-ṭuro**
swamp	*S:* **ṣyana**; *T:* **ʿawsho**
tree	*S:* **ilana**; *T:* **dawmo**; **ilono**
valley	*S:* **raghula**; *T:* **nirwo**
waterfall	*S:* **shamshuma**; *T:* **nodurto**; **maflo da-maye**; **shallal**
a wood	*S:* **ʿawa**; *T:* **ʿobo**

Some common expressions . . .

Here are a few expressions you'll hear in everyday conversation:

well now!; enough!	*S:* **ṭawa!** *or* **sapiq!**; *T:* **i-naqqa!** *or* **bas-yo!**
well...!	*S:* **khina!**; *T:* **asher!**
so!/indeed!	*S:* **hadkha!** *or* **bishrara!**; *T:* **aloh!**
I mean...; that is to say...	*S:* **Sukali le...** *or* **Awkith...**; *T:* **Qazdi...** *or* **Yaʿni...**
come on!	*S:* **yala khina!**; *T:* **yalla ...!**
okay!	*S:* **shapir!**; *T:* **tamam!** *or* **ṭrowe!**
hang on!; wait a minute!	*S:* **kli/klay** *(m/f)* **qaṭinta!**; *T:* **klay qaṭinto!**
in my opinion...	*S:* **briʿyani..!.**; *T:* **bu-renyaydhi...!**
all right!	*S:* **ma ṭawa oma shaapir!**; *T:* **ghamo layt!** *or* **tamam!**
bravo!	*S:* **aiyo!**; *T:* **afarim!** *or* **bravo!**
isn't that so?	*S:* **la ela hadkha?**; *T:* **latyawkha?**

20. WEATHER

Mesopotamian winters can be long and snowy, especially on the Tur-Abdin plateau and in the mountains of northern Iraq, whilst in the plains below it usually rains and is muddy. This is followed by equally long summers, which get extremely hot, particularly in the low-lying areas and plains. Certainly a good time to go to the region is in autumn, between September and October when the day-time temperatures are pleasant and the nights not to cold. Although Tur-Abdin, Urmia and northern Iraq are rugged and mountainous there are no skiing facilities. However, they are perfect for trekking, provided the security situation is stable enough to allow that.

What's the weather like?
S: **Dakhi le muzagha?**
T: **I-muzogho (*or* i-hawa) mishikil-yo?**

The weather is ... today.
S: **Ediom ... muzagha.**
T: **... yo ad-yawma.**

cold	*S:* **qura**; *T:* **quro**
cool	*S:* **payukha**; *T:* **qariro**
fresh	*S:* **basima**; *T:* **qariro**
cloudy	*S:* **ʿaymana**; *T:* **ʿaywo**
foggy	*S:* **ʿarpillaya**; *T:* **ʿarfeloyo/ ʿarfelayto**
freezing	*S:* **mqarṣana**; *T:* **jamudo**
hot	*S:* **shakhina**; *T:* **ḥemo**
misty	*S:* **khapuṭaya**; *T:* **ʿamuṭo**
very cold	*S:* **saggi qura**; *T:* **sagi quro**; **ghallabe quro**
very hot	*S:* **saggi shakhina**; *T:* **sagi ḥemo**; **ghallabe ḥemo**
windy	*S:* **hawana**; *T:* **hawa ghallabe**; **ʿalʿolo**

It's going to rain.
S: **Bed maṭra.**
T: **Gid-noḥet maṭro.**

WEATHER

It is raining.
S: **Bimṭare la.**
T: **Ko-noḥet maṭro.**

It's going to snow.
S: **Braye talga.**
T: **Gid-noḥet talgo.**

It is snowing.
S: **Ṭalga le biraya.**
T: **Ko-noḥet talgo.**

It's getting very cold.
S: **Sagi biqyara ela .**
T: **K-owe quro sagi.** *or* **K-owe quro sagi ghallabe.**

It is very sunny.
S: **Raba shimshante la.**
T: **Ghallabe k-muḥyo i-shemsho.**

It is cloudy.
S: **ᶜAywone ela.**
T: **I-hawa mᶜayamto-yo**

It is windy.
S: **Hawanta ela.**
T: **Kuthyo hawa.**

It is misty/foggy.
S: **ᶜArpillayta ela.**
T: **Kito mij.**

air	*S:* **hawa**; *T:* **hawa**
climate	*S:* **muzagha**; *T:* **muzogho; iqlima**
cloud	*S:* **ᶜayma**; *T:* **ᶜaymo; ᶜaywo**
fog/mist	*S:* **ᶜarpilla**; *T:* **ᶜarfelo; mij**
frost	*S:* **qirsa**; *T:* **ᶜaryo**
full moon	*S:* **khis aa**; *T:* **sahro kamilo**
hail	*S:* **barda**; *T:* **bardo; ḥarṣaftho**
heat wave	*S:* **makhshula d-khimma**; *T:* **maḥshulo d-ḥemo**
horizon	*S:* **upqa**; *T:* **ufqo**
hot wind	*S:* **poakha shakhina**; *T:* **hawa shaḥinto**

humidity	*S:* **raṭiwota**; *T:* **raṭibutho**
ice	*S:* **glida**; *T:* **glidho**
lightning	*S:* **Birqa**; *T:* **barqo**
moisture	*S:* **ṭaliluta**; *T:* **talilutho**
moon	*S:* **sahra**; *T:* **sahro**
new moon	*S:* **sahra khata**; *T:* **sahro ḥatho**
rain	*S:* **miṭra**; *T:* **maṭro**
rainbow	*S:* **qishti maran**; *T:* **qayso qadaḥ**; **qeshte d-moran**
season	*S:* **eqma**; *T:* **shuḥlofo**
sky	*S:* **shmayya**; *T:* **shmayo**
snow	*S:* **talga**; *T:* **talgo**
star	*S:* **kukhwa**; *T:* **kukwo**
stars	*S:* **kukhwe**; *T:* **kukwe**
storm	*S:* **ʿalʿala**; *T:* **ʿalʿolo**
summer	*S:* **qiṭa**; *T:* **qayṭo**
sun	*S:* **shimsha**; *T:* **shemsho**
thunder	*S:* **raʿma**; *T:* **raʿmo**; **rʿumyo**
thunderstorm	*S:* **ʿalʿala raʿmaya**; *T:* **ʿalʿolo raʿmoyo**
weather	*S:* **muzagha**; *T:* **muzogho**; **hawa**
wind	*S:* **hawa**; *T:* **hawa**
winter	*S:* **sitwa**; *T:* **sathwo**

21. CAMPING

Where can we camp?
S: **Ika masikh sharikh?**
T: **Ayko kiban shorina?**

Is it safe to camp here?
S: **Layt qinṭa d-sharikh lakha?**
T: **Mshayno-yo en shorina harke?** *or* **Amin-yo en shorina harke?**

Is there danger of wild animals?
S: **It qinta mkhaywate dwala?**
T: **Layto qenṭo da-ḥaywotho baroyotho** (*or* **waḥshiye**)**?**

Is there drinking water?
S: **It miya d-shtaya?**
T: **Maye d-shtoyo kito?**

May we light a fire?
S: **Masikh shirikh nura?**
T: **Kiban shughrina nuro?** *or* **Kiban maqithina nuro?**

—Kit

axe	*S:* **narʿa**; *T:* **nargho**
backpack	*S:* **ṣemda d-khaṣa**; *T:* **ṣemdo**
bucket	*S:* **ṣiṭla**; *T:* **siṭlo**; **dawlo**
campsite	*S:* **mashrita**; *T:* **mashritho**; **qampa**
can opener	*S:* **patkhan qupse**; *T:* **fotuḥo da-ʿulbe**
compass	*S:* **mṣawyana**; *T:* **mṣaybonitho**; **bawṣala**; **qompas**
firewood	*S:* **qayse d-nura**; *T:* **qayse di-nuro**
flashlight	*S:* **Bahrad d-ida**; *T:* **bahro d-idho**
gas canister	*S:* **pilla d-khapupa**; *T:* **shushaye d-hawfo**; **shushaye d-ghas**
hammer	*S:* **arzipta**; *T:* **akhlo**; **arzaftho**

ice axe	*S:* **nar^{c}a d-glidha**; *T:* **nargho du-glidho**
ice box	*S:* **ṣanduq qlida**; *T:* **ṣanduqo jamudo**
lamp	*S:* **shraya**; *T:* **fanso**; **lamfidho**
mattress	*S:* **shwita**; *T:* **teshwitho**
penknife	*S:* **skinta d-qanya**; *T:* **skino qanyoyo**
rope	*S:* **khula**; *T:* **ḥawlo**
sleeping bag	*S:* **kesta d-dmakha**; *T:* **kiso du-dmokho**
stove	*S:* **kanuna**; *T:* **qamino**; **ṣoba**
tent pegs	*S:* **sekyate d-yu^{c}arta**; *T:* **seke du-mashkno**
tent	*S:* **yari^{c}ta**; *T:* **mashkno**
water bottle	*S:* **basta d-miya**; *T:* **shushaye da-maye**; **barqub^{c}o**

ELECTRICITY — Turkey and Syria are 220-volt electric current. Iraq is also 220-volt. However it may not be constantly at full voltage strength. Although daily power cuts are a thing of the past they do occur occasionally, particularly away from the larger towns, where the local transformers of villages that have a supply can overload. Only the most remote villages are without power. Be sure to keep a flashlight or supply of candles.

22. EMERGENCY

Help *(m/f/pl)*!
S: **Ṣuyaᶜa!**
T: **Tokh lafe-li!/Tekh lafe-li!/Tokhu lafe-li!**

Could you *(m/f)* help me, please?
S: **En mbasmalukh masit mᶜadritli?/ En mbasmalakh masyat mᶜadratli?**
T: **Boᶜutho menokh, kibokh mᶜawnat-li?/ Boᶜutho menekh, kibekh mᶜawnat-li?**

Do you *(m/f)* have a telephone?
S: **Itlokh qaᶜya/etlakh qaᶜya etlokhon qaᶜya?**
T: **Kit-lokh telefon?/Kit-lekh telefon?**

Can I *(m/f)* use your *(m/f)* telephone?
S: **Masin maplikhin l-qaᶜyakhon?/ Masya maplikhan l-qaᶜyakhon?**
T: **Kibi mistaᶜmalno u-telefonaydhokh/u-telefonaydhekh?/Kibi mistaᶜmlono u-telefonaydhokh/ u-telefonaydhekh?**

Where is the nearest telephone?
S: **Ika et kha qaᶜya qariwa?**
T: **Ayko kit telefon qariwo?**

Does the phone work?
S: **Aha qaᶜya ypalikh?**
T: **U-telefon k-shoghil?**

Get *(m/f)* help quickly!
S: **Qri l-ᶜodrana lighayt!/Qre l-ᶜodrana lighayt!**
T: **Khayifo amṭay mᶜawanto!**

Call the police!
S: **Qri l-dakhshe!**
T: **Qrayu a-daḥshe (*or* a-polis)!**

I'll *(m/f)* call the police!
S: **Bid qarin l-dakhshe!/Bid qaryan l-dakhshe!**
T: **Gid-qoreno a-daḫshe (*or* a-polis)!/ Gid-quryono a-daḫshe (*or* a-polis)!**

Is there a doctor near here?
S: **Et kha asya qariwa l-lakha?**
T: **Kit osyo qariwo l-arke?**

Call a doctor.
S: **Qri l-asya.**
T: **Qrayu osyo.**

Call an ambulance.
S: **Qri l-radita d-ʿoshpa.**
T: **Qrayu radhayto d-ʿudrono.**

Where is the doctor?
S: **Ika le asya?**
T: **Ayko-yo u-osyo?**

Where is the hospital?
S: **Ika le bet-krihe?**
T: **Ayko-yo u-beth-krihe?**

Where is the pharmacy?
S: **Ika la bet-sammane?**
T: **Ayko-yo u-beth-samone?**

Where is the dentist?
S: **Ika le asya d-shin ne?**
T: **Ayko-yo u-osyo da-ʿarshone?**

Where is the police station?
S: **Ika la nuqazta dakhshe?**
T: **Ayko-yo mashryo (*or* qenṭrun) da-daḫshe?**

Take me to a doctor.
S: **Labili l-kha asya.**
T: **Mawbeli su-osyo.**

There's been an accident!
S: **Et hwiya kha gidsha!**
T: **Hawi gedsho!**

Is anyone *(m/f)* hurt?
S: **Et kha dskhipa le?/Et kha skhipta la?**
T: **Kit noshe kibe?**

This person *(m/f)* is hurt.
S: **Aha skhipa le./Hadhe skhipta la.**
T: **U-farşufano ʿajizo-yo./I-farşuftathe ʿajizto-yo .**

There are people injured.
S: **Et nashe mşulpe.**
T: **Kit noshe jriḥe.**

Don't *(m/f)* move!
S: **La mhalkhit!/La mhalkhat!**
T: **Lo rumshat!**

Go *(m/f/pl)* away!
S: **Krus mlakha!**
T: **Zokh m-arke!/Zekh m-arke!/Zokhu m-arke!**

Stand back!
S: **Dur Bara.**
T: **Klay tamo!**

I *(m/f)* am lost.
S: **Ṭliqa win./Ṭleqta wan.**
T: **Msakro-no./Msakarto-no.**

I *(m/f)* am ill.
S: **Kaiwa win./Kaiwta wan.**
T: **Kayiwo-no./Kayuto-no.**

I've been robbed.
S: **Ş-hwi lay qati.**
T: **Mashliḥḥalli.**

Thief!
S: **Ginawa!**
T: **Ganowo!**

My ... *(m/f)* has been stolen.
S: **... pishle gniwa./... pishla gniwta.**
T: **Gniw u-...-aydhi./Gniwo i-...-aydhi.**

I have lost my bags.
S: **Tolqli l-ṣimdi.**
T: **Msakar-li a-sefoqaydhi.**

I have lost my camera.
S: **Toliqli l-sayurti.**
T: **Msakar-li u-qameraydhi.**

I have lost my handbag.
S: **Toliqli l-simda d-idi.**
T: **Msakar-li i-janṭaydhi.**

I have lost my laptop computer.
S: **Toliqli l-khashuwi d-ida.**
T: **Msakar-li u-ḥoshubo meshtanyono didhi.**

I have lost my money.
S: **Toliqli l-zozi.**
T: **Msakar-li a-zuzaydhi.**

I have lost my passport.
S: **Toliqli l-maᶜbar tkhumi.**
T: **Msakar-li u-saqraydhi.**

I have lost my traveler's checks.
S: **Toliqli l-saki d-krukhya.**
T: **Msakar-li a-shekkat korukhoye didhi.**

I have lost my wallet.
S: **Toliqli l-simdi d-zoze.**
T: **Msakar-li u-jizdanaydhi.**

My possessions are insured.
S: **Midyani mᶜarwe ilay.**
T: **A-medonaydhi kitte shuroro (***or* **ta'min** *or* **inshurans).**

I have lost my group.
S: **Toliqli l-gudi.**
T: **Msakar-li u-gudaydhi.**

I have a problem.
S: **Ana et li kha qitra.**;
T: **Kit-li qeṭro (***or* **mushkile** *or* **problem).**

Forgive me.
S: **Pakhil li.**
T: **Shubqono.**

I *(m/f)* didn't realize anything was wrong.
S: **La dili it wa qiṭra.**
T: **L-adha^{c}no d-kito qeṭro./L-adhi^{c}ono d-kito qeṭro.**

I *(m/f)* want to contact my embassy.
S: **bayin d-qarin lazgaduti/ bayan qaryan l-azgaduti.**
T: **K-oba^{c}no qoreno li-izgaduthaydhi./K-ub^{c}ono quryono li-izgaduthaydhi.**

I *(m/f)* speak English.
S: **Msawtin Inglish./Msawtan Inglish.**
T: **Ko-mijghalno Inglishoyo./Ko-mijgholono Inglishoyo.**

I need an interpreter.
S: **Sniqawin l-mtargimmana.**
T: **K-lozam-li mtargmono.**

Where are the toilets?
S: **Ika lay bet-silye?**
T: **Ayko-yo u-beth-mayo (*or* u-tuwaylet)?**

23. HEALTHCARE

INSURANCE – Make sure any insurance policy you take out covers wherever it is in the Middle East that you plan to visit. Consult your doctor for any shots required or recommended when making any trip outside of North America and Western Europe.

What's the trouble?
S: **Mudi le hwiya?**
T: **Mun-yo u-qeṭro (***or* **i-mushkile** *or* **u-problem)?**

I *(m/f)* am sick.
S: **Kaiwa win./Kaiwta wan.**
T: **Kayiwo-no./Kayuto-no.**

My companion *(m/f)* is sick.
S: **Khawri kaiwa le./Khwarti kaiwta la.**
T: **U-ḥawraydhi kayiwo-yo./I-ḥwarthaydhi kayuto-yo.**

May I *(f)* see a female doctor?
S: **Masyan khazyan khda asita?**
T: **Kibi ḥuzyono ositho?**

I have medical insurance.
S: **Etli ᶜurawa kholmanaya.**
T: **Kit-li shuroro (***or* **ᶜarobutho) ḥulmonoyo.**

Please take off your *(m/f)* shirt/blouse.
S: **ᶜWud ṭawta w-shalikh l-panilokh/l-bluzukh./ ᶜWoed tawta w-shalikh l-panilakh/l-bluzakh.**
T: **Shlaḥ u-qamisaydhokh/u-bluzaydhekh, boᶜutho menokh/menekh.**

Please undress *(m/f)* .
S: **ᶜWud ṭawta w-shalikh l-lbushukh./ᶜWoed ṭawta w-shalikh l-lbukhakh.**
T: **Shlaḥ a-lwushaydokh (***or* **a-julaydhekh), boᶜutho menokh./Shlaḥ a-lwushaydhekh (***or* **a-julaydhekh), boᶜutho menekh.**

How long have you *(m/f)* had this problem?
S: **Min eman etlokh/etlakh aha qiṭra?**
T: **Hani m-ema d-kit-lokh/d-kit-lekh u-qeṭrano?**

How long have you *(m/f)* been feeling sick?
S: **Aha kma hwiya wit bir^{c}asha aha kiwa./Aha kma hwita wat bir^{c}asha aha kiwa?**
T: **Hani m-ema d-ko-maḥisat ruḥokh/ruḥekh bu-kewo?**

Where does it hurt you *(m/f)*?
S: **Ika la ykaywalukh/ykaywalakh?**
T: **Ayko ko-koyaw lokh?**/*T:* **Ayko ko-kayaw lekh?**

It hurts me here.
S: **Lakha la kyawi.**
T: **Ko-koyaw-li harke.**

I *(m/f)* have been vomiting.
S: **Hwiya win mad^{c}ure./Hwita wan mad^{c}ure.**
T: **ḥfiḥ-li.**

I *(m/f)* feel dizzy.
S: **Gashune win/wan.**
T: **Gayijno./Gayijono.**

I *(m/f)* can't eat.
S: **La win/la wan mṣaya d-akhlin/akhlan.**
T: **Laybi okhalno/ukhlono.**

I *(m/f)* can't sleep.
S: **La win msaya d-damkhin/la wan msaya d-damkhan.**
T: **Laybi domakhno./Laybi dumkhono.**

I *(m/f)* feel worse.
S: **Yatir khirba win bir^{c}asha/yatir khirba wan bir^{c}asha.**
T: **Maḥisno/maḥisono pis-tir (*or* zid ḥarbo).**

I *(m/f)* feel better.
S: **Taw byatir win/wan bir^{c}asha.**
T: **Maḥisno/Maḥisono sh-ṭow-tir (*or* zid ṭowo).**

Do you *(m/f)* have diabetes?
S: **Etlokh/etlakh shikar?**
T: **Kit-lokh/Kit-lekh kewo d-shakar (*or* sukkar *or* diabitis)?**

Do you *(m/f)* have epilepsy?
S: **Etlukh/Etlakh ṣriᶜuta?**
T: **Kit-lokh/Kit-lekh kewo di-mafultho (*or* sarᶜa *or* epilepsia)?**

Do you *(m/f)* have asthma?
S: **Etlokh/Etlakh leta?**
T: **Kit-lokh/Kit-lekh lhotho (*or* karyuth-ruḥo)?**

I have diabetes.
S: **Etli shikar.**
T: **Kit-li kewo d-shakar (*or* sukkar *or* diabitis).**

I have epilepsy.
S: **Etli ṣriᶜuta.**
T: **Kit-li kewo di-mafultho (*or* sarᶜa *or* epilepsia).**

I have asthma.
S: **Etli leta.**
T: **Kit-li lhotho (*or* sbisuth-neshmo *or* karyuth-ruḥo).**

I'm pregnant.
S: **Bṭinta wan.**
T: **ṭᶜinto-no.**

—Diagnosis

I *(m/f)* have a cold.
S: **Qrisha win./Qrishta wan.**
T: **Kit-li shawbo (*or* quro).**

I *(m/f)* have a cough.
S: **Ṣ-haᶜula win.**
T: **Ko-shoᶜalno./Ko-shuᶜlono.**

I have a headache.
S: **Yka'ew reshi.**
T: **Qarᶜi ko-koyu.**

I have a pain.
S: **Etli khewle.**
T: **Koyaw-li.**

I have a sore throat.
S: **Yka'ewa baluʿti.**
T: **Kit-li ḥis ḥarusho.**

I *(m/f)* have a temperature.
S: **Khamkhume win/wan.**
T: **Kit-li shḥuntho.**

I have an allergy.
S: **Etli khashushuta.**
T: **Kit-li nebutho (*or* ḥassasiye *or* alerji).**

I have an infection.
S: **Etli shulhawa.**
T: **Kit-li ḥubolo.**

I *(m/f)* have an itch.
S: **Etli khyuka.**
T: **Kit-li ḥyoko.** *or* **Ko-ḥoyakno./Ko-ḥaykono.**

I have a rash.
S: **It li shokhna.**
T: **Kit-li ḥemṭo.**

I have backache.
S: **Etli ka'iwa d-resha.**
T: **ḥaṣi ko-koyu.**

I *(m/f)* have constipation.
S: **Qapas ewen/ewan.**
T: **Qbath-no.**

I have diarrhea.
S: **Aqli plakha la.**
T: **Gawi k-izze.**

I *(m/f)* have fever.
S: **Shatana win./Shatanta wan.**
T: **Kit-li eshotho (ḥumtho *or* ḥemto).**

I have indigestion.
S: **Karsi le la mapshure.**
T: **Kit-li afthoro (*or* ʿasquth-fushoro).**

I have influenza.
S: **Etli enfluwanza.**
T: **Kit-li shʿolo ʿam shulhowo (***or* **inflawenza).**

I have a heart condition.
S: **Etli kiwa d-lebba.**
T: **Kit-li kewo du-lebo.**

I *(m/f)* have "pins and needles"/numbness.
S: **It li twinota.**
T: **Kit-li tonuwutho.**

I have stomach ache.
S: **Etli kiwa d-karsa.**
T: **Gawi ko-koyu.**

I have a fracture.
S: **Etli garma twira.**
T: **Kit-li tworo.**

I have toothache.
S: **Yka'o shinni.** *or* **Mra'a ele kaki.**
T: **ʿArshoni ko-kaywi.**

* * *

You (m/f) have a cold.
S: **Qrisha wit./Qreshta wat.**
T: **Kit-lokh/Kit-lekh shawbo (***or* **quro).**

You*(m/f)* have a cough.
S: **Etlokh/etlakh shʿula.**
T: **Kit-lokh/Kit-lekh shʿolo.**

You *(m/f)* have a headache.
S: **Etlukh/Etlakh kiwa d-resha.**
T: **Kit-lokh/Kit-lekh kewo d-qarʿo.**

You *(m/f)* have a pain.
S: **Etlukh khewle.**
T: **Koyaw-lokh/Koyaw-lekh.** *or* **Kit-lokh/Kit-lekh kewo.**

You *(m/f)* have a sore throat.
S: **Baluʿtokh/Baluʿtakh yka'ewa.**
T: **Kit-lokh/Kit-lekh ḥis ḥarusho.**

You *(m/f)* have a temperature.
S: **Khamkhume wit/wat.**
T: **Kit-lokh/Kit-lekh shḥuntho.**

You *(m/f)* have an allergy.
S: **Etlukh/Etlakh khashushuta.**
T: **Kit-lokh/Kit-lekh nebutho (***or* **ḥassasiye** *or* **alerji).**

You *(m/f)* have an infection.
S: **Etlukh/Etlakh shalhawita.**
T: **Kit-lokh/Kit-lekh ḥubolo.**

You *(m/f)* have a rash.
S: **It lokh/It lakh shokhna..**
T: **Kit-lokh/Kit-lekh ḥemṭo.**

You *(m/f)* have backache.
S: **Etlukh/Etlakh kiwa dresha.**
T: **ḥaṣokh/ḥaṣekh ko-koyu.**

You *(m/f)* have constipation.
S: **Qapas ewit./Qapas ewat.**
T: **Qbath-hat.**

You *(m/f)* have diarrhea.
S: **Aqlukh/Aqlakh plakha la.**
T: **Gawokh/Gawekh k-izze.**

You *(m/f)* have fever.
S: **Khamkhume wit/khamkhume wat.**
T: **Kit-lokh/Kit-lekh eshotho (***or* **ḥumtho** *or* **ḥemto).**

You *(m/f)* have indigestion.
S: **Karsukh/karsakh le la mapshure.**
T: **Kit-lokh/Kit-lekh afthoro (***or* **ʿasquth-fushoro).**

You *(m/f)* have influenza.
S: **Etlukh/Etlakh enfuwanza.**
T: **Kit-lokh/Kit-lekh shʿolo ʿam shulhowo (***or* **inflawenza).**

You *(m/f)* have "pins and needles"/numbness.
S: **It lokh/It lakh twinota.**
T: **Kit-lokh/Kit-lekh tonuwutho.**

You *(m/f)* have stomach ache.
S: **Etlokh/Etlakh ka'ewa d-karsa.**
T: **Gawokh/Gawekh ko-koyu.**

You *(m/f)* have a fracture.
S: **Etlokh/Etlakh garma twira.**
T: **Kit-lokh/Kit-lekh tworo.**

You *(m/f)* have toothache.
S: **Etlokh/Etlakh ka'ewa d-shinne.**
T: **ʿArshonokh/ʿArshonekh ko-kaywi.**

I *(m/f)* take this medication.
S: **Yshaqlin laha sam mana.**
T: **Ko-moyadno/maydono u-darmon-ano.**

I *(m/f)* need medication.
S: **Ṣniqa win lsam mana.**
T: **K-lozam-li darmono.**

I need medication for ...
S: **Sniqa win sammana qa .../Sniqta wan sammana qa ...**
T: **K-lozam-li darmono lajan ...**

What type of medication is this?
S: **Ma zna d-sam mana le aha?**
T: **Mun-shikil darmono-yo hano?**

What pill is this?
S: **Aya khabta d-mudi ela**
T: **Mun-ḥabtho-yo hathe?**

How many times a day must I take it?
S: **Kma zbate byawma wale d-shaqline?**
T: *—said by a male:* **Kmo kore bu-yawmo k-lozim moyadne?/**
—said by a female: **Kmo kore bu-yawmo k-lozim maydalle?**

How long must I take it?
S: **Qa kma wale d-shaqline?**
T: *—said by a male:* **Hul ema k-lozim moyadne?/**
—said by a female: **Hul ema k-lozim maydalle?**

When should I stop?
S: **Eman wali d-kalin minnay?**
T: —*said by a male:* **Ema k-lozim ṭorenolen?/**—
said by a female: **Ema k-lozim ṭuryalle?**

I'm *(m/f)* on antibiotics.
S: **Ṣ-hqalawin antibayotiks.**
T: **Ko-moyadno/maydono antibyotik.**

I'm allergic to ...
S: **Etli khashushuta min ...**
T: **Kit-li nebhutho men ...**

antibiotics	*S:* **antibayotiks**; *T:* **antibyotik**
penicillin	*S:* **penisilin**; *T:* **penisilin**

I do not need a vaccination.
S: **La win sniqa l-khmaṭa.**
T: **Lo k-lozam-li ṭᶜomo** (*or* **vaksin).**

I have my own syringe.
S: **Etli khmaṭa d-yati.**
T: **Kit-li mḥaṭo** (*or* **mosugho) d-ruḥi.**

Is it possible for me *(m/f)* to travel?
S: **Metmasyanta la qati d-karkhin?**
T: **Kibi korakhno/kurkhono hawkha?**

—Health words

AIDS	*S:* **ayds**; *T:* **aydz**
alcoholic	*S:* **awkhar/awkhrath dshakhra**; *T:* **shakhroyo; shatoyo**
alcoholism	*S:* **mawkhrut b-shakhra**; *T:* **shakhroyutho; shtoyo d-alkowol**
amputation	*S:* **prama**; *T:* **qṭoᶜo; qṣoyo**
anemia	*S:* **bṣirot dimma**; *T:* **mḥiluth-admo; fuqr-dam**
anesthetic	*S:* **mdakhyana**; *T:* **madimkhonitho; banch**
anesthetist	*S:* **mᶜaghuda**; *T:* **madimkhono**
antibiotic	*S:* **dalquw qurme**; *T:* **antibiyotik**
antiseptic	*S:* **mdakhyana**; *T:* **mdakhyono; antiseptik**

artery	*S:* **sheryana**; *T:* **sheryono**
artificial arm	*S:* **draᶜa ṣniᶜa**; *T:* **droᶜo mṣanaᶜto**
artificial eye	*S:* **ᶜayna ṣniᶜta**; *T:* **ᶜayno mṣanaᶜto**
artificial leg	*S:* **aqla ṣniᶜta** *or* **raghla ṣniᶜta**; *T:* **raghlo mṣanaᶜto**
aspirin	*S:* **asprin**; *T:* **aspirin**
bandage *medical*	*S:* **qmata ᶜaṣwaya**; *T:* **esoro; ᶜṣowo; fesqitho; qmoṭo**
Band-Aid	*S:* **smada**; *T:* **zulo ṭayfono; plaster**
bladder	*S:* **mtanta**; *T:* **mtonto**
blind	*S:* **samya/smita**; *T:* **samyo/smitho**
blood	*S:* **dimma**; *T:* **admo**
blood group	*S:* **adsha d-dimma**; *T:* **ṭuhmo admoyo**
blood pressure:	*S:* **rwisut dimma**; *T:* **rebṣo admoyo**
low blood pressure	*S:* **rwisut dimma nakhuta**; *T:* **rebṣo admoyo taḥtoyo**
high blood pressure	*S:* **rwisut dimma ᶜel laya**; *T:* **rebṣo admoyo ᶜeloyo**
blood transfusion	*S:* **nqalta dimma**; *T:* **nuqolo d-admo; shuḥlofo d-admo**
bone	*S:* **garma**; *T:* **garmo**
brain	*S:* **mukha**; *T:* **meḥo**
bug *insect*	*S:* **rekhsha**; *T:* **rakhsho**
burn *medical*	*S:* **yuqdana**; *T:* **yuqdhono**
cancer	*S:* **sarṭana**; *T:* **sartono; saratan; kanser**
cholera	*S:* **cholira**; *T:* **kolera**
clinic	*S:* **masᶜara**; *T:* **beth-osyutho; qenṭrun ḥulmonoyo**
cold: head cold	*S:* **qura; resha qarira**; *T:* **quro: quro d-risho**
constipation	*S:* **qapaṣ**; *T:* **qbath**
cotton wool	*S:* **ktana**; *T:* **ketono**
cough	*S:* **shᶜala**; *T:* **shᶜolo**
cream *ointment*	*S:* **meshkha**; *T:* **meshḥo**
dehydration	*S:* **yawshanuta**; *T:* **nashifutho**
dentist	*S:* **asya dshin ne**; *T:* **osyo/ositho da-ᶜarshone**

diarrhea	*S:* **plakhta daqla**; *T:* **mazlo d-gawo; rahṭo d-karso**
diet	*S:* **rajim**; *T:* **rejim**
dressing *(medical)*	*S:* **talwashta**; *T:* **lubosho**
drug *(medical)*	*S:* **sammana**; *T:* **darmono**
drug *(narcotic)*	*S:* **samma ᶜaghuda**; *T:* **samo; mukhaddar; drog**
dysentry	*S:* **dizenṭeria**; *T:* **dizenṭeria**
ear	*S:* **nata** *or* **adna**; *T:* **adhno**
ears	*S:* **natyate** *or* **adnate**; *T:* **adhnotho**
eardrum	*S:* **parda d-nata**; *T:* **ṭablo d-adhno**
epidemic	*S:* **pras-kurhana**; *T:* **mawtono; kurhono gawonoyo**
eye	*S:* **ᶜayna**; *T:* **ᶜayno**
eyes	*S:* **ᶜaynate**; *T:* **ᶜaynotho**
femur	*S:* **garma d-uṭma**; *T:* **garmo d-ᶜaṭmo**
fever	*S:* **eshatha**; *T:* **eshotho; ḥumtho; ḥemto**
flea	*S:* **pirṭana**; *T:* **furthaᶜno**
flu	*S:* **enfluwanza**; *T:* **shawbo; shᶜolo ᶜam shulhowo; inflawenza**
food poisoning	*S:* **sumama d-khalta**; *T:* **masmonutho d-muklo**
I ate this food.	*S:* **Khil li mhadhe khalta.**; *T:* **Akhili u-muklano.**
frostbite	*S:* **talguta**; *T:* **talgutho**
gall bladder	*S:* **mrarta**; *T:* **mrorto**
gently!	*S:* **nikha**; *T:* **hedi!**
germs	*S:* **qurme**; *T:* **mikrobe**
hand: left hand	*S:* **ida d-simmala**; *T:* **idho d-semolo**
right hand	*S:* **ida d-yammina**; *T:* **idho d-yamino**
hard! *vigorously*	*S:* **quya**; *T:* **qawyo!**
health	*S:* **khulmana**; *T:* **ḥulmono**
heart attack	*S:* **spakhta d-libba**; *T:* **shtoqo d-lebo**
heat stroke	*S:* **mkhuta d-libba**; *T:* **mḥoyo d-ḥemo; faliji**

hepatitis. *S:* **shaᶜatan**; *T:* **kabdho; shaᶜathan; hepatitis**

hernia *S:* **ptaqa**; *T:* **ftoqo**

hip *S:* **khruta**; *T:* **ḥrutho**

HIV *S:* **aych-ay-vi**; *T:* **aych-ay-vi**

hygiene *S:* **mriquta kholmanayta**; *T:* **nomuso ḥulmonoyo; qonuno ḥulmonoyo**

infant *S:* **yanuqa**; *T:* **ṭalyo/ṭlitho; zᶜuro/zᶜurto; naᶜimo/naᶜimto**

infected *S:* **ṭipya/ ṭpita**; *T:* **tafyo/tfitho**

It *(m/f)* is infected. *S:* **ṭipya le/ ṭpita la**; *T:* **Ṭafyo-yo./Ṭfitho-yo.**

infection *S:* **shukhama**; *T:* **ḥubolo; thaṭlushtho**

insect bite *S:* **nᶜaṣta d-rekhshe**; *T:* **dboṣo da-raḥshe**

  This insect bit me. *S:* **Aha rekhsha qam naᶜisli.**; *T:* **U-raḥshano dbiṣṣe-li.**

intestines *S:* **maᶜye**; *T:* **mᶜoye**

itching *S:* **khyuka**; *T:* **ḥyoko**

jaundice *S:* **yarqana**; *T:* **yarqono**

kidney *S:* **klita**; *T:* **klitho; kilwe**

kidneys *S:* **lilyata**; *T:* **kelyotho; killaw**

lice *S:* **qalme**; *T:* **qalme**

limbs *S:* **wasle**; *T:* **hadome**

malaria *S:* **malarya**; *T:* **malarya**

maternity hospital/clinic *S:* **bet-mawlada**; *T:* **beth-mawlodo**

milk *S:* **khalwa**; *T:* **ḥalwo**

  mother's milk *S:* **khalwa d-yimma**; *T:* **ḥalwo di-emo**

  cow's milk *S:* **khalwa d-tawiryate**; *T:* **ḥalwo da-tawrotho**

  goat's milk *S:* **khalwa d-ᶜeze**; *T:* **ḥalwo da-ᶜeze**

  powdered milk *S:* **khalwa ywisha**; *T:* **ḥalwo nashifo**

mosquito bite *S:* **nᶜaṣta d-baqa**; *T:* **dboṣo da-boqe**

mouth *S:* **puma**; *T:* **femo**

muscle *S:* **ʿaṣalta**; *T:* **ʿaṣalto**; **ʿadhale**
navel *S:* **shurta**; *T:* **shurto**
needle *S:* **khmaṭa**; *T:* **mḥaṭo**
nerve *S:* **gyade**; *T:* **gyodho**
newborn child *S:* **yaluda khata**; *T:* **yaludo**
nose *S:* **nahira**; *T:* **nḥiro**
nurse *S:* **yasupa/yasupta**; *T:* **samsemono/samsemonitho**; **oshufo/oshefto**
ointment *cream* *S:* **meshkha**; *T:* **meshḥo**
operating theater/room *S:* **tawana d-taʿwadtyate**; *T:* **tiyaṭron di-soʿurutho**; **tawono di-soʿurutho**
operation *surgical* *S:* **ʿaṣuwayta**; *T:* **soʿurutho**; **ʿoṣubayto**
organ *of body* *S:* **hadam paghra**; *T:* **hadomo**
oxygen *S:* **oksijin**; *T:* **oksijin**
painkiller *S:* **qaṭil khiwle**; *T:* **qoṭulo du-kewo**
palm *of hand* *S:* **kappa**; *T:* **kafo**
pancreas *S:* **shalpukhta**; *T:* **shalfuḥtho**
paralysis *S:* **msharyuta**; *T:* **msharyutho**
paralyzed *S:* **msharya/msharita**; *T:* **msharyo/msharyitho**
physiotherapy *S:* **awsaya kyanaya**; *T:* **fizyotherapya**
placenta *S:* **shlita**; *T:* **shlitho**
plaster *Bandaid* *S:* **ṣmada**; *T:* **zulo ṭayfono**; **plaster**
plaster cast *medical* *S:* **masmakh kilsha**; *T:* **masmkhono kelshonoyo**; **jibs**
pupil *of eye* *S:* **bawta *ḍ-ʿayna***; *T:* **bawtho *ḍ-ʿayno***
rabies *S:* **kurhan kalbuta**; *T:* **kurhono da-kalbe**; **kewo da-kalbe**
rash *S:* **ṭawsha**; *T:* **ḥemṭo**
rib (s) *S:* **elʿa (*plural* elʿe)**; *T:* **elʿo (*plural* elʿe)**
saliva *S:* **ruqe**; *T:* **ruqe**
shivers *S:* **rʿulta**; *T:* **rʿultho**
shoulder blade *S:* **katpa**; *T:* **kathfo**
shrapnel *S:* **qiṭʿate**; *T:* **falqe**; **shrapnel**

side *of body*	*S:* **dipna**; *T:* **dafno**
skeleton	*S:* **taghrumta**; *T:* **tagrumtho; hayklo**
skin	*S:* **gilda**; *T:* **galdho**
skull	*S:* **qirqipta**; *T:* **qarqaftho**
sleeping pills	*S:* **khabta d-nawma**; *T:* **ṭabbothe du-dmokho**
smallpox	*S:* **shalqo**; *T:* **shulfoḥo; shulfotho**
snake bite	*S:* **n^{c}aṣta d-khuwa**; *T:* **dboṣo d-ḥuyo**
This snake bit me.	*S:* **Aha khuwa qam na^{c}iṣli.**; *T:* **U-ḥuyano dbiṣṣe-li.**
spine; spinal column	*S:* **shishelta d-khaṣa**; *T:* **shishaltho d-ḥaṣo**
stethoscope	*S:* **shamu^{c}ta dasya**; *T:* **shomu^{c}to d-osyo; stethoskop**
stroke	*S:* **msharyuta**; *T:* **msharyutho**
stump *of limb*	*S:* **sharkana d-hadama qṭi^{c}a**; *T:* **sharkono d-hadomo qṭi^{c}o**
sunstroke	*S:* **mkhuta d-shimsha**; *T:* **mḥoyo d-shemsho**
surgeon	*S:* **ṣaruya**; *T:* **^{c}oṣubo/oṣubtho**
surgery *act of*	*S:* **mṣaruye**; *T:* **^{c}uṣobo**
syringe	*S:* **khmaṭa**; *T:* **mḥaṭo; mosugho**
syrup *medical*	*S:* **^{c}ṣara**; *T:* **^{c}ṣoro; sharab**
thermometer	*S:* **mashukhta d-khamimut**; *T:* **mkaylono di-shḥuntho; thermometer**
thigh	*S:* **^{c}uṭma**; *T:* **^{c}aṭmo**
throat	*S:* **ṣawra**; *T:* **ṣawro**
tibia	*S:* **garma d-shuqala**; *T:* **garmo d-shoqulo**
tiredness	*S:* **laweta**; *T:* **baṭilutho; t^{c}ishutho**
tooth	*S:* **shenna**; *T:* **sheno; ^{c}arsho; ^{c}arshono**
teeth	*S:* **shenne**; *T:* **^{c}arshone**
torture	*S:* **shenda**; *T:* **shendo**
trachea; windpipe	*S:* **yashṭa**; *T:* **yashṭo**
tranquilizer	*S:* **mshlyana**; *T:* **mshaynono**
tuberculosis	*S:* **ṭuberkulosis**; *T:* **tuberkulozis**
umbilical cord	*S:* **shurta**; *T:* **shurto**

urine	*S:* **jure/ tine**; *T:* **mazruqe; tafshirto**
vein	*S:* **warida**; *T:* **warido**
venereal disease	*S:* **kurhana myablana**; *T:* **kurhono** (*or* **kewo) gensonoyo**
vertebra	*S:* **khemra**; *T:* **ḥemro**
virus	*S:* **yukhla; virus**; *T:* **virus**
vitamins	*S:* **vitamin**; *T:* **vitaminat**
vomiting	*S:* **madᶜure**; *T:* **ḥfoḥo; gᶜoso**
whooping cough	*S:* **khnaqta**; *T:* **ḥaniqutho**

—Eyecare

I have broken my glasses.
S: **Ṭwiri l-khzayati.**
T: **Twiri-li a-ḥazoyothaydhi.**

Can you *(m/f)* repair them?

S: **Maṣit mṭarsitlon?/Maṣyat mtarsatlon?**
T: **Kibokh/Kibekh mtarṣat-len?**

I *(m/f)* need new lenses.
S: **Sniqa win l-ṭlawikhyate khate./Sneqta wan l-ṭlawikhyate khate.**
T: **Ko-luzmi-li ṭaliḥotho** (*or* **ᶜadasat) ḥathe.**

When will they be ready?
S: **Iman b-parqi?**
T: **Ema gid-owen ḥadhire?**

How much do I owe you *(m/f)*?
S: **Kma yṭalbinukh./Kma yṭalbinakh?**
T: **Miqqa ko-ṭolbat meni?**

contact lenses	*S:* **ṭlawikhyate bawaye**; *T:* **ṭaliḥotho ṭafyotho; ᶜadasat; kontakt lenz**
contact lens solution	*S:* **sam mana d-ṭlawikhyate bawaye**; *T:* **darmono da-ṭaliḥotho ṭafyotho**

24. RELIEF AID

Can you *(m/f)* help me?
S: **Maṣit mᶜadhret li?/Maṣyat mᶜadhrat li?**
T: **Kibokh mᶜawnat-li?/Kibekh mᶜawnat-li?**

Can you *(m/f)* speak English?
S: **Maṣit mṣawtit Inglish?/Maṣyat mṣawtat Inglish?**
T: **Ko-mijgholat Inglishoyo?**

Who *(m/f)* is in charge?
S: **Mani le mshalana?**
T: **Man-yo u-risho?**

Fetch the main person *(m/f)* in charge.
S: **Qri le mshalana.**
T: **Amṭay-li u-risho.**

What's the name of this town/village?
S: **Mudi le shemma d-hade mdita/qrita?**
T: **Mun-yo ishma di-mdhithathe/qrithathe?**

How many people live there?
S: **Kma nasdhe ykhayi lakha?**
T: **Kmo noshe k-ᶜayshi tamo?**

What's the name of that river?
S: **Mudi le shim ma d-aha nahra?**
T: **Mun-yo ishme du-nahrawo?**

How deep is it?
S: **Kma le ᶜamuqa?**
T: **Miqqa ᶜamuqo-yo?**

Is the bridge down?
S: **Gishra npila le?**
T: **Nafil u-geshro?**

Is the bridge still standing?
S: **Gishra hala rima le?**
T: **Hesh ko-kole u-geshro?**

Where can we ford the river?
S: **Mika maṣikh ʿawrikh l-nahra?**
T: **Kiban quṭʿina (*or* shufʿina) u-nahro?**

What is the name of that mountain?
S: **Mudi le shim ma d-awah ṭura?**
T: **Mun-yo ishme du-ṭur awo?**

How high is it?
S: **Kma le ʿellaya?**
T: **Miqqa ʿeloyo-yo?**

Where is the border?
S: **Ika le tkhuba?**
T: **Ayko-yo u-tḥumo?**

Is it safe?

S: **Et shaynuta?**
T: **Mshayno-yo (*or* amin-yo)?**

Show *(m/f)* me.
S: **Makhwili./Makhwayli.**
T: **Maḥway-li.**

Is there anyone trapped?
S: **Et nashe ʿeṣya?**
T: **Kito noshe maṣide tamo?**

Is the building safe?
S: **Mshayna ile aha benyana?**
T: **Mshayno-yo u-benyono?** *or*
Amin-yo u-benyono?

It's going to collapse!
S: **Bid napil!**
T: **G-nofil!**

Get out *(m/f/pl)* (of the building) now!
S: **Ploṭ/Ploeṭ/Ploṭon hadiya min binyana!**
T: **Nfaq** *(m/f)* **uʿdo! (***plural* **Nfaqu uʿdo!)**

Can you *(m/f)* hear any sound?
S: **Shmaʿa wit/wat kha mindi?**
T: **Ko-shumʿat mede?**

Silence *(m/f)*!
S: **Shtuq!/Shtueq!/Shtuqon!**
T: **Shtaq!** (*plural* **Shtaqu!)**

—Checkpoints

checkpoint	*S:* **nuqzata d-buqare**; *T:* **nuqzo d-buṣoyo; ṣayṭare; qonṭrol**
roadblock	*S:* **skhar urkha**; *T:* **skhoro du-darbo**

Stop *(m/f)*!
S: **Kli!/Kle!** (*plural* **Klimon!)**
T: **Klay!** (*plural* **Klayu!)**

Do not move *(m/f)*!
S: **La mhalkhit!/La mhalkhat!** (*plural* **La mhalkhiton!)**
T: **Lo malkhat!** (*plural* **Lo malkhitu!)**

Go *(m/f/pl)*!
S: **Khush!/Khoesh!/Khushon!**
T: **Zokh!/Zekh!/Zokhu!**

Who are you *(m/f/pl)*?
S: **Mani wit/wat/ton?**
T: *m/f:* **Man hat?**/*pl:* **Man hatu?**

Don't shoot!
S: **La darit!**
T: **Lo dorat!**

Help!
S: **ʿUdrana!**
T: **Tokhu lafe-li!**

Help me!
S: **Mʿader li!**
T: **Mʿawan-li!**

no entry	*S:* **layt maʿla**; *T:* **layto ʿboro**
emergency exit	*S:* **mapqa ʿriṣa**; *T:* **mafqo di-aliṣutho**
straight on	*S:* **tris**; *T:* **msawyo**
turn left	*S:* **ptul l-simmala**; *T:* **bram lu-semolo**

turn right	*S:* **ptul l-yamina**; *T:* **bram lu-yamino**
this way	*S:* **makha**; *T:* **u-darb-ano**
that way	*S:* **mtama**; *T:* **u-darb-awo**

Keep quiet *(m/f/pl)*!
S: **Shtuq!/Shtueq!/Shtuqon!**
T: *m/f:* **Shtaq!**/*pl:* **Shtaqu!**

You *(m/f)* are right.
S: **Ṭrisa wit./Ṭrista wat.**
T: **Shrolo k-immat.**

You *(m/f)* are wrong.
S: **Pawda wit/wat.**
T: **Ghalṭo hat.**

I *(m/f)* am ready.
S: **Mṭaywa win./Mṭayawta wan.**
T: **ḥadhiro-no./ḥadhirto-no.**

I *(m/f)* am in a hurry.
S: **Msarhu wewin/wewan.**
T: **Malizo-no./Malizto-no.**

What's that *(m/f)*?
S: **Mudi le aha?/Mudi la hadhe?**
T: **Mun-yo hawo/hayo?**

Come in *(m/f/pl)*!
S: **ᶜUl!/ᶜOl!/ᶜUlon!**
T: **Tokh ᶜbar!/Tekh ᶜbar!/Tokhu ᶜbaru!**

That's all!
S: **Layt mindi khina!**
T: **Bas-yo!**

—Food distribution

feeding station	*S:* **nuqazta d-tursaya**; *T:* **mashryo d-muklo**

How many people are in your family?
S: **Kma laye hadame diqartakhon?**
T: **Kmo noshe kito bi-iqarthathkhu?** *or* **Kmo noshe kito bi-ᶜa'ilathkhu?**

How many children?
S: **Kma shawre?**
T: **Kmo naᶜime?**

You *(m/f/pl)* must come back ...
S: **Wale d-atit/atyat/atiton ...**
T: m/f: **... k-lozim doᶜrat.**/*pl:* **... k-lozim doᶜrutu.**

this afternoon *S:* **ṭahra d-ediom**; *T:* **ad-ᶜaṣriye**
tonight *S:* **ramsha ediom**; *T:* **ad-lalyo**
tomorrow *S:* **qudme**; *T:* **ramḥel**
the day after tomorrow *S:* **qudme date**; *T:* **yawmo ḥreno**
next week *S:* **shawuᶜa d-bitaya le**; *T:* **shabtho d-uthyo**

There is water for you *(m/f/pl)*.
S: **An na miya qalukh/qalakh/qalawkhon elay.**
T: **Kito maye lajanokh/lajanekh/lajanayhku.**

There is grain for you *(m/f/pl)*.
S: **Et qalokh/qalakh/qalawkhon birzarᶜe.**
T: **Kito ḥeṭe lajanokh/lajanekh/lajanayhku.**

There is food for you *(m/f/pl)*.
S: **Et qalokh/qalakh/qalawkhon tursaya.**
T: **Kito muklo lajanokh/lajanekh/lajanaykhu.**

There is fuel for you *(m/f/pl)*.
S: **Et qalokh/qalakh/qalawkhon yaqdana.**
T: **Kito banzin lajanokh/lajanekh/lajanaykhu.**

Please form *(pl)* a queue (here/there)!
S: **En mbasmalawkhon klimun bdawra (lakha/tama)!**
T: **Boᶜutho menaykhu, klayu bu-rez (***or* **b-sirra) (harke/tamo)!**

—Road repair

Is the road passable?
S: **Hadhe urkha ᶜawurta la?**
T: **Kiban shufᶜina bu-darb-ano?**

Is the road blocked?
S: **Hadhe urkha ᶜṣita la?**
T: **Skhiro-yo u-darbo?**

We are repairing the road.
S: **Mtaquni wikh lurkha.**
T: **Ko-mṭarṣina u-darbo.**

We are repairing the bridge.
S: **Mtaqune wikh l-gishra.**
T: **Ko-mṣarṣina u-geshro.**

We need ...
S: **Sniqe wikh ...**
T: **Ko-lozam-lan ...**

wood	*S:* **qayse**; *T:* **qayse**
a rock	*S:* **isara; kepa**; *T:* **kefo**
rocks	*S:* **isare; kepe**; *T:* **kefe**
gravel	*S:* **bizqe**; *T:* **boqushe**
sand	*S:* **khaala; bizqe; baqlushe**; *T:* **ḥolo; qum**
fuel *(for fire)*	*S:* **yaqdana**; *T:* **yaqdhono**
fuel *(petrol)*	*S:* **banzin**; *T:* **banzin**

Lift *(sing/pl)*!
S: **Msalqana!/Msalqane!**
T: **Ma^{c}lay!/Ma^{c}layu!**

Drop it *(sing/pl)*!
S: **Marpi le!/Mrapimon le!**
T: **Marfaye-le!/Marfayu-le!**

Now!
S: **Hadiya!**
T: **U^{c}do!**

All together!
S: **Kula ^{c}am ekhdade!**
T: **Yalla!** *or* **^{c}Am ḥdhodhe!**

—Mines

mine *noun*	*S:* **paqu^{c}a**; *T:* **fetqo; lagham**
mines	*S:* **paqu^{c}e**; *T:* **fetqe; algham**
minefield	*S:* **khaqla d-paqu^{c}e**; *T:* **ḥaqlo da-fetqe**
to lay mines	*S:* **zra^c paqu^{c}e**; *T:* **droyo fetqe**
to hit a mine	*S:* **psa^c l-paqu^{c}a**; *T:* **mḥoyo fetqo**

to clear a mine	*S:* **msapiq l-paquʿa;** *T:* **shfoyo fetqe**
mine detector	*S:* **galyan paquʿe;** *T:* **mgalyonitho da-fetqe**
mine disposal	*S:* **zawluth paquʿe;** *T:* **mḥalaqto da-fetqe**

Are there any mines near here?
S: **Et paquʿe qurba mlakha?**
T: **Kit fetqe qariwe m-arke?**

What type are they?
S: **Mayna adsha laye?**
T: **Mishikil-ne?**

anti-vehicle	*S:* **dalqow-ʿaghule;** *T:* **luqbal-radhyotho**
anti-personnel	*S:* **dalqow-palkhe;** *T:* **luqbal-agire**
plastic	*S:* **plasṭik;** *T:* **plastik**
magnetic	*S:* **natupa;** *T:* **maghnaṭiqoye**

What size are they?
S: **Ma yurwa laye?**
T: *—How large are they?:* **Miqqa rabe-ne?;**
—How small are they?: **Miqqa naʿime-ne?**

What color are they?
S: **Ma gawna laye?**
T: **Mun gawno-ne?**

Are they marked?
S: **Rmize laye?**
T: **Kit mede rshimo aʿlayye?**

How?
S: **Dakhi?**
T: **Mun-shikil?**

How many mines are there?
S: **Kma parquʿe laye?**
T: **Kmo fetqe kit tamo?**

When were they laid?
S: **Iman ewa zriʿye?**
T: **Ema maḥitten-ne?**

Can you *(m/f)* take me to the minefields?
S: **Maṣit labliti/lablatli l-khaqla d-paquᶜe?**
T: **Kibokh/Kibekh mawblat-li la-ḥaqle da-fetqe?**

Are there any booby traps near there?
S: **Et pakhe ṭeshye qurba mtama?**
T: **Kito maṣidotho (*or* faḥe) qariwe me-tamo?**

Are they made from: grenades, high explosives, or something else?
S: **Mtursa laye min: mparqaᶜyate dida, purqaᶜe rabe, yan kha mindi khina?**
T: **Me-mun simene: mramye, mfajronyotho (*or* mparqᶜonyotho), aw medone ḥrene?**

Are they in a building?
S: **Go bibyana laye?**
T: **B-benyono-ne?**

... on paths?
S: **... ᶜal shwile?**
T: **... ᶜal a-darbone?**

... on roads?
S: **... ᶜal urkhate?**
T: **... ᶜal a-darbone?**

... on bridges?
S: **... ᶜal gishre?**
T: **... ᶜal a-geshre?**

... or elsewhere?
S: **... yan duktha khita?**
T: **... aw duktho ḥreto?**

Can you *(m/f)* show me?
S: **Maṣit makhwitli?/Maṣyat makhwatli?**
T: **Kibokh maḥwat-li?/Kibekh maḥwat-li?**

Stay (m/f) where you are!
S: **Push ika d-ewet!/Poesh ika d-ewat!**
T: **Fush b-dukthokh!/Fush b-dukthekh!**

Don't move *(m/f)*!
S: **La mhalkhit!/La mhalkhat!**
T: **Lo malkhat!**

Don't go *(m/f)* near that!
s: **La qarwit l-haw!/La qarwat l-haw!**
T: **Lozzokh su-med-awo!/Lazzekh su-med-awo!**

Don't touch *(m/f)* that!
s: **La gayshit b-haw!/La gayshat b-haw!**
T: **Lo gayshat bu-med-awo!**

—Other words

airforce	s: **zaynṭawsa**; T: **ḥaylo hawoyo**
ambulance	s: **raditha d-ushpa**; T: **radhayto d-ʿudrono; ambulans; asʿaf**
armored car	s: **radita zariditha**; T: **radhayto ʿa ifto**
army	s: **gaysa**; T: **gayso; askar; jaysh**
artillery	s: **mqalʿane**; T: **mqalʿono**
barbed wire	s: **khuʾa mṣalpana**; T: **ḥuṭo kubonoyo**
bomb	s: **parqaʿta**; T: **bomba; qunbala**
bomber	s: **mparqʿanitha**; T: **daroyo/ darayto da-bombe**
bomblet	s: **parqaʿta**; T: **bomba naʿimto**
bullet	s: **gulla**; T: **bughro**
cannon	s: **mqalʿana**; T: **madoqto ʿatiqto; kanon**
cluster bomb	s: **parqaʿtha sghulayta**; T: **bomba mbadronitho**
disaster	s: **tawhta**; T: **gunḥo**
drought	s: **yawshana**; T: **nashifutho**
earthquake	s: **nudhnadha**; T: **zawʿo; hyozo arʿonoyo**
famine	s: **kipna**; T: **kafno**
fighter	s: **qrawtana**; T: **qrabthono/ qrabthonitho**
gun: *pistol*	s: **glulita**; T: **pis ola; qurma; musaddas**
rifle	s: **isarta**; T: **chifta; tfanga; isorto**
cannon	s: **mqalʿana**; T: **madoqto ʿatiqto; kanon**
machine-gun	s: **rasosta; rasosyate**; T: **chifta makinayto**
missile	s: **ṣarukha**; T: **ṣoruḥo; ṣarukh**

missiles	*S:* **ṣarukhe**; *T:* **ṣoruḥe; ṣawarikh**
mortar *weapon*	*S:* **zayna d-sitta**; *T:* **madoqto na^{c}imto**
natural disaster	*S:* **tawhta kyanayta**; *T:* **gunḥo kyonoyo**
navy	*S:* **yamayuta**; *T:* **ḥaylo yamoyo**
nuclear power station	*S:* **nuqasta d-khayla grumanaya**; *T:* **qenṭrun d-ḥaylo fredtonoyo**
nuclear power	*S:* **khayla grumanaya**; *T:* **ḥaylo fredtonoyo; tuqfo fredtonoyo**
officer	*S:* **akhida**; *T:* **aḥidho; dhabiṭ**
parachute	*S:* **parashut**; *T:* **maṭlo; parashut**
peace	*S:* **shayna**; *T:* **shlomo**
people	*S:* **nashe**; *T:* **noshe; ^{c}amo**
pistol	*S:* **glulita**; *T:* **pisṭola; qurma; musaddas**
refugee	*S:* **galuya**; *T:* **gawsono/gawsonto**
refugees	*S:* **galuye**; *T:* **gawsone**
refugee camp	*S:* **mashrita d-galuye**; *T:* **mashritho da-gawsone**
relief aid	*S:* **suya^{c}a**; *T:* **m^{c}awanto ^{c}udronayto**
sack	*S:* **shray mshidta**; *T:* **saqo**
shell *military*	*S:* **qalwa**; *T:* **qlofo; qalwo**
shelter	*S:* **gawsa**; *T:* **beth-gawso**
submachine gun	*S:* **rasusta**; *T:* **chifta makinayto na^{c}imto**
tank	*S:* **rashupta**; *T:* **roshufto; dabbaba; tank**
troops	*S:* **khaylawate**; *T:* **qrabthone; fulḥe**
unexploded ammunition	*S:* **gulle la purqi^{c}e**; *T:* **asono lo mfajro** (*or* **mparq^{c}o**)
unexploded bomb	*S:* **marmita la mporqi^{c}ta**; *T:* **bomba lo mfajarto** (*or* **mparq^{c}to**)**; qunbala lo mfajarto**
unexploded ordnance	*S:* **mqal^{c}ana la mporqi^{c}a**; *T:* **mfajronitho lo mfajarto; mparq^{c}onitho lo mparqa^{c}to**
war	*S:* **qrawa**; *T:* **qrobo**
weapon	*S:* **zayna**; *T:* **zayno**

25. WAR

airplane	*S:* **ṭaysta**; *T:* **ṭayisto**
air-raid	*S:* **spukhya rqiᶜaya**; *T:* **ṣfoḥo hawoyo**
ambush	*S:* **kmina**; *T:* **kmino**
ammunition	*S:* **zawde**; *T:* **asono**; **zwodo**; **dhakhire**
anti-aircraft gun	*S:* **dalqiw taysyate**; *T:* **chifta luqbal-ayisyotho**
anti-tank	*S:* **dalqiw rashopyate**; *T:* **fetqo luqbal-roshufotho**
armored car	*S:* **radita arpansayta**; *T:* **radhayto ᶜaifto**
arms	*S:* **zayne**; *T:* **zayne**; **asliḥa**
army	*S:* **gaysa**; *T:* **gayso**; **askar**; **jaysh**
artillery	*S:* **shayudhta**; *T:* **mqalᶜono**
assault; attack	*S:* **spukhya**; *T:* **kwosho**
aviation	*S:* **malkhot a'ar**; *T:* **uyoso**; **ṭayyaran**
bayonet	*S:* **kallawa**; *T:* **shelfo di-chifta**
belt	*S:* **zunara**; *T:* **qamro**; **zunoro**
bomb	*S:* **parqaᶜta**; *T:* **bomba**; **qunbala**
bombardment	*S:* **qluᶜya**; *T:* **rghumyo**; **qṣofo**; **qaṣif**
butt *of rifle*	*S:* **rakhta**; *T:* **sakro**; **eshto**
captain	*S:* **akhida**; *T:* **dawqo**; **naqib**
ceasefire	*S:* **tashlita**; *T:* **kelyon-nuro**
chief of staff	*S:* **resh-gaysa**; *T:* **rish-baᶜle d-gayso**; **ra'is-arkan**
dagger	*S:* **gallawa**; *T:* **khanjar**
defeat *noun*	*S:* **twarta**; *T:* **twirutho**
detonation	*S:* **purqaᶜa**; *T:* **mfajronutho**
enemy	*S:* **bᶜildwawa**; *T:* **bᶜeldbobo**; **dijmin**
freedom	*S:* **khiruta**; *T:* **sharyutho**
general	*S:* **reshana**; *T:* **rab-ḥaylo**; **rishono**; **jeneral**
grenade	*S:* **parqaᶜta d-ida**; *T:* **mramyo**; **bomba d-idho**

gun barrel	*S:* **abub-glulita**; *T:* **shawṭo di-chifta**; **abubo di-chifta**
gun	*S:* **glulita**; *T:* **chifta**
helicopter	*S:* **ṭayupta**; *T:* **tayofto**
hostage	*S:* **meshkana**; *T:* **rahino**; **m^{c}aryo**
liberty	*S:* **khiruta**; *T:* **ḥirutho**
lieutenant	*S:* **qadhma**; *T:* **naqifo**; **mulazim**
lieutenant-colonel	*S:* **qadhma**; *T:* **mqadmono**; **muqaddim**
lieutenant-general	*S:* **reshana qadhmaya**; *T:* **neshro**; **fariq**
machine gun	*S:* **rasosta**; *T:* **chifta makinayto**
major-general	*S:* **resh tagha**; *T:* **foqudho**; **liwa^{c}**
martyr	*S:* **sahda**; *T:* **sohdo**
military school	*S:* **midrashta gaysayta**; *T:* **madrashto gaysayto**
military university	*S:* **bet-sawba gaysaya**; *T:* **beth-ṣawbo gaysoyo**
mine: anti-personnel	*S:* **dalqiw palkhe**; *T:* **fetqo luqbal-fulḥe**
munitions	*S:* **zwade**; *T:* **zuyone**
objective	*S:* **nisha**; *T:* **nisho**
opponent	*S:* **b^{c}eldara**; *T:* **saqubloyo**
patrol	*S:* **dayurta**; *T:* **methkarkhonutho**; **dawriye**
peace	*S:* **shayna**; *T:* **shlomo**
personnel *military*	*S:* **palkhe**; *T:* **agire**
pilot	*S:* **ṭayusa**; *T:* **ṭayostono**
pistol	*S:* **glulita**; *T:* **pisṭola**; **qurma**; **musaddas**
plane	*S:* **ayasta**; *T:* **ayisto**
prisoner	*S:* **asira**; *T:* **asiro**
raid	*S:* **spukhya**; *T:* **ṣfoḥo**
regiment	*S:* **pawga**; *T:* **ulqo**; **gudo**; **yahlo**
reinforcements	*S:* **^{c}uzaya**; *T:* **mḥaylone**; **maruḥone**
rifle	*S:* **isarta**; *T:* **chifta**; **tfanga**; **isorto**
rocket	*S:* **ṣarukha**; *T:* **giro nurono**
rocket-launcher	*S:* **ashid ṣarukhe**; *T:* **kashoṭo da-gire nurone**
shell *military*	*S:* **qlapa**; *T:* **qlofo**; **qalwo**
shelter	*S:* **gawsa**; *T:* **beth-gawso**

shrapnel	*S:* **ṣiwa**; *T:* **bughro mbadrono**
siege	*S:* **khṣara**; *T:* **ḥdhirutho**
soldier	*S:* **gaysaya**; *T:* **qrabthono**
spy	*S:* **gashusha**; *T:* **goshusho**
staff *army*	*S:* **gusha**; *T:* **ba^{c}le d-gayso**
submachine gun	*S:* **rasosta**; *T:* **chifta mikanikayto na^{c}imto**
tank	*S:* **rashupta**; *T:* **roshufto**; **tank**
to beat *overcome*	*S:* **zkaya**; *T:* **^{c}lobo**; **ghlobo**
to camouflage	*S:* **mkasyanuta**; *T:* **matloyo**
to command	*S:* **mpaqude**; *T:* **fqodho**; **ihobo fuqdhono**
to conquer	*S:* **mqanuwe**; *T:* **kubosho**; **kbishutho**
to defeat	*S:* **twara**; *T:* **tworo**
to destroy	*S:* **msakhip**; *T:* **maḥrowo**
to evacuate	*S:* **msapaqta**; *T:* **makhloyo**
to explode	*S:* **mparqi^{c}**; *T:* **mfajoro**
to free	*S:* **mkharir**; *T:* **shroyo**
to invade	*S:* **spakha**; *T:* **kwushyo**; **ṣfoḥo**
to kill	*S:* **qṭala**; *T:* **qṭolo**
to liberate	*S:* **mkharure**; *T:* **ḥuroro**
to loot	*S:* **shwaya**; *T:* **slobo**
to lose	*S:* **taluqe**; *T:* **khṣoro**
to make peace	*S:* **mshayin**; *T:* **syomo d-shlomo**
to pursue	*S:* **maqip**; *T:* **rdhofo**
to resist	*S:* **msaqolayuta**; *T:* **^{c}uzoyo**; **muqawama**
to retreat	*S:* **grashta**; *T:* **d^{c}oro**
to shoot down	*S:* **rmayta**; *T:* **manḥoto**
to surrender	*S:* **mtaslim**; *T:* **mashlomo**; **taslomo**
to surround	*S:* **mkarikh**; *T:* **ḥedhoro**
to take prisoner	*S:* **ma'asore**; *T:* **msoko d-asiro**
to take shelter	*S:* **mgawis**; *T:* **myodho gawso**
to win	*S:* **mzake**; *T:* **qmoro**
to wound	*S:* **msalip**; *T:* **jroḥo**
tracer bullet	*S:* **gulla d-bahranita**; *T:* **bughro samuḥo**
truce	*S:* **tashlita**; *T:* **tashlitho**
victory	*S:* **zakhuta**; *T:* **zokhutho**
war	*S:* **qrawa**; *T:* **qrobo**
weapon	*S:* **zayna**; *T:* **zayno**

26. POLITICS

aid worker *S:* **msayᶜana**; *T:* **ᶜudronoyo/ᶜudronayto**
ambassador *S:* **ezgada/ezgadta**; *T:* **izgado/izgadto; mshadro/mshadarto**
arrest *verb* *S:* **dmkhawish**; *T:* **msoko**
assassination *S:* **qiṭla bliqa**; *T:* **qaṭlo**
assembly *meeting* *S:* **knushya**; *T:* **knushyo**
assembly *parliament* *S:* **beth-sharire**; *T:* **knushto**
autonomy *S:* **sholṭan byata**; *T:* **shulṭono yothoyo; ḥukm dhati**
cabinet *S:* **mawtwa d-sharire**; *T:* **mawtbo d-sharire**
capitalism *S:* **reshmala**; *T:* **rishmeloyutho**
charity *organisation* *S:* **ᶜerwana**; *T:* **siᶜto maṭebonitho; ᶜudronayto**
citizen *S:* **barmata/bartmata**; *T:* **bar-athro/bath-athro**
civil rights *S:* **zidqe mdinaye**; *T:* **zedqe gawonoye; zedqe mdhinoye**
civil war *S:* **qrawa mdinaya**; *T:* **qrobo gawonoyo**
coalition *S:* **awyuta**; *T:* **awyutho gabayto**
condemn *S:* **dan**; *T:* **ḥromo**
constitution *S:* **namusa**; *T:* **qonuno shath'esoyo; dastur**
convoy *S:* **qapla dradiyate**; *T:* **luwoyo**
corruption *S:* **khwala**; *T:* **ḥwilutho**
coup d'etat *S:* **sukhapa gaysaya**; *T:* **qulobo; qyoṣo men-shelyo d-malkutho; enqelab**
crime *S:* **surkhana**; *T:* **ḥawbo**
criminal *S:* **msarkhana/msarkhanta**; *T:* **ḥayowo/ḥayowto**
crisis *S:* **ᶜasquta**; *T:* **ᶜoqtho; ᶜiqutho; ulṣono; kriza**
debate *S:* **durasha**; *T:* **kuthosho**
debt *S:* **dayna**; *T:* **dayno**

democracy — *S:* **dimoqraṭayuta;** *T:* **dimoqratutho; dimoqratiye**
development — *S:* **tuwara;** *T:* **ṭuworo; methṭawronutho**
dictator — *S:* **diktaturaya;** *T:* **ṭruno; diktator**
dictatorship — *S:* **diktaturuta;** *T:* **ṭrunutho; diktatoriye**
diplomatic ties — *S:* **isure suyasaye;** *T:* **esore diblomasoye**
displaced person — *S:* **tawtawa;** *T:* **mshanyo/mshanayto**
displaced persons/people — *S:* **tawtawe;** *T:* **mshanye**
election — *S:* **gubaya;** *T:* **guboyo**
embassy — *S:* **bet-ezgaduta;** *T:* **izgadutho; mshadrutho**
ethnic cleansing — *S:* **lkhayta ṭohmanayta;** *T:* **mandhafto ṭuhmayto**
ethnic minority — *S:* **qaliluta ṭohmayta;** *T:* **ḥsirutho ṭuhmayto**
exile *person* — *S:* **mizaṭra/misaṭrana;** *T:* **galwoyo/galwayto**
free — *S:* **khira;** *T:* **ḥiro/ḥirto**
freedom — *S:* **khiruta;** *T:* **ḥirutho**
government — *S:* **shulṭana;** *T:* **shulṭonutho; ḥukume**
guerrilla — *S:* **dar rara;** *T:* **gerilla**
hostage — *S:* **meshkana;** *T:* **rahino; mʿaryo**
human rights — *S:* **zidqe nashaye;** *T:* **zedqe noshoye**
humanitarian aid — *S:* **suyaʿa nashaya;** *T:* **ʿudrono noshoyo**
independence — *S:* **sharyuta;** *T:* **sharyutho**
independent state — *S:* **atra sharya;** *T:* **uḥdono sharyo**
independent — *S:* **sharya;** *T:* **sharyo/shritho**
jail — *S:* **bet-khwushya;** *T:* **beth-ḥbushyo; ḥabiss; sijin**
judge — *S:* **day yana;** *T:* **dayono**
killer — *S:* **qaṭula;** *T:* **qoṭulo**
king — *S:* **malka;** *T:* **malko**
law court — *S:* **bet-dayna namusaya;** *T:* **beth-dino**
law — *S:* **namusa;** *T:* **nomuso; qonuno**

lawyer *S:* **sinighra**; *T:* **snighro/snighartho**
leader *S:* **hadia**; *T:* **rishono/rishonitho**
left-wing *S:* **gazlaya**; *T:* **semoloyo/semolayto**
liberation *S:* **khurara**; *T:* **ḥuroro**
lower house *S:* **mawtwa takhtaya**; *T:* **bayto taḥtoyo**
majority *S:* **sagiyuta**; *T:* **yatirutho**; **aghlabiye**
member of parliament *S:* **hadama/hadamtha d-bet-sholṭana**; *T:* **hadomo/hadomto du-mawtbo d-shulṭono**
mercenary *S:* **razuqa**; *T:* **methrazqono**; **agiro**
minister *S:* **sharira**; *T:* **shariro**; **waziro**
ministry *S:* **shariruta**; *T:* **sharirutho**; **wazirutho**
minority *S:* **qaliluta**; *T:* **ḥsirutho**; **qalilutho**; **aqalliye**
minority vote *S:* **qala d-qaliluta**; *T:* **qolo di-ḥsirutho**
murder *S:* **qiṭla**; *T:* **qaṭlo**
opposition *S:* **saqulayuta**; **saqulaya**; *T:* **saqubloyutho**
parliament *S:* **bet-shulṭana**; *T:* **mawtbo d-shulṭono**; **barlaman**
party *political* *S:* **gabba** ***suyasaya***; *T:* **gabo** ***foliṭiqoyo***
peace *S:* **shayna**; *T:* **shlomo**
peace-keeping troops *S:* **khaylawate naṭure d-shayna**; *T:* **noṭure d-shlomo**
political rally *S:* **maqyapta suyasayta**; *T:* **knushyo foliṭiqoyo**
politician *S:* **suyasara/suyasartha**; *T:* **foliṭiqoyo/foliṭiqayto**
politics *S:* **suyasa**; *T:* **foliṭiqi**; **siyase**
POW camp *S:* **mashrita d-asire**; *T:* **mashritho d-an-asire d-qrobo**
president *S:* **reshquṭna**; *T:* **rish-quṭnoyutho**
prime minister *S:* **resh sharire**; *T:* **rish-wazire**; **risho d-sharire**
prison *S:* **bet-asire**; *T:* **beth-asire**; **ḥbushyo**
prisoner-of-war *S:* **asira dqrawa**; *T:* **asiro d-qrobo**
probably *S:* **kbar**; *T:* **balki**

protest — *S:* **mikhadh bᶜeltha**; *T:* **taglitho**
reactionary *adjective* — *S:* **hipkayuta**; *T:* **hefkoyo; rajᶜi**
Red Crescent — *S:* **Sahra Smuqa**; *T:* **Sahro Semoqo**
Red Cross — *S:* **Sliwa Smuqa**; *T:* **Ṣlibo Semoqo**
refugee — *S:* **galuya/galwayta**; *T:* **gawsono/gawsonto**
refugees — *S:* **galuye**; *T:* **gawsone**
republic — *S:* **qaṭnuta**; *T:* **quṭnutho**
revolution — *S:* **qawmaya**; *T:* **qawmo**
right-wing — *S:* **yaminaya**; *T:* **yaminoyo**
robbery — *S:* **shiwya**; *T:* **shloḥo**
seat *(in assembly)* — *S:* **mawtwa**; *T:* **kursyo**
secret police — *S:* **dakhshe razanaye**; *T:* **daḥshe rozonoye**
socialism — *S:* **shotapayuta**; *T:* **meshtawtfonutho; sosyalizm; ishtirakiye**
socialist — *S:* **shotapaya/shotapayta**; *T:* **meshtawtfonoyo/meshtawtfonitho; sosyalist; ishtiraki/ishtirakiye**
spy — *S:* **gashusha**; *T:* **goshusho/goshushto**
struggle — *S:* **kutasha**; *T:* **aghuno**
theft — *S:* **gnawta**; *T:* **gnowo**
testify — *S:* **s-hada**; *T:* **s-hodo; ihobo sohdutho**
trade union — *S:* **takhbarta**; *T:* **ḥuyodho da-tagore**
treasury — *S:* **shargaz za**; *T:* **beth-gazo; simto**
United Nations — *S:* **Emwate Mkhaydate**; *T:* **Emwotho Mḥaydotho**
upper house — *S:* **mawtwa ᶜellaya**; *T:* **bayto ᶜeloyo**
veto — *S:* **veto**; *T:* **vito; zedqo d-nkoro w-hfukhyo**
vote — *S:* **gubaya**; *T:* **qolo**
vote-rigging — *S:* **mzayupe l-gubaya**; *T:* **rukowo da-qole**
voting — *S:* **gabuye**; *T:* **guboyo**
world — *S:* **ᶜalma**; *T:* **britho; methᶜamronitho**

27. TOOLS

binoculars	*S:* **mkhawya**; *T:* **doyuqtho; mrawrwono mezdawgo; durbin**
brick	*S:* **lowna**; *T:* **lewno**
brush	*S:* **pirka**; *T:* **maknishto; fircha**
cable	*S:* **khuṭa**; *T:* **marsho; kabil**
cooker	*S:* **ṭawokha/kanuna**; *T:* **basholo**
drill	*S:* **naquwa**; *T:* **maqwo**
eyeglasses	*S:* **khazayate**; *T:* **ḥazoyotho**
gas bottle	*S:* **pilla d-khapupa**; *T:* **shushaye d-hawfo; shushaye d-ghas**
hammer	*S:* **arzapta**; *T:* **akhlo**
handle	*S:* **esit qa**; *T:* **qato; idho**
hatchet	*S:* **qurnasa**; *T:* **qurnoso**
hose	*S:* **kharsuma**; *T:* **kharṭumo; ṣonda**
insecticide	*S:* **mawdidh rikhshe**; *T:* **qoṭulo da-raḥshe**
ladder	*S:* **sim malta**; *T:* **sebeltho**
machine	*S:* **mziʿana**; *T:* **makina**
microscope	*S:* **mrawriw wana**; *T:* **mrawrwono; mḥawyono**
nail	*S:* **ṣiṣa**; *T:* **basmoro; ṣeṣo**
padlock	*S:* **qipla**; *T:* **quflo**
paint	*S:* **sawʿa**; *T:* **ṣwoʿo; boya**
pickax	*S:* **qazma**; *T:* **felqo; ṣaquro**
plank	*S:* **lukha** ***ḍ-qaysa***; *T:* **dafo; luḥo** ***ḍ-qayso***
plastic	*S:* **plasṭik**; *T:* **plastik**
pliers	*S:* **kaliwta**; *T:* **kalobto**
rope	*S:* **khola**; *T:* **ḥawlo**
rubber	*S:* **la khayta**; *T:* **maṭoṭo; maṭṭaṭ**
saw	*S:* **nasurta**; *T:* **masoro**
scissors	*S:* **msapranita**; *T:* **masfrono**
screw	*S:* **khalula**; *T:* **ḥolulo; quklo**
screwdriver	*S:* **patkhan khalula**; *T:* **dobar-ḥolule; qukloyo**
sieve	*S:* **ʿarbala**; *T:* **ʿarbolo**

spade	*S:* **mara**; *T:* **magraftho**
spanner/wrench	*S:* **spanar**; *T:* **qlidho ṣliḥo**
string	*S:* **yatra**; *T:* **ḥuṭo**
sunglasses	*S:* **khazayate shimshaye**; *T:* **ḥazoyotho di-shemsho**
telescope	*S:* **marwana**; *T:* **mrawrwono mqarwono; teleskop**
varnish	*S:* **varnish**; *T:* **seqlo; warnish**
wire	*S:* **khuṭa**; *T:* **ḥuṭo**

—Weights & measures

Turkey, Syria and Iraq use the metric system. Here is a list of international units – for reference translations are included for the most common imperial units.

kilometer	*S:* **kilomiṭra**; *T:* **kilomeṭro**
mile	*S:* **mila**; *T:* **mil; milo**
meter	*S:* **miṭra**; *T:* **meṭro**
foot	*S:* **durikta**; *T:* **raghlo; fut**
yard	*S:* **yard**; *T:* **yardo**
gallon	*S:* **galin**; *T:* **galon**
liter	*S:* **liṭra**; *T:* **liṭro**
ton	*S:* **ṭanna**; *T:* **ṭaᶜno** *or* **ton**
kilogram	*S:* **kilogram**; *T:* **kilogram**
pound	*S:* **pawnd**; *T:* **liṭro (pawand)**
gram	*S:* **gram**; *T:* **gram**
ounce	*S:* **awnsa**; *T:* **unqia**

28. THE CAR

Where can I *(m/f)* rent a car?
S: **Mika masin maghrin/masyan maghran radita ʿam mdawrana?**
T: **Ayko kibi makreno/makiryono radhayto?**

With a driver?
S: **ʿAm mdawrana?** *or* **ʿAm ṭaraya?**
T: **ʿAm qaloʿo?**

How much is it per day?
S: **Kma le aghra yawmaya?**
T: **U-yawmo b-miqqa-yo?**

How much is it per week?
S: **Kma le aghra shawoʿaya?**
T: **I-shabtho b-miqqa-yo?**

Can I *(m/f)* park here?
S: **Masin kalin lakha?**
T: **Kibi koleno/kulyono harke?**

Is this the right road for ...?
S: **ʿAl urkha tresta wikh?**
T: **U-darbo d-... hano-yo?**

Where is the nearest petrol station?
S: **Ika et noqazta d-banzin qurba?**
T: **Ayko kit nukasto (***or* **mashryo) d-banzin qariwo?**

Fill the tank please *(m/f)*.
S: **Mli l-tanki, en mbasmalokh/mbasmalakh.**
T: **Mlay u-tank, boʿutho menokh/menekh.**

normal/diesel *S:* **dizel/ʿyadaya**; *T:* **ʿyodoyo/dizel**

Check the oil/tires/battery, please *(m/f)*.
S: **ʿAqib lmishkha/gighle/ba ṭarita, en mbasmalukh/ en mbasmalakh.**
T: **Boʿutho menokh/menekh, ḥur bu-meshḥo/ban-ufne/bi-baṭṭaritho.**

I have lost my car keys.
S: **Tolqli l-qdile draditi.**
T: **msakar-li a-qlidaydhi.**

The car has broken down.
S: **Khrula raditi.**
T: **I-radhayto kalyo.**

There is something wrong with my car.
S: **Et kha pawda braditi.**
T: **Kit mede ghalṭo bi-radhaytaydhi.**

There is something wrong with this car.
S: **Et kha pawda b hadhe radita.**
T: **Kit mede ghalṭo bi-radhaytathe.**

I have a puncture (*or* flat tire).
S: **Nqule gighla d-raditi.**
T: **Kit-li panchar** (or **ufno naqiwo).**

I have run out of petrol.
S: **Preqle banzini.**
T: **Haw fayesh-li banzin.**

Our car is stuck.
S: **Raditan ʿsita la.**
T: **I-radhaytaydhan kalyo.**

We need a mechanic.
S: **Ṣniqe wikh mtaqnan radiyate.**
T: **K-lozam-lan mikanikoyo.**

Can you *(m/f)* tow us?
S: **Masit garshitlan/masyat garshatlan?**
T: **Kibokh/Kibekh gorshat-lan?**

Where is the nearest garage?
S: **Et khda dukana d-toqan radiyate?**
T: **Ayko kit garaj qariwo?**

There's been an accident!
S: **Et hwiya kha gidsha!**
T: **Hawi gedsho!**

THE CAR

My car has been stolen.
S: **Raditi pishta la gnawta.**
T: **Gniwo i-radhaytaydhi.**

Call *(m/f/pl)* the police!
S: **Qri l-dakhshe!/Qrae l-dakhshe!/Qrimon l-dakhshe!**
T: m/f: **Qray a-daḥshe!**/*pl:* **Qrayu a-daḥshe!**

—Car words

accelerator *S:* **banzin** *or* **msarhewana;** *T:* **makhifono; banzin**
air *S:* **hawa;** *T:* **hawa**
battery *S:* **rusaqa or batri;** *T:* **baṭṭaritho; rusoqo; baṭṭariye**
brake *S:* **makilyana or brayk;** *T:* **maklyono; fren; brayk**
car papers *S:* **waraqe d radida;** *T:* **warqe d-radhayto**
car registration/numberplate *S:* **seghla d-radita;** *T:* **seghlo d-radhayto**
clutch *S:* **akhudha;** *T:* **klach**
driver *S:* **mdawrana;** *T:* **qaloᶜo/qaloᶜto**
driver's license *S:* **sahduta d-dwara;** *T:* **sohdutho du-qloᶜo; fsoso du-qloᶜo**
engine *S:* **mziᶜana;** *T:* **moṭor**
exhaust *S:* **ekzuz;** *T:* **ogzos**
fan belt *S:* **qamra** *or* **zunar marwaha;** *T:* **qamro d-marwoḥo**
gas *S:* **banzin;** *T:* **hawfo; ghas**
gear *S:* **gir;** *T:* **gir**
hood *S:* **kasya;** *T:* **fagodho**
indicator light *S:* **bahra ramuza;** *T:* **bahro mawdhᶜono**
inner-tube *S:* **abuba gawaya;** *T:* **abubo gawonoyo**
insurance policy *S:* **akim ᶜarowota;** *T:* **shuroro d-gedshe; ᶜarobutho d-gedshe**
jack *S:* **marmana;** *T:* **maᶜlyono**
mechanic *S:* **mtaqnan radiyate;** *T:* **mikanikoyo**

neutral drive — *S:* **dwara lasṭraya**; *T:* **qloʿo meṣʿoyo**
oil — *S:* **meshkha**; *T:* **meshḥo**
parking lot — *S:* **makhimla d-radiyate**; *T:* **beth-kloyo**
passenger — *S:* **rakawa/ rakota**; *T:* **rakowo/ rakowto**
petrol — *S:* **banzin**; *T:* **banzin**
radiator — *S:* **radiyator**; *T:* **radyator**
reverse gear — *S:* **hpakhta**; *T:* **dʿoro**
seat — *S:* **mawtba**; *T:* **kursyo**
spare tire — *S:* **ghighla ʿatida**; *T:* **ufno zoyudo**
speed — *S:* **qaliluta**; *T:* **surhowo**
steering wheel — *S:* **sawkana**; *T:* **gighlo shabolo**
tank — *S:* **tanki d-banzin**; *T:* **tank**
tire/tyre — *S:* **gighla**; *T:* **ufno**; **tayer**
tow rope — *S:* **gam la d-grashta**; *T:* **ḥawlo du-grosho**
trunk/boot — *S:* **sanduq radita**; *T:* **ṣanduqo**
windshield wipers — *S:* **mkaprane d-zghugha d-radita**; *T:* **mandhifone di-zghughitho**
windshield/windscreen — *S:* **zghugha dradita**; *T:* **zghughitho**; **sakro d-hawa**

29. SPORTS

The Assyrians are avid followers of a wide variety of sports such as volleyball, tennis, basketball, netball, boxing, kickboxing, martial arts, bodybuilding, chess – but soccer is by far the most popular. Local tournaments are held in Turkey, Syria and Iraq and one international sporting event is held annually in Iran. Diapsora communities also have their own sporting teams and hold regular tournaments. The most popular Assyrian soccer team by far is Assyriska FF, a member of Sweden's first division. World-class sportsmen and women of Assyrian descent include former Iraqi soccer champion and now head of Iraqi Olympic Committee Ammo Baba, world tennis champion Andre Aghassi, Swedish champion basketball player Nina Baresso, and famous Swedish soccer player Kennedy Bakircioglu.

athletics	*S:* **she^{c}ye drishaye;** *T:* **athliṭoyutho**
ball	*S:* **guya;** *T:* **esfiro; ṭibbe**
backgammon	*S:* **she^{c}ya d-ṭablita;** *T:* **tesht^{c}inyo di-ṭablitho; she^{c}yo di-ṭablitho; ṭawla**
basketball	*S:* **spir sa la;** *T:* **esfir-saltho**
chess	*S:* **sheṭranj;** *T:* **qufso; sheṭranj**
cricket	*S:* **cricket;** *T:* **kriket**
football	*S:* **spir righla;** *T:* **esfir-raghlo; futbol**
goal	*S:* **nawpa;** *T:* **nawfo; gol**
golf	*S:* **kolf;** *T:* **golf**
hockey	*S:* **hoki;** *T:* **hoki**
horse racing	*S:* **moray sosye;** *T:* **muroyo da-susye; sibaqa da-susye**
horse riding	*S:* **par rashuta;** *T:* **rkowo da-susye**
match	*S:* **muraya;** *T:* **takhtusho**
pitch	*S:* **mashdakha d-gilla;** *T:* **mashtokho**
referee	*S:* **da yana;** *T:* **mfalghono; ḥakim**
rugby	*S:* **ragbi;** *T:* **ragbi**
skiing	*S:* **zakhputa;** *T:* **ski; rdhoyo ^{c}al u-talgo**

squash	*S:* **skwash**; *T:* **skwash**
stadium	*S:* **bet-sheᶜya**; *T:* **isṭadyon; beth-sheᶜyo**
swimming	*S:* **skhaya**; *T:* **skhoyo**
team	*S:* **guda**; *T:* **yahlo**
tennis	*S:* **tenis**; *T:* **tenis**
wrestling	*S:* **dar ra**; *T:* **kutosho**

Who won?
S: **Mani qrim le?**
T: **Man qmir le?**

What's the score?
S: **Mudi le kunasha?**
T: **Mun-yo menyono da-nuqze?**

Who scored?
S: **Mani mnupi le?**
T: **Man simle gol?**

30. THE BODY

ankle	*S:* ʿeqba; *T:* ʿeqbo
arm	*S:* draʿna; *T:* droʿo
back	*S:* khaṣa; *T:* ḥaṣo
beard	*S:* diqna; *T:* daqno
blood	*S:* dim ma; *T:* admo
body	*S:* paghra; *T:* faghro; gushmo
bone	*S:* garma; *T:* garmo
bottom	*S:* eshta; *T:* eshto
breast/chest	*S:* khadya/sadra; *T:* ḥadyo/ṣadro
chin	*S:* diqinta; *T:* daqinto
ear	*S:* nata; *T:* adhno
elbow	*S:* qursolta; *T:* yaṣilo
eye	*S:* ʿayna; *T:* ʿayno
eyebrow	*S:* gwina *or* qiṣṣa; *T:* gbino
eyelids	*S:* temre; *T:* temre
face	*S:* patta; *T:* fotho
finger	*S:* soʿa; *T:* ṣebʿo
fingers	*S:* sebʿate; *T:* ṣebʿotho
foot	*S:* aqla; *T:* raghlo; durakhtho
feet	*S:* aqle *or* reghle; *T:* raghle
hair	*S:* saʿra; *T:* sawko; saʿro
a hair	*S:* mina *or* mezta; *T:* mezto
hand	*S:* ida; *T:* idho
head	*S:* risha; *T:* risho
heart	*S:* lib ba; *T:* lebo
intestine	*S:* macye *or* miyure; *T:* maʿyo
jaw	*S:* laʿusa; *T:* fako; lughmo
kidney	*S:* kilita; *T:* klitho
knee	*S:* birka; *T:* burko
leg	*S:* aqla; *T:* raghlo
lip	*S:* sipta; *T:* saftho
liver	*S:* kawda; *T:* kabdho
lung	*S:* raata; *T:* rotho
mouth	*S:* pom ma; *T:* fumo
mustache	*S:* pesme; *T:* shwerib; zefe
nail *of finger/toe*	*S:* ṭepre; *T:* ṭefro
navel	*S:* shurta; *T:* shurto

neck	*S:* **qdala**; *T:* **qdholo**
nose	*S:* **nakhira**; *T:* **nḥiro**
rib	*S:* **el^{c}a**; *T:* **el^{c}o**
ribs	*S:* **el^{c}e**; *T:* **el^{c}e**
shoulder	*S:* **rusha**; **katpa**; *T:* **kathfo**
skin	*S:* **gilda**; *T:* **galdho**
stomach	*S:* **karsa**; *T:* **gawo**
teeth	*S:* **shi ne**; *T:* **^{c}arshone**; **shene**
throat	*S:* **gigarta**; *T:* **ṣawro**; **zagruro**
thumb	*S:* **krata**; *T:* **krotho**
toe	*S:* **saw^{c}a**; *T:* **ṣeb^{c}o**
tongue	*S:* **lishana**; *T:* **leshono**
tooth	*S:* **shin na**; *T:* **sheno**
vein	*S:* **warida**; *T:* **waridho**
waist	*S:* **khesra**; *T:* **dafno**
womb	*S:* **marib^{c}a**; *T:* **marb^{c}o**
wrist	*S:* **masurqa**; *T:* **qurṣlo**

31. TIME & DATES

century *S:* **dara**; *T:* **doro; mo-ishne**
decade *S:* **as sara**; *T:* **ʿsar ishne**
year *S:* **shata**; *T:* **shato**
month *S:* **yarkha**; *T:* **yarḥo**
week *S:* **shawuʿa**; *T:* **shabtho; showuʿo**
day *S:* **yawma**; *T:* **yawmo**
hour *S:* **shaʿta**; *T:* **shoʿtho**
minute *S:* **qaṭinta**; *T:* **qaṭinto**
second *S:* **rpapa**; *T:* **rfofo**

dawn *S:* **nughha**; *T:* **sloqo d-yawmo**
sunrise *S:* **saq yawma**; *T:* **dnoḥo d-shemsho**
morning *S:* **qidamta**; *T:* **qedimto; ṣafrayto**
daytime *S:* **imama**; *T:* **b-yawmo**
noon/afternoon *S:* **ṭahra**; *T:* **falge d-yawmo; ṭahro**
evening *S:* **ramsha**; *T:* **ʿaṣriye**
sunset *S:* **gnay yawma**; *T:* **ṭwoʿo d-yawmo**
night *S:* **lile**; *T:* **lalyo**
midnight *S:* **palga d-lile**; *T:* **falge d-lalyo**

four days before *S:* **mqam arbʿa yawme**;
T: **meqem arbʿo yawme**
three days before *S:* **mqam tlata yawme**;
T: **meqem tlotho yawme**
the day before yesterday *S:* **timmal d-ʿwere**;
T: **yawmo ḥreno**
yesterday *S:* **timmal**; *T:* **athmel**
today *S:* **ediom**; *T:* **ad-yawma**
tomorrow *S:* **qudme**; *T:* **ramḥel**
the day after tomorrow *S:* **qudme date**;
T: **yawmo ḥreno**
three days from now *S:* **akh edio tlata**;
T: **bithir tlotho yawme**
four days from now *S:* **akh edio arbʿa**;
T: **bithir arbʿo yawme**

the year before last	*S:* **teltath**; *T:* **shato ḥreto**
last year	*S:* **eshqat**; *T:* **ishqadh**
this year	*S:* **aya shita**; *T:* **ad-shato**
next year	*S:* **shita d-atya**; *T:* **shato d-uthyo**
the year after next	*S:* **shita d-bar hay d-atya**; *T:* **shato ḥreto**
last week	*S:* **shawuᶜa d-daᶜwar**; *T:* **shabtho d-shafiᶜo**
this week	*S:* **ah shawuᶜa**; *T:* **ad-shabtho**
next week	*S:* **shawuᶜa bitaya le**; *T:* **shabtho d-uthyo**
last night	*S:* **lilya d-daᶜwar**; *T:* **lalyo d-shafiᶜ**
this morning	*S:* **qidamta d-edio**; *T:* **ad-ṣafrayto**
now	*S:* **hadiya**; *T:* **uᶜdo**
just now	*S:* **hasha**; *T:* **har uᶜdo**
this afternoon/evening	*S:* **aya ṭahra aha ramsha**; *T:* **ad-ᶜaṣriye**
tonight	*S:* **ad lele**; *T:* **ad-lalyo**
yesterday morning	*S:* **tim mal qidamta**; *T:* **athmel ṣafrayto**
yesterday afternoon	*S:* **tim mal ṭahra**; *T:* **athmel ᶜaṣriye**
yesterday night	*S:* **tim mal bramsha**; *T:* **athmel b-lalyo**
tomorrow morning	*S:* **qudme qedamta**; *T:* **ramḥel ṣafrayto**
tomorrow afternoon	*S:* **qudme ṭahra**; *T:* **ramḥel ᶜaṣriye**
tomorrow night	*S:* **qudme bramsha**; *T:* **ramḥel b-lalyo**
in the morning	*S:* **bsapra**; *T:* **b-ṣafrayto**
in the afternoon	*S:* **bṭahra**; *T:* **b-ᶜaṣriye**
in the evening	*S:* **bramsha**; *T:* **b-lalyo**
past	*S:* **daᶜwar**; *T:* **da-ᶜbar**
present	*S:* **qaim**; *T:* **qoem**
future	*S:* **daᶜtid**; *T:* **da-ᶜtidh**

TIME & DATES

What date is it today?	*S:* **Edyom kma byarkha le?**; *T:* **Mun-yo u-siqumo d-ad-yawma?**
What day is it?	*S:* **mud yuma ile**; *T:* **Ayna yawmo-yo?**
What time is it?	*S:* **Mudi ila shaʿta**; *T:* **Miqqa-yo i-shoʿtho?** *or* **I-shoʿtho miqqa-yo?**
It is ... o'clock.	*S:* **Shaʿta d-... ila.**; *T:* **I-shoʿtho ... yo.**

—Seasons

summer	*S:* **qiṭa**; *T:* **qayṭo**
autumn	*S:* **teshreye**; *T:* **teshriyotho; teshritho**
winter	*S:* **sitwa**; *T:* **sathwo**
spring	*S:* **rbiʿa**; *T:* **rbiʿo**

—Days of the week

For Monday to Thursday in Turoyo, the most commonly used forms are given first, followed by their more classical versions.

Monday	*S:* **Troshiba**; *T:* **Yawme da-Tre** *or* **Trushabo**
Tuesday	*S:* **Tloshiba**; *T:* **Yawmo d-Tlotho** *or* **Tlothushabo**
Wednesday	*S:* **ʿArboshiba**; *T:* **Yawmo d-Arbʿo** *or* **Arbʿushabo**
Thursday	*S:* **Khamshoshiba**; *T:* **Yawmo d-Ḥamsho** *or* **Ḥamshushabo**
Friday	*S:* **ʿRuta**; *T:* **ʿRubto**
Saturday	*S:* **Shabta**; *T:* **Shabtho**
Sunday	*S:* **Khoshiba**; *T:* **. ushabo**

—Months

January	*S:* **Kanun Tray Yana**; *T:* **Konun Ḥaroyo**
February	*S:* **Ishwaṭ**; *T:* **Shbaṭ**
March	*S:* **Adhar**; *T:* **Odor**
April	*S:* **Nisan**; *T:* **Nison**
May	*S:* **Iyar**; *T:* **Iyor**
June	*S:* **Khziran**; *T:* **ḥziron**
July	*S:* **Tammuz**; *T:* **Tamuz**
August	*S:* **Ab**; *T:* **Ob**
September	*S:* **Ilul**; *T:* **Ilul**
October	*S:* **Teshrin Qamaya**; *T:* **Teshrin Qamoyo**
November	*S:* **Teshrin Tray Yana**; *T:* **Teshrin ḥaroyo**
December	*S:* **Kanun Qamaya**; *T:* **Konun Qamoyo**

—Star signs

Aries	*S:* **Emra**; *T:* **Emro**
Taurus	*S:* **Tawra**; *T:* **Tawro**
Gemini	*S:* **T'ame**; *T:* **Tome**
Cancer	*S:* **Aarṭana**; *T:* **Sarṭono**
Leo	*S:* **Arya**; *T:* **Aryo**
Virgo	*S:* **Btulta**; *T:* **Shebelto**; **Bthultho**
Libra	*S:* **Masata**; *T:* **Masato**
Scorpio	*S:* **ʿAqirwa**; *T:* **ʿAqrwo**
Saggitarius	*S:* **Kashshaṭa**; *T:* **Kashoṭo**
Capricorn	*S:* **Gadya**; *T:* **Gadhyo**
Aquarius	*S:* **Dawla**; *T:* **Dawlo**
Pisces	*S:* **Nuna**; *T:* **Nune**

TIME & DATES

—Time

What time is it?
S: **Shaʿta d-kma la?**
T: **Miqqa-yo i-shoʿtho?** *or* **I-shoʿtho kmo-yo?**

It is one o'clock.
S: **Shaʿta d-kha la.**
T: **ḥdho-yo.**

It is six o'clock.
S: **Shaʿta d-eshta la.**
T: **Sheth-yo.**

It is quarter to six.
S: **Eshta pyasha robʿa la.**
T: **Sheth noqiṣ ruwʿo-yo.**

It is quarter past six.
S: **Eshta ʿwara robʿa la.**
T: **Sheth w-ruwʿo-yo.**

It is half past six.
S: **Eshta o palge la.**
T: **Sheth w-falge-yo.**

It is twenty minutes past six.
S: **Eshta ʿawara ʿesri.**
T: **Sheth w-thultho-yo (***or* **w-ʿesri-yo).**

It is twenty minutes to six.
S: **Eshta pyasha ʿesri.**
T: **Sheth noqi? thultho-yo (***or* **ʿesri-yo).**

It is midday.
S: **Palga d-yawma le.**
T: **Salge d-yawmo-yo.**

It is midnight.
S: **Palga d-lile le.**
T: **Salge d-lalyo-yo.**

32. NUMBERS

Like other Semitic languages, Aramaic has a counting system where there are complex rules for masculine and feminine agreement. A simple easy-to-use system is given below. Where two forms are given the first is the (feminine) form that is used with masculine nouns, the second is the (masculine) form that is used with feminine nouns. Use the first form for counting.

0 *S:* **sipar**; *T:* **ṣifr** *or* **squt**
1 *S:* **kha/khda**; *T:* **ḥa/ḥdho**
2 *S:* **tre/tarten**; *T:* **tre/tarte**
3 *S:* **tlata/tlat**; *T:* **tlotho/tloth**
4 *S:* **arb^{c}a/arba^c**; *T:* **arb^{c}o/arba^c**
5 *S:* **khamsha/khamesh**; *T:* **ḥamsho/ḥammish**
6 *S:* **eshta/shet**; *T:* **ishto/sheth**
7 *S:* **shaw^{c}a/shwa^c**; *T:* **shaw^{c}o/shwa^c**
8 *S:* **tmanya/tmane**; *T:* **tmanyo/tmone**
9 *S:* **tesh^{c}a/tsha^c**; *T:* **tesh^{c}o/tsha^c**
10 *S:* **^{c}esra/csar**; *T:* **^{c}esro/^{c}sar**

11 *S:* **khadi^{c}sar**; *T:* **ḥdha^{c}sar**
12 *S:* **tri^{c}sar**; *T:* **tra^{c}sar**
13 *S:* **tilta^{c}sar**; *T:* **tlotha^{c}sar**
14 *S:* **^{c}ara^{c}sar**; *T:* **arba^{c}sar**
15 *S:* **khamsha^{c}sar**; *T:* **ḥamsha^{c}sar**
16 *S:* **eshta^{c}sar**; *T:* **shta^{c}sar e**
17 *S:* **shaw^{c}sar**; *T:* **shwa^{c}sar**
18 *S:* **tmani^{c}sar**; *T:* **tmona^{c}sar**
19 *S:* **tsha^{c}sar**; *T:* **tsha^{c}sar**
20 *S:* **^{c}esri**; *T:* **^{c}esri**

21 *S:* **^{c}esri kha**; *T:* **ḥa w-^{c}esri**
22 *S:* **^{c}esri tre**; *T:* **tre w-^{c}esri**
23 *S:* **^{c}esri tlah**; *T:* **tlotho w-^{c}esri**
24 *S:* **^{c}esri ^{c}arba**; *T:* **arb^{c}o w-^{c}esri**
25 *S:* **^{c}esri khamsha**; *T:* **ḥamsho w-^{c}esri**
26 *S:* **^{c}esri eshta**; *T:* **ishto w-^{c}esri**
27 *S:* **^{c}esri shaw^{c}a**; *T:* **shaw^{c}o w-^{c}esri**

28	*S:* ʿesri tmanya; *T:* tmanyo w-ʿesri
29	*S:* ʿesri teshʿa; *T:* teshʿo w-ʿesri
30	*S:* tlati; *T:* tlethi

31	*S:* tlati kha; *T:* ḥa w-tlethi
32	*S:* tlati tre; *T:* tre w-tlethi
33	*S:* tlati tlata; *T:* tlotho w-tlethi
34	*S:* tlati ʿarba; *T:* arbʿo w-tlethi
35	*S:* tlati khamsha; *T:* ḥamsho w-tlethi
36	*S:* tlati eshta; *T:* ishto w-tlethi
37	*S:* tlati shawʿa; *T:* shawʿo w-tlethi
38	*S:* tlati tmanya; *T:* tmanyo w-tlethi
39	*S:* tlati teshʿa; *T:* teshʿo w-tlethi
40	*S:* ʿarbʿi; *T:* arbʿi

41	*S:* ʿarbʿi kha; *T:* ḥa w-arbʿi
42	*S:* ʿarbʿi tre; *T:* tre w-arbʿi
43	*S:* ʿarbʿi tlata; *T:* tlotho w-arbʿi
44	*S:* ʿarbʿi ʿarbʿa; *T:* arbʿo w-arbʿi
45	*S:* ʿarbʿi khamsha; *T:* ḥamsho w-arbʿi
46	*S:* ʿarbʿi eshta; *T:* ishto w-arbʿi
47	*S:* ʿarbʿi shawʿa; *T:* shawʿo w-arbʿi
48	*S:* ʿarbʿi tmanya; *T:* tmanyo w-arbʿi
49	*S:* ʿarbʿi teshʿa; *T:* teshʿo w-arbʿi
50	*S:* khamshi; *T:* ḥamshi

51	*S:* khamshi kha; *T:* ḥa w-ḥamshi
52	*S:* khamshi tre; *T:* tre w-ḥamshi
53	*S:* khamshi tlata; *T:* tlotho w-ḥamshi
54	*S:* khamshi ʿarbʿa; *T:* arbʿo w-ḥamshi
55	*S:* khamshi khamsha; *T:* ḥamsho w-ḥamshi
56	*S:* khamshi eshta; *T:* ishto w-ḥamshi
57	*S:* khamshi shawʿa; *T:* shawʿo w-ḥamshi
58	*S:* khamshi tmanya; *T:* tmanyo w-ḥamshi
59	*S:* khamshi teshʿa; *T:* teshʿo w-ḥamshi
60	*S:* eshti; *T:* eshti

61	*S:* eshti kha; *T:* ḥa w-eshti
62	*S:* eshti tre; *T:* tre w-eshti
63	*S:* eshti tlata; *T:* tlotho w-eshti
64	*S:* eshti ʿarbʿa; *T:* arbʿo w-eshti

65 *S:* **eshti khamsha;** *T:* **ḥamsho w-eshti**
66 *S:* **eshti eshta;** *T:* **ishto w-eshti**
67 *S:* **eshti shawʿa;** *T:* **shawʿo w-eshti**
68 *S:* **eshti tmanya;** *T:* **tmanyo w-eshti**
69 *S:* **eshti teshʿa;** *T:* **teshʿo w-eshti**
70 *S:* **shawʿi;** *T:* **shawʿi**

71 *S:* **shawʿi kha;** *T:* **ḥa w-shawʿi**
72 *S:* **shawʿi tre;** *T:* **tre w-shawʿi**
73 *S:* **shawʿi tlata;** *T:* **tlotho w-shawʿi**
74 *S:* **shawʿi arbʿa;** *T:* **arbʿo w-shawʿi**
75 *S:* **shawʿi khamsha;** *T:* **ḥamsho w-shawʿi**
76 *S:* **shawʿi eshta;** *T:* **ishto w-shawʿi**
77 *S:* **shawʿi shawʿa;** *T:* **shawʿo w-shawʿi**
78 *S:* **shawʿi tmanya;** *T:* **tmanyo w-shawʿi**
79 *S:* **shawʿi teshʿa;** *T:* **teshʿo w-shawʿi**
80 *S:* **tmani;** *T:* **tmoni**

81 *S:* **tmani kha;** *T:* **ḥa w-tmoni**
82 *S:* **tmani tre;** *T:* **tre w-tmoni**
83 *S:* **tmani tlata;** *T:* **tlotho w-tmoni**
84 *S:* **tmani arbʿa;** *T:* **arbʿo w-tmoni**
85 *S:* **tmani khamsha;** *T:* **ḥamsho w-tmoni**
86 *S:* **tmani eshta;** *T:* **ishto w-tmoni**
87 *S:* **tmani shawʿa;** *T:* **shawʿo w-tmoni**
88 *S:* **tmani tmanya;** *T:* **tmanyo w-tmoni**
89 *S:* **tmani teshʿa;** *T:* **teshʿo w-tmoni**
90 *S:* **teshʿi;** *T:* **teshʿi**

91 *S:* **teshʿi kha;** *T:* **ḥa w-teshʿi**
92 *S:* **teshʿi tre;** *T:* **tre w-teshʿi**
93 *S:* **teshʿi tlata;** *T:* **tlotho w-teshʿi**
94 *S:* **teshʿi arbʿa;** *T:* **arbʿo w-teshʿi**
95 *S:* **teshʿi khamsha;** *T:* **ḥamsho w-teshʿi**
96 *S:* **teshʿi eshta;** *T:* **ishto w-teshʿi**
97 *S:* **teshʿi shawʿa;** *T:* **shawʿo w-teshʿi**
98 *S:* **teshʿi tmanya;** *T:* **tmanyo w-teshʿi**
99 *S:* **teshʿi teshʿa;** *T:* **teshʿo w-teshʿi**
100 *S:* **em ma;** *T:* **mo**

200	*S:* **tram-ma**; *T:* **mathe**
300	*S:* **tlat-ma**; *T:* **tloth-mo**
400	*S:* **arb^{c}a-ma**; *T:* **arḅa^c-mo**
500	*S:* **khamsham-ma**; *T:* **ḥammish-mo**
600	*S:* **eshtam-ma**; *T:* **sheth-mo**
700	*S:* **shaw^c-ma**; *T:* **shwa^c-mo**
800	*S:* **tmanyam-ma**; *T:* **tmone-mo**
900	*S:* **tesha^c-ma**; *T:* **tsha^c-mo**
1,000	*S:* **alpa**; *T:* **alfo**

10,000	*S:* **esra alpe**; *T:* **^{c}esro alfo** *or* **rebutho**
50,000	*S:* **khamshi alpe**; *T:* **ḥamshi alfo**
100,000	*S:* **em ma alpe**; *T:* **mo alfo**
1,000,000	*S:* **milyon**; *T:* **melyun**
10,000,000	*S:* **esra milyone**; *T:* **^{c}esro melyune**
1,000,000,000	*S:* **bilyon**; *T:* **belyun** *or* **bilyar**

first	*S:* **qadhmaya/qadhmayta**; *T:* **qamoyo/qamayto**
second	*S:* **trayanaya/trayanayta**; *T:* **trayono/trayonitho**
third	*S:* **tlitaya/tlitayata**; *T:* **tlithoyo/tlithayto**
fourth	*S:* **rwi^{c}aya/rwi^{c}ayta**; *T:* **rbi^{c}oyo/rbi^{c}ayto**
fifth	*S:* **khmishaya/khmishayta**; *T:* **ḥmishoyo/ḥmishayto**
sixth	*S:* **shtitaya/shtitayta**; *T:* **shtithoyo/shtithayto**
seventh	*S:* **shwi^{c}aya/shwi^{c}ayta**; *T:* **shwi^{c}oyo/shwi^{c}ayto**
eighth	*S:* **tminaya/tminayta**; *T:* **tminoyo/tminayto**
ninth	*S:* **tshi^{c}aya/tshi^{c}ayta**; *T:* **tshi^{c}oyo/tshi^{c}ayto**
tenth	*S:* **^{c}siraya/^{c}sirayta**; *T:* **^{c}siroyo/^{c}sirayto**
twentieth	*S:* **tre^{c}saraya/tres^{c}sarayta**; *T:* **^{c}esrinoyo/^{c}esrinayto**

once	*S:* **zbata;** *T:* **naqqa ḥdo**
twice	*S:* **tre zawnate;** *T:* **tarte kore; naqqawothe**
three times	*S:* **tla zawnate;** *T:* **tloth kore**
one-half	*S:* **kha palgaya;** *T:* **falgo**
one-third	*S:* **kha tlitaya;** *T:* **thultho**
one-quarter	*S:* **kha rwiᶜaya;** *T:* **ruwᶜo**
two-thirds	*S:* **tre tlitaye;** *T:* **tre-thulothe**
three-quarters	*S:* **tlata rwiᶜaye;** *T:* **tlotho-ruwᶜe**

33. VITAL VERBS

to be	*S:* **hwaya**; *T:* **hwoyo**; **ithutho**
to be born	*S:* **braya**; *T:* **hwoyo**
to give birth to	*S:* **mawlode**; *T:* **mawlodo**
to carry	*S:* **ṭʿana**; *T:* **ṭʿono**
to come	*S:* **taya**; *T:* **mathyo**
to cook	*S:* **bashule**; *T:* **busholo**
to cut	*S:* **qṣaya**; *T:* **qṣoʿo/qṣoyo**
to die	*S:* **myata**; *T:* **myotho**
to drink	*S:* **shtaya**; *T:* **shtoyo**
to drive	*S:* **mdawure**; *T:* **qloʿo**
to eat	*S:* **khala**; *T:* **muklo**
to fall	*S:* **npala**; *T:* **nfolo**
to finish	*S:* **praqa**; *T:* **shulomo**
to get	*S:* **shqala**; *T:* **mṭoyo**
to give birth to	*S:* **mabruye**; *T:* **mawlodo**
to give	*S:* **yhawa**; *T:* **ihobo**
to go	*S:* **khasha**; *T:* **mazlo**
to grow	*S:* **yrawa**; *T:* **irowo**
to have	*see page 26.*
to hear	*S:* **shmaʿa**; *T:* **shmoʿo**
to help	*S:* **mʿadure**; *T:* **mʿawanto** *or* **ʿudrono**
to hit	*S:* **mkhaya**; *T:* **mḥoyo**
to kill	*S:* **qṭala**; *T:* **qṭolo**
to know	*S:* **ydhaʿa**; *T:* **idhaʿto**
to learn	*S:* **ylapa**; *T:* **yulfono** *or* **ilofo**
to live	*S:* **bikhaya**; *T:* **ʿyosho**
to love	*S:* **makhube**; *T:* **rḥomo**
to meet	*S:* **pghaʿa**; *T:* **lqoyo**
to pick up	*S:* **shqala**; *T:* **myodo**
to read	*S:* **qraya** *T:* **qroyo**
to run	*S:* **rhaṭa**; *T:* **rhoṭo**
to see	*S:* **khzaya**; *T:* **ḥzoyo**
to sit	*S:* **ytawa**; *T:* **itawto**
to sleep	*S:* **dmakha**; *T:* **dmokho**
to smell	*S:* **nqakha**; *T:* **nqoḥo**
to speak	*S:* **msawte**; *T:* **imoro**

to stand	*S:* **klaya;** *T:* **kloyo; qyomo**
to start	*S:* **msharuye;** *T:* **shuroyo**
to stop	*S:* **klaya;** *T:* **kloyo**
to take	*S:* **shqala;** *T:* **mawbalto**
to talk	*S:* **msawte;** *T:* **jghaliye**
to taste	*S:* **ṭᶜama;** *T:* **ṭᶜomo**
to teach	*S:* **mawlupe;** *T:* **mawlafto**
to throw	*S:* **shdaya;** *T:* **mḥalaqto**
to understand	*S:* **parmuye;** *T:* **fhomo**
to wake up	*S:* **birᶜasha;** *T:* **maḥisto**
to walk	*S:* **mhalukhe;** *T:* **helkho**
to want	*S:* **bᶜaya;** *T:* **bᶜoyo**
to watch	*S:* **bikhyara** *T:* **ḥyoro**
to work	*S:* **plakha** *T:* **shgholo**
to write	*S:* **biktawa** *T:* **kthowo**

34. OPPOSITES

NOTE ON ADJECTIVES – As elsewhere in this book, adjectives are generally given in the masculine form only. For the most common feminine form replace the **-a/-o** ending with **-ta/-to**, e.g "high" *S:* **rama** → **ramta**, *T:* **romo** → **romto**.

beginning—end *S:* **shoraya—khutama**; *T:* **shuroyo—shulomo**
clean—dirty *S:* **dakhya—ṭawsha**; *T:* **nadhifo/nadhifto—ᶜjiqo/ᶜjiqto**
fertile—barren *land* *S:* **shamina—shaminta**; *T:* **shamino/shaminto—ᶜaqro/ᶜqartho**
happy—unhappy *S:* **psikha—dawya**; *T:* **fsiḥoyo/fsiḥayto—qḥiroyo/qḥirayto**
life—death *S:* **khaye—mawta**; *T:* **ḥaye—mawto**
friend—enemy *S:* **khawra—bᶜildara**; *T:* **ḥawro/ḥwartho—bᶜeldbobo; dijmin**
open—shut *S:* **ptikha—skhira**; *T:* **ftiḥo/ftiḥto—skhiro/skhirto**
wide—narrow *S:* **ptukha—ᶜiqa**; *T:* **fathyo/ftitho—ᶜiqo/ᶜiqto**
high—low *S:* **rama—kupa**; *T:* **ᶜeloyo/ᶜelayto** *or* **romo/romto—taḥtoyo/taḥtayto**
peace—violence/war *S:* **shayna—ᶜnupya/qrawa**; *T:* **shlomo—shghushyo/qrobo**
silence—noise *S:* **shitqa—rawba**; *T:* **shathqo—qolo**
cheap—expensive *S:* **shawya—dmaeya**; *T:* **lo ṭimo; arzon; rakhiṣ—ṭimo**
hot/warm—cold/cool *S:* **shakhina/qarira**; *T:* **shaḥino/ḥamimo—quro/qariro**
health—disease *S:* **khulmana—kiwa**; *T:* **ḥulmono—kurhono; kewo**

OPPOSITES

well—sick	*S:* **ṭawa—kaiwa**; *T:* **ḥlimo/ḥlimto; sagh—kayiwo/kayuto**
night—day	*S:* **emama—lilya**; *T:* **lalyo—yawmo**
top—bottom	*S:* **resha—eshta**; *T:* **risho—eshto**
backwards—forwards	*S:* **lbistar—lqodama**; *T:* **lakhalf—laqiddam**
back—front	*S:* **lbatra—lqamta**; *T:* **bithir—qum**
dead—alive	*S:* **mita—khaya**; *T:* **mitho/mithto—ḥayo/ḥaytho** *or* **ᶜayosho/ᶜayoshto**
near—far	*S:* **qurba—rikhqa**; *T:* **qariwo/qaruto—raḥuqo/raḥuqto**
left—right	*S:* **simmala—yamina**; *T:* **semolo—yamino**
in—out	*S:* **lghaw—lwar**; *T:* **lawghil—larwar**
up—down	*S:* **lᶜel—ltekhet**; *T:* **lalᶜel—laltaḥt**
here—there	*S:* **harka—tama**; *T:* **harke—tamo**
easy—difficult	*S:* **pshiṭa—ᶜasqa**; *T:* **fshiṭo/fshiṭto—ᶜasqo/ᶜasqtho**
quick—slow	*S:* **surhawa—nikha**; *T:* **khayifo/khayifto—hedi hedi**
strong—weak	*S:* **quya—mkhila**; *T:* **ḥaylono/ḥaylonitho—mḥilo/mḥilto**
thin—fat	*S:* **naqida—ṭrisa**; *T:* **dhaᶜifo/dhaᶜifto—taqinto/taqinto** *or* **raqiqo/raqiqto—khashino/khashinto**
success—failure	*S:* **kushara—rapyuta**; *T:* **kushoro—sqoṭo**
young—old	*S:* **ᶜlayma—sawa/ᶜlaymta—sawta**; *T:* **naᶜimo/naᶜimto—sowo/sawto**
new—old	*S:* **khatda—ᶜatiqa/khadta—ᶜatiqta**; *T:* **ḥatho/ḥathto—ᶜatiqo/ᶜatiqto**

OPPOSITES

question—answer	*S:* **shoaala—punaya;** *T:* **shuwolo—funoyo**
safety—danger	*S:* **shayna—qinṭa;** *T:* **mshaynutho —qenṭo; khaṭar**
true—false	*S:* **tris—pawda;** *T:* **shariro/sharirto—fawdo**
light—darkness	*S:* **bahra—khuya;** *T:* **bahro— ʿeṭmo; ḥeshukho**
well—badly	*S:* **ṭawa—khirba;** *T:* **ṭowo; kayiso—ḥarbo**
truth—lie	*S:* **shrara—dugla;** *T:* **shroro; shrolo—dugle**
comfortable— uncomfortable	*S:* **rwakhana—dla rwakha;** *T:* **rahat—rahatsiz**
handsome/beautiful —ugly	*S:* **shapir; shkhira;** *T:* **shafiro/ shafirto—natino/natinto; shkhiro/shkhirto**
rich—poor	*S:* **catira—paqira;** *T:* **ʿatiro/ ʿatirto** *or* **zangin— meskino/meskinto; faqiro/faqirto**
big—small	*S:* **raba—zʿora;** *T:* **rabo/ rabtho—naʿimo/naʿimto**
good—bad	*S:* **ṭawa—khirba;** *T:* **ṭowo/ṭowto; kayiso/kayisto— ḥarbo; bisho/bishto**
modern—ancient	*S:* **khata/ʿatiqa;** *T:* **ḥatho/ ḥathto—ʿatiqo/ʿatiqto**
yes—no	*S:* **eʾn—la;** *T:* **e—lo**
light—heavy	*S:* **qalula—yaqura; qalulta— yaqurta;** *T:* **khayifo/khayifto— yaquro/yaqurto** *or* **qalilo/ qalilto—tqilo/tqilto**
soft—hard	*S:* **rakikha—qishya; rakikhta- qshita;** *T:* **rakikho/rakikhto— qashyo/qshitho**
tall (long)—short	*S:* **yarikha—kirya; yarikhta- krita;** *T:* **yarikho/yarikhto— karyo/kritho**

THE MIDDLE EAST

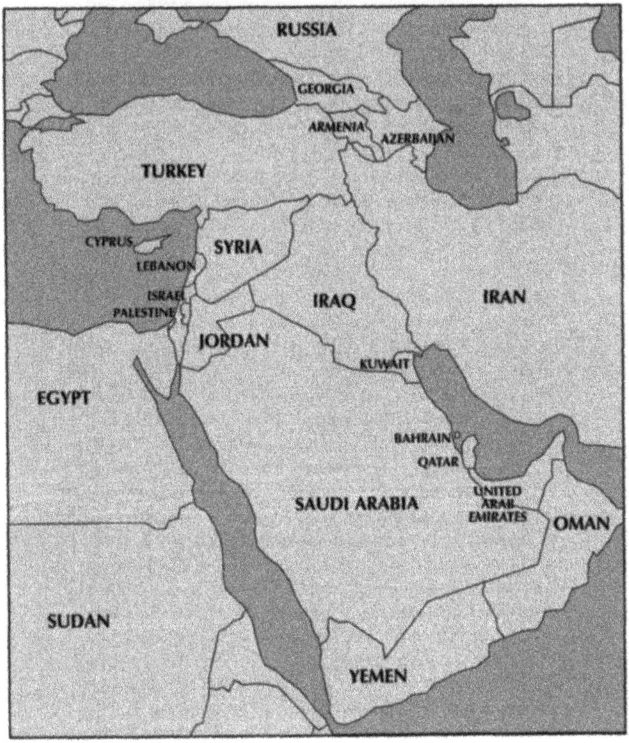

Map of Swadaya speakers

The map above shows areas where East Syriac (a.k.a. swadaya) is still spoken. There are over half a million East Syriac-speakers in Iraq with their centre in the capital Baghdad, and large homogenous concentrations in the northern provinces of Mosul, Dohuk, Erbil and Kirkuk. There are also smaller communities in Basra, Habbaniya, Hillah, Baquba, Amarah and other towns in southern and central Iraq.

In Syria there are more than 25,000 East Syriac speakers – not including as many as 20,000 or more refugees from Iraq. Here its heartland is the Gazarta (Jazira) region in the country's northeast corner, with Tell-Tamr being the centre of a concentration of 35 villages and groups in Hassaka, Qamishli, Dirbasiye, Malkiye, Ras al-'Ayn, Raqqa and Madinat al-Thawra. There are also communities of speakers in Aleppo, Damascus, Saydnaya, Homs and Hama – the bulk of these are refugees from Iraq.

There are less than 5,000 speakers of East Syriac in Turkey. Its former heartland was the region from the Tigris River to Lake Van and the border with Iran, but these communities ceased to exist after 1915. There are only one or two villages left in that area, as well as some families of speakers in Tur-Abdin, and Istanbul. There are also many Assyrian refugees from Iraq in Istanbul and Ankara that speak the language. There are also speakers of East Syriac amongst Assyrian refugees from Iraq (probably numbering 20,000) now residing in Jordan.

Apart from Assyrians, there are some 250,000 Jews worldwide that come from Assyrian areas in the Middle East and speak a Jewish form of East Syriac. They have a large concentration in Israel, especially in Jerusalem (Mahaneh Yehudah) and Tel-Aviv. There are also an estimated 50,000 people worldwide (Armenians, Kurds, Turks, Persians, Arabs) that speak East Syriac as a second language.

Note: Areas marked in red on the map denote regions and locations where East Syriac ceased to be spoken only within the last century and which due to successive political instability and conflicts have been emptied of speakers.

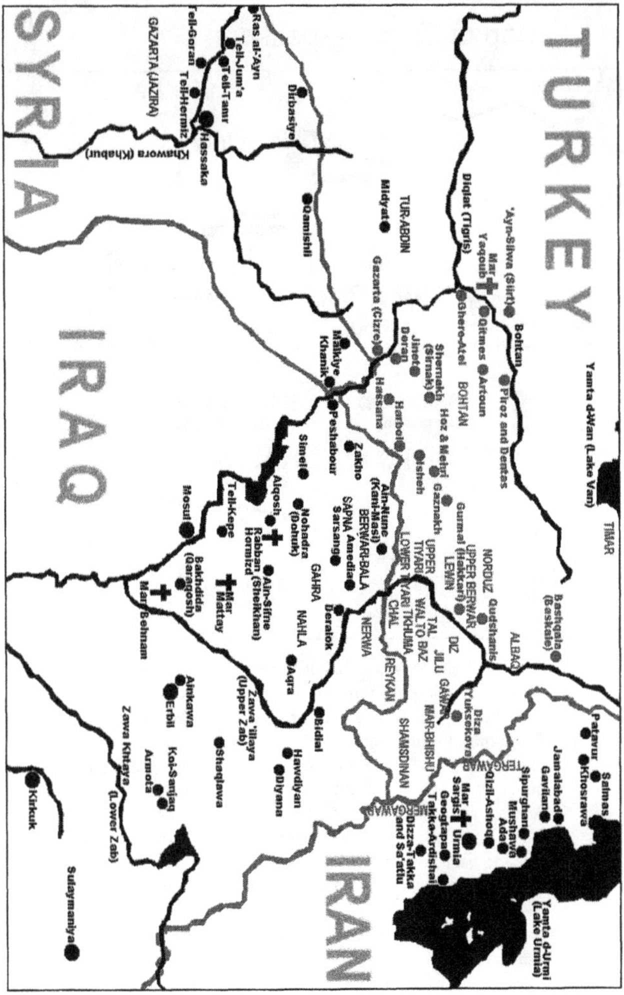
TURKEY
SYRIA
IRAQ
IRAN
Yamta d-Wan (Lake Van)
Yamta d-Urmi (Lake Urmia)
TIMAR
Bashqala (Baskale)
ALBAQ
Qudshanis
NORDUZ
UPPER BERWAR
Gurmal (Hakkari)
LEWIN
UPPER TIYARI
LOWER TIYARI
TAL
WALTO BAZ
TKHUMA
CHAL
DIZ
JILU
GAWAR
REYKAN
NERWA
Diza
Yuksekova
MAR-BISHU
SHAMSDINAN
TERGAWAR
MERGAWAR
Salmas
Khosrawa
Patavur
Jamalabad
Gavilan
Sipurghan
Qizil-Ashoq
Mushawa
Ada
Mar Sargis
Geogtapa
Urmia
Takka-Ardishai
Dizza-Takka and Sa'atlu
Bohtan
Piroz and Dentes
'Ayn-Silwa (Siirt)
Qitmes
Artoun
Mar Yaqoub
Ghero-Atel
BOHTAN
Shernakh (Sirnak)
Hoz & Meţri
Gaznakh
Jinet
Deran
Isheh
Harbol
Hassana
Diqlat (Tigris)
TUR-ABDIN
Midyat
Gazarta (Cizre)
Mankiye
Khanik
Peshabour
Zakho
Simel
Ain-Nune (Kani-Masi)
BERWARI-BALA
SAPNA
Amedia
Sarsang
Nohadra (Dohuk)
GAHRA
Alqosh
Rabban Hormizd
Ain-Sifne (Sheikhan)
Tell-Kepe
Mosul
Bakhdida (Qaraqosh)
Mar Mattay
Mar Behnam
NAHLA
Deralok
Aqra
Bidial
Zawa 'illaya (Upper Zab)
Ainkawa
Erbil
Shaqlawa
Hawdiyan
Diyana
Koi-Sanjaq
Arnota
Zawa Khtaya (Lower Zab)
Kirkuk
Sulaymaniya
Qamishli
Dirbasiye
Ras al-'Ayn
Tell-Jum'a
Tell-Tamr
Tell-Goran
Tell-Hermiz
Hassaka
Khawora (Khabur)
GAZARTA (JAZIRA)

MAPS

Map of Turoyo speakers

The map above shows areas where West Syriac (a.k.a. Turoyo) is still spoken. There are over 10,000 speakers of West Syriac in Turkey, and its heartland is in the villages of Tur-Abdin – the area between Nusaybin and Dargecit, with its centre at Midyat. There are also communities of speakers to be found in Mardin, Diyarbakir, Elazig, Adiyaman, Istanbul, Ankara, Izmir, Antalya and Adana. In Syria there are more than 50,000 West Syriac speakers. Here its heartland is the Gozarto (Jazira) region in the country's northeast corner, with Qamishli at its centre. There are also communities of speakers in Aleppo, Damascus, Homs and Hama. There are more than 5,000 West Syriac-speakers in Iraq with their centre in the provincial town of Sinjar, and there are also communities at Mosul, Kirkuk, Baghdad and Basra.